The Era of Trujillo

Generalissimo Rafael Leonidas Trujillo Molina

The Era of Trujillo

Dominican Dictator

by

Jesús de Galíndez

edited by
Russell H. Fitzgibbon

The University of Arizona Press
Tucson, Arizona

About the Author

JESÚS DE GALÍNDEZ taught international law in the Dominican Republic at the diplomatic and consular school operated by the Dominican foreign office. While serving as a legal adviser in the labor division of the Department of Labor and National Economy, he displeased Trujillo by arbitrating several strikes too favorably for the workers. As a result, he was singled out for constant harassment. In 1946 he obtained a visa to the United States. His sudden disappearance in 1956 became a *cause célèbre,* turning public opinion vehemently against the Dominican dictator.

About the Editor

RUSSELL H. FITZGIBBON, who had previously met Jesús de Galíndez in Costa Rica, was in 1962 a presidential election observer in the Dominican Republic for the OAS. Fitzgibbon has taught at UCLA, where he was Chairman of the Political Science Department and Director of the Center for Latin American Studies, and also at the University of California, Santa Barbara. He has served on the Editorial Committee of the Latin American Studies Center at Arizona State University. His many publications include *Cuba and the United States; Uruguay: Portrait of a Democracy;* and *Latin America: A Panorama of Contemporary Politics.*

F
1938.5
G313

THE UNIVERSITY OF ARIZONA PRESS

U.S. Copyright 1973
The Arizona Board of Regents
All Rights Reserved
Manufactured in the U.S.A.

All other rights to the original, unedited manuscript held by Fermín Galíndez Iglesias

I.S.B.N. 0–8165–0393–1 cloth
I.S.B.N. 0–8165–0359–1 paper
L.C. No. 72-79292

Contents

Jesús de Galíndez

. . . his memory is a luminous symbol
of the sacrifice of a life in defense of
the essential values of our civilization.

— President Rómulo Betancourt
of Venezuela,
New York Times, August 9, 1956.

Foreword

On February 27, 1956, Jesús de Galíndez, a forty-year-old part-time lecturer at Columbia University, presented his dissertation to a faculty committee as a candidate for a doctoral degree. His dissertation dealt with the reign of Trujillo, dictator of the Dominican Republic. Thirteen days later Galíndez disappeared forever. Although the case was never officially solved, Galíndez was almost certainly kidnapped in New York, taken to the Dominican Republic, and murdered, all on order of Trujillo.

Some seventeen years then elapsed from Galíndez's disappearance to this present publication of the dissertation for the first time in English. It is astonishing that we have waited so long. Galíndez's disappearance became a *cause célèbre* throughout the hemisphere, turning hemispheric opinion against Trujillo as nothing else had. The intricacies of his disappearance may have helped prepare the subsequent assassination of Trujillo himself.

Spanish editions of the dissertation sold widely throughout Latin America, but until now English-speaking readers have been denied it. We are, therefore, greatly in the debt of Professor Fitzgibbon and his publisher for making the manuscript available.

It is a remarkable book. Although its author was passionately opposed to Trujillo, he wrote with unusual restraint. Writing from exile in New York, he was, nevertheless, able to document his book from carefully researched Dominican sources, to produce a manuscript of compelling interest to anyone who cares about the Dominican tragedy or, indeed, about the problems of dictatorship versus democracy in all Latin America. Galíndez may or may not have been killed because of his book. But his book can stand alone.

Galíndez wrote at a time when the rule of the dictators in Latin America appeared to be coming to an end. A few years later Trujillo and other dictators had fallen, and, during the presidency of John F. Kennedy, the hemisphere entered what seemed to be a period of hope and democratic faith. But by 1970 other tides had set around the world, and we in North America seemed to be once more viewing with indifference the rise of new threats to liberty in Latin America. The publication now of the Galíndez book could not be more timely, for what he wrote — and how he died — reminds us once again of what ensues when a people delivers itself to a tyrant.

JOHN BARTLOW MARTIN
U.S. Ambassador to the
Dominican Republic, 1962–64

Editor's Preface

Doctoral dissertations normally do not make the best seller lists. The editor knows the son of a former Scandinavian foreign minister, who requested access to the ministry's archives for use in his doctoral research being completed in the United States. The initial response was a flat negative — it would involve the use of classified materials, and that obviously could not be allowed. He then explained his purpose and won an immediate reversal of the decision. The rationale? A doctoral dissertation would never be read, anyway!

In the present case, however, the study achieved early fame on two counts: it was an exceedingly well researched account of the first quarter century of a notoriously dramatic Middle American tyranny and, for a more macabre reason, its completion and imminent publication provided the cue for a widely publicized kidnapping and presumed murder.

The author of the work was Jesús de Galíndez Suárez, a Basque scholar who was studying and lecturing at Columbia University in the early and middle 1950s. His subject was Rafael Leonidas Trujillo y Molina, who contemptuously held the Dominican Republic in the hollow of his hand from 1930 to 1961.

The breaking of the tragedy of Galíndez came on the night of Monday, March 12, 1956. After delivering a lecture on the Columbia University campus, Galíndez was driven by a student some sixty blocks south to a subway entrance at Fifty-seventh Street and Eighth Avenue to go on by underground to his apartment on lower Fifth Avenue. He was in a typically cheerful and enthusiastic mood. He waved goodbye to the student and started down the subway stairs. From that moment, no friend ever saw him alive, or dead, again.

Within a few days the disappearance became a *cause célèbre,* one of the most publicized kidnappings to have occurred in many years. Investigations by university, city, state, and federal authorities went thoroughly into the case, but without tangible result. Galíndez was one of 142 persons reported missing to the New York City police during the week of March 12, 1956; more than two years later, he remained the only one of that number still officially listed as "missing." When the finger of suspicion during the investigations pointed too strongly to the Dominican dictator to be ignored, the latter's bland response was that the crime — if there were a crime — had occurred in New York City. It was therefore the responsibility of the New York police to solve it. Obviously, the Dominican authorities knew nothing about it!

The affair was complicated by the death in the Dominican Republic in early December of 1956 of a young aviator from Oregon, Gerald Lester Murphy, who was serving as a copilot in a Trujillo-owned Dominican airline. An Oregon congressman and a senator entered actively into the investigation of this case, which soon became tied with the disappearance of Galíndez. Dominican authorities quickly came forth with other bland, though sordid, explanations, an account that *Life* magazine in a thorough review of the dual case termed "shocking and ingenious but unconvincing."

The hypothesis that emerged from the various studies of the affair was that Galíndez had been abducted from Manhattan on the night of March 12, 1956, driven, possibly by ambulance (and probably drugged), to an airport at Amityville, Long Island, and flown from there by Gerald Murphy to the Dominican Republic. A too loquacious Murphy then perhaps later paid the ultimate penalty for his alleged talkativeness. The complex hypothesis had many ramifications and variations. Later sensational and probably irresponsible accounts had individuals claiming to have seen Galíndez alive after March, 1956, and also to have known people who had seen the body of a man "positively identified" as Galíndez dumped in an isolated ravine in the Dominican Republic. It was all, in Churchillian terms, a riddle wrapped in a mystery inside an enigma. And so it will doubtless remain.*

---

* Perhaps the most comprehensive account of the involved Galíndez-Murphy case is in Germán E. Ornes, *Trujillo: Little Caesar of the Caribbean* (New York, 1958), Ch. 19, "Unmysterious Mysteries," pp. 309–38. Additional information is included in Robert D. Crassweller, *Trujillo: The Life and Times of a Caribbean Dictator* (New York, 1966), Ch. 21, "The Galíndez Case," pp. 311–28 *passim*. A thoroughly unsatisfactory discussion of the affair, by one who undoubtedly knew much more than he told, is found in Arturo R. Espaillat, *Trujillo: The Last Caesar* (Chicago, 1963), Ch. 15, "Operation Galíndez," pp. 163–76. Edward R. Murrow organized, edited, and narrated a dramatic, hour-long radio broadcast, "The Galíndez-Murphy Case: A Chronicle of Terror," presented by the Columbia Broadcasting System on May 20, 1957.

If Trujillo assumed that the removal of Galíndez would prevent what would undoubtedly be a devastating critique of his regime by the early completion and possible publication of the study, he was ironically doomed to disappointment. It was not only a disappointment but possibly also, through the backlash of public opinion in many countries, the turning point in the whole evil career of the dictator.

Galíndez, although he had not yet received the degree from Columbia University, defended his dissertation in the traditional academic fashion on February 27, 1956. English copies were available for each member of his doctoral committee. They regarded the work highly and had only minor suggestions to make about it. At the conclusion of the examination, he collected the several copies in order to make the suggested changes. In the meantime — fortunate act! — he had given a Spanish copy to a Chilean acquaintance who, *only three days before Galíndez's disappearance,* turned it over to a prominent publisher in his own country, Editorial del Pacífico in Santiago, which, on June 15, 1956, brought out the first Spanish edition of *La Era de Trujillo*. The Spanish version had been trimmed to about 160,000 words, approximately half the length of the complete study.

So popular was the work and so sensational the circumstances surrounding the author's disappearance that six more printings were issued within a month and a half. In that same year, 1956, another Spanish edition, almost identical with the one issued in Santiago, was published by Editorial Americana in Buenos Aires. In his appraisal, Rómulo Betancourt, former president of Venezuela, said that "No other political publication in the Spanish language reached the same spectacular distribution in this century."

In 1962 the Librairie Gallimard in Paris published a French edition, *L'Ere de Trujillo*. In the late months of 1956, the New York periodical *Ibérica,* then published in Spanish and English versions but now only in Spanish, printed, by arrangement with the Santiago publisher, a series of seven extracts from the study, the translation being made by the staff of *Ibérica*. The total length of the excerpts, however, was not more than about 5 percent of that of the original study.

*   *   *   *   *   *

Jesús de Galíndez Suárez was born in Amurrio, Spain, on October 12, 1915. His father, also Jesús de Galíndez, was Basque and a distinguished opthalmologist. His mother, a Castillian, died soon after Jesús was born. As a youth, Jesús attended a Jesuit school in Bilbao for a time and then enrolled in the school of law of the University of Madrid, inasmuch as the Basque provinces had no university. His academic record was excellent and he received the degree of Licenciado in June, 1936.

A month later, the Spanish civil war broke out. The young university graduate — he was not yet twenty-one — became a staunch supporter of the Loyalist cause and served it in a number of capacities until the end of the civil war. His ideological orientation was toward the objective of an autonomous Basque republic within Spain, and it is reported on good authority that such an ideal was one he had formed early in life and to which he remained consistently attached. His will, found after his disappearance, closed with a tribute to both his Basque and Catholic attachments: *"¡Gora Euzkadi Azkatuta!* [Long live the free Basque country!] May *Jaungoikoa* [God] receive me in His bosom."

After Franco's defeat of the Loyalists, Galíndez fled to France, where he remained in exile for a little less than a year. On November 19, 1939, shortly before the Nazi occupation of France in 1940, Galíndez resumed his hegira, this time to the Dominican Republic along with other Spanish refugees who accepted political asylum in that odd haven.

Galíndez soon joined the diplomatic and consular school, operated by the Dominican Foreign Office, where he taught legal subjects. Subsequently he served as a legal advisor in the labor division of the Department of Labor and National Economy. In the latter capacity he allegedly first aroused Trujillist suspicion by being involved, as secretary of the department's minimum wage committee, in the settlement of a series of strikes among sugar workers, on terms that the regime felt were too favorable to the cane cutters. With the apparent strong possibility that he was marked for harassment — or worse — by the government, he obtained a visa for the United States, and on February 1, 1946, left for Miami, Florida.

Settling in New York City, he quickly became active among the exiled Spaniards living there, as an associate of various Latin American groups, and in collaboration with liberal, anti-Communist intellectuals. He became an official, registered representative in the United States of the Basque government-in-exile, centered in Paris after the end of the Spanish civil war. While still in the Dominican Republic, Galíndez had arranged for a visit to that country and a series of lectures by José Antonio de Aguirre, president of the Basque organization in Paris.

Galíndez wrote widely for Spanish newspapers and periodicals in the United States and Latin America. He lectured, participated in conferences on democratic problems in Latin America, and found time to write a book on Latin American historical and political development. His last published article was included in *Euzko-Deya,* a Basque review in Mexico, in February, 1956. He took an active part in the work of the Inter-American Association for Democracy and Freedom and served as a consultant to United States legal and business firms on complex questions of international law.

Galíndez began his association with Columbia University in 1951 as a part-time lecturer in Spanish and government. All the evidence indicates that he was highly regarded by both students and faculty. President Grayson Kirk of Columbia University later wrote to the *New York Times* that "He was a scholar well respected by his teaching colleagues and held in warm affection and regard as well by his students."

The fact that only inconsequential changes in his doctoral dissertation were suggested by his guidance committee rendered the study acceptable as a complete dissertation, even though the corrected version had not been officially resubmitted through academic channels prior to his disappearance two weeks after the formal defense of the dissertation. The Ph.D. degree was formally conferred *in absentia* on June 5, 1956, at which time Dean Jacques Barzun of the graduate faculties of the university cited "the name of our colleague, Jesús de Galíndez, whose unexplained absence for three months we all lament."

Investigations, official and unofficial, were all, in the absence of a *corpus delicti* of the missing person, formally inconclusive. Nonetheless, the overwhelming weight of circumstantial evidence was damning. Very respectable and responsible opinion maintains that the whole sensational and tragic denouement was the turning point for Trujillo and that thereafter his path to Avernus was as certain and irreversible as his earlier rise had been ruthless and conscienceless. Galíndez was, after an unresolved absence of seven years, declared legally dead by New York officials in 1963. His estate was transferred to Galíndez's father in Spain, and on his death, to his half-brother, Dr. Fermín Galíndez Iglesias, with whom arrangements for publication in the United States were made.

* * * * * *

Inasmuch as the study of Trujillo was originally written in Spanish and then, with the assistance of a number of the author's New York friends, translated into English for submission as a doctoral dissertation to Columbia University, the English version of the manuscript differs in various details from the printed Spanish editions. The basis of this published English edition is the 689-page manuscript used as a doctoral dissertation and, hence, the editor has, where it appeared necessary, carefully collated the Spanish and English forms and occasionally made changes in the latter, though these changes have been careful attempts to preserve the spirit of the original. Indeed, the underlying criterion in the absorbing task of editing has been to present the material as the editor is convinced the author would have wanted it presented.

The study in its dissertational form was organized in such a way that considerable repetition was inevitable. A long first chapter ("Part I") recounted chronologically, and with virtually no evaluative comment, the events of the period from 1930 to 1955, while the several chapters in Part II analyzed the same quarter century topically. In order to reduce that repetition to a minimum it has seemed desirable to condense the material severely, particularly in Part I, by omitting much detail that is now of little or no historical significance or that is adequately treated in other accounts of the Trujillo regime.

The author's documentation in his manuscript study is meticulous. His long first chapter, which constitutes Part I, contains no fewer than 1,123 footnotes, almost all of them citations to a wide variety of sources. In contrast, the three foreign-language editions of the work (Santiago and Buenos Aires, 1956, and Paris, 1962) almost entirely omit the original documentation but they do retain some of the author's explanatory footnotes, and the French edition adds occasional clarifying notes by the translator.

The editor's decision was to try to keep only as much of the chronology as was necessary, on the one hand, to provide continuity of narrative and, on the other, to demonstrate the careful nature of the author's documentation. The footnotes retained are given with sequential numbers, with the author's original footnote numbers inserted in brackets; in Chapter 1 the author began a new sequence of footnote numbers with each section but in this edition they are numbered sequentially for the entire chapter. In the few instances in which it has seemed desirable to insert an *editorial* footnote the insertion has been marked by symbols other than the customary footnote numbers, inasmuch as the latter have been reserved for the author's own notes.

For the sake of readability only the longer deletions from the original text have been marked by the customary symbols of ellipsis; in no case, however, whether so marked or not, does the deletion distort the original meaning of the author. Editorially inserted material is bracketed. If the bracketed material is of a supplementary rather than simply a clarifying nature it is italicized. In a small number of instances in which manuscript spellings show an obvious tendency to render Spanish orthography too literally into English (e.g., "negociation," "panegirist," "inmortal"), a corrected English form has been used without indication of the deviation. The author in a number of places used important quotations in the original Spanish and provided footnote translations into English (a mark of good scholarship, of course); for brevity's sake these normally have been rendered in this edition in the English form alone, but only after a careful comparison of the English and Spanish versions.

The editor is indebted to numerous persons who, in one way or another, have assisted in the long path toward publication of this study. A number of persons at Columbia University aided in various ways: Provost Jacques Barzun, Professors Wayne Wilcox, William T. R. Fox, and Charles Wagley. Miss Frances R. Grant, Secretary General of the Inter-American Association for Democracy and Freedom, and Miss Louise Crane, publisher of *Ibérica,* were exceedingly helpful in opening their respective extensive and valuable files on Galíndez for the editor's use. Mr. Morris L. Ernst of New York City generously provided a copy of his *Report and Opinion in the Matter of Galindez.*

Don Manuel de Irujo, president of the Basque government-in-exile (in Paris) was most generous, courteous, and helpful in providing biographical information and other assistance. Through his good offices the editor obtained pictures of Galíndez from Mrs. Miren Skipworth Button of Leigh-on-Sea, Essex, England, and Dr. Fernando Carranza Iza of Caracas, Venezuela. The editor is grateful to Dr. Santiago de Zarrantz of Santiago, Chile, and Mr. Jorge Nef, University of California, Santa Barbara, for assistance in obtaining a copy of the out-of-print Chilean edition of *La Era de Trujillo.* Mr. Michael Malek, University of California, Santa Barbara, supplied useful bibliographic information. The editor is also greatly indebted to his son, Alan L. Fitzgibbon of New York, for invaluable assistance in connection with illustrations and archival research. Mr. Marshall Townsend, director, Miss Stephanie Chase, editor, and others at the University of Arizona Press were uniformly helpful and insightful.

*   *   *   *   *   *

It was the editor's privilege and pleasure that, for a brief time, his path crossed that of the author. The occasion was in November, 1953, when both the author and he were guests at the first inauguration of José Figueres as president of Costa Rica. The vivid memory he retains of Galíndez is one of a vital and vivacious personality, warm, outgoing, and charming. He recalls the occasion one afternoon when Galíndez in a relaxed mood performed, solo, an intricate and strenuous Basque dance, executing the involved movements with precision and a verve that would have done credit to a man half his age. He remembers the mature and informed part that Galíndez took in numerous conversations that ranged over a wide variety of political areas and problems, consequential and inconsequential. He recollects the courtesy, the gregariousness, and the intense joy of living that Galíndez displayed. If ever the description "blithe spirit" could truly be applied to an individual, Jesús de Galíndez deserved it.

The case of *Society v. Rafael Leonidas Trujillo y Molina* on a charge of murder most foul (in the matter of one Jesús de Galíndez Suárez) must be based on circumstantial evidence. But it is a persuasive case. A cornerstone of it is the vast array of character witnesses — personal, documentary, circumstantial — which testify to the sordid, vicious, ruthless reality of the most cold-blooded and efficient dictatorship (or tyranny, if you will) that Latin America has ever seen. The evidence was first marshaled, as a lawyer would present it, by Galíndez, who was legally trained. He was cold and objective, not propagandistic; he gave credit when credit was due. The result was a devastating condemnation of the Caribbean Nero, the more overpowering because of its undoubted scholarship and unquestioned documentation. The price paid was the author's life, many weeks before the summation could be published in distant Latin American capitals or even accepted as a doctoral dissertation by Columbia University.

In death it was the fateful role of Jesús de Galíndez to stand alongside Emile Zola and repeat the pregnant phrase *"J'accuse!"* He was accusing one in high place of injustice and inhumanity, of defamation and torture, of imprisonment and slaying.

Galíndez also stood beside the spirit of Juan Montalvo, the liberal Ecuadorian polemicist who unrelentingly fought the dictator Gabriel García Moreno with his eloquent pamphlets written in exile. As the eminent historian Hubert Herring describes it, "When García Moreno accepted reelection in 1875, Montalvo answered with a tract, *La Dictadura Perpetua,* which was widely distributed despite the alertness of the police. In August, 1875, the dictator was cut down by an assassin's knife. Montalvo, hearing the news in exile, exclaimed: 'My pen killed him!'" Galíndez inherited that pen.

The Era of Trujillo was a uniquely valuable study, not only because of its pioneer contribution to scholarship but also because of its dramatic and tragic linkage with abduction and murder. It constitutes an overwhelming indictment. The case is presented in the following pages.

RUSSELL H. FITZGIBBON

Editor's Prologue:
The Evil That Men Do

On Saturday, May 16, 1970, Joaquín Balaguer, president of the Dominican Republic, was reelected to that office by a vote of 607,707 out of a total of 1,111,853 ballots cast. He had first been elected to the highest executive post in 1966, although he had served as president from August 4, 1960, to December 31, 1961, in succession to Héctor Trujillo, whose vice-president he had been.

It was that same Joaquín Balaguer who, on April 29, 1956, had cabled to the *New York Times* (published May 1) in his then position as Secretary of State of the Presidency, as follows:

I read with surprise and indignation your editorial of April 26, against whose terms I protest energetically, hoping that this denial which I am sending of the calumnious imputations contained in the editorial will be published in the same prominent form in which publicity was given to the gratuitous attack against the Dominican Republic. The imputations contained in this editorial are of great gravity without there being the slightest foundation for them.

These accusations, according to the import in the editorial itself, can only be attributed to a plan of Communist inspiration intended to depreciate a Government whose strong anti-Communist attitude is well known. Evidently the editorial to which I refer is part of the same campaign of calumnies that the Socialists in the United States and other countries in this hemisphere are putting into practice in accordance with the new policy of Moscow to introduce the Communist influence into the Americas by means of these political parties.

Joaquín Balaguer at that time was simply hearing his master's voice and doing his master's bidding. The master was Rafael Leonidas Trujillo, long the dictator of the Dominican Republic. Was Balaguer then a Mr.

Hyde and more recently a Dr. Jekyll? It is probably what the Dominican president would have us believe, but the ultimate decision must await the more remote verdict of history. We can certainly conclude, however, that Dr. Balaguer in 1956 was a puppet. He was no Pinocchio, dancing for Trujillo's Gepetto; there is too much gentle whimsy in Collodi's entrancing tale to make that simile apt, but he *was* a puppet. In fact, everyone who surrounded Trujillo during his thirty-one-year reign in the Caribbean state was forced into such a role; the alternatives were ruin — financial, social, political, moral — exile, or, in extreme cases, death.

Between 1956, when Balaguer sent his cable, and 1970, when he was triumphantly reelected president, lies as tortured a national political history, as full of inconsistencies and contradictions, as marked by heights of idealistic aspiration and troughs of despairing frustration, as any country in Latin America may have experienced in this century.

Trujillo did not leave a political testament, as Chile's Balmaceda and a few other prominent Latin figures did, and even if he had, it undoubtedly would have been an exercise in megalomania and egocentricity. It is desirable, then, to attempt an independent capsule assessment of what he bequeathed to a nation after three decades of iron rule.

It is customary to say that the assassination of Trujillo left a power vacuum in the Dominican Republic. That is accurate, but it stops short of telling the whole story. The Dominican people had not had simply a "lost weekend" — they had experienced a lost three decades plus, and that involved more than 1,600 weekends and all the days in between. Those who reached voting age at the time that Trujillo came to power were almost in their middle fifties by the time he was killed, and that, given Dominican life expectancy, meant that many of them were virtually through with life itself. They had passed that whole adult period with no meaningful participation in any significant and free political activity. Such activity, and then not free, was reserved to a dictator-designated elite, not to the commoners — theirs was not to reason why.

As a member of the Organization of American States observation team, the editor was privileged to see the voting in numerous precincts in the presidential election in December, 1962, the first free one that the Dominican Republic had had in well over three decades. He well remembers the poignancy and pathos of long lines of middle-aged men and women at the polls, voting freely for the first time in their lives, coming out of the polls with ink-dipped fingers (a technique to prevent "repeaters") proudly held aloft as "the mark of a Dominican." The unvoiced realization that each of them, as a tiny atom in the body politic, had finally had an impact on the political process was emotionally overwhelming to them.

The vacuum flowed from the fact, not merely that the electorate had performed its function only in travesty, but also from the fact that rotation in office — administrative, legislative, judicial, diplomatic, even military — had been so rapid and institutionalized that no one had a chance to learn the expertise of his job. An official could only be concerned with where the sordid game of musical chairs would next place him. If a permanent civil service could have carried on the administration even half as admirably as is done in Britain or France, at once above and below the political battle, an enormous asset would have been established but Trujillo dared not risk even that administrative achievement. An inevitable concomitant of the "system" was the corruption, graft, venality, greed,* infamy, attaching to almost every governmental act or process.

But perhaps worse than any of these other characteristics and consequences was what Galíndez called "the deterioration of all civic spirit." It was the stifling of the soul of a people, the atrophy of will and pride, certainly in the political realm, probably in most others as well. Trujillo perfected brainwashing to a fine art long before the word itself was devised. Men would be humiliated and insulted seemingly beyond human ability to bear, and then crawl fawningly back to the Benefactor like whipped puppies fearfully wagging their tails and licking his hands. The erosion of human self-respect and dignity, intangible though it was, was one of the heaviest liabilities to be charged against Trujillo.[†]

If Trujillo's good were interred with his bones an exhumation would reveal precious little of it, though Galíndez in all fairness looked thoroughly for what could be entered in black ink rather than in a bloody red.

This was the legacy of Trujillo.

* * * * * *

In the last of the conclusions with which the author closed his study he suggested that "the future of the country may well be chaotic, because there are neither social-political forces nor democratic instruments to facilitate a normal succession the day the tyrant disappears." How clearly he saw what was to come!

---

* Juan Bosch wrote in February, 1961, that "That which has given consistency and perdurability to Trujillism is not its character as a military and political tyranny, but the transformation of the country into a merciless capitalist enterprise, of which Rafael Leonidas Trujillo alone is the proprietor, and which the civil government and the armed forces serve as unconditional instruments." *Trujillo: Causas de una Tiranía sin Ejemplo* (Caracas, 1961), p. 174.

†Cf. Howard J. Wiarda, *Dictatorship and Development: The Methods of Control in Trujillo's Dominican Republic* (Gainesville, Florida, 1968), pp. 179–86, *passim.*

The events of the years following 1961 need be sketched only briefly. The bungled assassination plot was successful only in its first and most dramatic phase — the killing itself. As Wiarda points out,* successive phases were to include the capture of other key members of the family and the regime, to win control of the government, and to move on to a more normal system. This design very quickly fell apart, and all but two of the conspirators were soon captured and killed. Balaguer as president and Ramfis Trujillo as commander-in-chief of the armed forces were in the center of the picture, but neither had the will nor the ability of the departed dictator. The heavy burden of moral obloquy which the hemisphere loaded on the Dominican government, but even more, the international economic sanctions that had been imposed as a consequence of the 1960 foreign ministers' conference, resulted in reluctant concessions designed to persuade the world that a Trujillist leopard had changed its spots. Escalating domestic and foreign pressures finally forced the family clan into unwilling banishment in November, 1961, but Balaguer managed to survive the gathering storm until early in 1962; then he, too, went into asylum and then exile.

The unleashed military, built by Trujillo far beyond any needs of the country, attempted a take-over early in 1962, but it was only a forty-eight-hour interlude and then the council of state, now minus Balaguer, returned to power. Most of that year was spent in honest and valiant efforts at preparation for the presidential elections in December. The great need was for civic education of a very elementary sort. The elections on December 20, 1962, saw an easy victory by Juan Bosch, presidential candidate of the Dominican Revolutionary Party. Bosch was an intellectual and literary figure of considerable stature, who had long been in exile, and in terms of realistic experience in administration was a novice. He was a combination of idealism and naiveté.[†]

Bosch's unrealistic approach to the problems and pressures of his office, and above all, his failure properly to placate the army — an agency which Trujillo had never ignored or failed to control — gave him a poor rating as a political actuarial risk. His maverick and sometimes intransigent attitude antagonized one element after another. In late September, less than seven months after his inauguration, an army coup overthrew him.

---

*Howard J. Wiarda, *The Dominican Republic: Nation in Transition* (New York, 1969), p. 50.

†The editor had an opportunity for about an hour's conversation with President-elect Bosch, by himself, on the day after his great victory. When the editor reminded him that they had met in Costa Rica in 1953, Bosch beamed and asked, "And what did we talk about then?" The editor had to confess that he had forgotten, and Bosch interposed, "It must have been my poetry." In a moment of triumph he could be more interested in poetry than politics!

Reasons for his downfall were complex. In a later cogent analysis, Ambassador John Bartlow Martin concluded that, in effect, the failure and the failings of Bosch simply mirrored those of the Dominicans themselves.* At any rate, Bosch was out, and thinly disguised military control was in.

A businessman who had been a member of the council of state in 1962, Donald Reid Cabral, emerged after some three months as the central figure in the junta that succeeded Bosch. Attempts were made to move toward short and halting reforms but infighting among disparate and self-serving elements, especially the pampered military, became the order of the day. The crisis-point was reached in late April, 1965, with the launching of a revolt, allegedly aimed at returning Bosch to power. Confusing and competing forces almost immediately vied for control, and the whole situation was complicated by an official fear in the United States of Communist manipulation and possible capture of the picture. This led to massive landings of United States troops (at their peak, more than 20,000 men), ostensibly to protect United States nationals in the strife-torn capital city but actually to forestall the possible establishment of "another Cuba." The intervention was given a façade of being multi-national by the dispatch of contingents from several other American nations, the smallest of them consisting of *three* men.

During the virtual civil war that existed in the Dominican Republic from late April to the end of August, 1965, three groups contended for control at one time or another: the "constitutional" government, a military junta, and the "government of national reconstruction." Finally, after strenuous efforts to bring the warring factions together, a compromise regime was laboriously hammered out, headed by the relatively nonpolitical Héctor García Godoy. It remained precariously in power from early September, 1965, until the inauguration of a constitutional government on July 1, 1966.

García Godoy's most important task was to preside over presidential elections set for June 1, 1966. The principal candidates were Bosch and Joaquín Balaguer. By now, Bosch's image had become somewhat tarnished and his appeal diminished. In the hectic summer months of 1965, he had remained in safety in Puerto Rico and during the spring campaign in 1966 he stayed in his Santo Domingo house, ostensibly fearing assassination if he ventured out, and making his political pleas by radio from his home. Balaguer had succeeded in living down the incubus of earlier association with the Trujillo regime. His new Reformista Party made an especial appeal to women and the peasantry and he probably gained support from

---

* *Overtaken by Events: The Dominican Crisis from the Fall of Trujillo to the Civil War* (Garden City, N.Y., 1966), pp. 716–20.

their recollection of the largess that Trujillo had distributed to the Dominican disadvantaged, somewhat after the manner of Perón's cultivation of the Argentine *descamisados*. Balaguer won easily, receiving 745,409 votes to 517,784 for Bosch.

Balaguer's administration from 1966 to 1970 was in general moderate, reformist, and conciliatory. The new constitution permitted reelection of a president, though it could not be said that such a provision was the rationale for its having been written, as was the case with the peronista constitution in Argentina in 1949. At any rate, Balaguer took advantage of the provision and in early 1970 declared he would be a candidate for another term. This quickly aroused latent feelings and fears, and at one stage all opposing candidates threatened to withdraw if Balaguer remained in the presidency during the conclusion of the campaigning. He reluctantly took a leave of absence from the executive office for the last month of the contest.

The Dominican Revolutionary Party, again dominated by Bosch, persisted in boycotting the election, maintaining that the balloting would be manipulated and meaningless and that "representative democracy" was not an appropriate political prescription for this country. Georgie Anne Geyer, a veteran syndicated reporter, who interviewed Bosch at length after the 1970 election, recounted that he favored a "dictatorship with popular support."[*] This, she explained, was basically "a mixture of Mussolini corporativism, Nasseristic military insurrection as a road to power, Marxist utopianism, and Caribbean passion," though when she pressed him for details of the blueprint he became impatient and vague.

Conditions deteriorated within the next seventeen months. In a long analytical dispatch to the *Los Angeles Times* in October, 1971, a correspondent reported that the church, professional groups, labor organizations, and others were appalled by the rising tide of political violence and were increasingly clamoring for change. Protests were catalyzed by the mid-October murder of five Santo Domingo youths, allegedly by right-wing terrorists. Balaguer undertook another in a series of police force shakeups but killings continued; the number of political murders in 1971 to that date was asserted to be 139.[†]

The capital city's *El Caribe* speculated that the growing terror could "involve the Dominican society in a crisis of enormous proportions" and Bosch darkly predicted that an explosion "could come at any moment."

---

[*] "Bosch Five Years Later — Disillusion with Democracy," *Los Angeles Times,* May 31, 1970, p. G3.

[†] Francis B. Kent, "Discontent Mounting in Santo Domingo," *Los Angeles Times,* October 20, 1971, p. 25.

Leaders of various political parties were openly accusing Balaguer of dictatorial actions and trends.

*   *   *   *   *   *

In post-Perón Argentina it was customary for a long time to blame all the country's many and complex woes on the legacy of Perón. Undoubtedly he had distorted and well-nigh ruined the nation's economy, had thrown off balance the precarious alignment of Argentine political forces, had cried havoc in release of *descamisado* attacks on the established social order. As time passed, however, it seemed as if the shoulder-shrugging attribution of all Argentine ills to Perón wore a bit thin.

The Dominican picture and problem resemble in broad outline those of the vastly larger and more complex Argentina, though in matters of detail they differ enormously. Both countries were marked by serious internal social and political schisms, both were hopeful (in greatly differing stages and ways) of currents of modernization, both had long been under the heavy hand of dictators.

The historical development of any country, whether it be a reasonably well matured one like Argentina or a much less evolved one such as the Dominican Republic, is an unending process that can be likened to an interminable bolt of cloth. The colors and pattern in the warp and woof may change, sometimes violently, the closeness of the weave may vary, even the material may be altered as the bolt unfolds. But one part is conditioned by what has already been exposed to view and it in turn influences what the next unrolling of the bolt will display. In that larger sense, the Argentina of 1972 *is* indebted to the Argentina of 1955 and the Dominican Republic of 1972 to the Dominican Republic of 1961. Perón and Trujillo are still shadows over their respective lands, receding, it is true, but visible even yet without a telescope. The remaining Trujillist penumbra is doubtless the darker of the two because the blackness of the long Dominican eclipse was far more nearly total.

Bosch's idealism gave promise of the emergence of honesty and democracy. But there was poor soil in which to nurture such qualities. The Dominican background was a sorry record of authoritarianism alternating with anarchy, of foreign occupations and pressures from neighboring Haiti or by solicitation from one or another of the great powers (and United States pressure has been evident even within the past decade), of violent oscillation of governments, constitutions, and political systems. Small wonder, then, that the past decade has shown such difficulty in establishing a viable democracy.

An inchoate nationalism is apparent in the Dominican Republic, but it has not been accompanied by a disciplined democratic process that would make its manifestations most meaningful. Nascent nationalism often finds its outlet in xenophobia and the Dominican Republic offered a case in point, as the uncertainty of the popular reception of an inter-American conference scheduled for Santo Domingo in 1970 ominously footnoted.

Trujillo built up the armed forces beyond all reason. Both pre- and post-Trujillo, the upper-officer ranks were filled with venality and graft, and in the years after Trujillo, political ambition and adventuring have been added to the earlier corruption. It is not an earnest of orderly, stable politics, free of self-serving and manipulation. The armed forces have been strongly resistant to any suggestion or attempt that they be deflated. The specter of communism, whether bogey or real, is for them sufficient justification.

The oldest of the Republic's parties, the Dominican Revolutionary, is even yet only a third of a century old, no venerable age, certainly, even for Latin America. Many Latin American states have seen parties develop to the point where they show considerable continuity and even institutionalization. But not those in the Dominican Republic; even the largest and best organized are still highly personalistic. The names of Bosch and Balaguer are still almost synonymous with the Dominican Revolutionary and Reformist parties, respectively, and the same is true with lesser figures and weaker parties. Not only are the parties person-alistic, they are also, and almost by the same token, usually rigid and uncompromising in their positions. There is no faint reflection in the Dominican Republic of anything like "His Majesty's loyal opposition." Parties flourish like the green bay tree, and often wither almost as soon as they spring up; their very numbers make the smallest and weakest of them no more than froth that adds nothing to the palatability of the political soup.

In a number of Latin American countries the church and organized labor are factors of importance in politics. But not in the Dominican Republic. Neither one traditionally had significant strength in the country and of course during most of the Trujillo years both were kept sternly under control. In a freer, and now in some respects almost an anarchic society, they may be able to develop political muscle, but it will not be done overnight.

Middle class pluralism and values are often the connective tissue out of which an emergent nation can be bound together. In the Dominican Republic, however, class and group differences have been so deep-rooted and corrosive that mutual accommodation and compromise have been almost impossible; the situation has been worse since 1965 than even between 1961 and 1965. Violence is often born from the womb of frustration, and circumstances in "the land Columbus loved" seem peculiarly and tragically conducive to frustration. In the immediate future, at any rate, turbulence and violence, perhaps even revolution, are more likely to be normal than abnormal. That, too, is part of the legacy of Trujillo.

The reelection of Balaguer in 1970 was not to be regarded as what the Latins often call *imposición,* but it had enough of the appearance of a controlled and manipulated choice that it inevitably raised in some quarters the specter of a renewed dictatorship. After all, Balaguer had been Trujillo's surrogate at the time of the latter's assassination. At first glance Balaguer does not seem carved of the stuff dictators are made of, but he had expert tuition and he is a persistent and ambitious man. The clues to the future may well be found in the past. It is important, then, that we know a great deal about what Trujillo did and said and thought and wanted. We cannot do better than to turn to the thoroughgoing analysis of such matters that was made by the man who, by direct experience and thorough research, knew the nightmare of Trujillismo perhaps better than anyone else. Jesús de Galíndez was an objective though not a dispassionate student of that tyranny. He closed his study at the time of its apogee. Let us give him the floor.

RUSSELL H. FITZGIBBON

The Era of Trujillo

THE DOMINICAN REPUBLIC IN 1956

ATLANTIC OCEAN

MONTE
CRISTI
LUPERÓN
PUERTO
PLATA
PUERTO PLATA
SOSÚA
Río
Massacre
El Cibao
ESPAILLAT
DAJABÓN
MONTE
CRISTI
SANTIAGO
SAMANÁ
LIBERTADOR
SANTIAGO
SAMANÁ
SAN FRANCISCO
DE MACORÍS
Bahía de Samaná
LA VEGA
SAN
RAFAEL
DUARTE
ELÍAS
PIÑA
Pico Trujillo
(Pico Duarte)
LA VEGA
TRUJILLO
EL SEIBO
BENEFACTOR
SAN JUAN
LA ALTAGRACIA
AZUA
TRUJILLO
VALDEZ
Río
Jaina
SAN
PEDRO
DE MACORÍS
SANTO
DOMINGO
BAHORUCO
AZUA
SAN
CRISTÓBAL
LA ROMANA
NIGUA
JAINA
SAN PEDRO
DE MACORÍS
INDEPENDENCIA
CIUDAD TRUJILLO
(SANTO DOMINGO)
BANÍ
BARAHONA
CARIBBEAN SEA
BARAHONA

CUBA

CAP-HAÏTIEN

ST. MARC
HAITI

DOMINICAN REPUBLIC

PORT-AU-PRINCE

CIUDAD TRUJILLO
(SANTO DOMINGO)

HISPANIOLA

Author's Introduction

I. Latin American Dictatorship

As of midyear 1955, half of the Latin American republics were under dictatorships,* the majority of a military type. Only one of them was proclaiming itself as such: the Republic of Honduras, which was established as a result of the 1954 elections in which no candidate received the constitutionally required 50 percent of the votes cast. Another dictatorship which had just disappeared, that of Perón in Argentina, presented special characteristics, as did that of Vargas in Brazil some years ago. But all the others were following a very well-defined pattern.

The Latin American dictatorship, especially in the twentieth century, has presented certain characteristics which identify it and isolate it from other dictatorial regimes known to political science. It has elements in common with other types, but its essential difference and characteristic are the adoption of a formal structure similar to that of the western democracies. There is a constitution; periodic elections are held; the government is divided into the three classic powers [i.e., branches]; a detailed declaration of human rights is proclaimed. The structure of government is inspired by the Constitution of the United States, and the declaration of human rights is inspired by its French counterpart of 1789 plus some recent innovations of social tendency. But each and all of these democratic institutions have been distorted in practice, in order to transform them into mere tools of the omnipotent will of one strong man, who usually has been the president of the republic but who may sometimes act through a puppet ruler.

---

* Although the Galíndez manuscript does not list them, and some borderline and arbitrary decisions are necessary in cataloguing them, they may be assumed, as of mid-1955, to include Argentina, Colombia, Cuba, the Dominican Republic, El Salvador, Guatemala, Haiti, Honduras, Nicaragua, Paraguay, Peru, and Venezuela.

The Latin American dictatorship is a special type which deserves a place of its own in political science. In fact, and this will be further developed in the conclusion of this study, these regimes might better be called tyrannies in the sense that a dictatorship presupposes a formal structure of its own, and what exists in Latin America is a *de facto* situation in which the apparent formal law is violated. There is no ideological philosophy; there is only a regime of force. In order to facilitate the analysis, however, the current term — dictatorship — will be used in this study.

Dictatorships appeared early in Latin America, although the type dealt with in this study was not fully defined until the end of the nineteenth century. Analysis of its evolution does not belong in this study, but we must recall at least some of its milestones.[1]

After the wars of independence and following the defeat of certain monarchic trends (which existed in Brazil up to 1889, and occasionally in Haiti and Mexico), the new Latin American nations adopted constitutions inspired by the United States structure of government, based upon the division and balance of the three branches: executive, legislative, and judicial. They, likewise, incorporated the declaration of human rights taken from the French Revolution, either directly or through the Spanish version of 1812.

The only country which openly adopted the dictatorial form of government was Paraguay, in 1814, under the influence of Dr. José Gaspar Rodríguez de Francia who, one year earlier, had attempted another form inspired by classic Rome, that of a double consulate. This formal dictatorship lasted until Francia's death in 1840.

In the remaining countries, a balance of constitutional democratic institutions was attempted at first. But there soon developed the cycle of rebellions against the government, suspension of constitutional guarantees, bloody civil wars, *de facto* dictatorship to reestablish order, and revolution to oust the dictatorship. It was a process of instability and violence, the analysis of which does not belong here, but in many countries it has lasted up to mid-twentieth century or later. Very few countries have been able to escape this experience.

Examples of Latin American dictatorship in the days following independence are so many that it would be useless to mention them. Predominant among them were the following: in the first half of the nineteenth

---

[1] For fuller development of the Latin American political evolution and current forms of government, see the author's book, *Iberoamérica: Su Evolución Política, Socio-económica, Cultural e Internacional* (New York, 1954); especially see chapters XIII, XIV, XVII, XVIII, XXIV, XXV, and XXVII; also the extensive bibliography, covering the continental and national fields. [Fn. 1, Introduction.]

century the Argentine dictator, Juan Manuel de Rosas, from 1835 to 1852; in the second half of the century, the two Paraguayan dictators, Carlos Antonio López (father), from 1844 to 1862, and Francisco Solano López (son), from 1862 to 1870; and the Mexican dictator, Porfirio Díaz, from 1877 to 1911.

Countries where dictators were frequent included Paraguay, Bolivia, Peru, Ecuador, Venezuela, Central America in general, Haiti and the Dominican Republic. On the other hand, Chile, in 1830, was able to reach constitutional democratic stability — the first Latin American country to achieve this. Argentina followed in 1852, and, in general, Colombia, Costa Rica, and Brazil have held the democratic line, the latter even during its empire. At the beginning of the twentieth century, Uruguay joined this group and very soon became a "model state," as did Mexico.

The dictatorships of the nineteenth century paid no attention to the constitutions in force; occasionally the dictator did not hesitate to proclaim himself as such, even if he were only a *de facto* dictator, without the legal formality of Dr. Francia.

However, the methods which the special type of present-day Latin American dictatorship or tyranny were to adopt were introduced little by little. Perhaps the first symptom of these was the repeated changes of constitution, each aimed to grant more powers to the president and to diminish those of other organs of the state, to suspend constitutional guarantees and individual freedoms, and to extend the presidential term. Naturally, each revolutionary movement against the dictator usually meant another constitutional change to reverse this trend.

Finally, there arrived a period in which the dictator or tyrant no longer changed the formal structure of government, because he preferred to maintain democratic appearances while subjecting all state institutions to his caprice. The contemporary type of dictatorship or tyranny, which is disguised under a constitutional democratic appearance, has strengthened itself in this way. There are earlier and contemporary examples of this type, but its two masters were Porfirio Díaz in Mexico, from 1877 to 1911, and Juan Vicente Gómez in Venezuela, from 1908 to 1935. Both of their regimes extended sufficiently long to permit them to attain the needed stability to perfect their style and thus establish the model to be imitated by others. Gómez changed the constitution several times but Díaz did not bother to do so. Both of them also simulated elections, permitting no possible opposition, and occasionally preferring to have somebody else elected as "president," but always keeping the actual power themselves; both maintained the appearance of a congress and courts, although these were only tools to execute their dictates; both proclaimed individual rights, which did not exist in practice.

This type of dictatorship has had extraordinary success in the twentieth century. Almost without exception, Latin American dictators maintain this constitutional democratic appearance, which is as formal externally as their regime of force is ironclad. There are small variations from country to country; occasionally there is a pretense of a multiplicity of parties, although in reality only the government party has any freedom of action. During recent years, tolerance of labor unions has been fairly prevalent, although they are government-controlled. The dictatorship may be highly personal or partly shared with the army. But the basic characteristics of the regime repeat themselves everywhere.

The end of World War II seemed to mark a decline of these Latin American dictatorships. In 1944, Maximiliano Hernández Martínez was ousted in El Salvador, and Jorge Ubico in Guatemala. The receding tide continued in 1945 and 1946, and its climax was perhaps the collective inter-American quarantine against the puppet government imposed by Somoza in Nicaragua in 1947. By that year, only five dictators remained in Latin America,* and even Trujillo and Somoza were in danger. But this trend has changed radically since 1948. During that year, new dictatorships of military origin were established in Peru and Venezuela. Today, perhaps half of the Latin American republics are ruled by dictatorships of various shades; almost all of them follow in their basic lines the type perfected by Díaz and Gómez half a century ago.

It is impossible to foresee the evolution of democratic processes in Latin America in the future. Even with the most optimistic criteria, it is obvious that the unstable cycle of dictatorships and revolutions will continue in many countries for a long time. Hence, the Latin American dictatorship or tyranny merits study as a typical species existing in contemporary political science.

Such a study could be general in character, focusing on common features. But perhaps the picture then would be confused, because it would not present as perfect a design as the concrete study of any one of these regimes. For this reason, the detailed analysis of a single case seems preferable. Trujillo's Dominican Republic has been chosen as the prototype.

This regime has the advantage of being the oldest of all existing dictatorships in Latin America. Trujillo rose to power in 1930; twenty-five years of uninterrupted rule permit a study in depth of his regime, and even a consideration of small shifts of direction in response to changing world

---

* Galíndez probably is referring to: Juan D. Perón (Argentina), Rafael L. Trujillo (Dominican Republic), Tiburcio Carías A. (Honduras), Anastasio Somoza (Nicaragua), and Higinio Morínigo (Paraguay).

events. The author of this study has had the personal advantage of having lived for six years in the country, and has since maintained continuous contact with Dominicans of all political tendencies.

Hence, the political regime of the Dominican Republic during the twenty-five years of the Era of Trujillo (1930-1955) will be the subject of this study. It is not solely the analysis of a single country, but also an attempt to present the Dominican dictatorship as a prototype of a continental species. Details may vary, but the typical features are repeated from country to country.

II. The Dominican Republic to 1930

[*This section of the Introduction (pp. 10-20 of the manuscript) presents in a strictly factual manner a summary account of the ethnic composition of the Dominican population, the principal products of the country, a suggestion of the problems arising from coexistence with neighboring Haiti, and, somewhat more fully, the historical development from the time of discovery until 1930. The author cites as general historical sources J. G. García,* Compendio de la Historia de Santo Domingo *(Santo Domingo, 1867–69) and* Historia Moderna de la República Dominicana *(Santo Domingo, 1906); Gustavo Adolfo Mejía Ricart,* Historia de Santo Domingo *(Ciudad Trujillo, 1948-   ); A. del Monte y Tejera,* Historia de Santo Domingo *(La Habana, 1853); B. Pichardo,* Resumen de Historia Patria *(Barcelona, 1922); and Joaquín Marino Incháustegui Cabral,* Historia Dominicana *(Ciudad Trujillo, 1946 and 1948). For the United States occupation, 1916-24, he cites Sumner Welles,* Naboth's Vineyard *(2 vol., New York, 1928); Max Henríquez Ureña,* Los Yanquis en Santo Domingo *(Madrid, 1929); and Melvin M. Knight,* The Americans in Santo Domingo *(New York, 1928).*]

III. Sources Used for This Thesis

[*This section of the Introduction (pp. 21-33 of the manuscript) is reproduced as the Bibliography in this edition of* The Era of Trujillo, *p. 275.*]

Chapter 1: The Era of Trujillo

All official documents of the Dominican Republic must be dated, as decreed by Law No. 247 of April 16, 1940,[1] with special reference to the year of the "Era of Trujillo" which began on August 16, 1930. Another law requires that the current year, 1955, be called the "Year of the Benefactor" because it marks "the 25th anniversary of the transcendental period of History called by the name of Era of Trujillo."[2]

On August 16, 1930, Trujillo took the oath for the first time as president of the Dominican Republic; on May 16, 1930, he had been elected without opposition. Either of the two dates could be used to mark officially the beginning of his era. But in truth it really started in February, at the time of the bloodless coup which ousted President Horacio Vásquez. In order to get a better understanding of its development, one must probe more deeply into the past of Rafael L. Trujillo.

Personal Background of Trujillo Before 1930

"The genealogy of Trujillo is well known. He descends from a Spanish officer and a French marquis. Two conquerors who came to American lands with cloak, sword, and crest, and a cross on their

---

The first chapter is devoted to a recital of the most important events of the twenty-five years Trujillo had been in power. All analysis or comments will appear in the Second Part. As much as possible, statements are based upon both official and unofficial sources. Occasionally there may be reference to other sources or ones based on the direct knowledge of the author. Although at times it may appear that the facts have not enough general relevance, they are included because they initiate a process which becomes important later on in the study. [Fn. 1, Chap. I, Sec. 1.]

[1] Dominican Republic, *Gaceta Oficial* No. 5442. (Hereafter cited as *G.O.*) [Fn. 2, Chap. I, Sec. 1.]

[2] *El Caribe,* May 16, 1954. [Fn. 3, Chap. I, Sec. 1.]

chests," says the most often reprinted biography in praise of Trujillo.[3] Opposition authors gloat in emphasizing a much less glorious past of the closest ancestors of Trujillo.

Nevertheless, all of them agree on the identity of his grandfathers and parents. His paternal grandfather was an officer of the Spanish secret police, who during the four years of the Dominican annexation to Spain served in the island, and in 1865 went back to Cuba. Captain José Trujillo Monegas left behind in the Dominican town of San Cristóbal a son, José ("Pepito"), born in 1865 [1864?], whose mother was the young Silveria Valdez, a Dominican. His maternal grandfather was a Dominican, Pedro Molina, and his maternal grandmother was Luisa Ercina Chevalier of Haitian parentage. In 1865, a child, Julia Molina, was born to the couple Molina-Chevalier.[4]

José Trujillo Valdez and Julia Molina were married in San Cristóbal in 1885. They had seven boys (Virgilio, Rafael Leonidas, Aníbal Julio, José Arismendi ["Petán"], Romeo, Pedro, and Héctor Bienvenido ["Negro"]) and four girls (Marina, Julieta, Nieves Luisa, and Japonesa). Rafael Leonidas was born on October 24, 1891.

The career of Trujillo from early manhood is closely bound to the American military occupation. It seems that about the time he was sixteen years old, he obtained his first steady job, as a telegraph operator. A short time afterward he married Aminta Ledesma, mother of Flor de Oro. The landing of American marines offered him the opportunity to escape from such an obscure life.

In December, 1918, he approached the commander of the national guard organized by the United States military government, and on January 11, 1919, he took the oath as provisional second lieutenant and was garrisoned in the eastern area of the country, where the *gavilleros* (guerrilla forces) often fought against the authorities. He was a competent officer. A report by the district inspector, dated September 30, 1919, says in reference to Lieutenant Trujillo: "I consider this officer to be among the best in the service." Another report, in 1921, affirms that "his behaviour before and after the attack was excellent." On August 15, 1921, he entered the officers' school at Jaina and was graduated by Christmas of that year. A letter from Colonel Rixey informing him of his new assignment in Santiago says that the commander of the Northern Department

---

[3] Abelardo R. Nanita, *Trujillo,* 5th ed. (Ciudad Trujillo, 1951), p. 73. (This book and most of the books and pamphlets referred to are noted at length in the Bibliography.) [Fn. 4, Chap. I, Sec. 1.]

[4] The biographers favorable to Trujillo and those opposed to him agree on the facts. They disagree on details, silences, and adjectives. [Fn. 5, Chap. I, Sec. 1.]

"has full confidence in your ability."[5] In October, 1922, he was promoted to captain.

In accordance with the Hughes-Peynado Plan of 1922, the national guard, organized by the United States Marine Corps, remained as the national police force of the new Dominican government, and its native officers kept their ranks and assignments. Captain Trujillo commanded the Sixth Company garrisoned in San Francisco de Macorís until August, 1923. Then he was transferred with the same rank but as inspector of the First District. A few months later, Major J. César Lora, commander of the Northern Department, was murdered by a medical officer in defense of his honor, and Trujillo was promoted to his position as major commander on March 6, 1924. He was promoted again on December 6, 1924, to lieutenant colonel, chief of staff of the national police, with residence in the capital city. One year later, on June 22, 1925, Trujillo was appointed colonel, commander of the police, by President Horacio Vásquez.

His eulogists and his enemies agree that Trujillo did an outstanding work as chief of the police. He reorganized the force and made it efficient. A law passed in 1927 transformed this police into a national army, and at the same time its chief was promoted to the new rank of brigadier general. President Vásquez himself pinned the insignia on Trujillo's shoulders during a military review held on August 15. This same year, 1927, Trujillo again married, this time to Bienvenida Ricardo [Ricart]. Two years later, on June 5, 1929, his first son Rafael L. ("Ramfis") was born to him by María Martínez.*

Trujillo kept his position as general commander of the Dominican national army until the coup of 1930. President Vásquez never suspected him until it was too late.

The Coup of February, 1930

On March 2, 1930, Horacio Vásquez resigned as president of the Dominican Republic, and Rafael Estrella Ureña took the oath as provisional president, having been the victorious leader of a revolutionary movement which started in Santiago on February 22. The panegyrists of Trujillo are always very careful to point out that the commander of the army remained neutral in his military fortress in order to avoid useless bloodshed. The authors of the opposition affirm without hesitation that Trujillo was in fact the directing brain of the revolution and that his

---

[5] These three quotations are taken from Gilberto Sánchez Lustrino, *Trujillo: El Constructor de una Nacionalidad* (Havana, 1938), pp. 87–88. [Fn. 7, Chap. I, Sec. 1.]

* Trujillo was still married at the time to doña Bienvenida, who quickly passed into disfavor. Trujillo divorced her on April 30, 1935, and married María Martínez on September 28 of the same year.

behavior was a model of treason. In any event, General Trujillo was proclaimed on March 18 as a presidential candidate, and on May 16 he was elected president without any opposition.

There is not available a satisfactory account of what happened during the last days of February, 1930. And it is unlikely that in the future it will be possible to reconstruct an accurate narrative of these events. The main protagonists of the coup have been too cautious to do so until now, and many of them have long since died. However, one may attempt to summarize the unquestionable facts, one may add the verbal account the author received confidentially from one of the protagonists of the coup, and one may end with an objective reconstruction, based principally upon the diplomatic correspondence of the United States legation in Santo Domingo with the Department of State.[6]

President Horacio Vásquez went to the United States on October 31, 1929, for surgery. On January 6, 1930, he returned to the Dominican Republic. A decree on January 9 summarily dismissed Major Ernesto Pérez,[7] adjutant to the Headquarters of the Brigade (lieutenant of General Trujillo), because of "behaviour unbecoming an officer of the Army,"[8] but on January 15 the newspaper *Listín Diario* noted that the dismissed Major Pérez had been seen in Fortress Ozama dressed in uniform.

On January 28, Charles B. Curtis, the new minister from the United States, presented his credentials to President Vásquez. The *Official Gazette* on February 15 published a proclamation calling for general elections on May 16.

During this same period, different presidential candidacies were made public, sometimes in contradictory fashion. *Listín Diario* on February 11 published a letter addressed to Federico Velázquez, Rafael Estrella Ureña, General Desiderio Arias and Dr. Teófilo Hernández, the leaders of the Compactación de Partidos (Alliance of Parties), backing Velázquez as the presidential candidate, and proposing the joint nomination of a "national candidate." *Listín Diario* on the thirteenth made public the candidacies of the National party: General Horacio Vásquez for president and Dr. José D. Alfonseca for vice-president.

---

[6] U.S. Department of State, *Foreign Relations of the United States, 1930* 2: 699–717. The complete Report No. 22, dated March 1, is especially useful (pp. 709–17). [Fn. 3, Chap. I, Sec. 2.]

[7] *G.O.* 4171. [Fn. 4, Chap. I, Sec. 2.]

[8] *Listín Diario* of Jan. 11, 1930, in announcing this expulsion from the army, said that it had been due to the abduction of a minor, Ozama Petit, by Major Pérez in Monte Cristi. An account of this abduction can be read in Félix A. Mejía, *Vía Crucis de un Pueblo* (Mexico, 1951), pp. 20–25. Ex-Major Pérez acted prominently in the coup of 1930, and has always been one of the trusted men of Trujillo, although never a bright one, and at present holds the rank of brigadier general. [Fn. 5, Chap. I, Sec. 2.]

On February 23, 1930, the revolution broke out in Santiago. Some groups of the opposition had seized two military posts in Santiago. On February 25 *Listín Diario* carried a major headline: "Latest news about the movement agitating the Cibao. Neither President Vásquez nor Vice-President Alfonseca have resigned. The rebellious troops cry: Long live General Trujillo and General Estrella Ureña!" In the text it was said that President Vásquez had been persuaded to fight the revolution and that he went to the Fortress Ozama together with Vice-President Alfonseca and other members of the regime. It was also stated that the leaders of the revolution were General José Estrella, Licenciado [Attorney] Rafael Estrella Ureña, General Desiderio Arias and some others, but nothing was said about the attitude of General Trujillo.

On February 27, the same newspaper announced that the revolutionaries, under the command of General José Estrella, had already occupied the city, that Vásquez and Alfonseca would resign, and that all parties would agree on a new secretary of interior and police who would be provisional president in accordance with the Constitution. There was no mention at all of General Trujillo. In the March 1 edition it was said that Estrella Ureña had been selected as the new secretary of interior and police, and that President Vásquez would leave the country. *Listín Diario* of the third still said nothing about General Trujillo, although reference was made to a ceremony in the Fortress in which Brigadier Trujillo appeared together with Estrella Ureña. On the fifth, the exile of Vásquez and Alfonseca was announced, together with the formation of the new government.[9]

The *Official Gazette* is more scanty in data. There is nowhere official evidence of the resignation of President Vásquez. Decree No. 1258 on March 3, signed by Estrella Ureña as provisional president, appointed the members of the new provisional government, because of the resignation of the previous secretaries; nobody countersigned it. . . .

In the *Bulletin* of the Senate appears the record of the session held on March 2 at 10:23 A.M. by the National Assembly (joint meeting of both chambers of Congress)[10] in which the Assembly was advised of and accepted the resignations of President Vásquez and Vice-President Alfonseca. Five minutes later, at 10:28 A.M., the National Assembly met again to receive the oath of Lic. Rafael Estrella Ureña as provisional president.

---

[9] All the news mentioned day by day with reference to *Listín Diario,* has been taken from the pertinent editions of this newspaper of the capital city, at that time the most important in the Dominican Republic, and backer of President Vásquez and his National party. [Fn. 14, Chap. I, Sec. 2.]

[10] Dominican Republic, Senate, *Boletín del Senado* (hereafter cited as *Bol. Sen.*), March, 1930, pp. 140–43. [Fn. 23, Chap. I, Sec. 2.]

... Estrella Ureña promised free elections for the next constitutional period, beginning August 16.

This is the official evidence and the newspaper accounts of what happened, which cannot be refuted twenty-five years later. All other explanations which appear in subsequent books are contradictory and doubtful, because they are partisan and show wishful thinking. Nevertheless, a careful analysis of the documents allows a reconstruction of the main events, a reconstruction which is, at the same time, similar to the interpretation sent by the United States minister in his reports to the Department of State. Nor does it differ from a confidential statement the author had from one of the protagonists of the coup.

There is no doubt that Trujillo was implicated in the coup and that he intervened decisively but cautiously in its development. As that informant told the author, the "brains" behind what happened were Rafael Vidal and Roberto Despradel, who, being political prisoners in Fortress Ozama some time before, realized that Brigadier Trujillo could be the most efficient instrument to oust the government of President Vásquez. Vidal and Despradel indoctrinated Brigadier Trujillo in favor of the cause they considered to be just and democratic. Their error was not to take into account the personal ambitions of Trujillo, who could not advance in his military career beyond being head of the army.

A short time before the coup, large consignments of weapons were transferred in secret from Fortress Ozama in Santo Domingo to Santiago de los Caballeros.[11] The orders were given by Trujillo. From this moment on, the account of the informant coincides with the data that, clearly stated in the books written against Trujillo or interpreting silences and ambiguities in the books of his panegyrists, are repeated in all accounts and interpretations.

The revolution started in Santiago with an attack against Fortress San Luis, which presented a token defense. Rafael Estrella Ureña assumed the political leadership of the movement. The role of Trujillo in the capital was to paralyze the reaction of the government, feigning loyalty to President Vásquez at the same time that he controlled Fortress Ozama and the main part of the army.

It does not seem that President Vásquez suspected Trujillo's treachery until the end; but there are enough clues to indicate that prominent

---

[11] It is confirmed by United States Minister Curtis, in his Report No. 22, March 1: "Probably in December, he [Trujillo] stripped the fort in Santo Domingo City of practically all spare arms and shipped these arms to the fort in Santiago. He most certainly was in league with the revolutionists from the very beginning, and never severed his connection with them." (Dept. State, *Foreign Relations* 2: 711.) [Fn. 30, Chap. I, Sec. 2.]

members of his government had already suspected him and that they attempted to convince the president upon his return that Trujillo was a serious threat as the head of the army. On the other hand, the correspondence of the United States legation in Santo Domingo has proved *a posteriori* that the former minister, Young, knew of these suspicions and talked about these rumors with Trujillo himself. A cable sent by U. S. Minister Charles B. Curtis on February 26 read: "22. In spite of the solemn assurances given to my predecessor and the authorities, it is now absolutely certain that General Trujillo conspired with the revolutionary leaders and has repeatedly betrayed the government."

Nor were the aspirations of Rafael Estrella Ureña and the beginning of his machinations in Santiago a secret. On the eve of the revolution and before its first sparks, Third Secretary John Moors Cabot was sent to Santiago, where he spoke on the same night of February 22 with Estrella Ureña. Cabot returned to the capital convinced that the situation was not serious.

On the twenty-third General José Estrella started his advance towards Santo Domingo. President Vásquez called the chief of the army, still convinced of his loyalty. Trujillo answered that he was sick, and only then did the old president decide to go in person to the fortress. Trujillo reiterated his loyalty.

Early on the twenty-fourth, the secretary of foreign relations, Lic. Francisco J. Peynado, went to the United States legation requesting asylum for the president, his wife, and the vice-president, because the rebels were half an hour away from the city. One hour afterward, President Vásquez, his wife, Vice-President Alfonseca, and others arrived at the legation. In the meantime, Minister Curtis had spoken by telephone with General Trujillo, who again repeated to him his loyalty to President Vásquez.

The already obvious treason was confirmed when on the dawn of February 25, Minister Curtis himself decided to go by the main road to Santiago. He met the government soldiers only a few miles away from the city; not a shot had been exchanged with the enemy. In the meantime, President Vásquez had left Fortress Ozama, finally convinced of Trujillo's treason. During the following night the first revolutionary troops entered the city without any resistance.

A cable from Minister Curtis on the night of the twenty-seventh forwarded the contents of an agreement between President Vásquez and the rebel leaders: the appointment of a new secretary of interior and police who could be acceptable to all parties (it turned out finally to be Estrella Ureña) and would succeed as provisional president in accordance with the Constitution; the formation of a provisional government with participation by all parties; and the acceptance of the future election results in accordance with the Constitution and the laws in force; [etc.]. [12] One of these points read: "6. There shall be no restrictions as to candidates, except that neither Alfonseca or Trujillo shall run."

Subsequent public events confirm the fulfillment of this agreement in its first steps. Estrella Ureña was appointed secretary of interior; two days later President Vásquez and Vice-President Alfonseca resigned, and the new provisional government was formed with representatives of all parties. However, the immediate changes prove also that, despite the agreement reached at the United States legation, it was General Trujillo who occupied the key positions with his most trusted men; the new secretary of the presidency was none other than Rafael Vidal, the brains of the plot with Trujillo; and the second secretary of interior and police was Lic. Jacinto B. Peynado, who was to be the political lieutenant of Trujillo until his death in 1940.

Trujillo remained at the head of the army. [13] The way he used the position to impose, first, his candidacy as president, and then to eliminate all other leaders in the name of the 1930 revolution deserves special consideration.

The Provisional Government of Estrella Ureña

Rafael Estrella Ureña took his oath as provisional president after an agreement in which the ousted president, the supposed leader of the revolution, and the minister of the United States, who acted as mediator, agreed that General Trujillo should never be a presidential candidate. Five and a half months later, Trujillo was inaugurated as constitutional president of the Republic and Estrella Ureña became his vice-president. What happened during this intervening period provides one of the best keys for understanding the development of the "Era of Trujillo."

The incumbency of the provisional government may be divided into two quite distinct periods. During the first month, the Dominicans remained in political ferment with two groups competing for victory in the approaching elections, which all expected would be free. During the second period, Trujillo imposed his rule by violence, eliminating all opposition.

On March 2 Estrella Ureña took his oath; on the fourth his first cabinet was chosen, and former President Vásquez and his vice-president, Alfonseca, left as exiles. However, by a week later the leaders of the

---

[12] *Ibid.,* pp. 706 and 714–15. [Fn. 37, Chap. I, Sec. 2.]

[13] Despite what Bessault states [Lawrence de Bessault, *President Trujillo: His Work and the Dominican Republic* (Santiago, D.R., 1941)] (p. 76), Trujillo did not ask leave of absence as chief of the army until he was nominated as presidential candidate in the middle of March. His biographer and panegyrist Sánchez Lustrino (*Trujillo,* p. 164) says so. [Fn. 40, Chap. I, Sec. 2.]

National party had recovered and hastened to prepare their electoral
campaign. . . .

Listín Diario on March 19 announced the nomination by the Patriotic Coalition of Citizens of Rafael L. Trujillo as candidate for president
and Rafael Estrella Ureña for vice-president. Trujillo thus achieved his
first personal triumph only twenty days after the meetings in the United
States legation. [14]

Two days later, in its edition of March 21, *Listín Diario* announced
the first slate of the National party. On March 28 it published a joint
manifesto of the National and Progressive parties announcing an electoral
alliance. Five days later, on April 2, the new alliance presented its own
slate: for president, Federico Velázquez, and for vice-president, Angel
Morales.

The difference was felt very soon in the contrasting methods of electoral campaigning. Accounts of the abuses and even murders which from
then on were committed by Trujillo's henchmen may be read in any of
the books written against Trujillo. The so-called "The 42nd" acquired a
sinister reputation as a pro-Trujillo gang of army men. . . . Proof that
Provisional President Estrella Ureña was worried over the situation is
found in a cable from United States Minister Curtis to the Department of
State, dated March 18:

> This noon, I had a very frank and long talk with the President, who
> admitted that the General was dominating him and preventing him from
> promising real results from the army during the election with the result that
> it could not possibly be fair. The President asked me to make it publicly
> known that the United States would not recognize Trujillo as President in
> view of the agreement, reached through the mediation of the Legation, which
> ended the revolution; and he pointed out that any opposition on his part
> to Trujillo's candidacy would be ascribed by the latter to self-interest.[15]

There is documentary evidence that Trujillo was not sure of himself
until some weeks later. At the same time the terrorist campaign went on.
Listín Diario on April 8 stated that several houses and stores in Santiago
had been stormed. Two days later, it stated that in Barahona, one
person was killed and several were wounded. At this time also, the
new Dominican minister in Washington met with the acting secretary of
state to ascertain the attitude of the United States government toward
Trujillo's candidacy. The memorandum written on that occasion by

---

[14] One of the official biographers of Trujillo, Bessault, exposes better than anyone, Trujillo's personal ambitions in the latter's replies to questions, that he quotes:
"When did you first think of becoming President of the Dominican Republic?"
I inquired. Like a shot his answer came: "When I first began thinking at all, as a
child." "And when did you first decide definitely that you would be President?" "The
same day I began thinking about it." (Bessault, p. 36.) [Fn. 2, Chap. I, Sec. 3.]

[15] Dept. State, *Foreign Relations* 2: 718 [Fn. 6, Chap. I, Sec. 3.]

Francis White pointed out that the State Department had refused to give him any clear answer. This ambiguous attitude of the State Department was reflected even better in the correspondence of that period with the United States legation in Santo Domingo. Curtis feared a revolution initiated either by enemies of Trujillo if he would insist on being a candidate, or by Trujillo himself if he were forced to withdraw his nomination. The Department of State instructed its minister to follow a flexible policy. In case Trujillo were elected president the State Department had already decided to recognize him as such.[16]

The electoral campaign officially began in April. Seven parties were officially recognized: National, Progressive, Patriotic Coalition of Citizens, Liberal, Republican, Nationalist, and Independent Workers.

The report sent back by Minister Rafael Brache after his visit to the Department of State on April 23 must have been interpreted as favorable by Trujillo, because on the next day he addressed his now well known manifesto to the Dominicans accepting his nomination to the presidency:

> In permitting my name to be presented as candidate for President of the Republic for the coming term, 1930-34, I wish to address myself to all those whose efforts can assure the success of our campaign. . . . There is no danger following me, because at no time will the position with which I may be favored as the result of the May elections ever be used to tyrannize the popular will of which at present I am a servant and which I will loyally serve in the future. . . .[17]

A young dentist, Dr. José E. Aybar, made the most violent of all the speeches against Trujillo's candidacy: ". . . This revolution . . . has served only to abort a candidate who, like the fruit of all abortion, has no vitality." Two years later, Dr. Aybar went over to the ranks of Trujillo and in 1940 organized the short-lived Trujillista party. But during this earlier period he was known as the creator of the slogan *"¡No puede ser!"* (It cannot be!). By the last days of April it was apparent that a free electoral fight was impossible.

The Central Electoral Board, whose members had been appointed by common agreement of all parties, decided to act: "The Central Electoral Board requests that the Army be restricted to the barracks and the searching of individuals be ended." The request was obviously fruitless because on May 2 the resignation of the chairman of the board was announced; on the seventh, it was announced that the entire board had resigned. The government responded by appointing immediately another board, which supervised the elections one week later.

---

[16]*Ibid.*, pp. 717–22. [Fn. 10, Chap. I, Sec. 3.]

[17] Rafael L. Trujillo, *El Pensamiento de un Estadista* (Santiago, n.d. [1946–53]), 1: 3–5. [Fn. 14, Chap. I, Sec. 3.]

By that time Estrella Ureña no longer headed the government. On April 21 he had withdrawn from the presidency in order to devote himself to the election campaign. According to the Constitution, the secretary of interior and police, Lic. Jacinto B. Peynado, trusted man of Trujillo, took over the presidency.

From this time on events developed very rapidly. On May 14 *Listín Diario* published a manifesto by the Alliance announcing its abstention from the next elections "because of the acts of flagrant illegality." Two days later the elections took place, and the Trujillo-Estrella Ureña candidacy won by 223,731 votes in favor to 1,883 against (out of 412,711 registered voters). On May 18 Federico Velázquez (presidential candidate for the Alliance up to the time of its abstention) was arrested by high officers of the army; at the same time *Listín Diario* reported that Alfonseca and Morales had taken asylum in foreign legations. On May 30 the offices of *Listín Diario* were stormed by "a group of armed civilians belonging to the Coalition." [18]

A month and a half later, this series of post-electoral abuses ended with the arrest of Dr. Manuel de Jesús Troncoso de la Concha. [19] Ten years later Troncoso de la Concha was to be president of the Republic, and at the time of taking his oath as such, was to take another oath of loyalty to Trujillo.

Of all these events, the most far-reaching was the murder of Virgilio Martínez Reyna, perhaps the chief leader of the National party in the Cibao region. Ten years later, Trujillo was to use this murder as an excuse to take vengeance on General Estrella. The murderer remained unpunished, but the trials of 1940-41 taken from Trujillist sources serve as documentary evidence of its truth and shocking details. . . .

Trujillo was not only elected president but he was also able to eliminate all opposition. Numerous leaders of the Alliance were forced to go into exile; Martínez Reyna and others less fortunate were pierced with bullets; only the old and ailing caudillo, Horacio Vásquez, was respected in his slow agony in Tamboril. Trujillo sometimes rendered them posthumous honors. [20]

---

[18] *Listín Diario,* May 31, 1930. [Fn. 20, Chap. I, Sec. 3.]

[19] The report of the United States charge d'affairs a.i., Cabot, to the Department of State, on June 16, details several of these abuses and arrests, some murders, and the rebellion of General Cipriano Bencosme (Dept. State, *Foreign Relations* 2: 723–25). [Fn. 21, Chap. I, Sec. 3.]

[20] When former President Vásquez died in Tamboril, the Senate recessed in mourning on March 25, 1936. Former Vice-President Alfonseca, who died in February, 1933, was honored in a simpler way some time later by having a street named after him in the capital city. [Fn. 25, Chap. I, Sec. 3.]

The elections of May 16, 1930, deserve at least a brief analysis here. The new central electoral board certified the results: 412,711 voters were registered, of whom 225,614 voted, which means 55 percent of the total; of those votes, 223,731 were in favor and only 1,883 were against, which means 99 percent to 1 percent. It is obvious that the violence exerted in the preceding weeks insured the result; but in 1930, at least, it was admitted that 45 percent of the electorate had abstained and 1 percent of the votes were against. This is the last time such an admission occurs in the Dominican Republic. . . .[21]

On August 16, 1930, Trujillo took his oath as president of the Republic.

The First Trujillo Administration, 1930–34

The first decree of Trujillo as president on August 16 was the selection of his cabinet.[22] Vidal was back in the secretaryship of the presidency which he had left two months earlier because of misunderstandings with Estrella Ureña; together with him, the second Trujillist brain in the February revolution and president of the central electoral board during the climax of the May elections, Roberto Despradel, entered the cabinet; Lic. Peynado continued as secretary of interior and police; the fourth close associate of Trujillo in the cabinet was his uncle, Teódulo Pina Chevalier. Vice-President Estrella Ureña also received the portfolio of foreign affairs. The cabinet was now almost a homogeneous body of new Trujillist men. Significantly, the decree was signed in Fortress Ozama, which indicates that Trujillo's strength continued residing in the army. The same day, August 16, the new congress was inaugurated, with representatives present of all parties in the confederation.

Listín Diario of August 18 printed only a short report, without comment, of the inauguration of Trujillo. Among the personalities attending the ceremony, mention was made of the First Lady, Sra. Bienvenida R. de Trujillo. It is significant to observe the scanty political reporting from that

---

[21] The United States minister, Curtis, expressed a much harder opinion of these elections in his report to the Department of State on May 19: " . . . The Confederation announces that 223,851 votes were, according to the early reports, cast in favor of General Rafael Leonidas Trujillo for President of the Republic and Rafael Estrella Ureña for Vice-President. As the number given greatly exceeds the total number of voters in the country, further comment on the fairness of the elections hardly seems necessary; however, there is every reason to believe that, as anticipated by the Legation, the intimidation of the followers of the opposition had already been so great prior to the day of the elections that none was needed, and it would seem that none was practiced, on the day of the elections, in order to keep them away from the polls." (Dept. State, *Foreign Relations* 2: 723.) To check this comment of Curtis about the elections of 1930, see footnote 44 on page 27. [Fn. 26, Chap. I, Sec. 3.]

[22] Decree No. 1, *G.O.* 4280. [Fn. 1, Chap. I, Sec. 4.]

day on in *Listín Diario,* as a silent evidence of its opposition, which it did not dare to express publicly. This was not to last very long, however.

The panegyrists of Trujillo are accustomed to begin the history of his administration by referring to the San Cenón hurricane on September 3 as the starting point of the prodigious administrative work of their hero.[23] It is true that the hurricane was very severe; material destruction was great; hundreds or thousands of people died. However, the enemies of Trujillo point out that the hurricane also provided a good pretext for suspending constitutional guarantees at the right moment. Some of them even say that among the bodies cremated without identification in the *Plaza Colombina* might have been several political prisoners who disappeared forever at that time.[24] Four years later, the San Cenón hurricane and the "reconstruction" of the city were used as pretext for changing the name of the capital as a personal homage to Trujillo.

For the time being Trujillo's main reconstruction was political. The opponents of the first months had been previously eliminated. The last important incident to report was the death in combat of General Cipriano Bencosme, horacist, [i.e., a follower of Horacio Vásquez] and a candidate for deputy in February. This took place in the fields of Puerto Plata about the middle of November in a fight against Trujillo's soldiers.

During the first months of the new regime, the records of both chambers of Congress show activity and friendly differences of ideas. But very soon, in the language of both the *Bulletin* of the Senate and that of the Chamber it is possible to notice that a change is going on; even if one had not previously known what was simultaneously happening in the whole country, he could have suspected increasing dictatorship, by the caution of the legislators.

The first news of the new personal party appeared in *Listín Diario* on November 20, 1930, in a "Proclamation by the Provisional Organizing Committee of the Party of President Trujillo." Nine months later, on August 16, 1931, on the occasion of the first anniversary of the new government, the new "Party of General Trujillo" was officially constituted.

The confederation of parties which elected Trujillo was broken up permanently during that nine months, and all its most important leaders as of February, 1930, disappeared in one way or another.

The earliest evidence of uneasiness among the supporters of the new regime is found in *Listín Diario* of October 27, 1930. A few incidents were

---

[23] See, for instance, Bessault, *President Trujillo,* Ch. 6, "The Destruction and Re-creation of the Capital." [Fn. 4, Chap. I, Sec. 4.]

[24] See, for instance, Albert C. Hicks, *Blood in the Streets: The Life and Rule of Trujillo* (New York, 1946), pp. 42–44. The author is familiar with other details from persons who lived through the hurricane. [Fn. 6, Chap. I, Sec. 4.]

mentioned then, occurring in Puerto Plata, where the governor and several other persons had been placed under arrest, and two aides of the governor had been killed.

On December 18, 1930, the first resignation of a deputy occurred. The Chamber unanimously elected as a new deputy, Pedro M. Hungría, whose name was among the three proposed by Trujillo as "Chief of the Confederation of Parties."

By the end of January, 1931, the beginning of the submission of the judiciary was evident. In the session of the Senate on January 8, 1931, it was decided to reappoint in a body all magistrates and judges, on the ground that they had been elected in 1924 according to the Constitution for a period of only four years (a curious reflection three years after the constitutional crisis of 1928). However, the reelected president of the Supreme Court of Justice refused to take his oath again. In consequence, at its session of February 25, the Senate elected a new president of the Supreme Court and decided to retire Lic. Rafael Justino Castillo with a pension. [25]

The most serious clash between Trujillo and one leader of the confederation was that culminating in June, 1931, with the death of General Desiderio Arias. The symptoms of uneasiness were apparent from December 22, 1930, when *Listín Diario* published a statement by Arias addressed to his political friends (Liberal party) saying that, although he was not very active in politics, "we must support Trujillo." Only in the edition of May 11, 1931, was it made public for the first time (although in an indirect way) that Arias was in open rebellion.

An official announcement on June 17 disclosed the rebellion of General Arias. A release from the secretary of the presidency was reported in *Listín Diario* of that day as follows: "It is officially reported that Desiderio Arias, Fco. [Francisco] Morillo and Victoriano Almanzar, sought by the courts following their indictment for murder, . . . are escaping through the hills of the northeastern border."

Listín Diario of the twenty-second finally published a telegram from Trujillo, dated the day before: "In a combat which took place this morning, Desiderio Arias died. His body is being taken to Santiago. . . ." These are all contemporary references. In order to know the details of the rebellion and death of General Arias one must read later books, extracting from them the facts and eliminating epithets. [26]

---

[25] *Bol. Sen.,* Feb. 1931. [Fn. 17, Chap. I, Sec. 4.]

[26] See, for instance, Hicks, *Blood in the Streets,* pp. 207–12, Mejía, *Vía Crucis,* pp. 52–54, and Gregorio R. Bustamante, *Una Satrapía en el Caribe* (Guatemala, 1949), pp. 89–91. After his death, someone cut off the head of General Arias; it is usually said to have been Lieutenant Ludovino Fernández, who some years later became colonel, chief of police. [Fn. 22, Chap. I, Sec. 4.]

On August 16, 1931, Trujillo addressed three short messages to the Dominican people, to Congress, and to the delegates of his new party. At the end of the message addressed to the new party he gave this assurance: "As long as I occupy the first Magistracy of the State, I shall govern with the men of the Party. . . ."

On the same day, *Listín Diario* announced that Vice-President Estrella Ureña would depart for a trip abroad on a leave of absence. There was no explanation as to the reasons for this trip.

Not till long after was there any official report of the bloodless rebellion of Estrella Ureña. Previous clues indirectly confirm opposition to Trujillo by several leaders of the coup of February, 1930. As early as September, 1930, a decree, "expelling from the Dominican Republic" Dr. Ramón de Lara, the former president of the country's only university, Universidad Autónoma de Santo Domingo, and Dr. Leovigildo Cuello, disclosed that they were in Puerto Rico disseminating subversive propaganda.

In February, 1931, Congress passed a law punishing by civil degradation those who went to foreign governments or legations to complain against the measures taken by the Dominican government. . . .

Finally, at the session of December 7, 1931, the Chamber unanimously approved the prosecution of the vice-president of the Republic. The Senate agreed to this immediately; and at the next session of the Chamber, a letter was read from the president of the Senate notifying that body that Estrella Ureña had been dismissed as vice-president.[27]

This unanimity among the members of Congress attending the sessions did not necessarily mean that all of them agreed. At least two of them chose to withdraw from Congress, with some criticism of the new system which was on the march. On January 28, 1932, Lic. Rafael F. Bonnelly, a deputy from Santiago (belonging to the Republican party of Estrella Ureña) resigned, stating: ". . . I will not allow anyone, absolutely no one, to attempt to change the line of conduct I have decided for myself. . . ."[28]

One of the first laws of Trujillo's regime appears especially curious after the lapse of those many years. Law No. 40 of December 10, 1930, prohibited the naming of streets, towns, cities, etc., or the use of portraits on postage stamps, unless the persons thus honored "have been dead at

---

[27] Dominican Republic, Congress, *Boletín de la Cámara* (hereafter cited as *Bol. Cam.*), Dec. 1931; *Listín Diario,* Dec. 8, 1931. This newspaper stated that Estrella Ureña and Deputy Julián F. Grisanty "wait abroad on favorable events." [Fn. 35, Chap. I, Sec. 4.]

[28] *Bol. Cam.,* Jan. 1932. [Fn. 36, Chap. I, Sec. 4; Bonnelly served as president of the Council of State in 1962 and was a presidential candidate in 1966.]

least for ten years previously" and have rendered great services. Two short years later, Law No. 269 of September 29, 1932, repealed in part this earlier law in order to authorize the printing of a series of postage stamps commemorating the birthday of Trujillo. Since then, there has been a multiplicity of special laws sanctioning the use of Trujillo's name and, later, the names of his relatives. In the month of September, 1932, the Senate also approved unanimously the proposal of its president naming a new province planned around the city of San Cristóbal, Trujillo Province. . . .[29]

From the end of 1931, the country's submission became complete; and early in 1933 the conversions began. A topic suggested by Trujillo himself set the tone of this period. *Listín Diario* on August 28, 1931, stated that, according to reliable sources, Trujillo would announce shortly that he would not seek reelection in 1934. On September 7 the president himself issued a manifesto in which he solemnly confirmed the rumor:

> The principle of non-reelection, that seems daily to have more acceptance in the public conscience, is inherent to my ethics of Government and I will sustain it with the strength of my deep convictions even if, without any suggestion from my Government, the people will request my remaining in power, by an act of their sovereign will.

Listín Diario received this statement with pleasure, and on the ninth, printed an editorial praising it and hoping for free elections in 1934. It would very soon learn of its blunder. One year later the campaign for Trujillo's reelection was launched, led by former horacistas.

On February 27, as required by the Constitution, Trujillo addressed his annual message to Congress, giving a report of his administration during 1931. Despite his attempts at glamor, by emphasizing the increasing diplomatic relations of the Dominican Republic, the state of the nation he pictured was obviously bad; though the approved budget had been reduced by 25 percent, the fiscal year had ended with a deficit of $1,000,000 out of a total expenditure of $8,300,000. The external debt amounted to $16,592,500, and payments on its amortization continued in arrears.[30]

---

[29] *Bol. Sen.,* Sept. 1932. This territorial change could not be enforced until after the constitutional reform of 1934. [Fn. 41, Chap. I, Sec. 4.]

[30] It was suspended by Law No. 206 of Oct. 24, 1931. See Trujillo's later explanations in this connection, in his annual message of Feb. 27, 1933 (Rafael L. Trujillo, *El Pensamiento de un Estadista* [Santiago, D.R., n.d. (1946–53); hereafter cited as Trujillo, *Pensamiento*]), 1: 280–82. See also the United States point of view in Charles A. Thomson, "Dictatorship in the Dominican Republic," *Foreign Policy Association Reports,* April 15, 1931, pp. 37–39; and in Dept. State, *Foreign Relations of the United States, 1931,* 2:110–37; *ibid.,* 1933, 5: 589–671; and *ibid.,* 1934, 5: 189–202. [Fn. 57, Chap. I, Sec. 4.]

The new party of Trujillo, which was already called the "Dominican Party," was officially registered on March 11 with Trujillo as its director. On February 2 Trujillo's father, José Trujillo Valdez, was elected a deputy. The election was by standing roll-call of all deputies (including his son Virgilio). In April, Major Aníbal J. Trujillo was appointed military attaché in several European countries, replacing his brother Héctor; six months later this appointment was enlarged to include England, the Netherlands, and Denmark. On December 3 Trujillo's daughter Flor de Oro Trujillo Ledesma married Porfirio Rubirosa.[31]

Congress approved on November 8 as "urgent" a resolution, which has since become historic, granting Trujillo the title of "Benefactor of the Fatherland,"[32] officially bestowed upon him on August 16 of the next year during a very solemn ceremony. And on December 14, 1932, Trujillo was inaugurated as president of the Club Unión, which by a long tradition had been the exclusive gathering place of the best society in Santo Domingo.[33]

By the beginning of 1933, Trujillo had reached the height of his power; even *Listín Diario* began to use the new literary style of the Era. On January 23, for the first time, it published a front-page headline which said in reference to Trujillo: "Santiago extended a loud demonstration yesterday to the Honorable President of the Republic, General Rafael Leonidas Trujillo Molina." One of the speakers at the meeting, held at

---

[31] *Listín Diario,* Nov. 21 and Dec. 5, 1932. With this wedding, the fabulous career of Porfirio Rubirosa began; in April, 1933, he was appointed undersecretary of the presidency, in July of the same year undersecretary of foreign relations. [Fn. 62, Chap. I, Sec. 4.]

[32] *G.O.* 4601 (Special issue, which contains also some short biographical data about Trujillo and the speech delivered by the president of the Senate when he placed the Grand Collar of Benefactor on Trujillo, on August 16, 1933).

In the *Bulletin* of the Senate is found the stenographic record of the session held on Nov. 8, to approve this "urgent" resolution. It reads: "Senator Pérez: To introduce the following Motion (reading of the Motion granting to the President of the Republic the title of Benefactor of the Fatherland). I ask that the consideration of this project of Resolution be declared of urgency, in order that the Honorable Chamber of Deputies have time to approve it today. The President: Do you agree that urgency be declared and the discussion take place immediately? (Affirmative signs.) We agree. Let it be read by the Secretary (the Resolution is read). The President: The Senators have the floor to express their opinions about the read Resolution (silence). It is put to a vote (Affirmative signs). Approved." (*Bol. Sen.,* Nov. 1932, p. 192.) [Fn. 65, Chap. I, Sec. 4.]

[33] *Listín Diario,* Dec. 16, 1932. Before becoming president of the Republic, Trujillo had been blackballed as a member of the Club Unión. After imposing his election as president of the club in 1932, and his reelection in 1934, the club was "voluntarily" dissolved in May, 1935. [Fn. 66, Chap. I, Sec. 4.]

Santiago on the twenty-second, was the same Dr. José E. Aybar, who three years before had qualified Trujillo's candidacy as an "abortion." His new Trujillista effusions were as vigorous as had been his opposition in 1930. The "conversions" were frequent after that; and the converts were the most vociferous in the campaign for reelection.

This campaign was opened by Lic. Gustavo A. Díaz on March 12 and his words had the enchantment of the incredibly equivocal:

> Those who yesterday closed ranks with Trujillo in the legions of the old Horacism, can no longer live in a sterile and sentimental contemplation of the past, because politics is action and not inertia.[34]

Listín Diario devoted several columns to the meeting and the speech. On the twenty-second, someone launched the idea of "reelection without elections"; the newspaper limited itself to the comment that "the thesis is daring." Next day Dr. José E. Aybar reinforced the proposal by addressing a questionnaire to more than a hundred persons in regard to the idea, which he eloquently justified;[35] the newspaper said nothing, but printed the question and the answers in its pages. . . .

The poll was overwhelmingly favorable to reelection, although most of the answers preferred "reelection with elections." On April 18 the Chamber adhered unanimously to the reelection;[36] on the twenty-fifth, the Senate did the same. The same day, Listín Diario announced that Trujillo had accepted his reelection. Questioned by a newspaperman as to whether, during the elections, "there will be complete freedom at the polls as in 1930," the president answered: "As much freedom as at that time. I have already let the people know my love for Freedom."[37]

In the meantime, the name of a new personality appeared in the pages of Listín Diario. On April 18 a decree was published, by which,

---

[34] Listín Diario, March 13, 1933. This self-justification by a former leader of the National party attempted to take cover in the fact that Trujillo had been appointed chief of the army by President Horacio Vásquez. [Fn. 68, Chap. I, Sec. 4.]

[35] Among his reasons: "Will it not be more pertinent that instead of having general elections, and in view of the unanimous result of the spontaneous plebiscite favoring the reelection of Trujillo, who has been reelected already in the conscience of his people, that the Central Electoral Board declare him elected President of the Republic for the four-year period, 1934–38, thus sparing our impoverished national treasury the expenses which inevitably result from any electoral process, and at the same time giving complete satisfaction to the sovereign people who await anxiously the anticipated benefits expected from maintaining in force his glorious and insuperable Mandate?" (Listín Diario, March 23, 1933.) [Fn. 70, Chap. I, Sec. 4.]

[36] Bol. Cam., April 1933. [Fn. 72, Chap. I, Sec. 4.]

[37] Listín Diario, April 26, 1933. [Fn. 74, Chap. I, Sec. 4.]

"taking into account his services," the child Rafael L. ("Ramfis") Trujillo Martínez was appointed a colonel in the army.[38] Two months later, on June 5, the newspaper published a picture of Trujillo with his son "Ramfis," whose fourth birthday was celebrated that day.

The annual message of Trujillo, on February 27, 1933, continued to be somber, but at least he could announce that there had been no deficit at all during the past year, thanks to his having reduced by 10 percent the salaries of all public employees. It had been the lowest budget of the Dominican Republic since the United States Marines left the country ($6,398,043).

Contemporaneously, the widely known military plot, in which several army chiefs would lose their lives, was unfolding. Little documentary evidence may be found about this plot, headed by Colonel Leoncio Blanco,[39] but there is enough evidence concerning the fate of General Ramón Vásquez Rivera, who was accused of having known about the plot. *Listín Diario* on May 8, 1933, announced that General Vásquez Rivera had been dismissed as chief of the army and had been replaced by a brother-in-law of Trujillo. The name of Vásquez Rivera was not mentioned again until August 11, 1934, when *Listín Diario* reported that on the previous day Ramón Vásquez Rivera, former chief of the army, and others had been sentenced to five years in prison. It was admitted that the judge could not elicit any evidence except from one witness, despite the fact that more than twenty witnesses were on the stand. Four years later, in March, 1938, the Congress granted amnesty to Ramón Vásquez Rivera, together with other subsequent plotters.[40] The ease with which Trujillo discovered and smashed this plot, as well as others less organized in the following two years,[41] indicates that his power continued to be based upon the army.

---

[38] "Rafael Leonidas Trujillo Molina, General of Division, President of the Dominican Republic, Commander-in-Chief of the National Army, using the powers vested in me by Article 49 of the Constitution of the Nation and taking into account the merits of Rafael L. Trujillo Martínez, resolve to appoint him a Colonel of the National Armies and I hereby order all competent authorities to put him in possession of his office and to render him and make others to render the merited respect. . . ." (It was fully reprinted in *Listín Diario*, April 18, 1933.) [Fn. 75, Chap. I, Sec. 4.]

[39] In the books written against Trujillo one can find some data, sometimes vague and contradictory, about this plot and the later murder of Colonel Blanco together with some of his coplotters. See, for instance, Hicks, *Blood in the Streets*, pp. 52–55, and Bustamante, *Satrapía*, pp. 92–93. [Fn. 79, Chap. I, Sec. 4.]

[40] Former General Vásquez Rivera was reported "a suicide" about 1940 in Fortress Ozama, where he was jailed again. [Fn. 80, Chap. I, Sec. 4.]

[41] One notorious case occurred in 1933, when the victim was American and the Department of State intervened. Thomson, "Dictatorship," p. 33; and Dept. State, *Foreign Relations, 1934*, 5: 202–11. [Fn. 81, Chap. I, Sec. 4.]

On October 2, 1933, a law was approved declaring Rafael Estrella Ureña and others "traitors to the Fatherland."[42]

At the border, on October 18, Trujillo met the Haitian president, Stenio Vincent, for the first time. As a result, a mixed Dominican-Haitian commission was organized, entrusted with the study of the possible revision of the treaty on borders signed in 1929.

At the end of the first Trujillo administration in 1934, the economic situation of the Dominican Republic continued to be a difficult one, but it was already obvious that the regime had been politically consolidated. Trujillo's annual message to Congress, in February of that year, showed some optimism, announcing the first surplus for the fiscal period of 1933, $82,067 out of a total of $8,415,432 collected. The message ignored entirely the internal conspiracies and the activities of exiles abroad. Far more significant than this message were the two general elections of 1934.

Listín Diario on January 19, 1934, reprinted an interview granted by Trujillo to the Santiago newspaper, *La Información,* in which he already mentioned the name of Lic. Jacinto B. Peynado as the candidate for vice-president. On February 11 the nominating convention of the Dominican Party was held. "The Dominican soul vibrated with enthusiasm when Generalissimo Trujillo was proclaimed candidate for President for the period 1934-38"; thus *Listín Diario* headlined its report in its new Trujillist style.

Elections took place on May 16 and the results were published in the *Official Gazette* of the twenty-ninth.[43] Of course, there was never a thought of presenting any other slate than that of the Dominican party. A total of 286,937 voters were registered, and according to the official report, 256,423 voted in favor of Trujillo and all the names on the slate, including senators, deputies, governors,[44] mayors, and councilmen. Other elections were simultaneously held for delegates to the constituent assembly called one month earlier to amend the Constitution. The assembly met on June 5 and ended its work on the ninth. That same day the new constitution of the Dominican Republic was proclaimed, the twenty-third in its

---

[42] *G.O.* 4614. This law was caused by the intensification of activities carried on by Estrella Ureña and other exiles, especially in Cuba, where the former president went after the fall of dictator Machado. [Fn. 83, Chap. I, Sec. 4.]

[43] *G.O.* 4684. It is interesting to point out the discrepancy between the number of registered voters announced in 1934, and those announced in 1930; this contradiction seems to confirm the suspicions stated at that time by the minister of the United States, Curtis. [Fn. 89, Chap. I, Sec. 4.]

[44] According to the constitution of 1929, at that time in force, provincial governors were elected, but the president could replace them in case of resignation or death; the system was maintained in Trujillo's constitution of 1934, but it was changed in the 1942 constitution, since which date the governors are freely appointed by the president. [Fn. 90, Chap. I, Sec. 4.]

history. One of the amendments facilitated the "constitutional" creation
of the new Trujillo Province.

"Ramfis" sealed the first administration of his father. In May the
suspension bridge which bears his name was inaugurated. And in June
he celebrated his birthday for the first time in public, in the company of his
mother. *Listín Diario* published a picture of "Ramfis" dressed as a colonel
with this curious footnote:

> Today, the charming and beautiful child, Rafael Leonidas Trujillo
> Martínez, youngest Colonel of our National Army, beloved son of General-
> issimo Rafael Leonidas Trujillo Molina, Honorable President of the Republic,
> reaches and will magnificently celebrate his fifth birthday.[45]

No mention was made as yet of his mother; but in the next edition
there was a long and detailed report of the birthday party, in which the
hostesses were Sra. María Martínez, "mother of the greatly beloved honored child," and Sra. Peynado, wife of the elected vice-president. There
was no mention whatever of the First Lady and wife of the president, Sra.
Bienvenida Ricardo de Trujillo. . . .

The Second Trujillo Administration, 1934–38

On the inaugural date, August 16, the second congress of the Trujillo
Era was constituted. . . . [*Congressional officials were changed in several
cases.*] The only one who would finish his term two years later was Dr.
José E. Aybar. President of the Chamber Miguel Angel Roca would be in
jail by then.

The first outstanding event of the new term was the designation of
General José Estrella as "Special Commissioner of the President of the
Republic in the provinces of Santiago, Puerto Plata, Monte Cristi, La
Vega, Espaillat, Duarte, and Samaná." For six years, General Estrella
would be practically the viceroy of half of the Republic; at the end of 1940
he would be reviled and imprisoned.

The first weeks of this new term were dedicated to honor Trujillo.
Listín Diario began a poll in August as to the suitability of erecting a
statue of Trujillo; all agreed, except as to details. Some preferred an
equestrian statue, others an erect one of civic character. The doubts were
not resolved, but in the last week of October a campaign was launched to
collect the necessary funds for the erection of the statue. It was the week
of the "button for a statue."[46]

Meanwhile, the university came forward with honors. On October
3 a law was promulgated permitting the granting of doctorates *"honoris*

---

[45] *Listín Diario,* June 5, 1934. [Fn. 96, Chap. I, Sec. 4.]

[46] *Listín Diario,* Oct. 22, 1934. [Fn. 7, Chap. I, Sec. 5.]

causa." Six days later *Listín Diario* announced that a "great Assembly" of the university faculty had agreed to bestow upon Trujillo the title of honorary doctor, although after having discussed the point, they preferred not to grant it in any special school.

Henceforth, Trujillo would be known as Generalissimo Doctor Rafael Leonidas Trujillo Molina, Honorable President of the Republic, Benefactor of the Fatherland. . . .

At the beginning of November, 1934, Trujillo paid an official visit to the capital of Haiti. Three months later, on the occasion of the Dominican national holiday, Haitian President Stenio Vincent returned the visit in Santo Domingo. The main purpose of both visits was to smooth the negotiations concerning the frontier and to conclude the new treaty that would finally be signed a year later. At about the same time the ousted Cuban dictator, Machado, received temporary asylum in the Dominican Republic, and Trujillo refused to permit his extradition.

The campaign of honors was renewed during November. The statue was not enough, and the vice-president of the Chamber initiated an inquiry in *Listín Diario,* asking: "Which is the kind of apotheosis best suited to his condition [*postulados*] and greatness and to our duty in rewarding the eminent work of this worthiest servant of the Republic?" The first answer proposed to declare him by means of a large plebiscite "President for life of the Dominican Republic. . . ."

[*A number of alleged plots and cases of intrigue against Trujillo marked late 1934 and the early months of 1935; all failed. The allegations resulted in dismissal of several persons from public office and the expulsion of others from the Dominican party.*]

A law of April 24 decided that the State would be a party in any legal suit based upon attempts against the life or person of the president and granted it privilege over the properties of the guilty parties. [47]

There would be no more political news until the end of 1935. On December 12 *Listín Diario* declared that on the preceding day the accused parties found guilty in the court proceedings of those days had been condemned to the maximum prison penalty. A decree on October 31, 1935, had pardoned Juan Isidro Jimenes-Grullón and other prisoners convicted of political crimes. [48]

---

[47] *G.O.* 4788. [Fn. 24, Chap. I, Sec. 5.]

[48] *G.O.* 4848. The pardon of Jimenes-Grullón was annulled by a decree on April 6, 1937 (*G.O.* 5012); another decree, the day before, ordered his arrest upon his return to the Republic and accused him of being dedicated in Cuba "to a despicable and unjustified Communist activity." Jimenes-Grullón himself gives extensive information on his arrest, trial, sentence, pardon, and escape in his book, *Una Gestapo en América* (Havana, 1946). [Fn. 26, Chap. I, Sec. 5.]

To become acquainted with the scheme of these plots one has to resort to the later reports of some survivors; the majority of them are in exile since they were freed and managed to escape. [49] It seems certain that Trujillo's assassination was planned in one of these plots, a scheme that failed because of the information given by one of those involved. The most serious complication was the arrest of Amadeo Barletta, honorary consul of Italy in the Dominican Republic and a wealthy businessman. Mussolini's government intervened, threatening severe reprisals, and Barletta was freed, although he had to move to Cuba. [50]

Trujillo had emerged victorious from the last conspiracy against his regime in many years. The best proof of his renewed strength was the law of June 18, repealing the proceedings in 1933 by which Estrella Ureña and others in exile were declared traitors, and his call that same day for their return. None returned at that particular time; on the contrary, their number gradually increased.

It is very interesting to reread the "Whereas" of this law. The alleged reason for the measure was that the exiled survivors had in most cases somewhat rectified their conduct.

Meanwhile, new honors were being gathered for the Generalissimo. Numerous laws may be found in the *Official Gazette* of those months which authorized the giving of his name to streets and parks. [51] Various ladies proposed that his name be included in the words of the national anthem. Another law [52] authorized giving the name of Parque Ramfis (Ramfis Square) to the old Plaza Colombina at the capital, where the victims of the hurricane of 1930 had been cremated.

---

[49] See for instance, Hicks, *Blood in the Streets,* pp. 49–51; Bustamante, *Satrapía,* pp. 99–100; Thomson, "Dictatorship," pp. 32–33; and especially Jimenes-Grullón, *Gestapo.* [Fn. 28, Chap. I, Sec. 5.]

[50] Barletta was arrested on April 4, 1935. He was honorary consul of Italy, representative of General Motors, and president of the *Compañía Tabacalera.* On May 4, he was sentenced to prison and a fine. On the fifteenth, it was announced that the Italian ambassador in Washington had officially said to the State Department that Mussolini was ready to send a warship to the Dominican Republic. On the twentieth, Barletta was freed. See Dept. State, *Foreign Relations, 1935,* 4: 478–505; and Thomson, "Dictatorship," p. 33. The ultimatum by Mussolini was confirmed during World War II by the Dominican Secretaryship of Foreign Relations, in a pamphlet printed against Italy, which has not been available for this study. [Fn. 30, Chap. I, Sec. 5.]

[51] In the *G.O.* 4802 alone, four laws were printed (Nos. 919 to 922, on May 31), all of them declared to be "of urgency." [Fn. 35, Chap. I, Sec. 5.]

[52] *G.O.* 4752. The "Whereas" of this Law No. 812 says that "the illustrious man to whose patriotism, intelligence, and character the Republic has entrusted the supreme leadership of its destiny will feel pleasantly moved in his heart as a father by the homage so rendered to the son who will continue his prominent lineage." [Fn. 37, Chap. I, Sec. 5.]

On June 10, José Trujillo Valdez, deputy and father of Trujillo, died. He was rendered national honors, accorded by a law approved by Congress, and was buried in the Chapel of the Immortals at the Cathedral. During the following weeks his name was given to many streets and parks in the Republic.

During the second half of 1935, a campaign to grant the name of Trujillo to the capital of the Republic began. The idea was initiated . . . by the president of the Senate, Mario Fermín Cabral. A few days before, there was also originated the idea of asking the Nobel Prize for Peace for Presidents Trujillo and Vincent.

Listín Diario on July 20 published a letter by Trujillo in which he opposed Cabral's idea: "It is in clear opposition to one of my dearest aspirations as a patriot and ruler." Two days later, Cabral accepted Trujillo's decision, and Manuel A. Peña Batlle made the mistake of applauding Trujillo's gesture. [53]

Listín Diario on October 26, 1935, published statements by Trujillo announcing his intention of taking a trip abroad. A decree of October 27 entrusted the vice-president, Lic. Peynado, with the executive power during the absence of Trujillo. Peynado took office on November 1; ten days later the two chambers requested Trujillo not to leave the country; a meeting on November 17 renewed the request. A telegram from Trujillo was published in *Listín Diario* on the nineteenth announcing "that, because of the unanimous request of the Dominican people," he would spend his vacation at home. The joy at this decision was expressed in letters and in meetings in the days that followed. [54] But Peynado remained nominally at the head of the executive branch.

In *Listín Diario* on December 12 Cabral insisted on his petition, this time addressed to the acting president, asking that the plebiscitary campaign should be renewed favoring the change of the capital's name to Ciudad Trujillo. "It is the will of the country," he said. Immediately, this brought a deluge of adherences; first, Peynado, followed by the members of the cabinet and the two chambers. Trujillo remained silent. The Senate on January 8, 1936, and the Chamber on January 9 approved the law,

---

[53] *Listín Diario,* July 22, 1935. The author heard in 1940 from the lips of Peña Batlle himself (who died in 1954) that this letter put him in serious danger of death. At that time Peña Batlle prided himself on being one of the few opponents of Trujillo, although inactive. He later surrendered to the regime in 1941, and especially after 1942. [Fn. 44, Chap. I, Sec. 5.]

[54] The Senate approved in its session of Dec. 11 a law providing for "the placing of a plaque to perpetuate for future generations the spirit of generosity of President Trujillo, in renouncing his trip abroad." *Bol. Sen.,* Dec. 1935, p. 20. [Fn. 49, Chap. I, Sec. 5.]

thus changing the name of the capital;[55] on the eleventh, Acting President Peynado proclaimed it. [56]

A decree on February 5 returned to Trujillo the executive authority. *Listín Diario* on the eleventh gave an account of the Te Deum and other festivities celebrated the day before; it was an official "Día de Júbilo" (Day of Joy) declared by the council of the city.

The city founded by Columbus in 1496, with the name of Santo Domingo de Guzmán, has since then been called Ciudad Trujillo. But the change took place during a temporary absence of President Trujillo. The democratic appearance was fulfilled perfectly.

Meanwhile, Trujillo married for the third time. For awhile, Sra. Bienvenida Ricardo de Trujillo was not mentioned in the reviews of official functions, and in June, 1934, the name of María Martínez was mentioned for the first time as the mother of "Ramfis." *Listín Diario* on December 5, 1934, announced that the First Lady, doña Bienvenida, would go abroad on a pleasure trip for a few months; this is the last time that her name was mentioned. On February 19, 1935, a new law of divorce was passed, which introduced this unusual ground: "the will of either spouse, if they have not procreated any children during the first five years of marriage or later"; doña Bienvenida had not procreated. There was no mention of the divorce until *Listín Diario* noted on September 30 that "The Honorable President of the Republic celebrates his marriage to the charming lady doña María Martínez Alba." In October, 1935, Trujillo received the decoration of the Band of the Spanish Republic; and Congress approved a law describing in detail the insignia and baton of command of the Generalissimo. [57] In December the secretary of foreign relations officially requested the Nobel Prize for Peace for Trujillo and Vincent.

---

[55] *Bol. Sen.* and *Bol. Cam.,* Jan. 1936. Contrary to what had been usual in Congress since 1931, this time all senators and almost all deputies made speeches to "explain" their votes in favor. Printing of the speeches made in the Chamber required 17 pages of its *Bulletin. Bol. Cam.,* Jan. 1936, pp. 278–94. [Fn. 51, Chap. I, Sec. 5.]

[56] *G.O.* 4867. It is the "urgent" Law No. 1067. Its preamble says that "the universality of the Dominican people has manifested publicly its legitimate desire that the city of Santo Domingo, capital of the Republic, be called Ciudad Trujillo, in reverent expression of gratitude towards the famous Benefactor of the Fatherland, Generalissimo Doctor Rafael Leonidas Trujillo Molina. . . ." It was ordered that the law also be printed in the newspapers *Listín Diario* and *La Opinión.* When this change in the name of the capital city was made, it was decided that the old National Province — later District — be called National Province of Santo Domingo to keep the name given by Columbus. [Fn. 52, Chap. I, Sec. 5.]

[57] *G.O.* 4840. It is Law No. 1019. This law describes the insignia as follows: "A small cane of precious wood, with a golden handle that will have encrusted on one side a coat of arms of diamonds, sapphires, and rubies, and on the top five stars of diamonds . . . the bottom will be of gold with palms and laurels of green enamel in high relief." [Fn. 61, Chap. I, Sec. 5.]

The annual report to Congress by the executive on February 27, 1936, was a little more optimistic than in previous years. Prominently noted was the approval and forthcoming signature of the frontier agreement with Haiti. The budget of 1935 showed a revenue of $10,423,179 with a surplus of $49,322; the foreign debt amounted to $16,292,000.

The reelection campaign for the next term 1938–42 soon started, two years before the elections. *Listín Diario* on March 21 published the first message in that respect, signed by prominent people of the capital. The Chamber, in its meeting on March 24, adhered to a proposal by the commune* of Enriquillo that Trujillo should remain in power another twenty years. The campaign would continue in the provinces during 1936; the edition of *Listín Diario* of July 11 alone published four pages of signatures from the province of Barahona and its different communes. On October 25 a "large reelection demonstration" took place in the capital city. . . .[58]

[*In November, 1936, Héctor Trujillo, brother of the president, was promoted to the rank of brigadier general and designated chief of staff.*]

Thereafter, Héctor B. Trujillo would be the man most trusted by his brother, the Generalissimo, holding the highest rank in the army until 1952, when he was elected president. On June 16 his betrothal to Miss Alma McLaughlin was officially announced; up to the present time they had not been married.†

In March, 1936, the new boundary treaty was signed with Haiti, followed by the exchange of ratifications on April 14. For this reason, Trujillo again visited Port-au-Prince, duly authorized by Congress to leave the country, and the Haitians gave the name of Avenue President Trujillo to the old Grande Rue of their capital.

In April there took place one of the few civic rebellions recorded in the Era of Trujillo. In his annual message of 1936, Trujillo noted that in July, 1935, a contract had been signed between the State and the historian, Américo Lugo, for the writing of a "History of the Island of Santo Domingo." In the *Official Gazette* of April 8, 1936, a law was published cancelling the contract. The reason may be found in a letter written by

---

* A commune is a municipal district (*municipio*), roughly equivalent to a county.

[58] *Listín Diario,* Oct. 26, 1936. [Fn. 66, Chap. I, Sec. 5.]

† The marriage was finally celebrated on December 12, 1959. Cf. Robert D. Crassweller, *Trujillo: The Life and Times of a Caribbean Dictator* (New York, 1966), p. 267. The two Spanish-language editions of *The Era of Trujillo* include an identical footnote and the French edition a similar one to the effect that on the occasion of a visit by Vice-President Nixon in 1955 the newspaper *El Caribe* published a photograph (March 2) in which Miss McLaughlin was identified as "the fiancee of the [then] Chief of State."

Américo Lugo before cancellation of the contract;[59] Trujillo wanted a history as a pretext, ending the book with praise for the merits of his government; Lugo refused to write about contemporary events unless he had freedom of fair historical criticism. He was not imprisoned, but he became isolated in his own country until his death in 1952.

In September the name of Pico Trujillo (Trujillo Peak) was given to the highest point of the central mountain range of the island.[60] The preamble of the law made it clear that two small promontories had been discovered on the same mountain; the traditional name of La Pelona ["the Bald"] was reserved for the lower one. Naturally, frequent laws were passed to give the name of Trujillo's family to more streets and squares; even "Petán" [José Arismendi Trujillo Molina] got his in Bonao. But the prohibitive law of 1930 was never totally revoked; there were always partial repeals for a concrete case.

On November 4 a law was enacted suppressing communism, anarchism and other doctrines of the kind. The law would be repealed a year later at Trujillo's request.

We thus come to October 30, 1936, the day when one of the biggest scandals of the Era of Trujillo erupted. At the special session held that day by the Chamber, it was revealed that its president, Miguel Angel Roca, was the author of a series of anonymous letters that had been circulating against President Trujillo. The commotion was sensational; and as usual, the oratory of Dr. José E. Aybar was the highlight. It was debated whether Roca's "resignation" should be allowed or if he should be expelled from the Chamber. Finally the resignation was permitted. Immediately, the customary protests broke loose, and on November 3 more deputies insulted Roca at the Chamber's meeting.

The protests were not enough, nevertheless, and the uneasiness of Trujillo was evident in the mass "resignation" of fourteen deputies at the session of that day. The symptoms were of political madness, and the events proved it. The immediate court proceedings against Roca and his sentence to two years of prison on November 13 revealed that it was not a case of conspiracy, but a personal reaction by a man who loathed the work he had been doing since 1930, and who did not have the courage openly to oppose Trujillo.

The new chamber did not know how to show submission to Trujillo, apparently horrified at the risk incurred. A resolution sent a congratulatory message to Trujillo for his accomplishments during 1936; another gave

---

[59] The letter was recently reproduced in the publication of New York exiles, *Pluma y Espada,* Feb. 1952. [Fn. 82, Chap. I, Sec. 5.]

[60] It is specifically mentioned that Trujillo Peak has an elevation of 3,175 meters [10,416 feet] and La Pelona Peak 3,168 meters [10,393 feet]. [Fn. 83, Chap. I, Sec. 5.]

authorization to place a marble bust of Trujillo in both chambers. A law on December 23 ordered an annual celebration to be held on January 11 as the "Day of the Benefactor"; a decree instructed the issuance of a postage stamp commemorating the change of the name of the capital; another law bestowed on "Ramfis" the title of "Protector of Poor Children."

But Trujillo now had a new pastime. The story of Lina Lovatón is generally known in the Dominican Republic. *Listín Diario* of December 28, 1936, announced with fanfare her selection as Queen of the forthcoming carnival, and the fact that the designation had been made by the administrative council of Santo Domingo, with the assurance that the carnival would be an event of unusual importance by initiative of Trujillo; the Chamber had congratulated Lina Lovatón. *Listín Diario* in January published an extensive report concerning the festivities of the proclamation of Lina I: she had received the keys of the city; she had proclaimed Trujillo, his wife, and his mother as the "Great and Only Protectors of the Kingdom," as well as "Ramfis" her "Favorite Prince." At the same time, a colossal obelisk was dedicated near the seashore to commemorate the first anniversary of Ciudad Trujillo. The same newspaper, in its edition of February 8, gave a frontpage account of the coronation of Lina I and the official dance at the presidential palace.[61]

The annual message presented to Congress in February, 1937, noted, among other things: the establishment of a national police which unified the former municipal police and was distinct from the army; the signing of the boundary treaty with Haiti; attendance at the Inter-American Conference at Buenos Aires (where the Dominican delegation had introduced a plan for a League of American Nations);[62] the various foreign decora-

---

[61] Lina Lovatón was the daughter of a former attorney general in the Trujillo administration. Her "Kingdom" was continued at a villa in Miami, where she lives until the present day. Her brother, José Manuel ("Mencho") Lovatón was appointed vice-consul in Miami on August 25, 1943. *G.O.* 5964. [Crassweller quotes a lyrical, Trujillo-authored paean to "Queen Lina" published with her photograph in *Listín Diario* on September 23, 1937, on the occasion of her birthday. *Trujillo,* p. 134.

[On April 24, 1968 two New York City residents filed suit in a New York court against Yolanda and Rafael Lovatón, brother and sister living in Miami Beach, Florida (also naming a Washington attorney), alleging that the Lovatóns, acknowledged natural children of the Benefactor, had retained them to help locate portions of the Trujillo fortune that had been sent out of the Dominican Republic. The suit further alleged that through information supplied by the plaintiffs the Lovatóns had recovered "upwards of $900,000 from the estate" of Trujillo but that they had failed to pay the plaintiffs the agreed percentage. The plaintiffs in consequence asked in the suit for damages of $1,230,000, averring the Trujillo estate might be worth $800,000,000.] [Fn. 97, Chap. I, Sec. 5.]

[62] This plan was presented to different inter-American conferences, always under the title of the "Trujillo Project," until it was finally withdrawn at the Chapultepec Conference in 1945. [Fn. 99, Chap. I, Sec. 5.]

tions received by Trujillo; and a surplus of $238,669 out of a total revenue of $10,771,265; [etc.].

On February 26 a law, conferring upon Trujillo the "Grand Cross of Courage," related his "glorious deeds" in his military career, mostly limited to the campaign against General Desiderio Arias in 1931 (although his name was not mentioned).[63]

In the middle of 1937, the reelection campaign was resumed. The campaign continued with all intensity until the beginning of November when the first news of the massacre of Haitians became known. Afterwards, the campaign was absolutely silent.

But first, reference should be made to the important modifications introduced in the Dominican party, especially the statement published in *Listín Diario* on July 22, in which Party President Morel declared: "Complying with Article 39 of the Statutes of the Dominican Party, all the elective public officials of the Nation have presented their resignations so that the future conventions of the Party shall be free to fulfill the powers bestowed upon them by the said Article." As an example to be followed was cited the case of President Trujillo who was the first in signing his resignation. The system of "resignations" had been practiced since 1930, but this was the first public notice that indicated that the resignations were already signed for immediate use. . . .

The massacre of Haitians at the beginning of October, 1937, and its international repercussions were kept secret for more than a month. *Listín Diario* on November 9 published the first official notice, which declared:

. . . the incidents of the Northern frontier are not of an international character, nor are they invested with an importance and gravity which may impair the good relations between the two neighboring Republics. . . .

The same notice blamed the exiled Dominicans and some Haitians as enemies of Haitian President Elie Lescot for what happened; it requested the courts of justice to investigate the happenings, asserting that the events occurred the previous month. On November 13 a resolution of Congress declared four Dominicans traitors "because of their distorted declarations of the truth concerning the recent events about the frontier incidents between the nationals of Haiti and of this Republic. . . ."

---

[63] The preamble of this law said that "Generalissimo Trujillo has exalted with glorious deeds his military career. The following being outstanding among them: the personal and tenacious persecution of the rebels in the *Mogote* [Hummock] of Moca and the hills of Tamboril; his audacious entrance, alone, in Mao, focus of the armed sedition headed by one of the most fearful rebel leaders; his forced marches, from Copey to Montecristi, alone with four officers, through a field full of enemies, to block the passage of the conspirators against the public peace, deeds which deserve national gratitude." [Fn. 101, Chap. I, Sec. 5.]

Listín Diario on November 19 published an official notice assuring the fulfillment of the agreement with Haiti of October 15, 1937, and reproduced the documents exchanged on the occasion of the Haitian petition for inter-American mediation.[64] A month later on December 14 the same newspaper reproduced the Dominican memorandum to the governments of the United States, Cuba, and Mexico concerning this Haitian position. On December 16 Congress approved a resolution expressing its "vote of solidarity and its adhesion to his [Trujillo's] international policy" concerning the incidents with Haiti, and advocating safeguarding "the dignity, decorum, and the rights of the Dominican people."

A law on February 11, 1938, approved the Dominican-Haitian agreement signed in Washington on January 31 "which ends definitively and by compromise the differences between both Republics by reason of the events between nationals of both countries in the last months of 1937." The Dominican government expressed its regrets and assured that the guilty ones should be punished. Article 3 stipulated that "the Dominican Government is bound to pay the sum of $750,000 in United States currency," a sum that the Haitian government would invest in compensating the victims. Congress hastened to grant President Trujillo a "congratulatory vote" for the "triumph" attained in that agreement.

These are the only Dominican references by the government of Trujillo to the so-called "frontier incident," that cost the lives of more than 12,000 Haitians massacred in cold blood at the beginning of October, 1937.

A forced result was the punishment of the supposedly guilty parties. *Listín Diario* on December 16, 1937, announced the arrest of sixty persons involved in the events on the northern frontier. Three months later, it noted the trial and the sentences; the edition of March 15, 1938, published some details of the trial, presenting the acts as the impulsive reaction of some Dominican farmers whose properties had been plundered by certain Haitians.

The other consequence was his giving up his campaign for reelection as president in 1938. After a few weeks' silence following the publication of the news of the "incident," *Listín Diario* on January 10, 1938, published a speech by Trujillo in which he declined his presidential nomination:

---

[64] In this official release, the Dominican government disapproved what had happened and affirmed that an investigation would be made. It is obvious that this was a step attempting to stop the mediation (and investigation) by the governments of the United States, Cuba, and Mexico, shielding behind the agreement reached with the government of Haiti before the scandal broke out; for this purpose, some statements by Haitian President Stenio Vincent to the newspaper *Haiti-Journal* on Nov. 10 were also reproduced. In the following days it was hinted that riots had spread in Haiti against the government; and it was repeated that a Dominican investigation was going on, but nothing concrete was mentioned. [Fn. 119, Chap. I, Sec. 5.]

... I shall begin formulating a categorical reaffirmation of my purpose previously revealed on many occasions, to relinquish official investiture in order to enjoy the peaceful rest of private life. ... [65]

Listín Diario commented:

Dread transformed the faces of men of industry. The foreign colony was impressed. Anguish and intense silence drowned the hopeless cry that swelled the heart of the Republic. [66]

There was a general reaction against this announcement, although no one believed Trujillo was in earnest. At the capital on January 14, a meeting took place to ask Trujillo to desist from his purpose. ... [*It failed in its purpose.*]

Four months later, Peynado was elected president of the Republic, and Troncoso de la Concha, vice-president. This time it was not Trujillo's play. It seems that the reason that could not be made public was that the United States Department of State had expressed a certain veto towards the man responsible for the massacre of the Haitians. [67]

In his annual message to Congress in February, 1938, Trujillo tried to conceal the incident with Haiti by covering it with apparent diplomatic successes. He announced a surplus of $189,222 from a total of $11,561,-867 collected, [etc.].

The proclamation of the two candidates for the presidential term of 1938–42 was made on February 28 by the national convention of the Dominican party. A week previously, in *Listín Diario* on February 22, a curious official notice from the president of the Dominican party had appeared, regarding the "numerous petitions" received from persons who wished to be candidates in the next elections: the Supreme Chief, "at the same time that he regrets his inability to please all petitioners, will take into account their aspirations for future opportunities."

The elections took place on May 16; that same day *Listín Diario* published a headline that read thus: "People! Vote for the candidates of the Dominican Party, Peynado and Troncoso, suggested by the Honorable President Trujillo." The order was fulfilled; the *Official Gazette* on June 6 published the results: 319,680 had voted of the 348,010 registered electors; all the candidates received 100 percent of the votes cast.

Trujillo had some compensations. The Ateneo Dominicano awarded the prize for the best book of the year to *Reajuste de la Deuda Externa*

---

[65] Trujillo, *Pensamiento,* 3: 171–88. [Fn. 128, Chap. I, Sec. 5.]

[66] *Listín Diario,* Jan. 10, 1938. [Fn. 129, Chap. I, Sec. 5.]

[67] A direct source, whose name may not be revealed yet, confirmed to the author the active opposition of the Department of State against the reelection of Trujillo. [Fn. 131, Chap. I, Sec. 5.]

[*Adjustment of the External Debt*] signed by Trujillo. A resolution of Congress declared that Trujillo had been "the first and the greatest of the Heads of State that the Republic has had since its foundation until the present time." A law created the "Order of Trujillo" and awarded its highest decoration (the Collar of the Order) to Trujillo himself. . . .

On August 16, 1938, the new president of the Republic, Lic. Jacinto B. Peynado, took the oath of office. But the Benefactor continued in command.

The Peynado Administration, 1938–40

The speech by Peynado at his inauguration was symbolic of what the new period would be:

Blessed be the day of August 16, 1930, the lucky moment in which a Cavalier of the divine Order of Genius, whose insignia is granted by God alone, appeared for the first time in this august place with a brilliant torch in his hand, to offer his people this splendid gift: Civilization. . . . The bringer of light retires from Power leaving to his successor, whom he himself revealed to the people, the gleaming aura of his great work, the preservation of which will be the first duty of the Administration initiated today.[68]

Nothing had changed. Decree No. 1 confirmed all secretaries and undersecretaries of state; Decree No. 2 confirmed all remaining public employees; Decree No. 3 confirmed especially all members of the national army, military guard of the president, and the police; Decree No. 4 granted Generalissimo Trujillo the same privileges enjoyed by the president of the Republic, and to his wife and mother the same honors attributed to the First Lady. . . .

The pattern was not changed either. On the day after the organization of the new Congress, two senators and seven deputies resigned; fifteen days later, two more senators and two more deputies resigned.

And Decree No. 16, August 26, proclaimed that in recognition of "the services of Colonel Rafael Leonidas Trujillo Martínez" ["Ramfis"], he was promoted to the rank of brigadier general. The new general was nine years old.

No official document incorporated any other of the first measures taken by the new president, but one acquired fame quickly in the Republic and abroad, namely: the neon sign at the entrance of his house reading *Dios y Trujillo* (God and Trujillo). . . .

At the end of March, 1939, there was duly approved, with all the required procedure, a law granting the title of "Meritorious City" to San Cristóbal, because Trujillo was born there. On April 30 the "Day of the

---

[68] *Listín Diario,* August 17, 1938. [Fn. 1, Chap. I, Sec. 6.]

Workers" was celebrated with workers of the capital praising Trujillo but markedly without mention of the old Dominican Confederation of Labor. Every time that an important visit was reported or a message was printed in the press, its subject was regularly the Benefactor, and only by exception was it the president.

On June 28, 1939, the Senate received a letter from Trujillo requesting that the name Santo Domingo be given back to the capital. The senators decided to appoint a commission to draft the proper answer, but, of course, the name was not changed. *Listín Diario* of July 1 printed a full-page picture of the Benefactor with this information: Trujillo departs today for the United States and Europe; "in Washington, the illustrious statesman will meet President Roosevelt and Secretary Hull . . . in Europe, the Generalissimo will travel through different capitals to compare his ideas and methods of government with those of the most distinguished European statesmen. . . ." He traveled in his yacht *Ramfis*. On July 5 an announcement reported that the cabinet had sent a cable to Trujillo in Miami, reiterating their loyalty and requesting him to return soon; the Congress sent similar messages. Twelve days later, the creation of an "Executive Committee for the reception of the Benefactor" with Peynado himself as its chairman was announced.

There was a peculiar silence during the sojourn of Trujillo in the United States. There were no interviews with Roosevelt or Hull.* Only on August 8 was it said that Trujillo had arrived in Paris. The silence then continued; no European statesman paid him any attention. The best evidence of his colorless anonymity outside the Dominican Republic was two decrees of August 19, appointing him ambassador extraordinary to the governments of Great Britain and France. He had now at least a diplomatic status for official introductions.

The outbreak of World War II cut short his vacation. By September 4 he was on the high seas. But the yacht *Ramfis* did not seem to him safe enough, and on the ninth he switched at the Azores Islands to an American cargo ship. On landing in New York, he stated that the Dominican Republic had proclaimed its neutrality in the war, but "it will follow the policy of the United States in any direction that country may go. . . ."

Trujillo remained more than one month in the United States. He was still unable to meet Roosevelt or Hull.† But he interviewed one prominent exile, Rafael Estrella Ureña, who decided to return to the Dominican Republic.

---

* This is incorrect. Trujillo met with both President Roosevelt and Secretary Hull.

† See note above.

The return of Trujillo was an apotheosis. A law of September 25 had declared the date of his arrival a day of national holiday, and a decree on October 28 fixed the date as October 30, the day on which he would be in the capital. Vice-President Troncoso went to receive him in Puerto Plata. On Sunday, November 5 a great parade was held in the capital; more than 35,000 persons marched in line, headed by the secretaries of state, congressmen, and justices of the Supreme Court; towards the end marched the first Jewish and Spanish refugees recently arrived in the country.[69]

On December 2 the Estrella Ureña brothers, Rafael and Gustavo, returned from eight years of exile and conspiracy. *Listín Diario* of that day printed a cable addressed by Rafael Estrella Ureña to Trujillo announcing his arrival and ending with the word *"Abrazos"* ("I embrace you"). The trip was made in the yacht *Ramfis,* sent to pick them up. On landing, Rafael Estrella Ureña sent another telegram and more *"Abrazos."*

Listín Diario on the twenty-fifth printed another peculiar interview with Ricardo Paíno Pichardo, president of the Dominican party. Paíno Pichardo stated that Estrella Ureña had had an interview with Trujillo in Miami and expressed to him the desire to go back to his country and renew their friendship; that, as he had no money for the trip, Trujillo sent his yacht *Ramfis;* and that there had been no political bargain between them. He said also that it was not true that Estrella Ureña would receive any diplomatic post, because Article 65 of the statutes of the Dominican party provided that only its members may enjoy the advantages that the party offers. Gustavo Estrella Ureña had been elected a deputy on January 6, 1940, because he became a member of the Dominican party as soon as he arrived in the country but Rafael had not requested admission. *La Información* on February 16 announced that Rafael had opened a law office in Santiago. Before the year was out he was to be in jail, although for a brief period only.

The first official news about the illness of President Peynado was a decree on February 24, entrusting the executive power for the time being to Vice-President Troncoso de la Concha. Rumors about the seriousness of Peynado's illness spread quickly through the city, and guesses as to his successor began. The president of the university, Julio Ortega Frier, commented that Trujillo wanted to precipitate the resignation of Vice-President Troncoso in order to elect as the new president, Ortega Frier

---

[69] After this period, the direct experience of the author is added to the documentary evidence collected in his research for this study; he lived in the Dominican Republic from Nov. 19, 1939, to Jan. 31, 1946. [Fn. 39, Chap. I, Sec. 6.]

himself.[70] Lic. Jacinto B. Peynado died [of diabetes] on the evening of March 7. Troncoso de la Concha took the oath as president of the Republic on March 8. A picture taken at the moment of his approaching the building of Congress showed him flanked by Trujillo and surrounded by many colonels and military aides.

A few days previously, Trujillo had received another decoration, the Grand Cross of Malta. It was bestowed upon him by Prince Gaetano de Borbón Parma, dressed in the blue shirt and the red beret of the Spanish Falange. Trujillo reciprocated with the Golden Grand Cross of the Order of Trujillo. On the same day Trujillo received in a joint session of both chambers, the Grand Collar of the Order of Trujillo.

According to the *Official Gazette,* the budget approved for 1938 was $11,693,770, which meant a round increase of a million dollars over the previous one, and the budget for 1939 was $11,594,920, that is, similar to the previous one.[71] Another fact deserving mention here was the first issue of the new morning newspaper, *La Nación,* which appeared on February 19, 1940, more or less the property of Trujillo and thereafter the unofficial mouthpiece for his regime.

The Troncoso Administration, 1940–42

On March 8, 1940, Dr. Manuel de Jesús Troncoso de la Concha took the oath required by the Constitution as the new president of the Dominican Republic.[72] But in his speech to the National Assembly he added a second oath:

Honorable members of the National Assembly: I have just taken an oath to respect the Constitution and the Laws and to discharge with loyalty the position of President of the Republic. However, this oath is not enough. Gentlemen: I want also to swear that I will be a loyal follower of the political leadership started in 1930 by the Supreme Chief and Director of the Dominican Party, Rafael L. Trujillo Molina . . . and that only to him will I look for inspiration and support to continue this work that is his, and to which the Nation owes the happiness of its present and the insurance of its future.

---

[70] The author heard these comments directly from Ortega Frier; he may be mentioned as the source, since he died in 1953. Troncoso, as much as Ortega, had intervened very actively in the solution of the conflict with Haiti at the end of 1937 and beginning of 1938. [Fn. 49, Chap. I, Sec. 6.]

[71] *G.O.* 5108 and *G.O.* 5259. The Dominican budget would remain more or less similar until 1943, in which year it began to increase. Since 1947 these increases have been significant. [Fn. 55, Chap. I, Sec. 6.]

[72] *Listín Diario* on March 9 published a picture and a short biography of the new president. He was born on April 3, 1878; he graduated as a lawyer in 1899; he occupied for the first time a post in the cabinet during the last administration of General Ramón Cáceres (1911); he was later attorney general, president of the city council of Santo Domingo, president of the court of lands, president of the central electoral board, and president of the university. [Fn. 1, Chap. I, Sec. 7.]

Nothing was changed. On March 17 the delegates to the annual convention of the party elected two vice-presidents but its president, secretary, and treasurer continued to be appointed by decree by the Supreme Chief, Trujillo. On April 16 a law was approved according to which all resolutions by the congress, executive, courts, and municipal councils must be dated in the current year of the "Era of Trujillo," begun on August 16, 1930. A decree on April 13 confirmed the rank of secretary of state and member of the cabinet for the president of the Dominican party. The only thing that the new president allowed himself was the appointment of two of his sons as undersecretaries of state.

Everything remained quiet, until in May rumors about the serious sickness of Trujillo began. The press confirmed them only on May 31 in a brief notice of obvious official origin, saying that Trujillo was resting in his home after spending two days in the hospital. On June 11 another notice said that Trujillo was improving fast, and added that his illness "had never been serious."*

The newspaper said nothing more about this illness, but there is enough documentary evidence to back the rumors of those days. The rumors were based upon a remark imputed to his personal physician and secretary of health, Dr. Francisco Benzo, according to which: *"Esto huele ya a cadáver"* ("This [Trujillo] already smells like a corpse"). This belief awoke all kinds of desires as to the succession; President Troncoso was of no importance at all. On July 16 *La Nación* said that Trujillo had been out in the streets for the first time.[73] On the twenty-first, the same newspaper said that an investigation was going on inquiring into the conduct of the secretary of health and welfare, because there were "sound suspicions that serious irregularities have been committed in offices in his Department."

A decree the next day, July 22, appointed a new secretary of health. *La Nación* of August 9 stated in big headlines: "Former Secretary of Health and Welfare, Dr. Francisco E. Benzo, was arrested yesterday"; the proceedings had been sent to the attorney general.

The newspapers said nothing more about this first episode of a convulsive period that began at this moment, provoked by the illness of Trujillo and the ambitions that the possibility of his death awoke. Dr. Benzo was dismissed from his chair at the university; previously a delega-

---

*The medical problem was allegedly caused by anthrax on Trujillo's neck, developing into septicemia, and necessitating an operation. Cf. Crassweller, *Trujillo,* p. 180.

[73] Henceforth *La Nación* will be used as the main newspaper source. It seems that *Listín Diario* was kept alive during its last year with subsidies from the German legation; it was discontinued on January 15, 1942. [Fn. 13, Chap. I, Sec. 7.]

tion of the "President Trujillo University Guard" went to see him in jail
to request the resignation of that chair and all other honors he had accu-
mulated.[74] The trusted physician of Trujillo had committed the unpardon-
able error of being mistaken in the gravity of his diagnosis.

But Trujillo was not yet in good health; at least he was afraid of
not being in good health, and decided to depart for the United States to
look for American specialists. His trip was disguised by diplomatic formalities and later was transformed into Trujillo's greatest success; a decree on
August 28 appointed him as ambassador extraordinary on special mission
to sign, in Washington, the new Dominican-United States agreement which
abrogated the convention of 1924.

This agreement was signed on September 24, 1940. According to it,
the Dominican customs were returned to the administration of the Dominican government, and this entailed the obligation of paying the external
debt from its general funds. It was an indisputable success for Trujillo; but
in the Dominican Republic he personally received all the credit for it,
while the new Good Neighbor policy of President Franklin D. Roosevelt
and the measures which had preceded this step in other countries were
never mentioned.

A cascade of homages to Trujillo was at once unloosened. A law of
September 19 ordered two days of national holiday. Later laws ordered
a plaque to remind coming generations of this success of Trujillo, and
declared the pen with which Trujillo signed the agreement a national
jewel. On November 2 another law granted him the new title of "Restorer
of Financial Independence," which since then is always mentioned after
his title of Benefactor.

Trujillo returned on October 8. The special commissioner, General
José Estrella, announced his return the day before in an eloquent manifesto printed in *La Información* in Santiago, which said among other
things:

> ... The Dominican people, standing, receives full of enthusiasm and
> patriotic fervor its Illustrious Leader, and the regions of Cibao, all souls in
> festival, are ready to proclaim, heart in hand, their most decided adherence
> and eternal gratitude to the Supreme Chief.

On October 16 General Estrella was dismissed, and a few weeks later he
was in jail.

---

[74] The accusation was of irregularities committed as secretary of health and
previously as director of the Padre Billini Hospital. However, on January 28 of this
same year, 1940, Trujillo in person had congratulated him "because of his success
as the head of the Secretaryship of Health and Welfare during the last year." *Listín
Diario,* January 29, 1940. In addition on March 17 he had been elected second vice-
president of the Dominican party. [Fn. 17, Chap. I, Sec. 7.]

What had happened? One must go back to the rumors of the days when Trujillo was in the United States. Those rumors did not refer to the signature of the agreement, but to the persistent illness of Trujillo, and the name of General Estrella was the one most mentioned as his possible successor. It seems that José M. Bonetti Burgos, secretary to the president, told these rumors to Trujillo in the United States, and his reprisal was like lightning as soon as he came back.

La Información of Santiago announced on October 17 that Mario Fermín Cabral had been appointed governor of Santiago Province; on the next day, it announced that the office of the special commissioner had been done away with as being unnecessary.

La Nación on October 19, in the capital, gave extraordinary importance to the investiture of Governor Cabral. Governor Cabral stated at a political meeting in Santiago on November 3, 1940, "A new order of things now rules the destinies of Santiago."

Several days lapsed without any news about the arrest of General Estrella. The first news was peculiar: La Nación on November 2 said that, during the night of October 30–31, there had been an attempt to burn some judicial files of the court of appeals in Santiago, and that several people had already been arrested, among them two called Estrella and "a friend" of the former staff of General José Estrella. La Información on November 14 announced that the judiciary was investigating the double murder of Virgilio Martínez Reyna and his wife, which occurred in June, 1930; some arrests had been made. And it was added: "The double crime of San José de las Matas will not remain without punishment."

La Nación on November 17 reported that the day before, General José Estrella and Lic. Rafael Estrella Ureña [and others] "seriously implicated in the murder of Virgilio Martínez Reyna and his wife" had been sent to jail. La Información on the nineteenth announced that the day before, General Estrella had been insulted "by public censure" when he was taken from the court to the fortress through the streets of Santiago. La Nación during the next few days reported a number of civil complaints presented against General José Estrella and announced that the Dominican party had expelled from its ranks General Estrella, Lic. Rafael Estrella Ureña and other persons. Among the civil complaints against Estrella was mentioned the abduction of three minors.[75] The families

---

[75] On November 21 the authorities broke into the estate of General Estrella in La Herradura, "a place that Santiago society hears mentioned with justified horror." The newspaper account affirmed that General Estrella had there a "harem," and three minor sisters aged 18, 19, and 20 years were found there and have asked alimony for their children. La Información, November 22, 1940. [Fn. 44, Chap. I, Sec. 7.]

Martínez Reyna-Almánzar thanked Trujillo by letter and offered a mass for his health. A decree on November 29 deprived General Estrella of the Decoration of Military Merit; other decrees later removed the Orders of Trujillo and Duarte from General Estrella and Dr. Benzo.

On December 5 Trujillo departed again for New York. At the same time he requested to be admitted to the new Trujillista party. During his absence, the trials at Santiago developed in a peculiar way. *La Nación* on December 14 announced the coming hearing on a new murder, that of a photographer, José F. Roca, attributed to General José Estrella and others. On December 19 the trial for the murder of Roca took place in Santiago; General José Estrella pleaded guilty. He was sentenced to twenty years in prison; when he was taken back to jail, the people in the streets again insulted General Estrella.

During the following two months there was a surprising silence about the Martínez Reyna case. It was only on March 14 that this charge came to a hearing. The sentence could not be more surprising after such a scandal. General José Estrella and Lic. Rafael Estrella Ureña were indicted for the murder. The lawyer appointed by the court to defend them pleaded the statute of limitations, saying that more than ten years had elapsed since the murder; the judge accepted this pleading. General Estrella remained in jail, because he had already been sentencd for the murder of Roca. Lic. Rafael Estrella Ureña was freed, and hurried to cable to Trujillo, who was in New York;[76] Trujillo answered emphasizing the justice of his Era.[77]

On March 29, 1941, Trujillo returned to the Dominican Republic after the exchange of ratifications on March 10, 1941, of the Trujillo-Hull treaty. *La Información* on April 10 stated that he would suggest important changes in the cabinet as a consequence of some irregularities under investigation. Much more important had been the dismissal of José M. Bonetti Burgos as secretary of the presidency on February 5.

The sensational change did not happen until June 11. A decree on that day appointed Lic. Agustín Acevedo as new governor of Santiago Province in place of Mario Fermín Cabral. The importance of this change was revealed by the fact that President Troncoso himself went to Santiago to invest Governor Acevedo, just as had happened nine months before

---

[76] ". . . after being freed, I wish to send you my heartiest greetings ratifying my friendship and my offer to help you in anything you may think useful." *La Nación,* March 15, 1941. [Fn. 57, Chap. I, Sec. 7.]

[77] ". . . I am satisfied with your estimation of the Justice of my Era. . . ." *La Nación,* March 23, 1940. [Fn. 58, Chap. I, Sec. 7.]

when Estrella was dismissed and Cabral replaced him. Two days later, *La Información* reported that former Governor Cabral and former Lieutenant Colonel Veras Fernández had been arrested because there were "grave accusations against them."

La Nación on the eighteenth published two letters requesting amnesty, signed by General José Estrella from his cell in Fortress Ozama. In the first, he referred to the murder of Martínez Reyna, which he qualified as political and pinned upon Estrella Ureña, although "because of the unexplainable and rude interposition of Governor Mario Fermín Cabral and Lieutenant Colonel Veras Fernández" the statute of limitations was applied in order to save Estrella Ureña. In the second, he referred to the murder of Roca, which he qualified also as political and justified. The same day, the beginning of judicial proceedings against Cabral and Veras was announced. They were indicted for having exercised pressure upon the judge of Santiago, who had been dismissed.

The first news that Cabral and Veras were free appeared in *La Nación* of July 11; former Lieutenant Colonel Veras Fernández had been admitted as a member of the Dominican party. A decree on August 16 pardoned José Estrella. Mario F. Cabral would be reelected a senator on April 24, 1942. Trujillo had humiliated both of them, and neither dared to react with dignity.

But let us go back in this chronological summary, in order to record another surprising episode of this period: the creation of the Trujillista party, announced in *La Nación* on November 15, 1940. In order to have a better understanding of this step, one must remember the existence of one single party in the Dominican Republic since 1931, the Dominican party which has Trujillo as its chief. The newspaper used this headline: "At a historic meeting of University students, held yesterday in the Colón Square, the creation of the Trujillista Party was announced." And it added: "Ricardo Paíno Pichardo requests admittance into the ranks of the new Trujillista Party"; Paíno Pichardo had been the president of the superior directive council of the Dominican party since 1938. The new Trujillista party was organized by the "President Trujillo University Guard," and the main speech was delivered by its commander, Dr. José E. Aybar, at that time dean of the dentistry faculty and secretary of the Senate.

It was stated that the purpose of the new party would be "to cooperate in the political purification and education of the Dominicans"; and as reason for its constitution, the fact was alleged that the Dominican party did not accept as new members any adult person who had lived in the country during the last ten years without becoming a member of the party;

it was added that the Trujillista party would function inside the Dominican party and follow its structure and discipline.

The letter of Paíno Pichardo requesting his admission marked a model to be followed by all others; in that letter he detailed his past political life, and he affirmed that he had not belonged to any political party before 1930. Paíno Pichardo was accepted the next day. During the next few days, the acceptance of other individuals was announced; and March 31, 1941, was fixed as the last date to request admission to the party. *La Nación* on November 23, 1940, reported that the Trujillista party had already accepted 116 requests for admission and had returned 69; on November 27 it was announced that 2,559 requests had been received. On December 5, as stated above, Trujillo himself requested his admission to the Trujillista party; the University Guard answered that they had received his petition "with pride" and that they would consider it in "a special meeting, dressed in official uniforms." On the next day, they decided to appoint Trujillo as "the only Chief of the Trujillista Party."

The releases which appeared in the next few days show clearly that the Trujillista party was used to purge those persons considered to be weak or deserving a warning, more or less in relation to the trials of Santiago. Very few rejected requests, however, were made public; one of them was that of a former deputy from the province of Santiago, Francisco Pereyra, Jr., on March 10, 1941.[78] About April, 1941, news concerning the Trujillista party slowed down.

There is little more to say about the first year of Troncoso's nominal presidency. A decree on February 19, 1941, appointed Trujillo as special representative of the president with the rank of ambassador extraordinary and plenipotentiary in every country he could visit. The budget for 1940 reached $12,139,954, an increase of half a million over the preceding year. Congress, on January 3, 1941, approved the agreement between the Dominican Republic and the Export–Import Bank of the United States for a loan of $3,000,000 to the Dominican Republic. On April 1, 1941, the customs were transferred to the Dominican government in fulfillment of the agreement with the United States.

---

[78] He was rejected because his conduct as deputy from Santiago had shown inertia in face of the activities of certain politicians; "that weak and fearful attitude makes him unable to close ranks" with the men of the new party. *La Nación,* March 10, 1941. Pereyra "resigned" as a deputy on November 12, 1940; he remained in disgrace until September 21, 1943, the date on which he was again "elected" deputy. He was used, in 1947, during the maneuvers of the National Democratic party. [Fn. 72, Chap. I, Sec. 7.]

At the end of June, a feminist campaign began,[79] which was related to the new constitutional reform already in preparation and to be revealed at the end of the year.

In September, 1941, the constitutional reform was revived. A public poll about the possible suppression of the vice-presidency received a large favorable majority. On October 6 Trujillo — not President Troncoso — addressed a message to several congressmen proposing to them a number of constitutional amendments, among them the granting of equal political rights to women, the suppression of the vice-presidency, the extension of the presidential term, facilities to declare a state of emergency, and the easing of rules concerning exploitation of the subsoil. The Senate and the Chamber approved these reforms.[80]

About the same time, on September 4, Trujillo met with the new Haitian President, Elie Lescot, at the border (Villa Elías Piña).[81] President Troncoso did not attend the meeting.

On October 24, at an assembly in the capital, the president of the Dominican party proposed the presidential candidacy of Trujillo for the next term, beginning in 1942. President Troncoso made a speech saying that such a proposal made his heart beat "in a flood of joy and patriotism." Two days later, the Trujillista party also proclaimed Trujillo as its presi-

---

[79] A poll on the women's vote, which paved the way for its granting, had taken place during the previous month of December. At once, a struggle began among several groups of women who wanted to be the leaders of this movement. One of these groups was Acción Feminista Trujillista (Trujillist Action of Women) led by Abigail Mejía and Carmen Landestoy; another group was led in the capital by the widow of the late President Peynado. At the end, some other women got the leadership of this movement, among them Isabel Mayer and Milady Felix de L'Official. They had a big meeting in the capital, with speakers from all provinces. *La Nación,* June 20, 1941. After that, the movement was channeled through the new Trujillista party, as its feminine branch; on June 15 it was announced that Isabel Mayer and more than 1,000 women had already been registered in the party. *La Nación,* June 15, 1941. [Fn. 78, Chap. I, Sec. 7.]

[80] Trujillo read the message in person on the seventh. On the ninth, a special committee of the Senate recommended the reform. On Thursday, the tenth, the Senate approved it on first reading, and on Tuesday, the fourteenth, on second reading; on Wednesday, the fifteenth, the Chamber approved it on first reading, and on the seventeenth, on second reading. The Congress did not meet from the eleventh though the thirteenth nor on the sixteenth. *Bol. Sen.* and *Bol. Cam.,* October, 1941. The law was published in the *G.O.* 5656. [Fn. 88, Chap. I, Sec. 7.]

[81] Elie Lescot had been Haitian minister in Santo Domingo before the events of 1937, and Haitian minister in Washington during the same. It has always been pointed out that a personal friendship had existed between Trujillo and Lescot; when the latter was elected president of Haiti, it was also said that Trujillo had helped him in the campaign. After his election, there was an obvious improvement of relations between both countries, but step by step these relations became strained, until the Haitian legation in Ciudad Trujillo came under police surveillance. [Fn. 89, Chap. I, Sec. 7.]

dential candidate. There is no need to say that in the days that followed, adherences to that proposal rained from everywhere.

In December, 1941, Trujillo was in the United States once again, and from New York he sent a cable giving instructions to President Troncoso to declare war against Japan. *La Nación* of December 9 confirmed this detail: "A state of war between the Dominican Republic and Japan was declared. . . . The First Magistrate of the Nation, on receiving the recommendation made from the United States by Generalissimo Trujillo, requested authorization from the National Congress as required by the Constitution of the State." Three days later war against Germany and Italy was similarly declared.

The twenty-fourth constitution of the Dominican Republic was proclaimed on January 10, 1942. The vice-presidency of the Republic had disappeared; according to the new constitution, a vacancy in the presidency would be filled by the secretary of war and navy. A decree on January 2, 1942, had appointed Major General Héctor B. Trujillo as secretary of war and navy and commander-in-chief of the national army.

On January 1, 1942, the Dominican Republic signed the first joint Declaration of the United Nations. In the Third Meeting of Consultation of Foreign Ministers at Rio de Janeiro, also in January, the Dominican chancellor proposed a joint declaration of war against the Axis powers by all American republics, although he had to withdraw the proposal at once.

In February, the first attempted strike in the sugar fields took place and was at once suppressed by the army.[82] A memorandum from the secretary of interior and police, addressed to all governors, informed the workers "that the Government does not permit strikes."

In the same month, the electoral machine began to operate. The new Trujillista party was registered.[83] On the fifteenth, Generalissimo Trujillo was officially proclaimed as the presidential candidate of the Dominican party; at once the Trujillista party made him its candidate. A committee went to Estancia Fundación to tell Trujillo of his nomination; Trujillo

---

[82] The press said nothing about this; but the author himself saw trucks transporting troops with field guns. Some Spanish Communist refugees were accused of being the instigators of this strike, and several arrests were made; however, the Communists were finally freed, and only three Spanish anti-Communist leaders were expelled from the country. . . . [Fn. 104, Chap. I, Sec. 7.]

[83] *La Nación*, Feb. 15, 1942. The Trujillista party had been active again during the second half of 1941. *La Nación* of Aug. 23 said that it had received 4,685 petitions of admission in three days, and the edition of the twenty-eighth announced more than 4,000 petitions in a single day. In September, it was said that 29,815 petitions had arrived in fifteen days. And on Jan. 1, 1942, the same newspaper made a summary of the work of the Trujillista party in the fourteen months since its founding saying that it had 153,000 registered members among the men and 52,000 among women. [Fn. 107, Chap. I, Sec. 7.]

answered with a sibylline sentence: *"Y seguiré a caballo"* ("And I will continue on horseback").[84]

This sentence met with unbelievable success. *La Nación* on the seventeenth printed on its first page a picture of Trujillo on a horse, with these headlines: at the top "A sentence by the Chief which will enter History," at the foot *"Y seguiré a caballo."* Thereafter, it was the electoral slogan.[85] Even a *merengue* (a Dominican dance) was composed upon this line. . . .

Lic. Manuel A. Peña Batlle made his debut as president of the Chamber on April 26. In his speech he made an extraordinary proposal: that Generalissimo Trujillo occupy the presidency immediately after being elected in May, without waiting for the constitutional date of August 16. The Dominican party and the Trujillista party backed the proposal. On May 7 both chambers did the same. A letter from Major General Héctor B. Trujillo to President Troncoso started the required constitutional procedure: the secretary of war and navy offered his resignation, to be effective on May 15, the day before the elections.

Everything was ready for the great scene. The elections took place on May 16; the *Official Gazette* the next day published the results, incredible as they might seem: 581,937 votes [cast unanimously for the candidates of the Dominican and Trujillista parties]. Trujillo had been elected president for a third term; and his inauguration, according to the Constitution, was to be on August 16.

---

[84] *La Nación,* Feb. 16, 1942, gave an explanation of this sentence. It said that Lic. Porfirio Herrera notified Trujillo of his nomination, ". . . and as he made a reference to the fact that in that moment the Chief, with the same victorious impetus which led him through ways of success and glory, was riding on a nervous and noble colt, the Illustrious Leader answered: *Y seguiré a caballo* (And I will continue on horseback)." The author never did learn who had the idea of giving a political meaning to this sentence, as a symbol. It seems that what really happened was that, when the committee arrived at the *Estancia Fundación,* Trujillo was riding on a horse and did not want to stop to have a drink in celebration as suggested by the committeemen; it seems that he said more or less as follows: "You may have the drink, and I will continue on horseback." [It appears to be well established that the political novel on which Galíndez was working at the time of his disappearance in 1956 was to be entitled *Y Seguiré a Caballo.* The novel was of course left uncompleted and the text of what had been written cannot now be located.] [Fn. 109, Chap. I, Sec. 7.]

[85] One of the most typical editorials about this sentence appeared in *La Información* of Santiago, on Feb. 26, 1942; even Lanzarote [leader of a Genoese expedition in the latter thirteenth century credited with rediscovering the Canary Islands] and the Cid Campeador are mentioned next to Trujillo, all riding on horseback. The whole country was filled with pictures of Trujillo on horseback, the five stars of Generalissimo and this sentence. However, nothing reveals that *ambiance* better than a sign which the author himself saw in the main street of Ciudad Trujillo: "I will continue riding on horseback, you said, Chief. And we will follow you walking." [Fn. 110, Chap. I, Sec. 7.]

But on the next day, May 17, President Troncoso, using the previous resignation of Héctor B. Trujillo, appointed Generalissimo Trujillo as the new secretary of war and navy. *La Nación* on the eighteenth announced that on the same day President Troncoso would resign. That happened in a session of the National Assembly in which President Troncoso made a speech asserting that the elections of May 16, 1942, "have been the most comforting democratic spectacle within my memory." Trujillo took over; on the same day, his Decree No. 1 reappointed his brother Héctor as secretary of war and navy.

The presidential message of February 27, 1942, was not available for this study. According to the *Official Gazette,* the budget for 1941 was $12,167,050, more or less equal to the previous one; the fiscal year was closed with a surplus of almost half a million dollars. . . .

In June, 1942, the establishment of the feminine branch of the Dominican party was announced to be under the leadership of Carmita Landestoy.[86]

Troncoso de la Concha had gone through the presidency with neither pain nor glory. As he himself told the author some time later, if anything good happened during his administration "it was attributed to the Other One."[87]

The Third Trujillo Administration, 1942–47

On August 16, 1942, Trujillo again took the oath as president in the presence of many foreign special missions, although he had already held the office for three months. There were no changes in his cabinet, nor was there any sensational change in Congress.

Several legislative and administrative measures taken during the second half of 1942 revealed intense concern about the Haitian border. A

---

[86] Until then the feminine branch of the Trujillista party had been functioning under the leadership of Josefa Sánchez de González. From now on it was to be called for some time the "Feminine Branch of the Trujillista Party attached to the Dominican Party." In March, 1944, that fiction officially disappeared; the Trujillista party was only a summer night's dream. Carmita Landestoy would be an exile four years later, and she wrote a book against Trujillo. [Fn. 133, Chap. I, Sec. 7.]

[87] The best proof that nobody counted on President Troncoso was a release made public by the secretary for the affairs of the Generalissimo on Nov. 11, 1940, advising that requests for public offices must not be addressed to that secretaryship but to the honorable president of the Republic (*La Información,* Nov. 11, 1940). The only profit for Dr. Troncoso was the political advancement of several members of his family; about the end of April, 1941, his eldest son, Jesús María, was minister in Washington; his second son, Pedro, was minister in Buenos Aires; his third son, Wenceslao, was a member of the administrative council of Santo Domingo; and a son-in-law, Marino Cáceres, was secretary of agriculture, industry, and labor. But perhaps the initiative for these appointments was not always his. His comment to the author may be mentioned now, because he died in 1955. [Fn. 134, Chap. I, Sec. 7.]

law of September 16 created the new province of San Rafael (honoring *don* Rafael, naturally); [88] the partial elections, held on December 16, gave the traditional 100 percent in favor of the Dominican party. A decree on August 24 appointed the specialist in Haitian affairs, Anselmo A. Paulino, as governor of Libertador Province. On November 16 an important meeting took place in a border town in which the presidents of both chambers of Congress spoke. The speech by Peña Batlle was especially violent against the Haitians while praising the work of Trujillo. It was obvious that relations between Trujillo and Lescot were not as friendly as the latter had hoped they would be. . . .

On December 1, 1942, the second son of Trujillo was born and christened Radhamés. . . . On April 6, 1943, a resolution of the Senate approved the raising of the legation in Washington to the rank of embassy; Jesús María Troncoso was confirmed as first ambassador, and Flor de Oro Trujillo was appointed first secretary of the embassy. The government of the United States reciprocated the measure and promoted its minister, Avra Warren, as it first ambassador to the Dominican Republic. [89]

The army had received special attention the preceding year, on the pretext of the state of war. Much of the presidential message, dated February 27, 1943, was spent describing the country's diplomatic relations and the Dominican participation in the Third Meeting of Consultation of Foreign Ministers at Rio. The year's budget showed an income of $16,799,839, including $2,592,764 from customs, and a surplus of $2,155,136. This surplus was correctly described as "without precedent in the history of the National Treasury." A sum of $896,060 had been paid as interest on the foreign debt and $202,980 as amortization of bonds. The total of the foreign debt at the beginning of 1943 was $13,921,000.

At the beginning of September, another typical phenomenon of the Era of Trujillo took place. *La Nación* on the second published a headline: "Rafael L. Trujillo (Martínez) requests the abrogation of his nomination as general, granted by President Peynado in 1938. . . . President Trujillo has accepted with pride this noble gesture of his son in resigning the rank

---

[88] *G.O.* 5801. This name was justified by a petition by inhabitants of the new province "to link it in this way, now and in the future, to the memory of its illustrious author, Generalissimo Rafael L. Trujillo Molina." [Fn. 4, Chap. I, Sec. 8.]

[89] Ambassador Warren had presented his credentials as minister of the United States on July 4, 1942; he presented them again as ambassador on April 17, 1943. He remained in the country until the spring of 1944, when he was transferred by his government to investigate the situation in Bolivia before recognizing the new *de facto* government of Colonel Villarroel. The son of Ambassador Warren entered as a cadet in the Dominican air force and was promoted to a second lieutenacy before the departure of his father. (See picture printed in *La Nación,* April 23, 1944, on occasion of this promotion, in which Trujillo, Ambassador Warren, and Lieutenant Warren appeared together.) [Fn. 17, Chap. I, Sec. 8.]

of general." . . . "Ramfis" was fourteen years old when he resigned his first rank of general. Ten years later, at twenty-four years of age, he was to be again a major general and chief of staff of the air force, but only after having climbed one by one all the steps in the army hierarchy. . . .

The year 1944 was the centennial of the Republic; although judging from appearances it seemed to be the centennial of Trujillo himself. Preparations were long and expensive. It is important to note that the Dominican government decided to invite the government of the Soviet Union, although the lack of diplomatic relations caused many difficulties of protocol. The government of Moscow sent two diplomats; and in the Jaragua Hotel the red banner waved for the first time in the Dominican Republic.

The presidential message of February 27, 1944, continued to give special importance to the army. The total income of the treasury had been $17,206,787, creating a surplus this time of $3,701,458. Despite these two successive surpluses, the foreign debt continued to be $13,287,500. There was no explanation about the strain in the Dominican-Venezuelan and Dominican-Haitian relations.

At the beginning of March, the disappearance of the feminine branch of the Trujillista party, until then a part of the Dominican party, was decreed. From then on, there was only one party again, the Dominican party, of which the women's group became merely a section.[90]

On May 3 the fourth wedding of Flor de Oro Trujillo took place with great solemnity. This time she had been a widow, and her new husband was a wealthy Brazilian, Antenor Mayrink Veiga. . . .[91]

[*Pp. 184–85 of the manuscript recount details of the intricate and melodramatic interrelationship of horseracing and politics in the capital in 1944.*]

---

[90] *La Nación,* March 5, 1944. The newspaper report made explicit reference to a decree of June 3, 1942, which decided that the feminine branch of the Trujillista party would function as an affiliate of the Dominican party. This decree was abrogated, and at the same time the "feminine branch of the Dominican Party" was created. [Fn. 43, Chap. I, Sec. 8.]

[91] *La Nación,* April 30 and May 4, 1944. After the divorce from her second husband, the Dominican, Dr. Ramón Brea Messina (who ceased to be minister in Mexico), Flor de Oro married for a short time her third husband, a captain in the United States medical corps, who died in a fire in a Washington hotel. Mayrink Veiga had been in the Dominican Republic one year before, accompanying Major Napoleão Alencastro da Guimarães, who offered Trujillo the golden sword of a Brazilian general (*La Nación,* April 7, 1943). The fourth marriage of Flor de Oro lasted two years, two more marriages, with Frenchmen, lasted an even shorter time. In 1954 she married (for the seventh time) a Dominican singer. [Fn. 49, Chap. I, Sec. 8.]

On June 3, 1944, the new United States ambassador, Ellis O. Briggs, presented his credentials. His coldness towards Trujillo became known very soon; he lasted for only a short time. . . .[92]

At the beginning of October, 1944, the campaign for the reelection of Trujillo three years later was begun. The Chamber and the Senate declared their official support for the proposal. . . .

In January, 1945, something happened that might seem without importance, but that in the Dominican Republic meant much: Ricardo Paíno Pichardo fell into disgrace for the first time. On the twelfth *La Nación* printed prominently on its first page, a decree appointing Lic. Julio Vega Batlle as new secretary of the presidency in place of Paíno Pichardo. Other decrees on the sixteenth dismissed him from a number of other positions. The principal evidence of his total disgrace for the time being was the fact that he was not even elected a deputy after leaving the cabinet, where he had been the first lieutenant of Trujillo for five years. It was no secret that the cause of his fall was the offensive against him launched from the Secretaryship of Foreign Relations by Manuel A. Peña Batlle and Gilberto Sánchez Lustrino.[93]

The annual message by Trujillo in February, 1945, was of extraordinary length. The government's income in 1944 reached $21,789,750, and the fiscal year ended with a surplus of $5,254,796. The foreign debt was reduced to $12,652,000. The work carried on by the Departments of Foreign Relations, Public Works, and Agriculture received special and detailed attention. . . .

The summer of 1945 was a very agitated one. In the first place, World War II had ended in Europe. The different national groups of refugees living in the capital attempted to commemorate the surrender of Germany with a demonstration in the streets, but they did not receive the required permit. Secondly, Trujillo decided to establish diplomatic relations with the Soviet Union and to have a permanent mission in Moscow. . . .

---

[92] Briggs had been an assistant to Ambassador Spruille Braden in Havana, and his antidictatorial feelings were generally known. The United States embassy remained without a head for several months. Later, the Dominican government attacked Braden and Briggs over and over again, even alleging their "pro-Communist" sympathies. [Fn. 56, Chap. I, Sec. 8.]

[93] The fall of Paíno Pichardo was obvious, although he had ups-and-downs in the following weeks. However, those on the inside track in the regime were not sure how long his disgrace would last and were careful to maintain his personal friendship. They were right, although Paíno Pichardo never again became the strong man he had once been and finally faded from the front ranks of the regime until 1955. [Fn. 79, Chap. I, Sec. 8.]

In another interesting development, Trujillo on May 28 addressed a letter to Lic. Rafael Estrella Ureña, who was at this time a justice of the Supreme Court, but singled out as a member of the Dominican party, inviting him to reorganize the old Republican party.

Estrella Ureña accepted on the thirtieth and resigned as justice of the Supreme Court. *La Nación* reported on June 3 that some former leaders of the Republican party seemed to be opposed to reestablishment of the party.

The invitation of Trujillo on May 28 had also been addressed to former leaders of other old parties. P. A. Ricart answered from Curaçao that he could not reorganize the National party (horacist) because he was sick. But Dr. Wenceslao Medrano agreed to reorganize the Independent Workers party. And Rafael Espaillat announced that he was ready to organize a new National Democratic party, together with other personalities of second rank in the government of Trujillo.

It is obvious that this was a clever maneuver to simulate the existence of several political parties, and at the same time to undermine Rafael Estrella Ureña. No attacks at all were directed against Medrano or Espaillat; all attacks were concentrated on the Republican party.

A third aspect to notice was the sudden appearance of a labor movement, developed in the second half of 1945. It had been preceded in 1944 by an important law on labor contracts, approved on June 16, 1944. On August 7 a message praising the work of Trujillo was made public, addressed to the workers of the Americas by the reconstituted Dominican Confederation of Labor under the chairmanship of newspaperman Francisco Prats Ramírez. Very soon afterwards, Dominican delegates, paid by the government, attended the congress of the CTAL [Confederación de Trabajadores de América Latina — Latin American Confederation of Labor] in Cali, Colombia, at which the Communists got full control of this continental organization of workers.

Another law, on May 4, 1945, created a new secretaryship of Labor and Economy, the first incumbent of which was Jesús María Troncoso. The main constituent of this new Secretaryship was a Department of Labor, entrusted to Lic. Eduardo Matos Díaz[94] (today in exile in Mexico).

What was going on in the Dominican Republic? Trujillo appeared to be sending a minister to Moscow, to be reorganizing and rejuvenating the political parties, and to be creating a labor movement. . . . What was happening did not have the Dominican Republic as its main stage. Its cause was the end of World War II and its politico-social repercussions in

---

[94] The author was appointed legal adviser of this department; for this reason, he was a personal witness of many events reported in this and other chapters. [Fn. 107, Chap. I, Sec. 8.]

the entire world. Two Latin American dictators had already fallen in 1944, the Salvadorean Hernández Martínez and the Guatemalan Ubico. And Trujillo was trying to defend himself by adopting democratic appearances.

At the same time, it was obvious that there was considerable ferment inside the country. There are few documentary evidences of the clandestine activities carried on by a group of university students during that summer of 1945, but it is possible to find some indications.

Anybody who was active in the university at that time could guess the ferment which had been growing for several months.[95] Later it became clear that in 1945 there had been two different groups: one, the majority, backed by the vice-president of the university, Lic. José A. Bonilla Atiles, with clear democratic orientation, and a minority, with Communist peculiarities, led clandestinely by Pericles Franco Ornes, Jr. ("Periclito") who had recently returned from the University of Chile.

Shortly thereafter, the police were able to identify several students as possible authors of clandestine leaflets distributed at night.[96] Among those suspected was "Periclito" Franco. When a police officer went to Franco's home to arrest him, he feigned illness and profited by the hesitation of the officer, who returned to headquarters seeking further instructions. In the meantime, Franco slipped out and requested asylum in the Colombian legation. Concurrently, other young people were granted asylum in the Mexican embassy.

After at first refusing, the Dominican government was forced to grant a safe-conduct for all these young men to leave the country. Its reprisal was to request the retirement of those diplomats who had granted the asylum, and to sentence Lic. Pericles A. Franco, Sr. to three months in prison for a crime allegedly committed many years before.[97]

One of the consequences of these activities was the immediate purge of public employees. All of them were forced to fill in a long blank with

---

[95] The first symptoms of uneasiness appeared in the spring, just after the Third Congress of Youth. Several university students refused to sign a message supporting Trujillo to be addressed to the youth of the Americas, and their signatures were forged. The most serious incident came from the fact that the name of Dr. Gabriela Cifuentes, daughter of the Chilean chargé d'affairs and sister of the president of the Chilean Federation of Students, was included among the signers. Her brother made public and denounced this forgery. In addition, even in October, 1944, or before, a clandestine manifesto of the students began to be circulated (See *Boletín ARDE,* No. 16, Dec. 9, 1946). . . . [Fn. 109, Chap. I, Sec. 8.]

[96] There are a number of data about these events in Hicks, *Blood in the Streets,* pp. 201–26; Bustamante, *Satrapía,* pp. 104–8; several issues of the *Boletín ARDE;* and Pericles Franco Ornes, *La Tragedia Dominicana* (Santiago de Chile, 1946), pp. 77–82. The *Bol. Cam.* of June 26, records also the answer of the Dominican deputies to a message from Costa Rican deputies on behalf of political prisoners in the Dominican Republic. [Fn. 111, Chap. I, Sec. 8.]

[97] The author knows well the inside history of this case, because of his friendship with the Franco family at that time. . . . [Fn. 112, Chap. I, Sec. 8.]

seventeen questions, among them the following: "15. Who among your relatives are not registered in the Dominican Party? 16. If there are any such relatives, do you know the reasons why they are not registered? 14. If any relative of yours has been an enemy of the government, what has been your attitude towards that relative?" A committee studied the answers and in many cases questioned in person those employees under suspicion. . . .[98]

The labor movement increased its activities in the fall of 1945. And the game with the Communist party began, although there was not yet documentary evidence. In October, a new minimum wage law was passed, establishing a mixed committee of employers, workers and officers of the government to fix these wages. In January, 1946, a general strike exploded in the sugar fields of La Romana and San Pedro de Macorís. It has been the only important strike during the Era of Trujillo (another was attempted in the docks of Ciudad Trujillo). Hastily issued official decrees establishing minimum wages for sugar workers were documentary evidence of a well organized strike which Trujillo did not dare to break with the army as he had done before. At the same time such decrees indicated the low standard of living among Dominican workers.

In the meanwhile, a radio war between Venezuela and the Dominican Republic had started. The relations between Trujillo and the Venezuelan President Isaías Medina Angarita had become strained again during the summer of 1945, and the first news about the Venezuelan revolution in October, 1945, was received with joy. But the new Venezuelan government was headed by Rómulo Betancourt, who soon jailed several agents of Trujillo in Caracas.[99] At the same time, Venezuelan radio stations began to attack the Dominican dictatorship. The first reaction of Trujillo was a public meeting, on November 10, in which several speakers attacked the government of Venezuela.[100] In the following days, many articles under

---

[98] The *Boletín ARDE,* No. 17, Dec. 16, 1946, reproduced in photostat this circular. The author knows it personally, because he received it in the diplomatic school where he was a professor and in the Department of Labor. The questions not only inquired for possible enemies of the regime, but also required a definite proof of active collaboration, such as attendance at political meetings, articles in the press, and lectures. [Fn. 113, Chap. I, Sec. 8.]

[99] Some of those arrested were spies of the Dominican legation, whose files were violated in the first moments of the revolution. But more curious was the Dominican protest over the arrest of some Spanish Communist leaders who had fought in the streets of Caracas against Acción Democrática [the then dominant Venezuelan party]. [Fn. 136, Chap. I, Sec. 8.]

[100] *La Nación,* Nov. 11, 1945. Previously, *La Nación* had mentioned an article in the New York Communist newspaper, *Daily Worker,* attacking Betancourt as a "Trotskyite" and "dangerous character." Some days later, on Nov. 30, *La Nación* reported that, during their brief stop in the airport of Ciudad Trujillo on the way to exile in the United States, the ex-presidents of Venezuela, Medina Angarita and Eliázar López Contreras, had been greeted by the secretary of the presidency and the private secretary of Trujillo. [Fn. 137, Chap. I, Sec. 8.]

the pseudonyms of "Juan Primito" and "Máximo Manso" were printed in the press; there are sound reasons to believe that they were written by José Almoina, private secretary of Trujillo. Venezuela broke diplomatic relations with the Dominican Republic; this situation was to last until almost the end of 1948, when the Venezuelan government of Acción Democrática was ousted by the Venezuelan army.

Agitation for the reelection of Trujillo increased at the beginning of 1946. The evening newspaper *La Opinión* was for several weeks an escape valve and finally brought an explosion. About the middle of January, the secretary of the presidency visited the editor of *La Opinión* suggesting to him a campaign of "opposition"; the government wanted to inspire it and was ready to support it with money. The editor requested freedom of action and personal guarantees from Trujillo himself. Next morning he met with the president, and Trujillo promised those guarantees, with the only condition that the newspaper must not attack either the president or the army.[101]

La Opinión started its criticism in the social field, especially in a column headlined "We say what others silence." In February, in the middle of the campaign for reelection, a former vice-president of the university, Lic. José Antonio Bonilla Atiles, made public a letter explaining the reasons why he did not want to sign a manifesto of the intellectuals supporting reelection. Bonilla said that he understood that Trujillo was not the only possible candidate; a subsequent letter signed by about forty university students backed this position. This political rebellion was too much, and a muzzle was placed upon the newspaper. A few days later, Trujillo bought *La Opinión*. Bonilla Atiles was forced to seek asylum in the Mexican embassy and finally departed for New York as a political exile.

The strike in the sugar fields and the reaction provoked by the campaign in *La Opinión* seemed to show some weakness in Trujillo's regime. But the government reacted very quickly. On the one hand, strikes were restricted by law, and other measures of supervision over the labor unions were adopted; the law on minimum wages was also modified. On the other hand, university students and the relatives of those who had dared to face the regime were forced to declare their support of Trujillo.[102]

The annual message sent by Trujillo to Congress on February 27, 1946, has not been printed. The *Official Gazette* records that the budget

---

[101] The author had this information directly from Lic. José Ramón Estella, the editor. [Fn. 142, Chap. I, Sec. 8.]

[102] *La Nación,* March 14, 1946, reported the homage paid to Trujillo by 2,000 university students. It has been impossible to consult for this study the editions of *La Opinión,* in which many letters and comments of those days appeared. . . . [Fn. 147, Chap. I, Sec. 8.]

for 1945 was $20,943,133, five million more than the previous one. It is doubtful if the message referred to the worsening of relations with Haiti, especially after the denunciation of the possible connection of Trujillo with a plot against the life of Haitian President Lescot, as a consequence of which two persons were executed. Lescot was ousted as president in January, 1946, but the relations of Trujillo with the new government of Dumarsais Estimé became still more strained during the years to come. . . .

In June, 1946, two old lieutenants of Trujillo, Ricardo Paíno Pichardo and José María Bonetti Burgos, came back to the first row, but they lacked their old strength, and Virgilio Alvarez Pina continued to be predominant as president of the Dominican party.

"Cucho" Alvarez Pina played one of the roles in the tragicomedy developed during the second half of 1946 in connection with the organization and activities of the Dominican Communist party. The press did not report the secret steps behind the stage but there is left quite enough documentary evidence for reconstruction of the process.

The Dominican government had started its double game at the end of 1945. However, only on March 15, 1946, was there a first mention of Dominican Communists. An official release said that the government knew of the existence of a clandestine Communist party and ordered its members to appear within five days in order to regularize the party. The silence of the following days showed that the maneuver had failed; the party was not organized in public.

Then the tactics changed slightly, and an attempt was made to organize a labor party under Trujillist inspiration. The idea was already in gestation in 1945, but only in May, 1946, was it put into effect. On May 1 a political meeting of workers took place in Ciudad Trujillo; the main speaker was Francisco Prats Ramírez, president of the Dominican Confederation of Labor. One month later, the new National Labor party appeared in public.

La Nación on June 15 published two letters by Trujillo, addressed to the attorney general and the secretary of interior and police, admonishing them to respect all constitutional guarantees of free speech and organization of political parties. On the twenty-fourth *La Nación* printed another message by Trujillo inviting all exiles to return to the country, but three days later the same newspaper answered in an editorial: "These people must not return!" But the exiles did return.

Referring to a letter by the central committee of the Communist party printed in *La Opinión* on July 1, *La Nación* in its edition the following day expressed surprise that such a party could exist. But on August 27 *La Nación* printed a manifesto by the so-called Popular Socialist party (bearing the same name as the Cuban Communists), accompanied by a group picture of the signers of the manifesto. Its authors proclaimed them-- selves Marxist-Leninist-Stalinists and stated that their purpose was to seek to fulfill their program "through a struggle in accordance with the democratic rights and freedoms of the Constitution in force."[103]

On October 2 *La Nación* printed a letter by the Popular Socialist party (Communists) requesting permission legally to continue its activi- ties. The central electoral board rejected the request because it was not "in accordance with the provisions of Article 131, *et. seq.,* of the Electoral Law," although it did not explain the irregularity. *La Nación* on October 14 published a letter from Trujillo to the secretary of interior and police recommending that he take all necessary steps in order that the Com- munists might organize as a legal party; in this letter he praised the cooperation of the USSR during the war, adding that communism in the Dominican Republic "is already a fact of positive importance." The Com- munists hastened to thank Trujillo for this letter. But Alvarez Pina, as president of the Dominican party, opposed it energetically. The double game was obvious.

Another group appeared in the meantime, the Democratic Youth made up of non-Communist students. This group caused more alarm than the Communists, and *La Opinión* on October 17 printed a letter from several young Trujillistas calling these students and their president "Com- munists" and demanding: "Take down your mask, fakers!"

The tension provoked by all these maneuvers and the unexpectedly favorable reaction by the people, which was not reported by the official press, culminated in a meeting held in the Colón Square of Ciudad Trujillo on October 26. In order to know what actually happened in that joint meeting of the Popular Socialist party and the Democratic Youth, one must read the publications of the exiles. The *Boletín ARDE* of New York, edited by a former vice-president of the university, Lic. José Antonio Bonilla Atiles, printed a long report, which deserves to be taken as true at least in its essential parts: The meeting was authorized by the police, but several *agents provocateurs* of the government attacked the crowd, thus causing "incidents" in which several people were slightly wounded.

---

[103] *La Nación,* August 27, 1946. The same issue contained an editorial on the front page, commenting on the manifesto under this headline: "Communism comes into the light of day." Among other expressive things, it said: "What better answer about the existence of a democratic government than the very fact of the organiza- tion of the Popular Socialist Party and that its leaders can express themselves in such terms?" However, in the next issue it reproduced with the same prominence a letter insulting the signers of the manifesto because according to their picture they were "poor boys, hopeless ethnically and esthetically, with really troglodyte fea- tures." [Fn. 163, Chap. I, Sec. 8.]

What happened then was sufficient pretext for the measures taken immediately afterwards against both Communists and non-Communists.

This double game of Trujillo with the Communists served two ends in 1946: a simulation of democratic freedom on the eve of the 1947 elections and the pretension that the only enemies of the regime were the Communists. In 1946, a dictatorship supported by a single party was out of fashion; only one year before, the United Nations had defeated fascism, and the "cold war" had not yet started.

The pretense continued for half a year more; but now "the opposition" was limited to more obedient groups. The National Labor party was still alive, and it participated in the extraordinary elections held on December 14 to choose delegates to the third constituent assembly called under Trujillo. This time the elections were not 100 percent in favor of one single list; the Dominican party received only 662,340 votes and the National Labor party, 65,948.

The constituent assembly met December 26. The celerity of its proceedings was as usual and on January 10, 1947, the new constitution was proclaimed; it was the twenty-fifth in the Republic's history. The amendments were confined almost solely to financial provisions. . . .

According to the *Official Gazette,* the budget approved for 1946 was $26,333,644, which meant a five and a half million increase over the previous one. The one approved for 1947, in December, 1946, was for $39,625,628, which meant another jump of $13,000,000 or 50 percent over the 1946 budget.

The next four months were occupied with the "electoral campaign." Officially it was a three-sided contest. At the end of January, the third party, the National Democratic party headed by Rafael A. Espaillat, was launched.

On February 5, the declaration of principles of the National Democratic party was printed, which could not have been more similar to the declaration of the Dominican party. The central electoral board did not hesitate to recognize this new party on March 10.

The National Labor party announced at the end of March, 1947, the list of its candidates, without even wasting paper to explain the program of the party in case of winning.[104] Everything was ready for the elections.

La Nación of May 17 reported: "The candidacy of Honorable President Trujillo wins by a great majority in the polls." However, if one had

---

[104] *La Nación,* March 31, 1947. Despite the "Laborite" appearances of this party and its obvious official inspiration, the Dominican Confederation of Labor adhered to Trujillo's candidacy. *La Nación,* Jan. 30, 1947. [Fn. 202, Chap. I, Sec. 8.]

been reading the previous issues of this paper, one would hardly have guessed that elections were coming — elections with three rival candidates for the presidency: Rafael L. Trujillo Molina, Rafael A. Espaillat, and Francisco Prats Ramírez. Moreover, a few days before the elections, an announcement of support by members of the Chamber of Deputies for the candidacy of Trujillo, which was made public, contained among its signers the name of the candidate of the opposition Prats Ramírez (who at no time had resigned as a deputy of the Dominican party).[105]

The results were the most curious in the whole Era of Trujillo, and they surely meant a great job of calculation by the central electoral board or the agency deciding them. Province by province, county by county, the votes obtained by every one of the three parties were detailed. Of course, the candidacy of Trujillo and all candidates of the Dominican party won with the exception of two deputies reserved according to law for the minorities; these two deputies were equally assigned to the National Democratic party (the minority in the province of Santiago) and to the National Labor party (the minority in the province of Duarte). In total, the Dominican party received officially 781,389 votes; the National Democratic party, 29,765; and the National Labor party, 29,186. There was not a single abstention. At least none was mentioned in the board's certificate of election. On May 29 both chambers of Congress met solemnly in National Assembly to proclaim the victory of Trujillo.

In the meantime, the Communists, and some who were not, went to jail. A letter from Virgilio Alvarez Pina appeared in *La Nación* on January 29, denouncing to the attorney general the Communists as ready to intensify their activities on the occasion of the coming visit of the secretary general of the United Nations. Attacks against Communists were renewed in March on the occasion of the arrival in the country of "Periclito" Franco, and for the first time *La Nación* admitted the existence of a separate Democratic Youth, although it attacked them together with the Popular Socialist party.

In April, several accusations of terrorism were made against the Popular Socialist party and the Democratic Youth. The government then moved in on the Popular Socialist party and the Democratic Youth. Except for a few members who were able to escape in time, the rest were jailed

---

[105] The author has not been able to find in any of the public libraries of the United States the issue of the newspaper in which this statement was printed, with the name of Prats Ramírez (several issues of this period are missing). But he himself read it at that time, either in *La Nación* or *La Opinión*. He also read the immediate correction which was published saying that it had been a mistake of the typist who copies the list of deputies, admitting in this way, although indirectly, that the statement had not been signed at all. [Fn. 203, Chap. I, Sec. 8.]

immediately.[106] And they remained in jail until the beginning of 1950 when a commission of the Organization of American States went to the Dominican Republic.

This reaction was completed by the middle of June by a law prohibiting any Communist, anarchist, or similar groups. The tragicomedy was over; Trujillo was the author, but the Communists did not hesitate to play as extras; the true victims were the boys and girls of the Democratic Youth.

In July, Congress officially congratulated Trujillo for having paid off all the foreign debt of the Dominican Republic.[107]

The fourth inauguration of Trujillo as president of the Dominican Republic was soon to occur. However, in New York and Cuba many exiles were anxious to prevent it. It is impossible to find in the Dominican press traces of the "Cayo Confites invasion" until many months after the storm. Its participants were sentenced in absentia. But in the New York Spanish newspaper *La Prensa* and in other papers of both Americas there is evidence for those who would like to confirm it. It was an open secret. . . .[108]

The Fourth Trujillo Administration, 1947–52

The invasion from Cayo Confites failed in Cuban waters, without giving the invaders a chance to land in the Dominican Republic. The plan was delayed more than had been expected for several reasons, and none of the governments, related in any way to the clandestine operations, could ignore them for long. The United States stopped the purchase of war material; Cuba was forced to order the dispersal of the trainees. When the leaders of the invasion received the Cuban order, they decided to set sail in a suicidal gesture, but a few hours later were blocked by the Cuban navy. It was perhaps best for everybody involved. The revolutionaries were placed under arrest but only for a few hours.

On August 16, 1947, Trujillo took the oath for the fourth time. Though the president was the same as in 1930, the members of his cabinet

---

[106] In the Dominican press there was no report of these arrests, although *La Nación* mentioned at the end of December, 1946, some unimportant resignations from the ranks of the Popular Socialist party. It is in the *Boletín ARDE* of the New York exiles that it is possible to find data about this soon after the persecution started, especially in No. 22 on March 31, 1947, and in two leaflets of April 24 and May 10. . . . [Fn. 207, Chap. I, Sec. 8.]

[107] *Bol. Cam.*, July, 1947. However, this news was premature; in his annual message of Feb. 27, 1951, Trujillo announced again that the external debt had been fully paid in 1950. [Fn. 219, Chap. I, Sec. 8.]

[108] The activities of the exiles had been revived during World War II, and in the summer of 1943 a general congress took place in Havana which laid the ground for coordinated action. *Quisqueya Libre*, July, 1952. [Fn. 220, Chap. I, Sec. 8.]

were all of them different, although his brother, Héctor, had taken on the appearance of a veteran. . . .

The budget approved in December for the following year, 1948, reached $58,132,600, which meant another increase of $19,000,000 or 50 percent over the previous one.

The year 1948 opened with the trial in absentia of the Cayo Confites invaders.[109] The hearings began on January 28; chief defendant was Juan ("Juancito") Rodríguez, and the "criminal records" of other defendants were recalled. On January 30 sentence was passed, providing thirty years imprisonment and a joint penalty of $13,256,000 on all defendants except Rafael Brache and ten others. *La Nación* on February 14 printed the entire sentence with a list of all defendants, requiring a halfpage of the newspaper. . . .

On December 2 Aníbal J. Trujillo, a brother of the president, died. The newspapers covered the circumstances of his death with a veil of silence, the same as during the last years of his life. *La Nación* of the third stated that he died at home "in a tragic accident."* The issue of the eleventh reported the funeral services, with his brothers Héctor, Virgilio, "Petán," and Romero in attendance; the absence of Rafael Leonidas strikes the attention of the reader.

During the same days, Profirio Rubirosa [the playboy former husband of Flor de Oro Trujillo Ledesma] was transferred to a new post as ambassador to Italy.

The budget approved in December for 1949 was once again increased, this time to $66,735,260, or eight and a half million more than the year before.

In January, 1949, Anselmo A. Paulino appeared for the first time as the favorite; he was to be reaffirmed as such later after a brief disgrace. Three decrees, all dated January 24, appointed him secretary without portfolio, promoted him to the rank of "general," and gave him supervision of the national police, of the special motorized police and of another special inspection under the direct orders of the executive.

The annual message of Trujillo to Congress on February 27, 1949, announced that $64,421,569 had been collected in 1948, with a total of

---

[109] This trial was preceded by several other measures related to the Cayo Confites invasion. A law in October punished acts of piracy by sea or air (*Bol. Sen.* and *Bol. Cam.,* Oct. 1947). On Nov. 12, a joint session of the National Assembly was held to denounce the presidents of Cuba, Venezuela, and Guatemala for their protection of the "International Communist Brigade" (*Bol. Sen.,* Nov. 1947). And another law, Dec. 6, prescribes punishment for those who leave the country clandestinely for abroad (*G.O.* 6719). [Fn. 21, Chap. I, Sec. 9.]

* Cf. Crassweller, *Trujillo,* p. 228.

$92,918,900 as governmental income from different sources; the fiscal year had been closed with a surplus of $1,834,812. The same message reported at length on the difficult relations with Cuba, the Dominican contribution to the Ninth Inter-American Conference held at Bogotá, the increase of the war navy, and the development of social security.

At the end of February, the report printed in *La Nación,* concerning the reading of the annual message, had a surprise — it mentioned among those attending, "Captain" Rafael Leonidas Trujillo Martínez. The last previous picture of Trujillo's son, printed in the issue of January 26, had shown him in military uniform but without any rank.

On June 19 this tranquillity was interrupted by a second invasion, this time by air, known as the Luperón invasion, named for the town where the only attacking amphibian plane landed. The fact of the landing, which ultimately failed, and of the subsequent military incidents made it impossible to cover this attack with the silence that two years earlier veiled the Cayo Confites attempt. In *La Nación* and *El Caribe* of June 21 and editions following, there is extensive information,[110] although only from the point of view of the government; it must be rounded out with other reports appearing in the foreign press of those days.

The invasion was prepared in Guatemala, although it had the assistance of officials of other countries. Trujillo knew the plans very early. Several planes set out from Lake Izabal in Guatemala, but only one under the command of Horacio J. Ornes, reached the Dominican Republic.[111] A series of fortuitous circumstances precipitated the swift and tragic end of the coup, and only five prisoners survived of the fifteen invaders. A much publicized trial was held; the sentence was thirty years in prison. The Luperón air invasion had failed, as had the Cayo Confites maritime invasion two years before. But its balance was tragic.

On July 13, 1949, "Ramfis" received three decorations: the Grand Cross in Silver of the Orders of Trujillo, Duarte, and Colón. On this occasion, *La Nación* of the fifteenth printed his picture with a footnote summarizing the biography of the young "Captain of the Military Guard

---

110 See *La Nación* and *El Caribe* from June 21 to July 17, 1949. On the latter date, the government made public an official release concerning the event. On June 28 and 29, the newspapers printed complete information about the beginning of the process, with the individual questioning of the prisoners by the judge. [Fn. 56, Chap. I, Sec. 9.]

111 Horacio J. Ornes was a student of the author in the diplomatic school of the Dominican Republic. The author also spoke with him in Mexico City years after the invasion failed. His appointment as consul and secretary of the Dominican legation in Costa Rica has been previously noted; about 1945 he resigned all these positions and joined the exiles, after the arrest of his brother Germán for a few days in Ciudad Trujillo. He is at present living in Mexico. [Fn. 59, Chap. I, Sec. 9.]

of the President of the Republic. . . ."[112] In December, "Ramfis" sailed abroad; and his father appointed him inspector of embassies and legations with the full rank of ambassador extraordinary (he was twenty years old). He was accompanied by an escort of friends and his personal bodyguard, Captain J. Antonio Perrotta; the latter was named military attaché in France; the friends were all designated civil attachés.

Trujillo accompanied his son to a United States port but he came back immediately. The situation in the Caribbean area was more tense than ever. The Haitian government had denounced to the Organization of American States the serious machinations of Trujillo; simultaneously the Dominican government denounced the machinations of the governments of Cuba, Guatemala, and Costa Rica against Trujillo's regime. And, in order to dramatize the situation, President Trujillo asked from his congress full powers to declare war without mentioning any enemy country in particular. The Congress granted him those powers with an enthusiasm which contrasted notably with its silence in 1941 when the Dominican Republic entered into war against Japan, Germany, and Italy.

The Organization of American States resolved to send a commission to investigate the situation in the Caribbean. Its effects in the Dominican Republic were reflected in a message from Trujillo to Congress on February 21, requesting the abrogation of the full powers granted to him to declare war, an amnesty law, and a further law limiting the activities of political refugees. The three laws were approved at once.

The budget approved for 1950 was $72,668,840; the Dominican Republic now had an air force and a "war navy" [marina de guerra]. The message of Trujillo to Congress in February, 1950, announced that $62,218,383 had been collected (more or less the same as in the preceding year) and that the total income for the government was $81,795,943 ($11,000,000 less than in 1949); the fiscal year was closed with a surplus of $1,017,865. . . .

In June, 1950, the usual campaign for reelection began — two years before the elections. La Nación of June 23 said that the secretary of interior had addressed himself to the presidents of the Dominican, National, and Labor parties, advising them to start the campaign. The two parties supposedly in opposition did not seem to be impressed. The Dominican party started its propaganda in July, and on August 27 a great reelection meeting took place in the capital city with an attendance, according

---

[112] The footnote, appearing together with the picture of "Ramfis," in La Nación of July 15, 1949, deserves to be included in any anthology of the regime. It summarized the biography of the boy. [Fn. 69, Chap. I, Sec. 9.]

to *La Nación,* of more than 80,000 people. The campaign thereafter diminished.

On July 1 *La Nación* printed a message from Trujillo addressed to President Truman, on the occasion of the start of the war in Korea: "My Government is absolutely identified with the resolute attitude adopted by the Government of the United States." However, the Dominican Republic never sent troops to Korea. .. .[113]

The budget approved in December for 1951 was $74,606,200, which meant only a small increase of two million, the first such slowdown in six years. The message of Trujillo to Congress in February, 1951,[114] announced $73,566,403 collected (which meant $11,000,000 more than in 1949) and a total income of $98,986,160 ($17,000,000 more than in 1949 and $6,000,000 more than in 1948); the fiscal year was closed with a surplus of $2,715,872. The surprising statement was Trujillo's announcement of having fully paid the external debt of the Republic, despite the previous statement of such full payment in 1947; $354,112 was still due on January 1, 1950. . . .

In February, 1951, the reelection campaign was suddenly renewed. The Chamber declared the nomination of the Generalissimo for the term 1952–57 to be "of the highest national desirability";[115] the Senate did the same in another resolution; and on the seventeenth, the justices of the Supreme Court and all officers òf the Ciudad Trujillo courts made the same decision. The usual adherences poured in at once.

On February 19 Trujillo met with the new Haitian president, Colonel Paul Magloire. And on the twenty-eighth, he took a leave of absence as president, entrusting the executive power to the secretary of war, his brother Héctor. At the end of March, Trujillo congratulated Argentine President Juan D. Perón for his atomic "successes," and Perón answered, putting them at the service of his "noble friend."

La Nación on May 28 revealed another of the surprises concerning Trujillo's family. They were four pictures of the baptism held the day before of two grandchildren of the president, the children of "Captain Rafael Leonidas Trujillo Martínez and his honorable wife, Sra. Octavia

---

[113] Nevertheless, in one statement made to the press during his trip to the United States in December, 1952, Trujillo gave assurances that the Dominican Republic was ready to send troops to Korea if needed; he made his statement at the time of the final discussions for the truce. *Hispanic American Report,* Dec., 1952. [Fn. 102, Chap. I, Sec. 9.]

[114] Rafael L. Trujillo, *Pensamiento,* 10: 77–192. [Fn. 113, Chap. I, Sec. 9.]

[115] *G.O.* 7247; *Bol. Cam.,* Feb. 1951; and *La Nación,* Feb. 9, 1951. Francisco Prats Ramírez, opposition candidate in 1947, was a member of the special committee that drafted and proposed this motion. *La Nación, op. cit.* [Fn. 120, Chap. I, Sec. 9.]

de Trujillo"; the age of the children was not mentioned, but judging by the pictures, Ramfis Rafael must be less than one year old and María Altagracia must be about two years old. Trujillo, Sr., his brother Héctor, his wife *doña* María, and his mother *doña* Julia attended the ceremony. There is no mention in any previous official or social report of a wedding of "Ramfis"; only of his trip as inspector of embassies in December, 1949, a year and a half before the double baptism.

In the middle of July, 1951, another theatrical coup took place, this time of a political nature and very important. The secretary of interior presaged it in a release published on July 7 in *La Nación,* inviting all political parties for the second time to participate in the elections of 1952. Ten days later Trujillo addressed a message to the convention of the Dominican party declining his nomination as a presidential candidate, "despite the popular demand," and suggesting the name of his brother Héctor B. Trujillo; of course, this suggestion was accepted and confirmed by the convention. Rafael A. Espaillat wrote to the secretary of the interior stating that he could not lead the National Democratic party in the coming elections because he was sick; Espaillat was elected a deputy on August 14. Francisco Prats Ramírez, who had been a deputy since 1947, did not even answer on behalf of the Labor party. . . .

On November 11 Trujillo promoted "Ramfis" to the rank of lieutenant colonel *ad honorem,* without previous mention of his promotion to the rank of major.[116] At the same time, Trujillo's brother, José Arismendi ("Petán"), was promoted to the rank of brigadier general *ad honorem.* . . .

The budget approved in December for 1952 rose to $82,796,500, again with the considerable increase of six million. The message of Trujillo to Congress in February, 1952, announced $89,104,467 collected, a total income of $116,840,056, which meant extraordinary increases, and a surplus of $4,058,012. This report detailed at length the accomplishments of the whole Era of Trujillo until that date.

A decree on February 6 appointed Felix W. Bernardino as alternate delegate to the United Nations, a position which his sister Minerva already enjoyed; he retained simultaneously his position as consul general in New York, a more effective post than the other.[117] On the sixth, also, the Chamber approved at first reading a law "which points out the general utility of drafting and publishing a work which shall record, summarize,

---

[116] At least, in the pictures printed on July 18, reporting the act in which his father refused the presidential candidacy, "Ramfis" was still mentioned as "Captain Ambassador." *El Caribe,* July 18, 1951. [Fn. 152, Chap. I, Sec. 9.]

[117] Bernardino became very active following his arrival in New York. His main success was in turning several exiles over to Trujillo. . . . [Fn. 168, Chap. I, Sec. 9.]

interpret and affix in worthy form the prodigious governmental work" of Trujillo. . . .

The elections of May 16 could not have been more colorless; there was not even a pretense of a preceding electoral campaign. The only curiosity was the presence of fourteen members of the Cayo Confites invasion, lured there by Consul General Bernardino through his New York consulate; a decree of May 12 pardoned fourteen *confiteros;* [118] *La Nación* on the fifteenth published their picture together with Bernardino and their statements expressing admiration for Trujillo.

The electoral results were not surprising: 1,038,816 votes in favor of Héctor B. Trujillo; once again the votes were 100 percent in favor of all candidates of the Dominican party (including Francisco Prats Ramírez and Rafael A. Espaillat, elected deputies).

The last important decision by Trujillo before ending his fourth presidential term was to promote his son "Ramfis" to the rank of brigadier general on his twenty-third birthday, June 5; at the same time, he appointed him chief of staff of the air force. The same day Trujillo "promoted" his other son Radhamés to the rank of honorary major (he was ten years old).

Preparations for the new term were completed by the passage by Congress of a law, at the end of June, creating from the coming August 17 the new position of "Commander-in-Chief of the Armed Forces of the Republic." Trujillo himself had proposed this law in a message that argued as follows: "The creation of this position responds to the fact that, in practice, the need has been shown for a superior Command, to head the three great branches." The appointment to this position of Trujillo himself some days later illuminated the real reason for its creation.

In this way ended the fourth, and, for the time being, the last administration of Rafael L. Trujillo Molina. During this term the rush of resignations in Congress continued. But as a whole, the average of stability among legislators and justices elected for this term was slightly superior to that reached in the period 1942–47, which holds the "turnover" record to date.

The Administration of Héctor B. Trujillo Since 1952

On August 16, 1952, the new president of the Dominican Republic, Héctor B. Trujillo, took the oath of office. The picture, reprinted in all the official organs of publicity, was at best symbolic; the nominal president of the Republic appeared taking his oath from a nominal president of the

---

[118] *Confiteros* is the popular name used to refer to those who took part in the unsuccessful invasion of Cayo Confites. Among this group converted to Trujillo's regime, most of them returned to New York where they have since acted publicly close to Bernardino. . . . [Fn. 180, Chap. I, Sec. 9.]

Senate, but two other characters in the photograph dominated the scene, Rafael L. Trujillo, dictator of the Dominican Republic, and Anastasio Somoza, dictator of Nicaragua. Somoza had arrived in Ciudad Trujillo five days before to attend the ceremonies.

The new president confirmed all the present public employees in their positions. But he made a new appointment as expected; Rafael L. Trujillo was to be the commander-in-chief of the armed forces of the Republic. He named his nephew, Lieutenant Colonel Virgilio García Trujillo, the "Personal Assistant to the Commander-in-Chief." In Congress, the same faces mostly remained. At the inaugural ceremony, the address of the new president contained little of interest. What was quite curious was the address by the outgoing president, who took the occasion to attack the Colombian historian, Germán Arciniegas,[119] accusing him of "serving his masters in Moscow."

That no one might doubt the peculiar hierarchies in the Dominican Republic, a decree on August 26 declared that "the provisions in force concerning protocol do not affect the Benefactor of the Country and Commander-in-Chief of the Army"; everything related to his attendance at public ceremonies shall be governed by the official provisions which the director of protocol specifies in each case. The newspapers subsequently offered documentary evidence of this peculiar protocol; on many occasions they printed pictures of both Trujillo brothers at public ceremonies, and the footnotes usually mentioned them in the following order: Generalissimo Rafael L. Trujillo and President of the Republic, Héctor B. Trujillo.

After the inauguration, Trujillo did not remain for long in the Dominican Republic. At the end of 1952, he traveled to the United States as special ambassador at large and delegate of the Dominican Republic to the United Nations.[120] From this moment on, the Dominican newspapers

---

[119] Trujillo referred to the recent book *The State of Latin America* (New York, 1952), by Germán Arciniegas, the widely known Colombian writer and professor at Columbia University, a liberal and anti-Communist, accusing him of being dedicated "to the infamous task of discrediting his own country and brother countries, in books translated by others which he does not dare to publish in Spanish. Desiring to serve his masters in Moscow, he throws mud without any consideration." *La Nación,* August 17, 1952; and Trujillo, *Pensamiento* 11: 198–215. A short time later, Arciniegas' book appeared in Spanish under the title *Entre la Libertad y el Miedo;* three subsequent editions have already been printed, two in Mexico and one in Chile. [Fn. 9, Chap. I, Sec. 10.]

[120] *G.O.* 7502. At the time the Senate ratified this appointment, all senators requested the floor to support it. *Bol. Sen.,* Dec. 1952. The American writer, Cholly Knickerbocker, stated two months later in his syndicated column that Trujillo had intended to be appointed Dominican ambassador in Washington, but that at the last hour the invitations, already distributed for a party to introduce him as such in the embassy, were cancelled without explanation. *New York Journal and American,* Feb. 10, 1953, column "Smart Set." To the best of our knowledge, nobody denied this statement. [Fn. 12, Chap. I, Sec. 10.]

dedicated greater space to reports of the activities and social functions of Trujillo the Benefactor in the United States than to report the activities of Trujillo the president in the Dominican Republic. One of these reports concerned his purchase of a "flying yacht," meaning a private plane provided with bath and other comforts.[121]

However, the Dominican newspapers failed to report several other items, not so agreeable, which happened in the United States before and during Trujillo's stay there. Of course, they did not report in any detail the murder in New York of the exiled writer, Andrés Requena, on the night of October 2. Neither did they report picketing, organized by New York exiles in Washington and New York to protest against Trujillo's regime, in which participants carried a symbolic coffin.[122] They did not report that Trujillo was not received with any special honors in the Organization of American States, the United Nations, or by the United States government. Trujillo was officially considered only another delegate to the United Nations.

But there is some official Dominican evidence of the repercussions that these events produced. A decree in December appointed Adolfo ("Pito") Camarena as Dominican consul in Los Angeles, although Camarena remained for several weeks accompanying Trujillo and Bernardino in New York and Washington.[123] La Nación printed a cable addressed by President Trujillo to Benefactor Trujillo begging him to return to the Dominican Republic before departing for Europe, "in order to discuss matters that require your personal opinion and experience." A decree on February 28 appointed the Benefactor as secretary of foreign relations and worship, and secretary of public welfare.

The Dominican press purposely magnified the other activities of Trujillo in the United States. On his one visit to the General Assembly of the United Nations on February 24, 1953, Trujillo arrived protected by

---

[121] El Caribe, Dec. 30, 1952. After mentioning all the comforts of this flying yacht, the newspaper added that Trujillo was ready to go to New York, where "he will continue his fight against Communist infiltration in the Caribbean. . . ." [Fn. 13, Chap. I, Sec. 10.]

[122] Cf. for instance, Time, Feb. 16, 1952. One repercussion of these pickets, in reprisal, was a decree on Feb. 14, cancelling the appointment of Dr. Alina Romero de Florén as professor of the university (G.O. 7533). She is the sister of Dr. César Romero, an exile in whose home in Washington the pickets of the capital city were organized. A short time afterward, the Florén family had to leave for Colombia. Lic. Luis Florén, the husband, a Spanish refugee, had been the librarian of the university since 1940. [Fn. 15, Chap. I, Sec. 10.]

[123] The author keeps in his files some unpublished pictures proving this fact. [Fn. 18, Chap. I, Sec. 10.]

about twenty bodyguards, among them Lieutenant Colonel César A. Oliva ("Olivita"), future chief of the Dominican police, who was dressed as a civilian.[124] The press gave broad coverage to this and to his brief meeting with newly-inaugurated President Eisenhower. On February 22, 1953, the Dominican consulate general in New York arranged a demonstration in honor of Trujillo, for which the Dominican press reported 6,500 Dominicans turned out. However, the press remained silent as to what actually occurred during the demonstration.

In the meantime, everything was quiet in the Dominican Republic. The budget, approved in December for 1953, was $89,086,570, another increase of six and a half million. Trujillo returned to the the Dominican Republic on March 15. His arrival was a veritable apotheosis.

On May 8 Manuel de Moya was appointed secretary without portfolio. Three days later, he was appointed ambassador extraordinary on a special mission to attend the coronation of Queen Elizabeth of England; but he was not the only ambassador; the younger daughter of Trujillo (María de los Angeles del Corazón de Jesús) and her cousin were also appointed as ambassadresses extraordinary on the same special mission, although the girls were not yet fourteen years old.* Tulio Franco y Franco became permanent delegate to the United Nations. Trujillo returned to his role as Benefactor and commander-in-chief, plus his new sugar business. . . .[125]

A decree on September 28, 1953, promoted "Ramfis" to the rank of major general (he was twenty-four years old); he continued to be chief of staff of the air force, although he spent a great part of his time in the United States playing polo.[126] A decree on September 14 promoted Pedro

---

[124] New York Times, Feb. 25, 1953; Time, March 9, 1953. Although the name of Lieutenant Colonel Oliva was not mentioned, it is easy to identify him in several pictures next to Trujillo, especially in moments of possible danger. In the picture taken on Feb. 22, he appeared in the first row, holding his right hand in his coat pocket as though ready to fire. El Diario de Nueva York, Feb. 24, 1953. [Fn. 24, Chap. I, Sec. 10.]

* Cf. Crassweller, Trujillo, p. 362.

[125] A U.P. cable, August 18, announced that Trujillo would relinquish his duties as commander-in-chief of the armed forces of the Republic, in order to devote his activities to the management of the Río Haina Sugar Central, "which is the most important enterprise of the whole world in this field." La Prensa, August 19, 1953. [Fn. 41, Chap. I, Sec. 10.]

[126] For instance, La Nación, August 30, 1953, announced that "Ramfis" had returned "after a period of studies in the south of the United States." There are pictures of him playing polo on the Gulfstream Polo Fields of Delray Beach, Florida. [Fn. 57, Chap. I, Sec. 10.]

V. Trujillo (brother of the Benefactor) to the rank of brigadier general.
Another decree, on the twenty-sixth, combined into one single undersecretaryship those formerly of war, navy, and aviation, and appointed to
that position General José García Trujillo (nephew of the Benefactor). . . .

La Nación on November 10 announced that "Trujillo distributes
among the *colonos* (peasants) of five Dominican sugar centrals more than
one million *tareas* of land" [one tarea = .155 acre]. At the beginning of
1954, a strenuous campaign was launched against the American sugar
centrales (mills) of La Romana, which had repercussions in the United
States press.

The budget approved in December for 1954 amounted to $96,822,-
330. The year 1954 was to be a quiet one in the Dominican Republic;
Trujillo would travel through Europe. The previous year had ended with
the publicized wedding of Porfirio Rubirosa and Barbara Hutton, who
became a Dominican citizen by privileged naturalization. Major General
"Ramfis" was the best man. Porfirio was again renamed minister counselor
in Paris despite the fact of having been dismissed some days previously.

On May 14 a law was passed ordering that the year 1955 be officially
called the "Year of the Benefactor" and that the twenty-fifth anniversary
of his regime be celebrated with due magnificence.[127]

Trujillo departed in June for Europe. The two highpoints of his trip
were Spain and the Vatican. In Madrid he was officially received by
Franco; the Generalissimos embraced and bestowed decorations upon
each other.[128] Less noisy but more efficacious was his visit to the Pope;
Trujillo signed a concordat with the Holy See,[129] according to which
divorce was to be abolished some weeks later in the Dominican Republic
for those marrying under church laws. In the other countries through
which Trujillo passed, he became again only a tourist, although in the

---

[127] Law No. 3838, May 14, 1954. *El Caribe*, May 16, 1954. Virgilio Alvarez
Pina was appointed chairman of the organizing committee for the festivals to be
held during the Year of the Benefactor. He was back in the first row after a long
ostracism. [Fn. 78, Chap. I, Sec. 10.]

[128] Many issues of Dominican newspapers referred to the official stay of Trujillo
in Spain. As a sample, see *El Caribe*, June 6, 12, and 13, July 5, 21, and 22, 1954.
Trujillo vested upon Franco the Gold Grand Cross of the Order of Trujillo, and
Franco bestowed upon Trujillo the Collar of the Order of Elizabeth the Catholic.
[Fn. 79, Chap. I, Sec. 10.]

[129] *El Caribe*, June 17, 1954. . . . The Pope granted Trujillo the Grand Cross of
the Pian Order and his personal benediction in a private interview. The concordat
was submitted to the Senate for ratification on July 6; the ratification was granted
the next day unanimously. [Fn. 80, Chap. I, Sec. 10.]

United States he expounded his own "anti-Communist" experience to the press.[130]

On August 14 Trujillo returned to the Dominican Republic; the result was a new glorification. A consequence of his return was the new law on religious marriage, enacted on September 20, and the simultaneous abolition of divorce for such marriages. (Trujillo had been twice divorced; his daughter, Flor de Oro, five times).

At the end of September, Trujillo again went to the United States; on this occasion he offered his "anti-Communist" experience to a congressional committee and proposed the organization of another "United Nations for Peace" without Communists. Again, hero worship on his return.

As 1954 drew to a close, a press campaign in favor of constitutional reform was going on actively; the aim was to restore the vice-presidency and to reduce the age requirement for the president and high officers of the nation. "Ramfis" seemed to be the obvious candidate; and those who in 1941 had expressed themselves against the vice-presidency now stated they were in favor of it. *El Caribe* printed almost daily the list of visits received by Generalissimo Trujillo; the visits received by President Trujillo were not even mentioned, except in the case of some foreign diplomat forced to present his credentials to the nominal head of the state.

At the beginning of November, an unbelievable incident occurred in the Dominican Republic. A gang of robbers held up the branch of the Royal Bank of Canada in Santiago, killing two employees and wounding the assistant manager; they escaped with almost $150,000. The next day they were arrested by the military, and it was discovered that they had previously murdered two policemen to get their guns. Lacking a death penalty, the leader and six of the gangsters were sentenced to thirty years of hard labor and five other gangsters to twenty years. But on the next day, ten of them "attempted to escape" and were killed by the guards. The dismissal of the chief of staff of the army, Major General Virgilio García

---

[130] Before Trujillo returned to the Dominican Republic from this trip, the center of information of the Dominican Republic in New York distributed a statement by Trujillo from Miami attacking the United Nations because the USSR is a member: "I withdraw from the United Nations after attending its sessions in the winter of 1952–53, because it is a center where, in all or in the majority of its offices, Communist ideology prevails." (He attended only one afternoon and did not enter even one meeting room.) He also attacked in the same statement "some centers of education in the United States which should be investigated because there are many hidden Communists who are or were Spaniards, or from other countries, displaying activities in favor of the Soviet" (the distributed text was very careful not to mention any names). These statements appeared in, among other newspapers, *El Caribe*, August 12, 1954, and *El Diario de Nueva York*, August 13, 1954. [The Spanish-language editions of *La Era de Trujillo* state at this point that "allusion to Columbia University is evident."] [Fn. 81, Chap. I, Sec. 10.]

Trujillo, and his demotion to brigadier general were announced, because
he had not taken "the required preventive measures to avoid the killing
of the ten gangsters in Santiago. . . ."[131]

The budget approved in December for 1955 was $105,510,935.[132]
On December 26 Generalissimo Trujillo (not Trujillo the president)
announced that the Dominican government would buy the public utility
enterprises of Electric Power and Telephone; it was approved at once
by Congress. And on January 2, 1955, it was officially announced that the
fiscal income in 1954 had reached $110,418,837.

The Dominican Republic was ready to celebrate 1955 as the "Year
of the Benefactor" — the twenty-fifth anniversary of his Era. The year
began with the purchase of the Electric Company of Santo Domingo,
bought by the government for $13,200,000. . . . About the same time, the
Dominican press attacked the Costa Rican president, José Figueres, on
the occasion of the invasion of his country by rebels approaching from
Nicaragua.[133]

On February 11 a law granting Trujillo the "Collar of the Fatherland" was approved; twenty-five jeweled links were to form this collar,
one for each year of his Era. A few days earlier, *El Caribe* published an
article stating that foreign reviewers had declared the book *Meditaciones
Morales* by Sra. María de Trujillo "one of the three books of highest moral
value published in recent times" and comparable to the book *Life is Worth
Living* by Monsignor Fulton J. Sheen.

A workers' congress was called for May as one of the events of the
program of the Year of the Benefactor; it was mentioned as the fourth
congress, thus repeating the deliberate omission of those held before the
Era. The announced agenda had no items concerning the problems of
workers but only tributes to the deeds of Trujillo on behalf of the
workers.

---

[131] *G.O.* 7788; and *El Caribe*, Dec. 26, 1954. This demotion continued in force
at the time this study was completed in the middle of 1955. [Fn. 103, Chap. I,
Sec. 10.]

[132] *G.O.* 7787. There is a difference of about three million between the figure
published in the *Official Gazette* and that mentioned in *El Caribe*, Dec. 22, 1954, as
approved by Congress ($108,124,235). No explanation was given for this difference,
but it does not seem to be important. [Fn. 115, Chap. I, Sec. 10.]

[133] See, for instance, *El Caribe*, Jan. 27, 1955, in which appears an editorial
signed by its editor, Germán Ornes, and the reproduction of an alleged letter written
by Figueres to a Nicaraguan in 1950 explaining his plans of action. [Fn. 127, Chap. I,
Sec. 10.]

On March 2 Vice-President Nixon of the United States arrived in Ciudad Trujillo, one of the stops in his Caribbean tour. One of his official visits was to Generalissimo Trujillo. . . .[134]

In early May Congress approved another honor and title for Trujillo, that of "Father of the new Fatherland." The official ceremony to bestow the title upon him took place on May 14, during the first week of the year-long festivities to celebrate the twenty-fifth anniversary of his first election as president on May 16, 1930. Another of the events during this week was a magnificent parade with participation by land, air, and sea forces.

The reelection campaign for 1957 was not opened until May 22, when a congress of journalists requested the reelection in a document addressed to the Dominican party.[135] The party accepted the idea at once.

Sra. Trujillo also had received special honors one month earlier. The directive council of a so-called Pan American Round Table, made up of Dominican women, on April 28 proclaimed her as the "First Woman of the Americas in the Dominican Republic." The Virgin of Altagracia, patroness of the Republic, also received official honors: two decrees of May 6 accorded to this image the Gold Grand Cross of the Order of Trujillo and of Duarte-Sánchez-Mella.

On May 12 a law of political amnesty was enacted, to remain in force during the Year of the Benefactor for those enemies of the regime who returned to the country and promised not to relapse.

The Dominican Academy of Language announced on June 18 that it had named Trujillo as an active member (with the accompanying honor of being correspondent member of the Spanish Royal Academy). Two weeks before, the second expedition of Spanish immigrants, numbering 764 and coming directly from Spain, had arrived in Ciudad Trujillo; on the deck of their ship, they carried large banners greeting "the Chief." . . .

The nomination which received the widest publicity was that accorded Trujillo's daughter, Angelita, as Queen of the Fair of Peace and Confraternity of the Free World on June 24. The official proclamation was made by Virgilio Alvarez Pina as chairman of the organizing committee of the fair and was personally announced to the honored girl in the presence of

---

[134] *El Caribe,* March 2, 1955. Some United States newspapers printed photographs in which Nixon is embracing Benefactor Trujillo, but the captions made the mistake of calling him the president of the Dominican Republic. [Fn. 132, Chap. I, Sec. 10.]

[135] *El Caribe,* May 23, 1955. The document ended as follows: "Trujillo is our happiness. Let us embrace him with warm civic love and strong loyalty." [Fn. 141, Chap. I, Sec. 10.]

her father by a committee composed of the secretaries of foreign relations and education, the president of the Dominican party, and other high personalities. *El Caribe* reported this news with a full page banner headline in color. The Senate and the Chamber officially congratulated Angelita in two documents signed by all congressmen; the officials of other departments of the administration did the same.

El Caribe continued to report almost daily the list of interviews granted by Generalissimo Trujillo "in the National Palace." On August 2, the same newspaper began a curious public poll: Could Congress, by law, create the position of vice-president of the Republic? Three days later, Benefactor Trujillo himself answered the query, expounding the theory that, in view of the silence of the Constitution in regard to this question, Congress could create the position; the only constitutional obstacle lay in the matter of presidential succession, since the fundamental charter of the nation cites several successive secretaries in turn; this, however, could be obviated if the president would also appoint the vice-president as secretary of war, navy, and aviation. This maneuver purposely overlooked the fact that the constitutional reform of 1942 had eliminated the position of vice-president after a wide preparatory campaign.

The most peculiar answer was that of Lic. Jesús María Troncoso, secretary without portfolio, who began by stating that he had already finished a letter opposing the proposal made by *El Caribe* as being against the Constitution, when he read the letter from Trujillo and had changed his mind, convinced by the "ingenious formula" presented.

Another tribute took place in the city of Santiago, this time not in honor of Trujillo, but Lic. Federico C. Alvarez, one of the best lawyers of the Republic, on the occasion of his fortieth anniversary in the profession. Many lawyers and some legislators attended the dinner, which appeared to have no political character whatever. Lic. Sánchez Cabral offered a tribute in the main address, answered by the guest of honor.

The next day, August 10, *El Caribe* published a letter insulting Lic. Sánchez Cabral and calling attention to the dinner and the addresses. . . . [*Other critical letters and editorials were published.*] The Dominican party ordered a "court of honor" to pass judgment upon the participants at the dinner. If one carefully reads all these letters and the printed comments, the reason for this scandal becomes readily apparent; Lic. Sánchez Cabral and Lic. Alvarez had not mentioned Trujillo's name in their speeches. Another editorial in *El Caribe* on the eighteenth explicitly referred, as its single point of attack, to their "most reprehensible omission."

During the days following, the newspapers were full of items revealing the unexpected consequences of this omission. The two chambers of Congress officially condemned, on August 17, what had happened at the dinner; a decree on the fourteenth cancelled the appointments of Alvarez and Sánchez Cabral as professors of the university. Protests came from everywhere; some other participants in the dinner lost their positions; the persons involved attempted to excuse themselves and again were insulted in *El Caribe*.[136]*

On August 16, 1955, Trujillo, in a very solemn ceremony, received the Grand Collar of the Fatherland from the president of the Senate. On the same day, Angelita Trujillo received the keys of the capital in a magnificent parade. And in New York, a group of Dominican exiles again picketed in a symbolic gesture. Thus elapsed twenty-five years since Trujillo took his first oath as president on August 16, 1930. Thus passed a quarter of a century.

Historical Summary of the Era of Trujillo

Up to this point, a series of events, more or less significant, that mark the twenty-five years of the Era of Trujillo, has been set forth. The scholar could find himself lost in the multiplicity of these events, without reaching any general conclusions. Is it possible to summarize this material in an intelligible line of evolution?

In the author's judgment, it is possible to point out eight successive periods in the Era of Trujillo, each one showing slightly different trends; occasionally reflecting the impact of world events.

The first period was very brief: it extended from the coup of February, 1930, to the elections of May, perhaps to the first inauguration of Trujillo as president in August. During this period, the parties victorious in the elections of 1924, the National party (horacistas) and the Progressive party (velasquistas) were swept out. The new Confederation of Parties which apparently came to power with Trujillo was formed of two types of men and forces; on the one hand, there were small groups such as the Liberal party of Desiderio Arias and the Republican party of Rafael Estrella Ureña; on the other, there were some individual personalities who, in search of new ways, looked to a breaking of the old systems and politicians. The world-wide economic crisis, which severely affected the Dominican Republic, contributed to this renovation.

---

[136] . . . Among the attacks, some . . . are notable for their offensive wording: on the tenth, eleventh, thirteenth and eighteenth, Sánchez Cabral was called *"borracho"* (drunkard); on the thirteenth, Alvarez was referred to as *"demente"* (insane); on the fourteenth Senate Vice-President Rafael Vidal was treated as *"un negro"* (a Negro); and on the twenty-sixth, Lic. Federico Nina, secretary of the Chamber of Deputies, was called *"setemesino"* (prematurely born). [Fn. 173, Chap. I, Sec. 10.]

* Cf. also Crassweller, *Trujillo*, p. 285.

The second period was also brief, although less so. Its climax took place in 1931, but its trend was obvious almost from the time Trujillo became president. His intention was to impose his personal will, eliminating the parties and leaders who backed him in 1930. In some cases, their elimination was violent, as happened with Desiderio Arias; in other cases, it was bloodless but scandalous, as with Estrella Ureña; in still others, it was silent and almost unnoticed, as happened with Rafael Vidal. Trujillo was able at the same time to attract a group of submissive men who organized the new personalist party of General Trujillo, later called the Dominican party, and adapted themselves to the new political fashion in which Congress was only an automatic machine to approve the projects prepared by the executive. By the beginning of 1932, the parties of the Confederation had disappeared, and there was only the new Trujillo party. During all this period, economic difficulties continued to increase.

The third period lasted until the end of 1937 and reached its climax about 1934–35. On the one hand, many elements from the Horacist regime ousted in 1930 were converted to the Trujillist line and replaced in many positions the new men of good faith (the case of Dr. José E. Aybar is typical). On the other hand, the impossibility of maintaining any democratic opposition provoked a series of internal plots to oust Trujillo through violence. In this process, Trujillo strengthened his personal power; the elections of 1934 were typical, as was the reelection campaign of 1937. Economic difficulties continued, but Trujillo was master.

The fourth period, very brief, took place unexpectedly. It was caused by the massacre of Haitians at the end of 1937 and the international repercussions that this act provoked. Trujillo was forced to renounce his reelection in 1938, and the first opportunity of a possible evolution appeared. However, President Peynado did not repudiate the trust placed in him, and Trujillo overcame the crisis (or rather he lost the opportunity to permit the regime to evolve towards a more democratic form, although he could have remained as a fatherly adviser).

The fifth period was coincident with, and profited from, the outbreak of World War II. The moment was not propitious for the United States Department of State to show displeasure towards friendly (although dictatorial) governments, and Trujillo knew how to follow the new currents. From the return of Trujillo to the country at the end of 1939 until the World War was well advanced, his regime gained strength and his personal power was more obvious than ever before. Typical episodes of his political strength were the punishment of General Estrella and the elections of 1942 with their "constitutional" compromises, in order that Trujillo might assume the presidency immediately in May. At the same time, Trujillo benefited from the new United States policy of the Good Neighbor.

From 1939 to 1944, Trujillo was never in danger, and his political style developed with its typical enforced resignations of congressmen and justices.

The sixth period was one of serious danger for the Trujillist regime, as a consequence of the victory of the United Nations in World War II. New trends shook Latin America, and the Dominican Republic could not remain untouched. The first symptoms of agitation appeared in 1945, with symbolic activity by university students; though this did not mean a real danger, it showed evidence of spirit. Trujillo was forced simultaneously to adopt some appearances of democratic advances, such as the workers' movement which was allowed and encouraged, the more or less insincere play of calling back old political parties, and the brief limited opposition requested from La Opinión. The game became dangerous, and both the sugar strike of January, 1946, and the political outbursts in the pages of La Opinión suggested new methods to Trujillo. Nevertheless, the pretense continued in 1946 with the double game of the Communists and the use of the National and Labor parties in the elections of 1947. At the same time, the exiles prepared the unfortunate invasion of Cayo Confites. However, Trujillo outlived this period in which he was close to being destroyed. The new international situation and the anti-Communist reaction, which started about 1946 in consequence of Soviet aggressiveness, helped him while the increase of foreign trade after the end of the war also eased the Dominican economy and permitted Trujillo to reinforce the army.

The seventh period lasted from 1947 until 1952 and perhaps beyond. Trujillo was again master of the Dominican Republic; "anti-Communism" offered him an easy cover to destroy all opposition; he did not need even to simulate appearances of freedom; the very invasion of Luperón in 1949 helped him. And the economic prosperity of those years tied powerful groups to the regime.

An eighth period seems to be indicated since 1952 and has become obvious in the most recent months. Trujillo seems to be thinking seriously of his succession. There is no doubt that Héctor B. Trujillo is only a transitory figure without any strength of his own and that the obvious candidate for the future is "Ramfis."

The tones have varied slightly according to each period. Nevertheless, some general characteristics which define the regime persist. Its chronological evolution has been summarized in this First Part. Its systematic analysis will be the subject of the Second Part of this study.

Chapter 2: Value of the Constitution

[Here, in their 1955 setting, are the observations of Galíndez on the Dominican constitution.]

In Latin America, a constitution seems to be a symbol which all venerate but which very few follow. It is almost never a basic document of government in the sense that citizens generally agree upon it; it is a partisan apparatus — a program of political action imposed by the predominant group. For this reason it changes as political fortunes change, with every new regime hastening to make amendments appropriate for its purposes and its methods.

New constitutions are very frequent in most Latin American countries, even where they may require the approval of a dictator. Occasionally two different texts may be approved in two succeeding years. Some constitutions never enter into force; some are revived after abrogation; very often, what is referred to as a new constitution is in fact an old one, duly amended. As a consequence of such instability, a constitution loses its meaning and strength.[1]

The Dominican Republic holds, up to now, the record for the number of new constitutions as well as for various other manifestations of constitutional instability. Trujillo's regime has maintained a tradition of awesome respect for constitutional procedures. It has also maintained a tradition of

---

[1] See author's article, "La Inestabilidad Constitucional en el Derecho Comparado de Latinoamérica," *Boletín del Instituto de Derecho Comparado,* México, May–August, 1952, pp. 45–65. There is a reprint and a French translation in *Cahiers de Legislation et Bibliographie Juridique de l'Amérique Latine,* Paris, April–June, 1952, pp. 9–28. [Fn. 1, Chap. II.]

numerous constitutional changes. The Constitution has already been changed three times during his Era — 1934, 1942, and 1947 — and a forthcoming change now seems apparent. New needs require new organic provisions. More obvious than this, however, has been the idolatry toward constitutional appearances, even though their purpose has sometimes been to disguise childlike caprices.

Perhaps it would be sufficient to recall Trujillo's play with the presidential veto defeated by Congress in 1932 before giving his name to the new province, Trujillo, with mention of the pertinent Article 37 of the Constitution in the *Official Gazette.* Or to recall his opportune leave of absence in 1935 in order that Vice-President Peynado would exercise the executive power — using Article 52 of the Constitution, printed in the *Official Gazette* — before changing the name of the capital to Ciudad Trujillo.* And the complicated game of resignations in May, 1942, in order that Trujillo as secretary of war and navy for one day could become president, using Article 51 of the Constitution, three months before the date of his official inauguration. More seriously it should be recalled how, in the settlement of the coup of 1930, the façade of constitutionality was meticulously maintained (Article 53 of the 1929 constitution was the respected provision) and Estrella Ureña was appointed secretary of interior before the resignation of President Vásquez, although the latter had been ousted by an act of military violence.

It is obvious, then, that Trujillo's regime, as is generally true of all Latin American dictatorships during the twentieth century, attempts to disguise a man's all-powerful will under the constitutional appearances of elections, congress, laws, courts, and civil and social rights. Political life in the Dominican Republic, the same as in other Latin American countries, is such that no one can be fooled by these appearances. But, let us turn our attention more directly to an analysis of the meaning and value of the Constitution itself.

---

*The relevant portions of the constitutions referred to by Galíndez were as follows:

Constitution of June 20, 1932, Article 37: "Every law approved in both Chambers will be sent to the Executive. If the latter does not make objections, he will promulgate it . . . ; if he makes objections he will return it to the Chamber from where it proceeded. . . . The Chamber . . . will discuss the law anew. If, after this discussion, two-thirds of the total. . . approve it again, it will be remitted to the other Chamber, and if this Chamber approves it by an equal majority it will definitively be considered a law."

Constitution of June 9, 1934, Article 52: "In case of the temporary or permanent absence of the President of the Republic he will be supplanted, with full powers, by the Vice-President. If the absence be permanent, the substitution will continue until the end of the presidential term.

"Further, by virtue of a decree by the President of the Republic, the Vice-President will temporarily exercise the presidential power."

Constitutional History of the Dominican Republic[2]

During a century of independent life, the Dominicans have enacted twenty-five constitutions which were different from each other at least in name. In most of the cases they were only amendments of previous constitutions. Several provisional documents, one constitution which did not enter into force, one additional act, plus two Spanish constitutions, two Haitian constitutions, and several United States organic orders which were in force during the respective occupations can be added to the list. . . .

[*The remainder of Section I, pp. 300–306 of the manuscript, summarizes lucidly the constitutional annals of the Dominican development, intertwined with relevant political considerations, from colonial times up to 1930, with almost no attempt at interpretation.*

For the dual reason that it embodies a personal reference and also sheds light on the governmental instability of the Republic at various times, it seems appropriate to reprint Note 5, included in the omitted portion (MS. pp. 302–4) as follows:]

5. During this period [1863–82], two different Governments coexisted at times in the Dominican Republic, and their members changed in a vortex. In 1944, the author prepared for the Secretaryship of Foreign Relations of the Dominican Republic a complete list of all previous Secretaries. The finding of this research in the *Official Gazettes* of the past was that from Sept. 14, 1863, on which date the Provisional Government of Salcedo was organized to fight against the Spaniards, until Sept. 1, 1882, on which the first Government of dictator Ulises Heureaux ("Lilís") was organized, there were fifty changes of Secretaries (in more than one instance there was a triumvirate); that from 1864 to 1868 there were twenty-seven; and that in 1878 there were seven. During this same period, from 1863 to 1882, there were eleven "constitutional Presidents" and fourteen "provisional" Presidents; in 1878 alone there were three "constitutional" and three "provisional" Presidents; and in more than one instance, there were simultaneously at least two Governments, according to the different texts printed in the *Official Gazettes* and the Collection of Laws (See *Memoria de la Secretaría de Relaciones Exteriores para el Año 1944*, (Ciudad

---

[2] The data presented here are an almost literal reproduction of Chapter 7 bis of the author's work, *Elementos de Ciencia Jurídica* (Ciudad Trujillo, 1940–41; plus two appendices in 1945; mimeographed). (Edition of his lectures in the diplomatic school of the Dominican Republic.)
  The text of the first twenty-four constitutions, new or amended, until that of 1942, plus the Additional Act of 1876, the Spanish Constitution of Cádiz (1812), the Constituent Act (of Independence) in 1821, a constitutional project by Juan Pablo Duarte in 1844, and the 1916 constitution (which did not enter into force), have been published in the first two volumes of the *Colección Trujillo*, which appeared in 1944 on the occasion of the centennial of the Republic. They are under the title of *Constitución Política: Reformas Constitucionales, 1844–1942*, two vols. (Santiago, 1944). The constitution of 1947 was printed in the *Official Gazette* (*G.O.* 6569) of Jan. 19, 1947; an English translation was printed by Prof. Russell H. Fitzgibbon, *The Constitutions of the Americas* (Chicago, 1948), pp. 297–320. [Fn. 2, Chap. II.]

Trujillo) pp. 687-700). This instability in the Government explains some changes of constitutions.

The Reform and Constitution of 1934 *

The first proposal for this reform came in a message addressed to the Senate by President Trujillo on March 29, 1934. He recommended the amendment of nine articles and the addition of the transitory provisions. The alleged reason for the reform was the need to correct conflicts between articles, as well as other errors, and generally to provide a text which would more nearly allow the realization of "the purposes which inspire our political and administrative organization."

Once the project was received by the Senate, it was declared to be urgent and it was approved on second reading on April 3. On the same day it gained approval on the second reading by the Chamber. The law was enacted the following day and signed by Trujillo as president and by all members of his cabinet. This law provided for a constituent assembly.

The assembly met in the capital on June 5. Two days later a "General (study) Committee" reported, advising approval of the amending project with very minor alterations. On June 9 the new constitution of the Dominican Republic was proclaimed, the twenty-third since independence.

In appearance, Article 4, dealing with the administrative division of the Republic, was only slightly modified. The purpose was to simplify the constitutional mechanics of the creation of the new Trujillo Province. Later, this provision would also facilitate the rechristening of the capital as Ciudad Trujillo.

Paragraph 2 of Article 6 was also amended. It read originally: "The following are established as inherent to human personality: . . . 2nd. Freedom of labor, prohibiting, consequently, the establishment of monopolies." Now the sentence was completed as follows: ". . . prohibiting, consequently, the establishment of monopolies for the benefit of private persons." The report of the committee was very explicit on this point: "The general interest should, in some cases, require the establishment of monopolies in the hands of the government. . . ."

Several paragraphs of Article 49, which concerns the powers of the president of the Republic, were also amended. A new paragraph, 21, was added, giving the president the power "to approve or not to approve taxes established by municipal councils." A new paragraph, 22, was added to give the president the power to grant pardons or reprieves on February 27, August 16, and December 23, to prisoners sentenced by the courts.

---

* The three published foreign-language editions of *La Era de Trujillo* all omit the sections dealing with the constitutional changes of 1934, 1942, and 1947; they include pp. 306–29 of the manuscript.

The reform of Article 57 was more important than it appeared to be, and it reflected the new manner of Trujillo's regime. The article concerned the judiciary and the establishment of its different organs. The old text said: "The judges of the courts of Justice shall be in office four years, and may be indefinitely reelected." That statement disappeared in the constitution of 1934, which meant that judges could now be removed at will. The committee had advised that this statement be retained, except as it applied to *alcaldes,* the justices of the peace.

The change in Article 89 was also important since it permitted taxes on exports and, thus, the alleviation of the financial deficit. The earlier text prohibited export taxes: "There shall be no tax imposed upon exports; this provision shall not prohibit the imposition of taxes upon the products of the land or industry." The statement which replaced this did not prohibit export taxes.

The provision of the old Article 100, which specified that salaries of judges could not be decreased during the period for which they had been elected, disappeared in its entirety in the 1934 constitution. A new Article 100 appeared, replacing the old one and giving another indication of what was to be expected from Trujillo's rule. The new article provided that the terms of all elected officers, "whatever the date of their election, end uniformly on August 16 of every fourth year . . . and in consequence they need to have been the object of a new election in order to occupy their offices validly." In consequence, in case of any vacancy "because of death, resignation, dismissal, disqualification, or any other cause, the person who substitutes for him will remain in the office until completing the term"; it meant another constitutional guarantee for the increasing pattern of resignations and subsequent elections in Congress, governorships, and courts.

These were the major amendments to the Constitution introduced by the constituent assembly of 1934. As can be seen, there was no new constitution, even though the end product was proclaimed such, but merely amendments to provisions of the old constitution. The most important modifications are those found in Articles 57 and 89, which made judges removable and allowed the use of taxes on exports. The new Article 100 reaffirmed this provision of Article 57 and expanded it to cover other "elected" officers. Most of the remaining amendments slightly increased the powers of the executive. Finally, the amendment of Article 4 was only the constitutionalizing of the methods of the Benefactor used to christen future provinces and towns with his name and those of his relatives. In general, all of this constitutional renovation was but to constitutionalize what was already the distinctive political style of the Era of Trujillo.

One may also emphasize not only the speed with which the Assembly attacked and finished its task but also the fact that even minor deviations recommended by the general committee were rejected in order to follow faithfully the suggestions made by the president. The spirit of this reform would be re-encountered in the changes of 1942 and 1947.

The Reform and Constitution of 1942

Although Dr. Troncoso de la Concha was the president of the Republic in 1941, when this reform began, it was not he but Generalissimo Trujillo who officially initiated it. The initiative came in a message dated October 6, which the Generalissimo read to a group of legislators on October 7. In order legally to begin the procedure, the six senators in that group made the project theirs and introduced it into the Senate on October 8. The approval came readily — on the first Senate reading on the tenth and the second on the fourteenth, and on the first Chamber reading on the fifteenth and the second on the seventeenth. It was published in the *Official Gazette* No. 5656 three days later.

Among the proposed amendments the only one which it was felt required a campaign of preparation was that to eliminate the vice-presidency. In a public poll carried on in the pages of *La Nación,* by official initiative, the proposal received the enthusiastic backing of the persons consulted because it was obvious that such was Trujillo's desire. Without any public poll, the granting of equal political rights to women had support and precedent, since Law No. 390, which granted equal civil rights to women, had been passed on December 14, 1941, and there had been subsequent activities by the feminine branch of the Trujillista party. The remaining proposals came relatively abruptly, although some of them were a consequence of the new times and new needs of the regime.

Elections for members of the Constituent Assembly were held on December 16, 1941. The Assembly met on December 27 and decided at once that it should constitute itself as a general committee. On January 5, 1942, the Assembly met in plenary session to discuss and approve in public the amendments to be effected by this reform. The work was over on the ninth. The new constitution — officially the twenty-fourth in the history of the Republic — was proclaimed and published in the *Official Gazette* No. 5692 (bis)[3] on the tenth.

The law providing for the reform had mentioned specifically thirty-five articles and two chapters to be amended and had asserted that it might

---

[3] Its text is also printed in *Constitución Política* 2: 507–51, together with a brief historical introduction, plus the complete text of the law determining the need for this reform and of the report of the general committee as appendices. [Fn. 29, Chap. II.]

be wise to look over the transitory provisions and other articles which might need revision. Of those provisions specifically mentioned, Article 11 and one paragraph of Article 8 were left untouched. Altogether, about forty articles and thirty-five paragraphs, several chapters, and the transitory provisions were revised. Palpably, this 1942 reform was very wide; in some aspects it was quite deep. Nevertheless, it is not proper to consider the text approved in January, 1942, to be a new constitution in any strict sense, for neither the structure of the government nor its main principles were substantially modified.

First, it is important to point out the elimination of the vice-presidency, not so much for the fact itself as for the importance given to this step by the public poll that indicated its deep political implications. The 1934 constitution had devoted Chapter II of Title VIII to the Vice-Presidency. That chapter was deleted. The matter was then dealt with in Articles 51 to 53 of Chapter I of the same title, which concerned the presidency.

According to Article 51, any vacancy in the presidency, temporary or otherwise, would be filled by the secretary of war and navy;[4] in his absence, by the secretary of interior and police; and in his absence, in turn, by the secretary of the presidency. Article 52 provided that the president might, temporarily and by decree, entrust a secretary of state to exercise the executive power.

The matter of presidential vacancy was further covered by Article 47, which provided that the president of the Supreme Court assume the office of the president of the Republic whenever a president-elect was unable to take over the duties until the president-elect could take office or until a new president was elected.

Another substantial amendment, which had had its beginnings some time before, was the concession of equal political rights to women. The new text of Article 9 read: "All Dominicans of either sex more than eighteen years of age, and those who are or have been married, although they have not reached that age, are citizens." The prior text had referred only to "male Dominicans."

Two amendments of great importance because of their implications for the economic life of the country (Articles 90 and 96) were quietly added. According to the new text of Article 90, "private individuals may acquire, by means of concessions that the law authorizes, or by means of contracts that the national congress approves," the irrevocable right to

---

[4] The idea seemed to be, on the one hand, to avoid the possible risk of a vice-president politician without any active duty, which might always awake ambitions and, on the other hand, especially to have ready Trujillo's brother Héctor available for any temporary absence of the president, as secretary of war and navy. [Fn. 30, Chap. II.]

exemptions from or limitation of taxes in "certain works or enterprises of public utility, to which it is fitting to attract the investment of new capital for the development of the national economy, or for any other object of social interest." This reform was a radical change and was contrary to the amendment made in 1934 to this same article. The new provision was general and could apply to industrial, agricultural, or any other kind of enterprise.

But the new Article 96 showed a special concern for mineral deposits: "Mineral deposits belong to the State, and may be exploited by private individuals only by virtue of concessions or contracts granted under the conditions that the law determines." This principle was not an invention of the Dominicans. It simply adopted a device frequently found in twentieth century Latin American constitutions.*

A similar development was found in the new text of Paragraph 2 of Article 6, which concerned the rights of workers. The earlier provision proclaimed "freedom of labor." The new one repeated this principle but qualified it immediately: "The law may, as the general interest may require, establish the working day, days of rest and vacation, minimum wages and salaries and their methods of payment, social insurance, preponderant participation of nationals in all labor, and, in general, all the measures of protection and assistance by the State that are considered necessary in support of workers."

The remaining substantial amendments reinforced in many cases the powers of the president. The new Article 79 provided that provincial governors were to be appointed and might be removed by the president of the Republic. A similar amendment was found in Paragraph 27 of Article 49, under which the power to designate the president and the members of the administrative council of the District of Santo Domingo belongs to the president of the Republic.

Many amendments, aside from those already mentioned, increased the powers of the president at the expense of those of the Congress. . . . [These included a restatement of "national emergency" and the executive powers flowing from it, "complete and exclusive jurisdiction over the Army," regulation of ocean and river zones, ports, and coasts, and others.]

Two former provisions failed to reappear in the 1942 constitution. One was the former Paragraph 5 of Article 61, according to which the Supreme Court had the power to make final decisions concerning the constitutionality of laws and executive orders; the deletion could raise, in theory, serious problems of interpretation. It was not likely, however, that this sort of thing would happen in Trujillo's regime. The other deletion was

---

* Influenced, of course, by Article 27 of the Mexican constitution of 1917.

that of former Article 99, which had required the use of arbitration before any declaration of war.

Finally, two paragraphs, 4 and 5, were added to Article 104 (formerly 101) on the law of public expenditures. According to the first, if Congress were to close the legislative period without having passed the annual budget, that of the previous year would continue in force. By the second, if the Congress is recessed, the executive may make budgetary adjustments, with the obligation of submitting these changes to Congress later.

Article 8, concerning nationality, was modified in two respects: the children of Dominicans born abroad might request the nationality of their parents during the year after having reached the age of civil majority; Dominicans who attempt to use another nationality in the Dominican Republic were to be punished. Articles 23 and 26, taken together, required a majority of two-thirds in Congress for a projected law to be declared urgent.

A new paragraph of Article 45 altered the residence requirements for the president, changing from ten to twenty years the time which presidents must have lived in the country. Also important was the conferring upon the president the power to deny admission to the country to foreigners and to expel those already admitted.

Title IX, concerning the judiciary, received a number of changes, the most important one being the integration of a new chapter entitled "Land Courts."

In Article 97, September 24, the anniversary of the Financial Restoration, was set aside as a national holiday.

The new Article 103 allowed the free organization of political parties, "providing their tendencies conform with the principles established in the second article of this Constitution."

The new Article 107 prohibited titles which connote social distinction, but allowed, for life, "titles of honor that the national Congress gives or has given to citizens who lend or have lent eminent services to the Republic to assure its peace and well-being, or to guarantee or recover its liberty and independence"; this would include, of course, the title of "Benefactor" and any other bestowed, or which may be bestowed, on Trujillo.

There was added, finally, a double transitory provision which stated that the new five-year term was not to affect the elected officers for the term ending on August 16, 1942, but that the new political rights given to women were to become effective immediately — in time for the coming May elections.

In closing these comments, it is worthwhile to emphasize again the rapidity with which the Constituent Assembly consummated its share of the task, even though the breadth of the reform undertaken permitted its members a certain freedom in wording the amendments. The 1942 reform was fairly substantial, although it did not result in either a new structure of government or a new constitution, as was proclaimed. It should also be pointed out that the reforms were initiated by Trujillo as Benefactor and not by President Troncoso de la Concha, although an attempt was made to meet the formalities by the immediate adoption of the reforms as their own by the senators to whom Trujillo read his message. The constitutional politics of the Era continued unchanged.

The Reform and Constitution of 1947

Once again, the initiative for reform came from Trujillo, now president, who on October 7, 1946, made a statement proposing to amend Articles 94 and 95 of the Constitution, dealing with the national currency. The Congress . . . called a constituent assembly. The restricted purpose of this reform was . . . merely to allow constitutionally the issuing of Dominican bills instead of the dollar bills used up to that time, to avoid inflation. A month later (November 15), however, two laws were passed, which expanded the scope of the reform to include additional articles dealing with the powers of the president over municipal matters and with municipal administration, and secondly, the representation of minorities in the electoral process, a matter which was directly related to events then transpiring concerning the National and Labor parties and the 1947 elections.

The Constituent Assembly met on December 26, 1946. Its committees reported and the Assembly finished its work on January 9, 1947. On the tenth the new constitution of the Dominican Republic — the twenty-fifth — was proclaimed and the text was published in the *Official Gazette* of January 19.[5]

The major reforms of 1947 concerned the currency system. The new Article 94 is very long. It begins by saying that the national currency is the golden peso. Immediately after, four detailed paragraphs about the monetary and banking system were added. The new Article 95 provides that any modification in the money or banking system must have the approval of a two-thirds majority of each chamber unless it has been

---

[5] *G.O.* 6569. An English translation of this 1947 constitution can be found in Fitzgibbon, *Constitutions,* pp. 297–320. [Fn. 44, Chap. II.]

initiated by the executive on the proposal of the monetary board or has the board's approval.

The second reform, much less important, concerned the financial powers of the municipal councils. The third reform was so minor that it appears to have been unnecessary. It added one sentence to Article 84, which deals with elections; the new sentence declares that the law will determine the standards of minority representation.

Another small amendment referred to the requirements to be president of the Republic, stated in Article 44. The former text required one to have been a resident in the country for at least twenty years. The new text requires only five years, but they must be immediately preceding the election.

The constitutional reform of 1947 was important in respect to the Dominican monetary system. The other three amendments were, in fact, unnecessary. One of them did not alter the Constitution at all. It is almost too obvious to deserve comment that this was no new constitution. Of course, the procedure — Trujillo's initiative and the immediate approval — was maintained.

Fourth Reform on the March

Since the end of August, 1954, and especially during September of that year, the Dominican press published a series of letters written in response to a poll concerning the restoration of the vice-presidency.[6] The similarity of the answers recommending such restoration — even from men who in 1941 opposed the vice-presidency with the same enthusiasm now shown in its defense — and the recommendations at the same time that the age qualification required by the Constitution to occupy the highest positions of the state be reduced (it has been thirty years since 1942) are obvious signs that a constitutional amendment concerning these matters could be approaching. Is this reform on behalf of a prospective dynastic succession?[7]

The Dominican Constitutional System

The constitutional system of the Dominican Republic, under Trujillo as during previous regimes, is basically inspired, as are most Latin American constitutions, by the Constitution of the United States and the Decla-

---

[6] El Caribe, several issues from August to October, 1954. In June, 1955, the same newspaper referred vaguely to studies under way for the coming constitutional reform. El Caribe, June 22, 1955, p. 14. And in August, Trujillo suggested the creation of the vice-presidency by law. [Fn. 48, Chap. II.]

[7] The symptoms seem to point in favor of "Ramfis," who will be twenty-eight years old at the time of the 1957 election. [Fn. 49, Chap. II.]

ration of Rights of the French Revolution. Only the details have been changed to adapt to different periods. The basic system has persisted since the constitution of 1844.

In the following chapters, the constitutional structure of each institution, and the distortion of such structure in practice, will be examined. It is useful here, however, to present a general picture of the system.*

The Constitution is divided into fifteen titles, which are, in turn, occasionally subdivided into chapters.

Title I refers to the nation and its government and to the territory.

Title II includes the enumeration of individual rights.

Title III concerns nationality and citizenship.

Title IV has an interesting sentence which appears in Article 12: "Only the people is sovereign."

Titles V, VI, and VII set up the legislative branch.

Title VIII deals with the executive power.

Title IX deals with the judiciary.

Title X sets up the chamber of accounts.

Title XI deals with the municipal councils.

Title XII concerns the provinces.

Title XIII refers to elections.

Title XIV deals briefly with the armed forces.

Title XV embraces a series of general provisions.

This, in brief, is the contitutional structure of the government of the Dominican Republic. However, a very close reading of the constitutional text is one thing; government in practice is quite another. Both will be the subject of the following chapters.

---

* Because the Dominican constitution which Galíndez analyzes in the rest of this section has since been replaced, this portion (pp. 330–33 of the manuscript) has been skeletonized. The present constitution, dated November 28, 1966, differs internally to some extent from that analyzed by the author. Its main subdivisions are:

Title	I.	The Nation, the Territory, and the Frontier System.
Title	II.	Individual and Social Rights and Duties.
Title	III.	Nationality and Citizenship.
Title	IV.	The Legislative Branch.
Title	V.	The Executive Branch.
Title	VI.	The Judicial Branch.
Title	VII.	The Accounting Commission.
Title	VIII.	The National District and Municipalities.
Title	IX.	The Provinces.
Title	X.	Electoral Assemblies.
Title	XI.	The Armed Forces.
Title	XII.	General Provisions.
Title	XIII.	Constitutional Amendments.
Title	XIV.	Transitory Provisions.

Chapter 3: Elections and Resignations

[*Writing in 1955, Galíndez describes the patterns of elections and resignations through that year.*]

According to Article 12 of the Dominican constitution in force in 1955, "Only the people is sovereign." According to Article 2, . . . the government of the Republic "is divided into the Legislative Power [Branch], Executive Power, and Judicial Power. These three branches are independent in the exercise of their respective powers."

This is the letter of the Constitution, the democratic facade. The reality of the Dominican Republic under Trujillo is entirely different. There are no independent powers, no officials elected for a term of five years; there is one single power, that is, Trujillo, as chief of the Dominican party, whether or not he happens also to be the president of the Republic.

The key to the Trujillo system, necessary in order to understand the perfect working of this regime, is in the Constitution itself: it is Article 16, together with Article 39 of the statutes of the Dominican party. According to Article 16, "When vacancies of Senators or Deputies occur, they will be filled by the respective Chamber, which will choose a substitute from the panel presented by the appropriate organization of the political party to which the Senator or Deputy who gave rise to the vacancy belonged." As a complement to this provision of the Constitution, Article 39 of the statutes of the Dominican party provides that: "The Party maintains that all elective positions belong not to the person elected, for his personal benefit, but to the Party so that they may serve the political program and the discipline of the Party. In consequence, in order to fulfill this high purpose of political ethics, the candidates chosen for elective positions and the members of the Party that now occupy elective positions, when they accept the nomination in the first case, and with the approval of these statutes in the second instance, must send in writing their undated resignations to the Chief of the Party."[1]

This means that Trujillo, as chief of the Dominican party, has the undated resignations of all elected officials (including legislators and judges). When he chooses to remove one of these officials, he needs only to add a date and send in the resignation.

If this resignation affects a legislator, Article 16 of the Constitution becomes applicable and the chief of the Dominican party simultaneously sends a letter to the respective chamber proposing a panel with three names as possible substitutes. As the Congress is made up of members of the party, the resignation is accepted automatically without discussion, and the person who is at the head of the list is elected unanimously as the substitute. In this way, the legislators change periodically, but always in accordance with the Constitution.

Article 16 of the Constitution was not invented by Trujillo. It was an amendment introduced in the 1924 constitution. Vacancies were previously covered by vote of the pertinent electoral body, within sixty days of the occurrence of the vacancy. It might be a wise principle in countries where the victorious party in an election has a very small majority, which can thus be maintained for the duration of a constitutional term without the risk that occasional deaths might modify the slight balance of power.

What Trujillo has introduced is the trick of undated resignations. The procedure was imposed in fact before being written down in the statutes of the party. It was practiced in the Chamber of Deputies in 1930–34 and was intensified in the whole congress of 1934–38. But in July, 1937, it became official: *Listín Diario* of July 22 published a notice by Morel, at that time president of the superior directive council of the Dominican party, stating: "According to Article 39 of the Statutes of the Dominican Party, all elective officers of the Nation have presented their resignation, in order that the next conventions of the Party may be free to exercise the powers conferred in that Article." The same notice refers to the case of Trujillo, who had been the first to sign his resignation as president.

In the following pages we will see how this device is applied in the daily life of the Dominican congress.

The same device is also applied to all other elective positions in the state, although the constitutional article that facilitates it changes from case to case. In the case of the judiciary, Article 19, Paragraph 1 of the

---

[1] It is worthwhile to remember that Article 39 of the statutes of the Dominican party was made public in July, 1937, that is, about the time preparations for the 1938 general elections began. [Fn. 2, Chap. III.]

Constitution is applied. According to this article, the Senate has the power
to appoint all judges. In the courts, the procedure is simpler than in Congress: Trujillo fills in the date and sends in the resignation without need
of submitting simultaneously three names for the substitutes; it is enough
to make known to the senators informally the name of the person who
must be elected as replacement. A similar procedure is followed in the
chamber of accounts.

In the case of governors and secretaries of state, the substitution is
very simple because they are freely appointed and dismissed by the president of the Republic. Before the constitutional reform of 1942, however,
when the governors were elected by the respective provinces, this device
of the resignation and substitution was also applied in accordance with
Article 78, Paragraph 1 of the Constitution, that gave the executive the
power to fill these vacancies.[2]

Elections 100 Percent Unanimous

According to Title XIII of the Constitution now in force, "the Electoral Assemblies shall meet of their own right three months before the
end of the constitutional term" (i.e., on May 16 every five years), and
sixty days after any extraordinary call for partial elections (in case of
new provinces being created, for example). "It is the function of the
Electoral Assemblies to choose the President of the Republic, the Senators
and Deputies, Councilmen, Mayors and Alternates in the City Councils,
and any other officer so determined by law." "Elections shall be by direct
vote . . . and with representation of minorities when more than two candidates are to be elected." "Elections shall be directed by a Central Electoral
Board and by local boards dependent upon it."

An electoral law regulates the application of those principles and the
details of the electoral mechanism.

Nothing can better evaluate Dominican elections during Trujillo's
regime than an analysis of the electoral results announced in issues of the
Official Gazette, since he rose to power in 1930. Since then, six ordinary
general elections were held in 1930, 1934, 1938, 1942, 1947, and 1952;
three extraordinary elections in 1934, 1941, and 1946 to elect delegates
to constituent assemblies; and several partial elections.

The results of the 1930 elections were published in the *Official
Gazette,* No. 4257 on June 13. These were the elections in which the Tru-

---

[2] This apparent division of powers in the Constitution and its inefficiency in
practice is a common characteristic of all Latin American dictatorships. But there is
no other in which the trick of "resignations" is practiced as it is in the Dominican
Republic. This is the most peculiar characteristic of Trujillo's regime. [Fn. 4,
Chap. III.]

jillo-Estrella Ureña ticket won, after a hard electoral campaign in which numerous abuses forced the final abstention of the Velázquez-Morales ticket, presented by the National-Progressive Alliance. The central electoral board certified in that year the results county [común] by county, listing the number of registered electors, the number of votes cast, the number of votes in favor of the ticket headed by Trujillo, and the number of votes cast "against" this candidacy without mentioning who received them. The total figures for the Dominican Republic showed this result: registered electors, 412,711; votes cast, 225,614; votes in favor of Trujillo's ticket, 223,731; votes against, 1,883.

As suggested previously, it seems that this result may reflect the actual decision at the polls, although perhaps the figures were exaggerated. It was the only time during Trujillo's regime that negative votes were announced. Because of the numerous abuses preceding it, the elections were not free; but it was worthwhile to emphasize the great number of abstentions, and even the courage of those who voted negatively. In summary, and according to the official figures, 55 percent of the registered electors voted, 99 percent of the votes were in favor, and 1 percent were against. However, as the United States minister, Curtis, pointed out, the number of votes announced in favor of the Trujillo-Estrella Ureña candidacy was in excess of the number of possible voters; the electoral results announced in 1934 confirm the possibility of this electoral fraud because there were only 286,937 registered voters (that is, almost 40 percent fewer than in 1930).

It is worthwhile to look at some details of the vote by provinces. The provinces in which more votes against were announced were those of Barahona (649 against and 10,604 in favor), Samaná (326 and 3,379), and Puerto Plata (336 and 14,415). In the province of La Vega not one single vote against was announced (28,688 in favor), and only twenty votes against in the province of Santiago (35,860 in favor). In the province of Santo Domingo, including the capital, the result was 38,938 in favor and 160 against. By counties, there were twenty-six in which not a single vote against was announced (in a total of sixty-two counties). In the capital city, the results were 14,868 in favor and 50 against (in a total of 25,736 registered electors).

The results of the 1934 elections were published in the *Official Gazette,* No. 4684 of May 29. This time the certificate of the electoral board was much simpler than in 1930 because it did not announce one single vote against; all the votes cast were in favor of the candidates presented by the Dominican party (the only one entered in the elections, and the only one existing in the country). The total showed 286,937 registered electors and 256,423 votes cast in favor of the Dominican party; which meant 88.65 percent of the electors voted. Moreover, 100 percent of the votes were cast in favor of the whole list of candidates, including president, congressmen, governors, and councilmen.

The results of the 1938 elections were printed in the *Official Gazette,* No. 5180 of June 6. The certificate of the electoral board was virtually identical to that in 1934; there was a small number of abstentions, and all the votes were in favor of the solitary list presented by the Dominican party. In total, 348,010 registered electors and 319,680 in favor were announced in 1938; which meant 91.85 percent of eligible voters cast their votes.

The results of the 1942 elections were published in the *Official Gazette,* No. 5749 of May 17, the day following the elections, strange as that may seem. The result was also identical to the 1934 and 1938 elections in respect to its unanimity, but there is an interesting detail to be noted, according to the certificate of the electoral board itself. This year, two parties officially went to the polls, although their lists were exactly the same, the Dominican party and the Trujillista party. Another detail in the mechanism was that this time the certificate of the electoral board did not waste space in making any distinction between registered electors and votes cast; it simply announced "the total of votes cast, which is at the same time the number of votes received by every candidate included in the lists presented by the Dominican and Trujillista Parties." The total of votes announced for the whole Republic was 581,937; the increase over 1938 was due to the fact that this time women voted.

The general elections of 1947 were the only complicated ones in the history of Trujillo's regime, because of the game carried on with the National and Labor parties. That necessitated a four-column certificate from the electoral board, listing respectively the total votes cast, the number of votes received by the Dominican party, those received by the National Democratic party, and those received by the National Labor party. The totals announced for the whole Republic were: votes cast, 840,340; votes in favor of the Dominican party, 781,389; votes in favor of the National party, 29,765; votes in favor of the Labor party, 29,186. The results were published in the *Official Gazette,* No. 6632 of May 27.

One cannot believe the announced results reflected the votes in fact cast at the polls. It is clear that the results in every province and especially the "success" of one candidate for each "opposition" party was prepared beforehand. Nevertheless, it is worthwhile to examine some official details of these elections. The Dominican party was recognized as casting 92.85 percent of the total votes; and each of the two opposing parties was recognized as getting almost 4 percent of the total. Good care was taken that the votes of the "opposition" parties be similar although not exactly the same. Distribution of the minority votes by provinces was very careful, in order that each of the minority parties receive one deputy; the National party got the third deputy in the province of Santiago with 22,120 votes, against 87,508 votes for the Dominican party and only 789 for the Labor party; the latter got the third deputy in the province of Duarte with 21,942 votes, against 41,696 for the Dominican party and only 1,865 for the National party.

The latest general election, in 1952, followed the old routine. Its results were published in the *Official Gazette,* No. 7428 on May 31. The certificate of the electoral board said simply: "Total number of votes cast and received by every candidate of the Dominican Party." The figure for the whole Dominican Republic was 1,038,816 votes, without mention of the number of registered electors or abstentions. The unanimity was perfect.

The three elections for constituent assemblies were an exact reflection of what happened in the ordinary general elections. In 1934 the elections took place simultaneously with the general elections of that year; the results were published in the *Official Gazette,* No. 4682 on May 25; these results were 100 percent unanimous and were identical. In 1941, the constituent assembly elections were held five months before the regular elections of 1942, and the number of electors was slightly smaller because women did not yet vote. The *Official Gazette,* No. 5683 on December 20 announced a total of 361,463 votes, all in favor of the Dominican party.

The special elections of 1946 had a complication similar to those of the regular elections of 1947, because the Labor party took part in them. The results were published in the *Official Gazette,* No. 6556 on December 19, announcing the victory of all candidates of the Dominican party plus two minority candidates of the Labor party, one in La Vega and another in Santiago. If we compare this distribution with that of 1947, it is easy to verify the obvious difference in the votes counted for the Labor party. In December, 1946, the Labor party received almost 25,000 votes in the province of La Vega and five months later it received only 3,142; in the province of Santiago, it received in December more than 24,000 votes, but in May it received only 789, the minority votes being counted for the new National party. On the contrary, the Labor party received in May a minority deputy in the province of Duarte with almost 22,000 votes, but in December the votes received by the Labor party in this province were not even mentioned. These data are enough to prove the falsification of the results in these two polls. . . .

The figures and data already mentioned make unnecessary any comment about the "honesty" of the Dominican elections during the Era of Trujillo. Neither Hitler, Stalin, Mussolini, nor Franco ever dared to announce results so nearly unanimous; at least they allowed a small percentage of contrary votes or abstentions; at least they established some differences of votes between the chief and the remaining candidates in the list.

But it is useful to cite other data about the electoral procedure. The author cannot prove this procedure by documentary evidence, but he knows most of it from a direct source whose name he can not disclose.

We will say very little about the call for elections, which is made officially by the central electoral board in the *Official Gazette*. Neither shall we discuss the nomination of candidates by the convention of the Dominican party, whose delegates limit themselves to applauding the proposal made by the president of the superior directive council as suggested by Trujillo. Neither shall we deal with the electoral campaign, which often does not exist at all. What is more significant are the details of procedures at the polls.

These details are generally known in the Dominican Republic because its citizens have lived them. The vote is compulsory, and every identity card must have a rubber stamp that its holder voted in the last elections, or else he may be punished and may have trouble even in cashing a check. But this compulsion does not mean that the voter goes to the polls; it is enough that he send his identity card with a servant. The ballots are printed by the Dominican party, and the voter does not always put his into the box.

We shall refer now to details of the latest general elections, held in 1952, as they were told to the author by the chairman of a local electoral board in a county of the inland Cibao, during his temporary stay in New York some weeks later.

The provincial council of the Dominican party notified the author's informant of his appointment, although he was not a resident of that county. The council gave him the instructions, ballots, books, and seals. He left the capital of the province on horseback and arrived at dawn at the county seat. The local members of the electoral board were waiting there for him, and they met together in the school. Its doors were carefully closed while the voters waited in line outside.

When the hour scheduled to begin the election came, an assistant half opened the door and collected the identity cards of the first ten voters in line, none of whom was allowed to enter the school; the assistant brought their cards to the chairman of the board, who noted their names and numbers one by one in the registry book, stamped the cards, and dutifully put ten ballots of the Dominican party into the box. The procedure was repeated, ten by ten, until no more electors were in line.

When the hour scheduled to close the election came, the chairman wrote the required certificate with mention of candidates and votes received by them. But before writing it, he checked carefully the number of electors noted down in the registry book and the number of ballots put into the box, and as he found that there were two fewer ballots than names he put two more ballots into the box to make it even. Once verified that everything was all right, the members of the local board signed the certificate. Our informant went back to the capital of the province on horseback, just in time for the provincial electoral board to send a telegram to the capital of the nation with the "results" in order that the "exact" total of votes in the whole Republic could be printed next morning in the newspapers.

We have forgotten to add one detail. On his way back to the capital of the province, this informant met an elector who, because of certain difficulties, had arrived too late at the school and had not gotten his identity card stamped as required. However, there was no legal possibility to help him; the certificate was already signed and the informant could not afford the risk that some time later someone would find one stamped identity card more than electors noted down in the registry book. Nobody had voted in that county, but the apparent legality was ironclad.

Congressmen Who Resign by Letter

According to Article 14 of the Constitution, senators and deputies are elected "by direct vote" (of the people). By Article 102, their term lasts five years, from August 16 of the year in which the general elections take place.

If there is any section of the Constitution without effectiveness in practice, it is the one containing these provisions. No congressman is sure of remaining five years in office, and in fact there are very few who serve until the end of their terms. Many more congressmen are elected by the Chamber or the Senate itself on the suggestion of the chief of the Dominican party, than are officially elected by direct vote of the people. Changes among officers for both chambers do not occur only on August 16, but at any time convenient for a readjustment in the government. In other words, congressmen are entirely at the mercy of Trujillo as chief of the Dominican party.

The author has noted one by one all the resignations of senators and deputies which can be found in the pertinent *Bulletins* of the Senate and the Chamber during the quarter of a century covered by the Era of Trujillo. It will be enough to give here the general statistics, plus mention of the more significant details, to understand the hard truth about Trujillo's congress. The author has in his files the complete and detailed list of the names of resigning congressmen, with dates of resignation and provinces they represented in Congress, but it would be excessive to repeat all of them. It must be added that these figures are a minimum. It could happen that some resignations have been overlooked, especially during the present administration of Héctor B. Trujillo because the *Bulletins* of this period have not yet been received in the public libraries of the United States, and one cannot be sure of the information contained in available newspapers. But all the figures stated can be proved with the mention of names and dates.[3]

We shall begin with the Senate. The details of its resignations will be analyzed more carefully, because the upper chamber seems to have deserved a certain respect; nevertheless, its progressive instability shows the general trend of Congress during the Era of Trujillo.

1930–1934: During this period, the Senate kept its traditional stability; there were only two vacancies. (During this same term, the resignations in the lower chamber had already started, and one of the new senators had previously been a deputy for a month.)

1934–1938: During this term, the Senate lost its stability and followed the trend of resignations already prevalent in the lower chamber. Thirteen vacancies occurred, one by death . . . and twelve by resignation. Eight senators ended their term, including the president and the two secretaries. The senatorship of Puerto Plata changed four times, and that of La Vega three times.

1938–1942: On August 16, 1938, thirteen senators took the oath; eleven were already senators at the end of the previous legislative term and two were new. On January 3, 1939, three senators were added, representing the new provinces of Benefactor, Libertador, and Monseñor Merino. The instability of the Senate increased in this period. During its four years, thirty-two vacancies occurred, two because of death, one because of a resignation caused by fatal illness, and twenty-nine because of simple resignations (almost twice the number of senators). Only three senators completed their terms. The secretaryships were changed five times.

The senatorships of Puerto Plata and Monte Cristi changed four times, and those of Santo Domingo, Barahona, and Santiago three times. On August 17, 1938, the next day after the inauguration of the new

---

[3] The source of each of these statistics will not be noted, because it would be tedious. Almost all are taken from the pertinent *Bulletin* of the Senate or of the Chamber of Deputies. Since June, 1953, for the Senate and November, 1952, for the Chamber, the source (incomplete) is the Dominican newspapers available for consultation. [Fn. 8, Chap. III.]

Senate, two senators had already resigned, and two weeks later two more senators did the same. Seven of the eight resignations that were given from April 24 to May 26, 1942, were a consequence of the general elections of May 16 and occurred in order to advance the inauguration of new senators.

1942–1947: On August 16, 1942, sixteen senators took the oath. Eight former senators continued, but only two had been such since 1938. The instability of this term was similar to that of the previous one. Thirty-two vacancies occurred, all of them because of resignation; even the president resigned as senator (on the same day he became president of the lower chamber). Only six senators ended their term. The senatorship of Puerto Plata changed five times, that of Monte Cristi four times, and those of Benefactor, Duarte, and Seybo three times each. . . .

1947–1952: On August 16, 1947, nineteen senators took the oath. It could be said that they were the same senators who ended the previous period, because the only three newcomers resigned the next day and were replaced by the substitutes elected at the end of the previous term. However, only four senators were survivors from 1942. On January 1, 1950, another senator was added, representing the new province of Independencia; and on January 9, 1951, another for the new province of Santiago Rodríguez.

Instability continued in this period. Forty-two vacancies occurred, one because of death and forty-one because of resignations, which sets the record in the Senate up to the present. This time, the president and vice-president ended their terms, but the secretaryships changed five times (four because of resignations and once because of death). Only six senators ended their terms (including the president and the vice-president). The senatorships of Trujillo Valdez and Monte Cristi changed hands six times each, that of Samaná five times, and those of Puerto Plata, Espaillat, and Duarte four times each. . . .

1952–1955: On August 16, 1952, twenty-three senators took the oath (including the representatives of two new provinces). Almost all of them had been in the previous Senate; four were new, . . . but only four had survived since 1947. During this period, which is the current one, it is not possible to offer accurate figures because the official *Bulletin* of the Senate has not been fully available for this study. According to the newspapers, at least ten resignations and one death occurred in three years; the presidency changed hands twice (once because of the death of Troncoso de la Concha), the vice-presidency three times, and the secretaryships twice.

Let us now consider the lower chamber. It would be tedious to analyze changes of deputies with the same detail given to the Senate, because the legislators involved were three times as numerous as in the Senate. Therefore, the statistical data will be reduced to a minimum:

1930–1934: On August 16, 1930, thirty-three deputies took the oath. The first resignation occurred four months later; and on the occasion of the annual elections on August 16, 1931, all officers except the president were changed. A similar change of officers occurred on August 16, 1932. On the contrary, no changes at all occurred in 1933. In total, twenty-one vacancies occurred, nineteen because of resignations (some of them true resignations) and two because of dismissal.

1934–1938: On August 16, 1934, thirty-three deputies took the oath; two more were later added for the new province of Trujillo. In total, fifty-one vacancies occurred, forty-six because of resignation and five because of death. Seven constituencies changed hands three times, and several changed twice. President Miguel Angel Roca was forced to resign, before being arrested and tried. Fourteen deputies "resigned" on that occasion.

1938–1942: On August 16, 1938, forty-nine deputies took the oath; one more was added later for the new province of Libertador. In total, 100 vacancies occurred, 98 because of resignations and 2 because of deaths. The presidency changed twice, the vice-presidency six times, and the secretaryships three times. Five constituencies changed four times each, and several three times each. The day after being organized, on August 17, 1938, the Chamber accepted the resignations of seven deputies. One deputy was such for only a month, another for a month and a half.

1942–1947: On August 16, 1942, thirty-six deputies took the oath (their number had been reduced after the constitutional reform according to which the new proportion was one deputy for every 60,000 inhabitants instead of one for every 30,000). Eight deputies were added later for newly created provinces.

In total, 143 vacancies occurred, 139 because of resignations and 4 because of death. The presidency changed once; the vice-presidency changed four times, as did the secretaryships. One constituency changed hands eight times, another seven times, four changed six times each, five changed five times each, and several four times. Two days after the new Chamber was constituted two deputies resigned, including a secretary. . . . One deputy held office for only seven days — a record in both chambers.

1947–1952: On August 16, 1947, forty-five deputies took the oath; four more were later added for new provinces. In total, 129 vacancies occurred, 126 because of resignation and 3 because of death. There were two changes of vice-president and four of secretaries.

One constituency changed hands seven times, three changed six times each, one five times, and several four times. On two occasions, the resignation came immediately after permission had been granted by the Chamber to indict the resigning deputies. On the same day the Chamber was organized, seven deputies resigned. The novelty of this period is that not only the deputies of the Dominican party resigned, but also the woman deputy elected in 1947 for the Labor party and the deputy elected in 1947 for the National party. The Labor deputy was replaced three weeks after the inauguration of the new chamber by her husband, Francisco Prats Ramírez, defeated pseudo-candidate for the presidency of the Republic.

1952–1955: On August 16, 1952, fifty deputies took the oath, including the representatives of two new provinces. Only incomplete data, taken from newspapers, are available. At least eighty-four deputies have resigned in three years. Among the changes were one of the presidents, three of the vice-presidents, and five of the secretaries. At least one constituency changed hands four times in two years. Attention should be drawn to the resignation on July 21, 1953, of three of the four deputies of the Santiago Province, plus three more deputies in other provinces, in an obvious collective punishment.

These are the statistical data, dry but impressive in their raw truthfulness. It is useful to add some general comments.

The first resignation occurred in the lower chamber on December 18, 1930, four months after it was organized. During the first Trujillo administration, the Senate was respected (except for one senator killed in battle, and another removed), but since the second Trujillo administration both chambers have suffered the same instability.

Almost all vacancies have occurred because of resignation; only a very small percentage was because of natural death, one case because of violent death. There have been numerous cases of legislators who took the oath on August 16, the opening day of a new congress, and then resigned on the same day or on the next day (usually because they had already resigned at the end of the previous term, after having been candidates in the May elections). There have been deputies who held their seats for only one month or even for a few days; and many legislators in both chambers have been such for only a few months.

The presidents of both chambers have had a certain permanence; but not the vice-presidents and secretaries, who have changed often. The stability of Mario Fermín Cabral as president of the Senate from 1930 to 1938, that of Manuel Troncoso de la Concha as president of the Senate from 1943 until his death in 1955, and that of Porfirio Herrera as president of the Chamber from 1943 to date, and before as president of the Senate after 1938, are notable. A similar stability marked the tenure of the first president of the Chamber, Miguel Angel Roca, from 1930 until his arrest at the end of 1936.

Some individual senators and deputies are remarkable because of their continuance but, in general, the pattern is that no legislator remains in his seat for a long time; the Congress is used as a place of rest or partial recovery, according to individual needs,[4] for personalities of the regime who sooner or later come back to active positions.

At times there have been resignations en masse, which seems to suggest situations of political uneasiness, either national or local. Such cases occurred in November, 1936, after the Roca scandal was disclosed, and in November, 1940, after the arrest of General José Estrella.

How do these resignations take place? The procedure is very simple: one secretary reads the letter by which the affected legislator resigns, without explanation, his seat for a given province; the Chamber or the Senate accepts the resignation. Immediately afterwards, a secretary reads a letter from the chief or the president of the Dominican party submitting three names to fill the vacancy; a secret election takes place, and the first name in the list is elected unanimously.[5] Finally, the president of the Chamber

---

[4] Among the symptoms of the disgrace into which a person may fall are his selection to the upper chamber or the lower chamber. In general, members of the cabinet who are dismissed in friendly terms are elected senators. To the Chamber would go former governors (often exchanging positions with a former deputy) and other high public employees who retire from their active jobs. On some other occasions, a first election as a deputy shows that the political star of a less known person is rising; even the fact of being mentioned among the three names proposed for alternate is a good sign. The same thing happens to persons who have previously been punished by ostracism. On the contrary, a former secretary of state who resigns his senatorship or seat in the Chamber without coming back to active service knows that his political star is setting, although perhaps some years later it may shine again. José M. Bonetti Burgos has been a good example of all these ups and downs. [Fn. 12, Chap. III.]

[5] We shall transcribe, as documentary evidence, the full text of the session held by the Senate on Feb. 27, 1936, as characteristic, because the only item on the agenda was the approval of a resignation and the election of a substitute. It says, literally:

"Senator Secretary Brea: A letter from Sr. Luis Ginebra, Senator from Puerto Plata, in which he resigns his high position, has been received. (Secretary Brea reads it.) The President: If there is no objection, those who are in favor, please let it be known. (All Senators make affirmative signs.) Accepted. The resignation has been accepted. Senator Secretary Brea: A letter from the Dominican Party has been received, in which the following names are sent to fill the vacancy caused by the resignation of Senator Ginebra: General José Fermín Pérez, Lic. J. H. Ducoudray, and Lic. Emilio Espínola. The President: A recess is in order to reach agreement on the candidate we must choose. (It is 9:40 a.m.) The session is reopened. (It is 9:45 a.m.) Let the ballots be distributed. (The ballots are distributed and every Senator places his vote in the box.) The President: There are twelve ballots, corresponding to the twelve Senators. The Secretary will read them. Secretary Brea: All ballots are in favor of General José Fermín Pérez. The President: General José Fermín Pérez has unanimously been named as Senator for the province of Puerto Plata, in place of the resigning Luis Ginebra. Being in the corridors, the elected Senator Pérez is invited to take the constitutional oath. (Senator Pérez takes the oath, all Senators standing.)." Immediately afterwards the session was closed, because there were no more items to be discussed. (Bol. Sen., Feb. 1936.)

It must be added that the same General J. F. Pérez had resigned the same senatorship of Puerto Plata on July 2, 1935, being replaced by Luis Ginebra, now resigning. [Fn. 14, Chap. III.]

learns that the new congressman is in the building;[6] he appoints a commission to invite him to enter the floor of the Chamber. The new legislator takes the oath, and he makes a speech thanking Trujillo.[7]

Only on very exceptional occasions, has a congressman resigned his seat orally. Such was the case of Deputy Aníbal J. Trujillo [a brother of the dictator] on December 26, 1936, in almost exalted terms.[8] The most remarkable case was that of Deputy Bienvenido Gimbernar because of its symbolic importance. This newspaperman had been elected a deputy from Trujillo Province in 1938, and in December of the same year he became a deputy from the new province of Monseñor Merino. Five months later he read in person a letter of resignation which did not contain the usual brief formula, but a long discussion:

> My desire to devote all my time and energies to work in journalism . . . takes me out of this Chamber . . . which I leave today with the conviction that I have not been an accomplice to any weakness or hesitation, and most of all that I have not used my seat here like a bench in a public square for chatting or gossiping, for petty politics among pals. . . . Some not very nice incidents led to my being called, in the gossip of the corridors, impertinent and impolitic. Impertinent, sometimes, because I requested more attention in this Chamber to the activities carried on here, activities that, because all actions are carried out virtually unanimously by reason of emanating from a Power directly tied to the political party led by that Power, requiring for the same reason, the disciplined attention of all those present and voting, as a demonstration of perfect approval, good sense, and legislative decency. . . . My satisfaction with my own behavior, and my gratitude towards the only Chief, show that I never act for the mere purpose of cashing a monthly salary, or for political protection. . . . I desire only that my alternate in this position

---

[6] This detail is mentioned occasionally, not only in the *Bulletin* of the Chamber, where it is often found, but also in the press reporting what happened the day before in Congress. [Fn. 15, Chap. III.]

[7] This speech is simple routine and usually is brief. But on occasion it sounds like a tragicomedy; such was the case of Deputy José Hungría, resigning on July 21, 1953, on the occasion of the collective punishment against the deputies of Santiago and others of the Cibao region, and then reelected one month later. His reaction in face of the punishment was in these terms: "Here I am again as deputy from the province of Santiago, where I was born. . . . What greater happiness is there than to follow, with courage tempered and the soul opened, in the phalanxes of that victorious *Caudillo* who stops the hands of the clock when he is at work." *La Nación*, August 27, 1953. [Fn. 16, Chap. III.]

[8] Aníbal J. Trujillo had been elected deputy three weeks before in the readjustment following the Roca scandal. He did not only resign orally, but it was announced that he was transferred to another position. Almost all deputies requested the floor to express their regrets; one among them proposed to salute him with the Masonic greeting; it was finally decided to close the session in order to accompany Trujillo's brother to his home.

Even more impressive was the session of Feb. 2, 1932, in which Trujillo's father, José Trujillo Valdez, was elected deputy from La Vega on the occasion of a vacancy. This time the election was by roll call, with all members standing (even his son, Virgilio). *Bol. Cam.*, Feb. 1932. [Fn. 17, Chap. III.]

understand . . . that the Republic, believe-it-or-not, pays too well . . . the function of being legislators of the Republic.

This resignation was so unexpected and the content of the letter
reflected such criticism of the activities of the deputies, that it at once
provoked alarm among other members of the Chamber. Instead of accepting it in the usual routine, the secretary proposed to delay its consideration
"in order to study it. . . ." A deputy called attention to the statutes of the
Dominican party and said that "the most appropriate thing would be to
address this resignation to the Director of the Party." The resignation of
Gimbernar was not accepted that day.

On the next day, it was obvious that there had been "consultation"
concerning the resignation, because it was approved by forty-six votes.
Immediately after, a letter from Trujillo was read proposing three names
to fill the vacancy. Everything thus returned to the routine procedure.
But the resignation of Gimbernar and the reaction it provoked is the best
proof of how the resignations of deputies are usually carried out in the
Dominican Republic. . . .

We do not need to extend these data. In the Dominican congress, all
appearances are respected and all the rules are followed; but absolutely no
legislator is sure of his seat. All of them run the risk that Trujillo as chief
of the Dominican party[9] will send in their letters of resignation.

The Legislative Process

Article 33 of the Constitution enumerates in twenty-four paragraphs
the powers of the Congress. . . . [*The author identifies them and related
provisions on pp. 376-77 of the manuscript.*]

Again, this is the letter of the Constitution which, in appearance, is
followed word for word.

Let us begin with the power to approve taxes and expenditures. It
is true that every year, in December, the congress approves the budget
and the law of public expenditures for the next year. But neither the
budget nor the law is ever discussed; a secretary reads in each chamber
the project sent by the executive, and the legislators approve it as a whole;
the stenographic record printed in the *Bulletin* of both chambers offers the
documentary evidence of this fact year after year.

Mention will be made only about the legislative period 1945–46,
taken as an example in this study. The Chamber of Deputies considered

---

[9] This omnipotent power of Trujillo is personal, not exercised as president, and
he likes to remind the nation of this at times. The announcement he made as
"Benefactor" in February, 1940, about coming changes in the cabinet and the
Congress, was typical. It has not been the only case. We must also remember the
repeated experience during the trips of Trujillo while out of the presidency; during
his absences, there are usually no resignations in Congress; they begin again after
his return. [Fn. 24, Chap. III.]

the budget for 1946 in its ordinary session of December 19, 1945, begun at 10:40 a.m. During this session, a mission of the UNRRA [United Nations Relief and Rehabilitation Administration] was formally received, a bill without importance was considered on first reading, a state contract was considered on second reading, and finally the draft budget was considered on first reading, being declared urgent. The session ended at 11:35 a.m. Five minutes later the Chamber met again in extraordinary session, begun at 11:40 a.m. and ended at 12 noon, after having passed on second reading the budget and another law.

On the next day, December 20, the Senate met in ordinary session at 11 a.m.; in this session a diplomatic appointment was confirmed, the draft budget was considered on first reading, after being declared urgent, and several senators asked the floor to praise the work of Trujillo; a message of congratulation was sent to him, and the session ended at 11:55 a.m. Five minutes later the Senate met again in extraordinary session, which began at 12 noon and ended at 12:40 p.m., after passing the budget on second reading. The stenographic records of these four sessions prove that it was merely a "reading," never a discussion; and that this reading did not cover even the figures of the budget but only its formal introduction.

But all appearances were fulfilled. And they continue to be fulfilled throughout the whole year. Numerous special laws are approved every year with the sole purpose of transferring sums from one chapter to another of the law of public expenditures. The decision in each case is made by the executive, but Congress legalizes it. In the period from August 16, 1945, to August 16, 1946, at least twenty special laws authorizing such transfers were approved. What is more curious is the fact that in these cases all figures were read and transcribed, which was not done with the general law in December.

Let us consider now the legislative process. There is not one single law of importance that is not initiated by the executive, usually drafted by the office of the legal adviser, which in any case supervises the projects prepared by other departments. It is very rare that the Supreme Court introduces any project, and the motions presented by legislators are few.

It is important to study the procedure for approval of laws. The bills almost never are discussed, and if the legislators ask the floor it is because a given bill refers in one way or another to Trujillo.[10] Many laws

---

[10] Among the laws which provoked most speeches in eloquent style, the following deserve to be mentioned: that of 1936 which changed the name of the capital to Ciudad Trujillo, that of 1938 which created the Trujillo Prize for Peace, and that of 1940 which requires mention of the year of the Era of Trujillo. . . . We must remember also the numerous laws passed for the exclusive purpose of providing an exception to the law of 1930 which prohibited the use of names or faces of persons still alive, in order to name after Trujillo or one of his relatives some town, street, or bridge, or to erect statutes in their honor. [Fn. 26, Chap. III.]

are declared to be "urgent," for the only purpose of getting them approved in two subsequent sessions the same day, the second one lasting from five to ten minutes. In any case, it is very rare that a law is not approved in two following sessions. Usually, a secretary reads the bill submitted by the executive, the presiding officer puts it to vote as a whole, and the legislators "signify in the affirmative."[11]

When the Dominican Republic declared war against Japan, Germany, and Italy, the previous constitutional authorization granted by Congress to the executive was approved without discussion or even comment.

Again statistics, in their hard reality, will be the best proof of these statements. The legislative period 1945–46 is taken as a sample for this study, because during this term several international treaties of worldwide importance and a number of labor laws were approved. All of them should have deserved at least a minimum discussion, though they did not receive it.

During that year, as is customary, two ordinary legislative periods and two extraordinary ones took place. In total, the Senate met in 131 ordinary meetings and 50 extraordinary ones. The Chamber of Deputies met in 137 ordinary sessions and 35 extraordinary ones.

During that legislative year, the following work was completed: at least 170 laws, 25 contracts of state, 20 transfers of assignments in the law of public expenditures, 9 resolutions of municipal councils, and 7 international treaties were approved. Both chambers accepted many resignations and elected the alternates; the Senate elected several judges and approved a number of diplomatic appointments, and several messages were addressed to Trujillo. In addition, the budget and law of public expenditures for 1946, the statement of accounts for 1945, and the annual report of the executive for 1945 were approved. Some of these laws and treaties were of great importance, such as the law of maximum hours, that of minimum wages, two laws restricting strikes, as well as the conventions establishing the UNESCO and the FAO, and the monetary-financial agreements of Bretton Woods.

If we read the *Bulletins* of both chambers to check the time spent

---

[11] As an example, we shall transcribe the stenographic record of the session held by the Senate on May 24, 1933, in which the law conferring upon Trujillo the rank of Generalissimo was approved. It continues as follows, after noting the reading of the bill:

"The President: The draft law just read is opened to discussion. (Silence.) After this silence we shall put the project to a vote. Senator Pérez: I propose that we vote this project standing. The President: The proposal of Senator Pérez is put to vote. (All Senators make affirmative signs.) Approved. The proposal of Senator Pérez has been approved. The project of law is put to vote. (Affirmative signs.) Approved." *Bol. Sen.,* May, 1933, p. 38. [Fn. 27, Chap. III.]

during this period — as the author did and noted — we shall see that the average time for every ordinary session varied from thirty to forty-five minutes, the average time for every extraordinary session between five and ten minutes, and that only rarely did the meetings last an hour. The record was a session of the Senate on February 21, 1946, which lasted two hours; but, on the other hand, there were ordinary sessions that did not last even fifteen minutes, and in more than one session the legislators did nothing but read and approve the minutes of the previous meeting.

Let us consider in particular the time spent to approve some of the more important laws and treaties. The previous extraordinary period in August, 1945, will also be taken into consideration, because the Charter of the United Nations was approved then:

(1). Charter of the United Nations and statutes of the International Court of Justice: The Senate approved them without discussion in the ordinary session of August 1, 1945, which lasted one hour forty-five minutes (on the same day the extraordinary period was opened). The Chamber approved them without discussion in the ordinary session of August 9, which lasted fifty-five minutes.

(2). Convention of the UNESCO: The Chamber approved it without discussion in the ordinary session of April 3, 1945, lasting twenty minutes. The Senate approved it in the ordinary session of April 9 that lasted forty-five minutes (other laws were also approved).

(3). Monetary and financial agreements of Bretton Woods: Both the Senate and the Chamber approved them in the ordinary sessions of December 28, 1945, without discussion. The Senate met for one hour, the Chamber for one hour and twenty minutes.

(4). Convention of the FAO: The Senate approved it in the ordinary session of June 25, 1946, lasting thirty minutes; and the Chamber in the ordinary session of the twenty-seventh, that lasted forty-five minutes.

(5). Law on Maximum Hours: It was approved in both chambers on January 3, 1946. It was declared "urgent," and the second reading took place immediately after the first. The Senate met for twenty minutes on the first reading, and ten minutes on the second reading; the Chamber met for fifty-five minutes on the first reading (some other matters were considered), and five minutes on the second reading; in neither chamber was the project discussed, despite its important repercussions.

(6). Law on Minimum Wages: The Senate approved it on the first reading in the ordinary session of October 10, 1945, that lasted forty minutes, and on the second reading in the extraordinary session of the same day that lasted twenty-five minutes (some other long laws were also considered). The Chamber approved it on the first reading on October 16 in an ordinary session that lasted forty minutes, and on the second reading on the seventeenth, in another extraordinary session that lasted also forty minutes without any discussion.

(7). Law restricting strikes, after the general walkout of January, 1946: It was approved in both chambers on January 17 in subsequent ordinary and extraordinary sessions. Those in the Senate lasted thirty and ten minutes, and those in the Chamber lasted one hour fifteen minutes and ten minutes (one deputy asked the floor to speak about the strike in the sugar fields).[12]

One must add that, although there are in both chambers standing committees which theoretically must study draft bills before their formal discussion, and although from time to time the committee reports are read in plenary sessions, in many cases even this formality is not fulfilled. The laws are declared to be "urgent" and considered at once in plenary meeting of the chambers. Very rarely is any previous routine report of the pertinent committee mentioned.

We shall not extend these comments further. The data presented indicate what is a well known "secret" in the Dominican Republic (and Deputy Gimbernar denounced it clearly in his letter of resignation): congress is simply used to sanction constitutionally the bills decided upon and drafted in their entirety by the executive. The legislators do not discuss those projects, they simply vote "yes."

The Executive

The Constitution devotes Title VIII to the executive branch. According to Article 44, it shall be exercised by a president elected every five years by direct vote; Article 49 enumerates in twenty-seven paragraphs his powers; Article 51 provides that during his temporary or permanent absence his post shall be filled by the secretary of war and navy, and in the absence of that official by other high officers who are mentioned. The remaining articles, 45 to 53, regulate other details of the presidency of the Republic.

In this case, the Constitution is followed quite closely, although not fully. The exceptions are the periods during which Trujillo is not president, and pulls the strings of the presidency from behind the scenes. But in general, the wide powers granted constitutionally to the president facilitate the mechanism of Trujillo's regime. Let us remember that the constitutional reform of 1942 slightly increased these powers. Moreover, the

---

[12] Although it does not belong to this period, it is worthwhile to mention also the case of the approval in a single vote of the very long Trujillo labor code, considered by Congress in May, 1951. This code required two sessions because 693 articles had to be read; but it did not receive any discussion at all. (*Bol. Sen.* and *Bol. Cam.*, May, 1951.) [Fn. 31, Chap. III.]

fact that the secretaries are freely appointed and dismissed by the executive obviates the need of pretended "resignations" and lessens the importance of frequent substitutions. Nevertheless, we must analyze this instability, because it further illustrates the nature of the regime.

It begins with the lack of continuity in the administrative structure. During the twenty-five years of the Era of Trujillo, there have been many changes in the organic law of the Secretaryships of State [i.e., cabinet positions] in order to suppress, increase, merge, separate, or reorganize them. Perhaps the only ones that have not changed much are the Secretaryship of Foreign Relations and that of the presidency, which, despite the name and being close to Trujillo, is not officially the first one in rank. Officially those of war, navy, and aviation, and of interior and police have priority. On one occasion, these were merged, but they were separated later. The remaining secretaryships have had greater instability in name, number, and powers.

An important detail to be pointed out is that some other officials heading different departments of the central administration have also had the rank of secretaries of state. These include the president of the university, the governors of the District of Santo Domingo and of Trujillo Province, the president of the Dominican party, and others. During recent years, some secretaries without portfolio have been appointed. Among all these special secretaries, the president of the superior directive council of the Dominican party should be pointed out, because his membership in the cabinet is typical of the confusion between government and party.

Instability among the secretaries has been obvious since the first Trujillo administration in 1930–34. The first change to be found in the *Official Gazette* occurred on October 27, 1930, when a substitution was made in the Secretaryship of Development and Public Works. Three months later, in January, 1931, the Secretaryships of Interior-Police and War-Navy were merged. On May 8, 1931, Roberto Despradel ceased to be secretary of the treasury and was appointed minister in Washington. In August, 1931, Dr. Max Henríquez Ureña replaced Rafael Estrella Ureña as secretary of foreign relations, and his brother Pedro became superintendent of education. Since then, the replacements have been periodic; so much so that in the cabinet named by Trujillo at the beginning of his second administration, 1934–38, only two persons from the 1930 cabinet remained.

We cannot detail all the changes in the cabinet; it would be too tedious. Only certain cases will be mentioned as symptomatic. The only person who has lasted for a long time in a secretaryship is the youngest brother of Trujillo, Héctor Bienvenido, who was at the head of the Secretaryship of War and Navy from its reestablishment in January, 1942, until he was inaugurated president of the Republic in August, 1952. Besides this case, exceptional and understandable because of the relationship, loyalty, and lack of personality of Héctor B. Trujillo, the secretary of state who has the record of permanence in the same post is Lic. Arturo Despradel who was secretary of foreign relations from July, 1938, to September, 1943.

One may also point out some of the ruler's favorites, although their own strength made them on occasion more intensely vulnerable at the end: Lic. Jacinto B. Peynado, secretary of the presidency from May, 1932, to August, 1934, vice-president from 1934 to 1938, and president from 1938 until his death in 1940; Ricardo Paíno Pichardo, president of the Dominican party from December, 1938, until May, 1942, and secretary of the presidency from this date to February, 1945; Virgilio Alvarez Pina, president of the Dominican party from May, 1942 to 1949; and Anselmo A. Paulino, in different cabinet positions from 1949 to the end of 1954. We shall detail later the final fate of these favorites.

Passing from individual cases to the general trend, we may consider the third Trujillo administration, 1942–47, as a sample because it is the central period of the Era. It was opened with the immediate change in the Secretaryship of War and Navy in May, 1942, that allowed Trujillo to occupy the presidency the day after the elections. On August 16, 1942, Trujillo confirmed all members of the cabinet in their positions. In 1943, we find four changes in the cabinet. In 1944, there were five changes of ministers and seven interim appointments; in 1945, six changes and three interim nominations. In 1946, eleven changes of ministers took place (including the brief comeback of Paíno Pichardo), and seven interim appointments were made.

This instability is also reflected in other high officers of the nation having the rank of secretaries of state, such as the attorney general, the legal adviser to the president, the president of the administrative council of the district of Santo Domingo, and the president of the university. No one remains in office long enough to become politically important.

It is interesting to note the fate of some of the most outstanding lieutenants of Trujillo. Lic. Jacinto B. Peynado was a favorite and died as president of the Republic, but he never reached a position of real personal strength. Later, three members of the cabinet did have real political strength as lieutenants of Trujillo in different positions: Paíno Pichardo, Virgilio Alvarez Pina, and Anselmo A. Paulino. All three ended in disgrace, and the last one was sentenced to ten years in prison. Although not members of the cabinet, the fate of other lieutenants has been much the same, such as General José Estrella as special commissioner in the northern provinces from 1934 until his imprisonment in 1940, and

Mario Fermín Cabral, president of the Senate from 1930 to 1938 and governor of Santiago in place of Estrella in 1940 (but imprisoned for a short time in 1941). So has that of several chiefs of the army. One could even add the cases of two brothers of Trujillo, Virgilio and Aníbal Julio, who during the first years of the regime had important positions and later fell into disgrace.

Not only is the tenure in secretaryships unstable, but during their holding of office the secretaries are mere heads of departments for the time being, obeying instructions from above. The official biographer of Trujillo, Abelardo R. Nanita, takes care to emphasize that as one of his "virtues."[13]

But Trujillo is the master of the regime not only when he is president of the Republic, but also when he is officially out of the government. Some of the facts already pointed out in Chapter I are enough to prove this, such as the existence of the Secretaryship of the Office of the Generalissimo from October, 1940, to May, 1942, his title of commander-in-chief of the armed forces, his mention in all newspapers, with priority over the president himself, and his announcement of coming changes in the cabinet.[14] The most symbolic case of all was the resignation of President Troncoso in May, 1942, so similar to the usual resignations of congressmen.

The only immovable position in the Dominican Republic is that of the Benefactor of the Fatherland and Generalissimo of the armed forces. "President" Peynado was right when he proclaimed: "God and Trujillo."

The Judiciary

In accordance with the Constitution, the courts form the third branch of the state. Title XI regulates the hierarchic organs of justice: the Supreme Court, courts of appeal, land courts, courts of first instance, municipal judges, and other courts the law may create. According to Article 19, Paragraph 1, all justices and judges are elected by the Senate. Articles 58 to 70 enumerate their powers. In 1931, it was clearly established that the

---

[13] "Trujillo has no advisers. Concentrating everything in himself, he is more impenetrable than a Chinese wall. Several of his subordinates may be at the same time developing a plan conceived by Trujillo; but every one knows only the part entrusted to him; the others are ignorant of it. . . . His distrust, his innate suspiciousness, will always free him of the political error that ruined so many leaders in the Americas, where the president himself arms the hand and prepares the prestige of the one who shall oust him." Abelardo R. Nanita, *Trujillo,* 5th ed. (Ciudad Trujillo, 1951), p. 124. [Fn. 36, Chap. III.]

[14] He did this during the Peynado administration in February, 1940, during the Troncoso administration in April, 1941, and during the administration of his brother, Héctor, in Dec., 1952. Let us also remember the message he addressed to the Dominicans and to all authorities after the death of Peynado, advising them to obey Troncoso as the new president. [Fn. 37, Chap. III.]

term of all these judges is the same as that of the Senate which elects them every four years (now five years).

What is the position of justices and judges in the Era of Trujillo? It is convenient to make a distinction between their routine judicial activities, their activities with possible political repercussion, and the stability of their positions.

With regard to stability, it may be noted that at the beginning of the Era it seemed that the Supreme Court would be respected; justices elected in 1931 and in 1934 ended their terms without any more incident than that in January, 1931, when the Senate "reelected" the justices named by the previous Senate, making it clear that their term could not exceed the constitutional four years, an incident that provoked the replacement of the court president and the election of a new justice.

This stability ended in 1938. During the period 1938–42, at least eleven resignations and replacements occurred, plus the elimination of two justiceships in February, 1942. Some of the justiceships changed hands two and even three times. During the period 1942–47, at least eleven resignations and thirteen substitutions took place (one because of retirement and another because of death), plus an increase by two justiceships in June, 1946. During the period 1947–52, at least ten resignations and substitutions took place, including that of the president of the Court.... [*Similar instability is to be noted in judicial incumbencies at lower levels.*]

The procedure for these resignations and substitutions is in essence similar to that used for legislators, except that the proposal of the three names by the party is unnecessary because the naming of the justices and judges is subject only to decision by the Senate. The letter of resignation is read, and immediately afterwards the Senate names the substitute. Very often the resigning judge is named for another position, which may be superior or inferior; for instance, it is usual that a president of a court of appeals is promoted to become a justice of the Supreme Court, although occasionally it happens in reverse.

We shall not give more details; those mentioned are enough to show the instability in the judiciary. Under the threat of being "resigned" at any time, the justices and judges cannot be independent in their activities, despite the statements made by Trujillo to that effect for external use.[15]

Still more significant is the fact, which can not be proved by the official records, that the Dominican courts never dare to issue decisions

---

[15] "You are, by a constitutional provision, one of the three Powers that compose the State.... You are independent and you are responsible. Nothing or nobody must influence you...." (Speech to the assembly of judges held on Jan. 9, 1933.) Rafael L. Trujillo, *Pensamiento*, 1: 243–51. [Fn. 44, Chap. III.]

which imply a constitutional criticism of the laws approved by Congress or the measures taken by the government.[16] In fact, the courts are not the third power of the state, but only one more instrument of the executive. The key to the system continues to be undated resignations in the hands of Trujillo, in accordance with Article 39 of the statutes of the Dominican party.

As we earlier noted, the attorney general — head of the judicial police and of the local state's attorneys, according to Article 58, Paragraph 3 of the Constitution — has the rank of secretary of state and in consequence a position of similar instability, perhaps not so great because of its technical character.

A few last words about the *Tribunal de Cuentas* (chamber of accounts), which, according to Title X of the Constitution, must verify every year the accounts of the government and render a report to Congress. In accordance with Article 72 of the Constitution, its members are elected by the Senate from a tripartite proposal made by the Chamber. Again, the resignations are repeated; during the period 1942–47, at least six resignations occurred.

Local Administration

According to Article 79 of the Constitution, in every province there shall be a governor "appointed and dismissable by the Executive." This free designation by the president was introduced by the 1942 constitutional reform, in order to simplify the previous use of resignations; according to Article 78 of the 1934 Constitution, the provincial governors were elected by the inhabitants of every province, and, in case of the "resignation, disqualification, or death" of the office holder, his vacancy was filled by the executive.

The *Official Gazette* seems to indicate that during the first years of Trujillo's regime the governors were respected. The first appointments by the executive to be found in the *Gazette* were in April, 1936. Later they became frequent.

In view of these free appointments by the executive, and the nature of the governors' roles which must be that of close collaboration with the central government, we shall not dwell for long on their changes. Only as an indication of their instability, we shall mention the changes found in the same period 1942–47: five in the second half of 1942, nineteen in 1943,

---

[16] Until the 1942 constitutional reform, the Supreme Court had power specifically "to decide, in last resort, about the constitutionality of laws, resolutions, and rules in all cases of controversy between parties." This power disappeared in the 1942 and 1947 constitutions. [Fn. 45, Chap. III.]

twenty-eight in 1944, twenty-seven in 1945, fourteen in 1946, and fourteen in the first half of 1947. (In 1942 there were fifteen provinces with a
governor in each, and eighteen after 1945.)

Besides the governors, occasionally the executive names special commissioners for several provinces of one whole area. These commissioners
are used to carry out special policies for a given area.

We shall not enter into a study of the municipal councils. Mayors
(síndicos) and councilmen are elected every five years by direct vote of the
inhabitants of the *común* (county or district) (Articles 76 to 78 of the
Constitution). If there is any vacancy, it is covered by their alternates. The
only difference is that in the counties the game of resignations is usually
handled by the local council of the Dominican party, although a personal
decision by Trujillo may be a factor in important towns.

Combination of Powers in One Single Chief

According to the Constitution, the Dominican Republic follows the
United States system of division of powers. They are three: legislative,
executive, and judicial, elected in different ways and in appearance acting
in balance. In practice, not only do two of those branches lack all power
(as we have already analyzed), but there is not even a real functional
difference between officeholders in the three branches.

It is normal that an outgoing secretary of state becomes a legislator,
and the legislators are a quarry from which can be mined candidates for
governors, diplomats, and judges. In fact, Congress is a resting place for
an official who for months or years has exercised a position that requires
hard work, and at the same time the human reserve from which to obtain
at any moment the persons required as substitutes for other active
positions.

We shall mention some examples of these interchanges between the
three branches of the state. . . . [*Transfers of membership from one chamber to the other were frequent.*] Interchanges between the cabinet and the
Congress are also frequent. If one secretary retires without falling into disgrace or even if he is in relative disgrace, it is normal for him to be elected
as a senator or deputy. The first of those changes occurred on May 13,
1931, when a former secretary of war was elected deputy; [*many later ones
followed*]. . . . Exchanges between deputies and governors, in the same or
different provinces, are so frequent that it would be pointless to detail
cases. There have also been exchanges of members of the other branches
of the government with the Supreme Court. The changes also involve the
Dominican party.

Less frequent are shifts involving commanders of the army, because
this means their transfer to civilian life. Nevertheless, it has happened at

times. On November 3, 1936, the chief of staff, Aníbal J. Trujillo, became a deputy; on January 3, 1942, General José García ceased to be secretary of war, and on the next day was elected a senator; in July, 1944, General Fernando A. Sánchez was transferred from being chief of staff to a senatorship, and in January, 1945, was restored as a general. Also interesting is the case of Federico Fiallo, a senator between two periods as general, and a deputy before being named chief of police.

No more data are necessary to show the pattern. Secretaries of state, congressmen, justices of the Supreme Court, and governors come and go, exchange positions among themselves, and accordingly lack any stability whatsoever. Under these circumstances, any division of powers is impossible, and, even less, a balance among them. Each one fulfills a mechanical role at a given moment, and all of them simply obey instructions coming from above.

The only power in the Dominican Republic is Trujillo, because it is not even possible to speak of the supremacy of the executive. If the president of the Republic is not Rafael L. Trujillo, the occupant of the post may at any time "be resigned." With the exception of Peynado, who died while president, the other two presidents have also been subject to the game of political musical chairs: Troncoso de la Concha resigned as president of the Republic in May, 1942, and in January, 1943, was elected president of the Senate (not by the people, but in a manipulation of resignations). In the other case, Héctor B. Trujillo was promoted from being secretary of war and chief of the army for about twelve years to be titular president of the Republic; he had also resigned in 1942 as secretary of war and navy, in order to facilitate the constitutional game which made his brother president of the Republic three months before the official inauguration.

With good reason, then, the Dominicans when they refer to Trujillo do not call him president if he is such, or Benefactor if he is resting. They call him simply: The Chief. This position is not mentioned in the Constitution, but it is the only one which needs neither election nor resignation.

Territorial Changes

Although this aspect of Dominican political life seems to have nothing in common with the powers of the state, it is wise to consider here the changes of provinces and of territorial names because they also reflect another symptom of instability.

The constituent assembly of 1942 purposely modified Article 4 of the Constitution in order to facilitate these changes by law of Congress, having as a goal the creation of the new Trujillo Province carved out of the national district, as it had been established in 1932.

On January 1, 1935, this new Trujillo Province was created. At the same time the remaining territory of the former province of Santo Domingo was transformed into the new national district of the same name. On January 1, 1939, three new provinces were established: Libertador, Benefactor, and Monseñor Merino. On January 1, 1943, the new province of San Rafael came into existence, and in May of the same year the new province of Bahoruco. In January, 1945, the province of Monseñor Merino disappeared, and the new provinces of Trujillo Valdez and La Altagracia were organized. On January 1, 1950, the new province of Independencia was inaugurated, and one year later that of Santiago Rodríguez, and in August, 1952, those of Salcedo and Sánchez Ramírez.

This means that during the Era of Trujillo, eleven new provinces have been created, almost doubling the number of those existing in 1930 (at that time they were twelve). At the same time, many readjustments of counties occurred.

As a complement of this, let us remember the change of name of the capital from Santo Domingo to Ciudad Trujillo, by law on January 11, 1936.

Chapter 4: Insecurity Instead of Freedom

[*The status of human rights and freedoms in 1955 is described herein.*]

It is difficult to document an analysis of human rights and basic individual freedoms in a long dictatorship like Trujillo's, as is true in other Latin American dictatorships. It is possible to mention individual cases of persecution; but those acute cases reveal nothing more and leave no trace, but that vague atmosphere of terror that seals lips and perverts souls. The pretense that characterizes the Dominicans today can not be proved with documentary evidence; it can only be felt by living among them for some months.

There is, however, something symptomatic that can be established. The freedom or the tyranny of a regime is revealed in the daily press. If, in any country, it is possible to criticize the government in the press and qualify as arbitrary its decisions, there is reason to believe in the existence of freedom. But if, in any country, one reads and hears only praise of the ruler and never a criticism, there would be good grounds for suspecting tyranny.

For this reason, the best evidence of the dictatorship of Trujillo in the Dominican Republic and especially of its increase during the first years of the regime is to be found in the pages of its newspapers; in the silence of *Listín Diario* after the middle of 1930, and its new literature of eulogies after the arrest of its editor in 1933; in the limitless praises of Trujillo (especially in *La Nación* and *El Caribe*); and in the absolute lack of any criticism (but for a short interlude in *La Opinión* in 1946).

For those living in the Dominican Republic there are many other evidences in the university lectures, in which controversial topics are avoided; in the sudden silence of any group if somebody who is not fully trusted approaches; and in the public praises of Trujillo by those who criticize him in private.

[121]

Today that vague terror is so deep-rooted, that in very few cases are public warnings necessary — although from time to time they occur. The main weapons of the regime continue to be the army and the police force, against which no resistance at all is possible, but the most effective one is the widespread espionage system.

The dictatorship of Trujillo is not so bloody as exiles affirm. Some cases of murder occur. But the Trujillist style is more characterized by another kind of bloodless domination: starvation and the certainty that it is not possible to earn a living without full proof of active adherence to the regime. Trujillo prefers forcing the collaboration of a former enemy, which humiliates him, to eliminating him violently, for in the end, this reflects upon the regime. Such cases are numerous.

In this chapter, we shall attempt only to describe in the most objective and documentary form possible the restriction of individual freedoms, mentioning some of the more notorious cases of violence. In other chapters we shall complete the study with an analysis of political parties, labor unions, the press, the university, and other areas of control.

Constitutional Principles Regarding Human Rights

In the classical manner of constitutional law in Latin America since its first texts were drafted, the Constitution of the Dominican Republic has always contained a chapter devoted almost in its entirety to enumerating the basic individual rights. They are imported directly from the French Declaration of the Rights of Man and of the Citizen and are characteristic of peoples who achieved their independence in a colonial regime in which the king had absolute power and the individuals had no rights.[1] What happened is that very soon after those declarations, individual rights were ignored in daily practice.

The Dominican constitution in force enumerates these individual rights in its Title II, Articles 6 and 7. The first contains twelve paragraphs

---

[1] This characteristic seems to be one more symbol which reflects the origin of the Latin American republics. In the Constitution of the United States, civil rights were introduced later as amendments to a constitution whose purpose had been to organize the new federal government of a people with a certain tradition of freedom. In Latin America, the new republics were born out of a colonial period in which the king had concentrated in himself all power "by divine right," and the people had no rights of their own. The greatest care of the constituents was not so much to organize a government but to guarantee the new individual freedoms, and for that purpose they wrote them down in constitutions, believing, perhaps, that such a solemn proclamation would make them stronger and permanent. The initial symbolic meaning remains; even in the constitutions of retrogressive regimes, the declaration of individual rights is repeated, although in practice such rights are ignored. [Fn. 1, Chap. IV.]

enumerating concrete rights; the second affirms that this enumeration is not restrictive. It is fitting to add other articles of the Constitution referring to rights of a political nature. . . .

[*There follows (pp. 409–10 of the manuscript) a summary paraphrase, or quotation of personal rights as embodied in Articles 6, 88, 89, 90, 93, and 103 of the prevailing constitution.*]

In general, all these individual rights reproduce with slight variations the classical declaration in constitutional laws of French origin. The most important modification is contained in Article 2, where, since 1942, a series of rights of the workers is listed, adopting the new labor trend initiated in Latin America by the Mexican constitution of 1917 and reaffirmed by the Cuban constitution of 1940.

According to Article 33, Paragraphs 7 and 8, and Article 49, Paragraph 8, it is possible to declare a state of siege and suspend some of these individual freedoms, or to declare a state of national emergency with suspension of all of them except that of the inviolability of life. This suspension of constitutional guarantees has been declared only once during the Era of Trujillo — on the occasion of the 1930 hurricane. Not even in periods of international war, as in 1941–45, or in moments of possible invasion, as in 1947 and 1949, have they been suspended again; it has not been necessary.

Neither do laws exist in the Dominican Republic restricting these freedoms in general, as is typical in the ideological European dictatorships. The only restrictive law we know of is that approved in June, 1947, prohibiting communist, anarchist, and similar groups. Aside from this, democratic appearances are respected.

Individual Rights in Practice

One should establish that different degrees exist among these individual rights. Some of them have an almost normal application, others are merely restricted, some do not exist in practice.

The only individual right that the author found to be more or less fully allowed in practice, during his six-year stay in the country and in his subsequent research, was that proclaimed in Paragraph 3 of Article 6, dealing with freedom of conscience and worship, and in Article 93 which defines the relations between the state and the Catholic church.

Officially, almost all Dominicans are Catholic. There is an official separation of the church and the state, but in fact the Catholic religion has an unofficial status. There is no national holiday nor any tribute paid to the present regime that does not include a Catholic ceremony, almost always performed in the Cathedral of Santo Domingo. But at the same time, freedom of worship for the Protestant minority is respected, and in the last few years, for some Jewish refugees. The only limitation (which is constitutional according to the last sentence of Paragraph 3) is that affecting the practices of African origin usually called voodoo,[2] but as a matter of fact they are also practiced in private by some people of the lower class.[3]

There is another freedom that is almost fully applied, if we view it with a Latin mind and not a Saxon one. We refer to the freedom of education embodied in Paragraph 4 of Article 6. It is not the freedom of education of the United States, because in the Dominican Republic, as generally in the Latin countries, the government determines the lines of education at all levels; but within these broad limits, there are private schools and colleges. Up to now, there is only one governmental monopoly in education, that of the University of Santo Domingo.[4]

The restriction upon the freedom of education is of a different kind, a vague one. It consists in the difficulty of teaching or discussing in the classrooms any ideas that might directly or indirectly stir up dissatisfaction with the policies of the Trujillist regime.

There is a third group of individual rights, normally respected although in concrete instances they may be openly violated. These refer to the right of property (Paragraph 7), that of literary and artistic property (Paragraph 11), and the inviolability of the home (Paragraph 9).

The right of property, in its normal form as well as in the special connotation of Paragraph 11, is not usually endangered except if the private interests of Trujillo and his relatives or favorites enter into play. If such an interest appears, it has been proved repeatedly that it is useless to attempt any legal action and it would even be difficult to find a lawyer

---

[2] Paragraph 3 of Artcle 6 says: "Freedom of conscience and of worship without any other limitation than the respect owed to public order and good customs." A law of September, 1943, established punishment for those practicing *voudou* or *lua*. *Bol. Sen.*, Sept. 1943. [Fn. 4, Chap. IV.]

[3] The voodoo (or *voudou*) of Haitian origin is not the only religious practice of African origin that the author found in the Dominican Republic, practiced more or less clandestinely. In one of his trips he found traces of another religion called *congo*, on the borders of the Ozama River near the village of Las Minas; it seemed to be two different specimens, the *congo criollo* and the *congo holandés*. Besides these religious practices, there are also many hybrid superstitions mingled with the Catholic ceremonies of the interior, especially on the occasion of deaths and other important events. [Fn. 5, Chap. IV.]

[4] There is reason to believe that at present and profiting from the recently signed concordat with the Holy See, the archbishop of Santo Domingo is negotiating the opening of a free Catholic university, perhaps to be located in Santiago. For the time being, some lectures are given at the so-called Free University, in the nearby city, La Vega. [Fn. 6, Chap. IV.]

ready to defend the case.[5] In 1939, a Spanish refugee started a fishing business in the capital city; a short time afterward, he received a visit from two unofficial agents who suggested that he share his possible profits in exchange for protection; he thereupon decided to abandon the enterprise and leave the country. About 1944 or 1945, a fruit-juice factory was started, which a Spanish refugee who had a patent for a chemical formula entered as a partner; this refugee visited the author some years later in New York and showed him documents proving that he had a contract with a personal agent of Trujillo for this joint business, despite which he had been forced to leave the business and the country because of personal threats.

Inviolability of the home is, in fact, generally respected. But nobody doubts that this right will not be respected at all if, one day, the police decide to search a house or to make an arrest. Such cases have become so routine that they are no longer surprising. It is also natural among Dominicans to suspect that the servants or a visitor may be a spy of the regime; the fact is that not even in the intimacy of the home are they accustomed to speaking freely if somebody who is not of the utmost confidence is present. To engage in conversation it is preferable that two persons be alone, and better still, out in the open.[6]

The fourth group of this category is formed by two political rights, so nonexistent for years that the regime does not even bother to restrict them. These are the freedom of speech (Paragraph 5) and the freedom of assembly (Paragraph 6, completed by Article 103). It would not occur to anyone in the Dominican Republic to hold a meeting, public or private, in which this pretended freedom could be interpreted as meaning the right to criticize the regime and its policies; much less to organize a political party or similar association, without previous approval from the government.

The fifth group is formed by four other freedoms which apparently are respected, but are so restricted or violated that they are practically nonexistent. They are the inviolability of life (Paragraph 1), the inviolability of correspondence (Paragraph 8), the freedom of movement (Paragraph 10), and individual security (Paragraph 12).

---

[5] The author can personally vouch for this fact. [Fn. 7, Chap. IV.]

[6] See Bustamante, *Satrapía*, pp. 87–89. In 1946, a newspaperman living in New York went to the Dominican Republic, to come to some agreement with Trujillo regarding a press service for propaganda, which lasted for more than a year. He had dinner one evening in the home of José Almoina, private secretary of the president, and Almoina took him to the garden before talking because he was uncertain whether a microphone had been installed inside the house (data given by this newspaperman to the author). [Fn. 10, Chap. IV.]

Inviolability of life: According to the Constitution, death sentences cannot be imposed except in cases of treason or espionage during time of war. This is the principle, and, in fact, not a single death sentence has been imposed during the Era of Trujillo. But the case is not so simple as that. Some people have died "in battle" against the public forces, such as General Desiderio Arias in 1931 or some seven invaders of Luperón in 1949. In other cases, they have died in prison, without any explanation about their disappearance. In still other cases, they have been found dead on the roads after peculiar accidents, or they seem to have been "suicides," like some leaders of the 1946 strike in La Romana.

We must discuss another matter that bears upon Paragraph 1, Article 6 of the Constitution, because it reveals the style of legal simulation in the regime; it is the well known *ley de fuga* (law of escape). If a common criminal deserves the death sentence because of his crimes or because he is potentially dangerous, it is simply pretended that he attempted to escape and that the police or the soldiers watching him were forced to shoot and kill him. In general, the victims of this system are murderers and many are robbers.[7] In the Dominican Republic everybody knows this trick; but it recently received wide publicity in the press, on the occasion of the holdup of the branch of the Royal Bank of Canada in Santiago in November, 1954.

In this case, it was a question of a holdup which resulted in four deaths, at least two of them premeditated. However, as there is no death sentence in the Dominican Republic, the criminals were sentenced in December to thirty and twenty years in prison. The next morning, ten of them "attempted to escape," and the guards were forced to shoot and kill them; to make matters easier, the "escape" was attempted on the rifle range of the army. *La Nación* printed individual pictures of the ten corpses; *El Caribe* limited itself to printing two pictures. Legal appearances were maintained, and a warning was served.

Inviolability of the mail: The author himself saw during his time in the Dominican Republic how censorship is practiced in the central post office. During his stay, there were two different censorships, one for letters and another for books and magazines. Censorship of letters was exercised in person by the superintendent of the post office in a small room in the

---

[7] The author knew of some cases during his stay in the Dominican Republic. One of them was reported by a certain physician in the eastern region. He had examined, in the past, the corpse of a person murdered under mysterious circumstances but obviously the victim of a common crime; suspicion pointed to a cousin of the victim, who denied the accusation. Some time later this physician asked the local sergeant of police about the results of this investigation, and the latter answered bluntly: "The sharks have eaten him already" (referring to the suspected murderer). [Fn. 12, Chap. IV.]

basement; the envelopes were examined one by one before being distributed. This does not mean that all are opened; it seems that the rule is to allow those to pass which come from and are addressed to persons who are not suspect at a given moment.[8] A certain percentage of all letters is always opened, just in case.

Correspondence coming from or addressed to dubious persons is read. Of course, this censorship is secret, and the envelopes do not usually show traces of having been opened; proof of the violation of this right becomes evident only when somebody is called by the police or goes to jail as a consequence of an indiscreet letter. As for censorship of books and periodical publications, it is divided into two categories. Publications arriving in packages for general distribution and sale are always examined before delivery to the bookstores is permitted, so that several issues of *Time, Bohemia,*[9] and other magazines have been confiscated in their entirety. As for newspapers and magazines addressed to individuals, they pile up in the office of the censor, who if he has time reads them carefully before destroying them or allowing them to circulate; but often they wind up in a purifying bonfire when too many numbers accumulate.[10]

Freedom of movement: On the surface there are no public restrictions except those which pertain to entering or leaving the country; in both cases, great difficulty is experienced. The consulates do not grant visas without previously checking the political ideology of the visitor, and in this regard, documentary evidence exists.[11] Not even the Office of Foreign Relations issues a passport without a previous investigation, which is often delayed indefinitely; the airports are closely watched.

---

[8] As a consequence of this percentage of letters not being opened, it happened, for instance, that the issue of *Reader's Digest* for April, 1946, in which an article against Trujillo appeared was not allowed to circulate in the Dominican Republic, because the censor confiscated the packages; but a Jewish refugee received his clipping by air mail without being suspected by the censor. [Fn. 13, Chap. IV.]

[9] It seems that the circulation of the Cuban magazine *Bohemia* has been prohibited during the last years. In the forties it used to arrive weekly, except for issues in which references were made to Trujillo. [Fn. 14, Chap. IV.]

[10] One of the censors himself explained to the author this system, and one day showed him the pile of packages ready for the fire. This lack of time to inspect all packages made it possible for the issue of *Foreign Affairs* of July, 1941, in which an article by John Gunther about "Hispaniola" (Dominican Republic and Haiti) was printed including a reference to the massacre of Haitians of 1937, to be discovered some time later in the library of the Secretaryship of Foreign Relations; the issue was returned to the library after the part containing the accusing pages had been carefully removed. On the censorship of correspondence, see Bustamante, *Satrapía,* pp. 72–73. [Fn. 15, Chap. IV.]

[11] Circular letter from the undersecretary of foreign relations to the members of the Dominican foreign service, on October 14, 1946 (reproduced in photostat by the *Boletín ARDE,* No. 9–10, Oct. 21, 1946).... [Fn. 16, Chap. IV.]

Special documents are not required for travel within the country, but the police exercise careful supervision of all traffic from town to town. On the roads there are numerous stationary army patrols that halt vehicles to request the identity cards of the travelers and to note the number of the passing vehicle. These patrols are found especially at the exits from the capital and other important cities, as well as at strategic spots on the main highways. The alleged reason for this supervision is the desire to facilitate the investigation of any possible accident on the road and to make certain everyone is carrying his identity card and paying his annual fee. In fact, it is an efficient method of controlling the movements of people under suspicion. Another form of police supervision is the obligation to fill out a form upon arriving at any hotel or guest house, a form that the owner must send in every day to the police mentioning all personal data regarding transients; there is also documentary evidence of this supervision.

Individual security: According to Paragraph 12, Article 6, nobody may be arrested without a previous judicial order except in the event of being surprised in the very act of a crime. All arrested persons must be delivered to a judge within forty-eight hours after arrest or be set free, and every person arrested without cause or without the required legal formalities must be released immediately, either at his own request or at the request of any other person (habeas corpus). The reality during the twenty-five years of the Era shows that not one of those provisions is applied, and nobody would dream of presenting a writ of habeas corpus in case of political arrests. If the police decide to arrest someone, he is arrested; sometimes the police detention is prolonged for months before the case is solved by freeing the prisoner or by a trial that provides a delayed legality for everything that has happened.

The question of freedom of labor, with its new rights for workers, has purposely been left for final consideration. These rights are a recent acquisition, embodied in the 1942 constitutional reform. Their development up to 1946 was quite different from their development since that time. In general, it can be said that they have benefited the working classes and that they are applied as long as they do not conflict with official interests of the regime or the private interests of Trujillo as a businessman.

A few words more about the general principles mentioned in Articles 88 and 89. They are remnants of previous liberal regimes. Today they have no meaning. What rules is not the law, but the will of the Benefactor. Nobody would think of demanding the annulment of a governmental decision because it lacked legality.

Political Freedoms

According to Paragraph 5, Article 6 of the Constitution, "the right to express thoughts without subjecting them to previous censorship" is inherent to human beings, restricted only by this limitation: "The law will establish penalties applicable to those who act against the honor of persons, the social order, or the public peace." According to Paragraph 6 of the same article, "freedom of association and of assembly for peaceful ends" is also inherent in human beings. And according to Article 103, "the organization of political parties and associations is free, in accordance with the principles established in the second article of this Constitution."

Let us note the application of these constitutional principles in detail.

The hard truth is that freedom of speech has not existed since May, 1930; the last use of this freedom during the election campaign of that year was crushed by the terror of "the 42nd" and the post-electoral arrests of leaders of the National-Progressive Alliance. Reading the Dominican press during these twenty-five years would suffice to prove this, but perhaps it will be useful to analyze some concrete cases of relative freedom of public expression in order to evaluate its nuances; the exception proves the rule.

The author personally witnessed some of these cases during his stay in the Dominican Republic. In October, 1942, the president of the Basque government-in-exile, José A. de Aguirre, visited the Dominican Republic for two days. His visa was requested and granted with difficulty. Then it was suggested that he give a lecture in the university; the president of the university favored the idea but he did not dare approve it without previous authorization by the president of the Republic, which was also granted. When the arrival of President Aguirre was announced in the press, the minister of Franco Spain made an oral protest to the Office of Foreign Relations, which relayed the protest to the organizers of the trip and warned them not to mention Aguirre's title as president and not to have him speak in public about Spanish politics. The Chamber of Deputies appointed a committee of three of its members to attend all functions honoring Aguirre, including the lecture in the university and a semi-private dinner. Not the slightest restrictions were imposed for the lecture on "The Spirit of Freedom in the Peoples of the World"; Dr. Troncoso de la Concha presided, and the room was full of people who enthusiastically applauded the lecturer. The Office of Foreign Relations only requested advance copies of the speeches to be delivered at the dinner by some refugees resident in the country.[12] One can say with all justice that in this case a freedom prevailed which the Dominicans lack.

In the same way, Spanish refugees enjoyed freedom to hold political meetings in private places; they included, remarkably enough, the activities of the Communists through their front, Centro Democrático Español.

---

[12] Some documentary evidence of this trip can be found in *La Nación* in October, 1942, and the *Bol. Cam.*, session of Oct. 8. [Fn. 22, Chap. IV.]

This club was watched discreetly by the police, but its activities were not curtailed until 1945. Non-Communist groups had no difficulties until 1947. Fascist Spaniards also had the same freedom to act during the period of the Spanish civil war, and the local branch of the Falange Española was active until it disbanded of its own accord at the end of 1939.

Foreigners thus enjoyed in general a freedom of speech that the natives could not even dream about.

On the debit side of the record, one must point out that street demonstrations which the different national groups of exiles had planned in Ciudad Trujillo to celebrate the surrender of Germany were never allowed by the authorities, although they used delaying tactics instead of openly prohibiting them. It seems that in this case the government feared the fact of a public demonstration in which Dominicans might participate. On the other hand, the Americans in La Romana held a similar public demonstration in the streets after the surrender of Japan.

Concerning the Dominicans, the only variation from this silence, except to voice praise of the regime, was during the period in 1946 when, first, *La Opinión* for a few weeks, and, afterward, the Popular Socialist party (Communist) and the Democratic Youth, for another short period, were able to carry on a moderate campaign of opposition. The political nuances of this period are worth analyzing.

Let us consider, first, the campaign of *La Opinión*. It started in January, 1946, as suggested by the president. The secretary of the presidency himself visited the editor to request that campaign, adding that the government desired to direct it and was ready to subsidize the editor personally. The editor, a former Spanish refugee, did not accept those conditions and requested an interview with Trujillo himself. In this interview, Trujillo agreed to the requested freedom of action on condition that neither the president nor the army be attacked. The first evidence of the new stand was the printing, as authorized by Trujillo himself, of a letter signed by several Spanish non-Communist exiled leaders against the person hiding behind the generic pen name of "A Spanish Republican," attacking the new Venezuelan government of Acción Democrática and the ambassador of the Spanish Republican government-in-exile in Caracas; no name was mentioned at all, but it was generally known that he was the private secretary of Trujillo, José Almoina.

During the following weeks, *La Opinión* carried on an active campaign of criticism of social and labor problems, including the cost of living. Among other things, it published the stenographic record of the national committee on wages in which it was affirmed that some Dominican sugar cane workers were at that time making twenty-five cents a day without meals. When this campaign of *La Opinión* entered the political field by printing a letter saying that Trujillo was not the only possible presidential candidate, the government became alarmed because of the favorable reaction it produced among wide groups of students and others. The campaign was then stopped, and a short time later Trujillo bought the newspaper. A new editor amended its policy to conform to the usual Trujillist line, but finally the newspaper disappeared permanently.

With regard to the campaign of the Popular Socialist party, for several weeks the party was allowed to hold public meetings until that riotous one in Ciudad Trujillo which offered a pretext for repressive measures. The formation of the party and its first activities were encouraged by Trujillo's agents, who went to Cuba to discuss terms with Communist exiles; but a similar freedom of speech in favor of the majority of Dominicans who wanted a change of policies and abhorred communism was not permitted. The campaign was presented in these terms: the only enemies of the regime are the Communists, and Trujillo is saving the democratic and spiritual values of the Dominican people against the threat of a disturbing and atheistic communism.

During twenty-five years, these are the only known examples of free speech and political activities not exclusively concerned with mere praise of Trujillo and his work. The Trujillista party as well as the National Democratic and National Labor parties later, were no more than fronts organized and backed by the government to simulate an appearance of multiplicity of political parties during a period in which world events were moving towards wider democracy.

Not only is there no freedom of speech, but on the contrary it is possible to cite countless instances in which public opinion favorable to Trujillo and his regime is forcibly created. Instances include those public demonstrations in the streets in which public employees are asked to participate by departmental order; one of the best examples was the demonstration against the Venezuelan government held on November 10, 1945. But there are more concrete cases.

The blank that all public employees were forced to fill out and send to the "Purification Commission for Public Employees" in 1945 sought not only information about relatives and other people not friendly to the regime, but also the answers to such questions as the following: "11. What political work have you done? 12. Details about your cooperation with the present government: (a) meetings you attend; (b) meetings you do not attend; (c) propaganda you have carried on in favor of the Government; (d) how many nonpolitical articles have you written? (e) how many political articles? (f) how many talks, lectures, and speeches have you made on topics of interest for the Government? (g) what other demonstrations of loyalty have you given? (h) do you attend punctually the *Te Deums* on National Holidays, political-cultural meetings, agricultural meetings, assemblies of the Dominican Party, etc.? (i) what special work of a political character have you done during the current year? (j) which activities did you carry on before being a public employee? (k) before being a member of the Dominican Party, what were your political activities?"

In the second place, was the circular addressed by Trujillo himself to all public employees one year later,[13] in which he said: "I want to know if you have had conversations with persons who are enemies, unfriendly, or neutral towards the Government, and what efforts you made to influence those persons in its favor. If you did not, what was your reason?"

In the third place, a question was included in almost every government blank, including passports or permits for imports, requesting the number and date of registration in the Dominican party.

Given these circumstances, it is not surprising in the Dominican Republic to see letters printed in the newspapers, in which a close relative — even a parent — repudiates those who have made statements abroad or have carried on activities of opposition to Trujillo's regime. These statements have also been occasionally forced from foreigners for different reasons.

Arrests Without Indictment, and Murders

Despite the guarantees offered in Paragraph 12 of Article 6 of the Constitution, everybody in the Dominican Republic believes that he may be arrested by the police without any judicial order and that his arrest may be prolonged indefinitely. In some cases the arrest is brief, if there are only suspicions or it is in the nature of a warning; in other cases the arrest ends finally in a trial which legalizes the situation, although the alleged crime occurred many years before; and in still others, the individual just disappears.

It is difficult to prove this with documentary evidence but in the highest positions of the Dominican government there are persons who know these facts from personal experience such as Dr. Manuel de Jesús Troncoso de la Concha, president of the Republic from 1940 to 1942 and president of the Senate from 1943 until his death in 1955, who had been arrested in 1930; or such as his successor as president of the Senate and holder of the same office from 1930 to 1938, Mario Fermín Cabral, who was arrested in 1941 after carrying out his duty of sending to jail and humiliating General José Estrella; or such as the editor of *El Caribe,* Germán Ornes Coiscou, who was arrested for a few days in 1945.

---

[13] Letter, June 21, 1946, reproduced in photostat by the *Boletín ARDE* No. 16, Dec. 9, 1945. [Fn. 27, Chap. IV.]

The best description of the prisons during the Era of Trujillo is the book *Una Gestapo en América,* by Juan Isidro Jimenes-Grullón. He describes his own experiences from the time of his arrest on July 19, 1934, on suspicion of being implicated in the conspiracy of Santiago, until his pardon on October 31, 1935. During that year he was sent to the penitentiary of Nigua, so well known at the beginning of the regime, and to the solitary cells of Fortress Ozama in the capital. He suffered for a long time as a political prisoner at the mercy of General Fiallo and finally went through a trial and sentence; he was beaten and witnessed the more serious tortures suffered by other prisoners. He mentions by name and gives details of the cases of prisoners who were killed in prison. His book seems objective and at the same time dramatic; it has an authenticity stemming from direct sources of information.

The novel *Cementerio sin Cruces* by Andrés Requena is essentially true, but it cannot be mentioned as a source because the author was not an eyewitness and uses hearsay evidence. The events belong to a later period, when the young boys of the Popular Socialist party and the Democratic Youth were arrested after their activities in 1946–47. Requena was himself murdered a few months after the publication of this novel.

The author of this study had also occasion to speak with some persons who were in the penitentiary of Nigua during the first years of the regime, such as Lic. José A. Bonilla Atiles, and with others who have been in Fortress Ozama in more recent years. He has also spoken with one of the survivors of the 1935 plot against Trujillo in the capital, Ing. J. C. Alfonseca.

The penitentiary of Nigua was closed in April, 1938. Its disappearance marks the end of a period. Its prisoners were reportedly tortured in order to force confessions; most of the time they worked in the fields cutting grass with machetes.[14] It is not surprising that some persons, after being there a few days, preferred to surrender unconditionally to the regime, and from the penitentiary, went on to occupy positions of great importance in the government; one among them was the nephew of the ousted President Horacio Vásquez.

This susceptibility to conversion may explain the relative benignity of the Trujillo regime. Hicks mentions 134 victims by name in his book;[15]

---

[14] It is customary for prisoners, the common as well as the political ones, to be put to work on private farms of members of the Trujillo family or of chiefs of the army. [Fn. 36, Chap. IV.]

[15] Hicks, *Blood in the Streets,* pp. 228–30. There is another long list of murders in the *Boletín del Partido Revolucionario Dominicano,* New York, March, 1954. [Fn. 37, Chap. IV.]

but that is a small number compared with the victims of that other vague terror to which we will refer later. Trujillo and his agents resort to extreme measures infrequently; it is more efficient to subdue the will, in order later to humiliate people by forcing them into collaboration.

However, there are also cases of presumed political murders. The best known case was that of Virgilio Martínez Reyna and his wife in June, 1930. *Listín Diario* denounced it at the time, but the best official confirmation of this crime was made public by the regime itself ten years later, when General Estrella was arrested in 1940 and tried because of that murder, which he admitted.

Detailed reference will be made to only one of the most notorious public murders during recent years. It is that of the businessman Porfirio Ramírez and seven other persons on the night of June 1, 1950. Porfirio Ramírez died because he was the brother of the chief of staff of the 1949 invasion. He was in the trucking business. That evening he departed from the capital in a truck loaded with flour, together with his driver Juan Rosario, an assistant driver, and three handymen; at the last moment, an old man and a woman requested that he take them also. About two miles from the city, they stopped at the usual military police post, and a sergeant ordered him to take six soldiers to the bridge of the Nizao River between San Cristóbal and Baní. This was the place chosen for the murder. When the truck arrived there, Lieutenant General Federico Fiallo in person (at that time chief of staff of the air force) and several officers stopped the truck, while the soldiers held the travelers at gun point. Ramírez was killed on the spot. The remaining persons were carried to a nearby curve to simulate an accident on the road, where they were beaten to death. But the driver, Juan Rosario, did not die then, although he pretended to be dead even when the criminals set the truck on fire; this time, a victim and witness survived for a few hours and could tell what had happened before he was finished off at the Baní hospital.[16]

Murders Abroad

Enemies of Trujillo have also been murdered in foreign countries on at least three occasions; and in these three cases it is possible to prove the crime, although the authors still remain unpunished.

---

[16] The Cuban magazine *Bohemia,* July 2, 1950, published a detailed report of this murder. Another brother of the victim, Dr. Víctor M. Ramírez, left the country with his family and signed a complete affidavit in Havana on June 17 (this affidavit was fully reproduced by the publication of New York exiles, *Pluma y Espada,* July 20, 1950). [Fn. 44, Chap. IV.]

The first murder took place in New York City on April 28, 1935.[17] That evening, an unknown person went to a modest rooming house at 87 Hamilton Place and asked for Dr. Angel Morales. Morales had been vice-presidential candidate for the Alliances in the 1930 elections and was forced to escape into exile afterwards; he had been declared a traitor to the Fatherland because of his activities against Trujillo abroad. Morales was not at home, and his fellow roomer, Lic. Sergio Bencosme, appeared when the landlady told him that somebody was asking for Morales; Bencosme was shaving at the moment, and it seems that the murderer thought that it was Morales himself when he shot Bencosme to death. Ten months later the district attorney's office was able to get an indictment from the grand jury against Luis ("Chichí") de la Fuente Rubirosa as the murderer of Bencosme;[18] when the required action was started to extradite him from the Dominican Republic, where he went after the murder, the official answer was that no such individual existed there.[19]

The second case can not yet be qualified officially as murder (because the body was never recovered) but its complete disappearance is doubtless evidence of what happened. This time the victim was Mauricio Báez, a labor leader who was given asylum in the Mexican embassy after the strike of 1946 and was later a leader of the Popular Socialist party, and who again went into exile in Cuba some time later (breaking with the party at

---

[17] See *New York Times*, April 29, 1935, front page, and other New York newspapers of those days. Recently, the magazine *Confidential*, July, 1954, revived the case, profiting by the publicity received by Porfirio Rubirosa on the occasion of his brief marriage with Barbara Hutton. [Fn. 45, Chap. IV.]

[18] *La Prensa*, New York, Feb. 19, 1936. This newspaper referred to "Chichí" as "supposed to be an officer in the Army in Santo Domingo." [Fn. 46, Chap. IV.]

[19] The author has plenty of confidential information concerning this case, received from a person who at that time was a member of the staff of the district attorney in New York City. He has also spoken with Dr. Angel Morales. The identity of "Chichí" de la Fuente Rubirosa as the actual murderer who shot Bencosme to death was fully confirmed; that source affirms that "Chichí" appeared later dressed in the uniform of a Dominican lieutenant in a picture with several co-officers. When the official representatives of the New York police went to the Dominican Republic to start the negotiations for the extradition of "Chichí," they were shown the list of officers in the Dominican army to prove to them that such a Lieutenant Fuente Rubirosa did not exist at all. It was generally believed that he also was eliminated. A fascinating aspect of this case was the peculiar presence in New York City at that time of Porfirio Rubirosa, a cousin of the murderer. Porfirio arrived in New York on the S.S. *Coamo* on April 16, and departed in a hurry the day before the murder. The office of the district attorney wanted to question him about the case, but he has been protected since then by diplomatic immunity every time he comes to New York. He is a very peculiar diplomat; officially a minister counselor in the Dominican legation at Paris, but living in every other part of the world. [Fn. 47, Chap. IV.]

the same time). On December 10, 1950, three individuals went to his home in Havana and persuaded him to go with them apparently to see Congressman Enrique C. Henríquez (a Dominican by birth and an enemy of Trujillo); it seems that Báez at the beginning suspected something and refused to go, but he finally agreed.[20] He has never been found, dead or alive. The Dominican legation in Havana attempted to place the blame upon other exiles, because Báez was said to be in communication with the chargé d' affairs, Felix W. Bernardino (appointed consul general in New York a few days before), so that he might be granted amnesty to return to the Dominican Republic.

The third murder was that of Andrés Requena in New York City.[21] On the evening of October 2, 1952, Requena left his home about 9:00 p.m. after saying to his fiancée: "I'm going to see the people you know." About 10:30, he took a cab on the corner of Sixth Avenue and 57th Street; a man "in a raincoat" accompanied him, who later never gave himself up to the police. He gave the taxi driver the address of 243 Madison Avenue in the downtown section of the city, and as soon as he entered the hall he was killed with five bullets. Again in this case the Dominican consulate general attempted to blame Dominican exiles because Requena was in communication with the consul; but Requena himself had brought to the printing shop where an anti-Trujillo paper was published an article in which he told the whole story.[22] Two months before, he had tried to get his mother and sister out of the Dominican Republic, and a travel agent had told him that Consul General Bernardino wanted to discuss the matter with him. They agreed that the Dominican government would allow the exit of the two women if Requena accepted the compromise of not writing any more articles against either Trujillo or the Bernardino family; Requena accepted the proposal, but at the same time he reported to his exiled friends that as soon as his relatives arrived in the United States, he would again start his campaign. Finally he lost all hope that the Dominican gov-

---

[20] See the Cuban newspapers and magazines of that time, especially *Bohemia*, Dec. 17, 1950. The Báez case was denounced to the International Bureau of Labor, in a document signed on March 10, 1951, by three Dominican labor leaders in exile (*Quisqueya Libre*, August, 1951). [Fn. 48, Chap. IV.]

[21] See *New York Times*, Oct. 4, 5, and 7, 1952; *Time*, Oct. 13, 1952; *La Prensa*, Oct. 4, 1952, *ff.*; *El Diario de Nueva York*, Oct. 5, *ff.*; and all other New York newspapers of those days. [Fn. 49, Chap. IV.]

[22] This article was translated into English and printed by *The Daily Compass*, Oct. 7, 1952. The original Spanish article was printed in *Pluma y Espada*, Oct.–Nov., 1952. [Fn. 50, Chap. IV.]

ernment would fulfill its promise, and decided to renew the fight without waiting longer. It seems that this article was read in the presence of too many persons. The murder of Requena continues officially unsolved.[23]

Just at the time of closing this study, on August 8, 1955, another Dominican exile was murdered in Havana. He was Manuel de Jesús ("Pipí") Hernández Santana, who escaped from the Dominican Republic in 1931 and until his death was active in revolutionary groups.[24]

---

[23] The author knew Andrés Requena personally, and followed very carefully the investigation of this still unsolved murder. It seems that in the beginning the police suspected the exiles, especially the coeditor of *Patria,* Juan M. Díaz; but Díaz was also threatened with death on the next day by telephone, and he remained under police protection for several weeks. The investigation was later directed towards the *confiteros* who had been attracted and were being used by Consul General Bernardino (see *El Diario de Nueva York,* Oct. 9, 1952). There are sound grounds to believe that Requena met from 9:30 to 10:30 with persons who intervened in the negotiations to get the required permission for the exit of his mother and sister from the Dominican Republic; and that he went immediately afterward to an appointment which was a death trap. There is the suspicion that a feminine bait was used for this appointment. Of course, it is believed that the man in the raincoat who accompanied him to a taxicab and never did appear before the police afterwards was what in gangster slang is called "the finger man," and his duty was to confirm that Requena went to the murder place at the right moment. If, then, one considers the place of the crime and other circumstances, it also seems obvious that the murderer must have been very sure of the hour; he could not expose himself to being seen in the hall of a small building.

In connection with this case, there was brought to light the personal background of the Dominican consul general and alternate delegate to the UN, Felix W. Bernardino. He had been sentenced on Jan. 14, 1934, to three years in prison for a homicide committed in the Dominican Republic and later had been restored to all his civic rights by a presidential decree at the beginning of 1939 (*G.O.* 5272). He had been Dominican chargé d'affaires in Cuba during the period immediately preceding the disappearance of Mauricio Báez. One year after Requena's murder, Bernardino was to shoot a Venezuelan at a seaside near Caracas (*Visión,* New York, Nov. 13, 1953). Requena had bitterly attacked in the pages of *Patria* not only Trujillo but also Consul General Bernardino and his sister Minerva; and his friends have reported that he was ready from the very beginning to double-cross Bernardino at the end of the negotiations to get the permit in favor of his mother and sister.

Some New York converted *confiteros* deserved attention those days, and were questioned by the police. One was Adolfo ("Pito") Camarena, named a few weeks later as consul in Los Angeles (*G.O.* 7511), although for some months he did not get there and acted as trusted agent of Bernardino during the subsequent stay of Trujillo in the United States. The *New York Times* (Jan. 6, 1953) printed comments about his sudden success, rising from the position of fruit peddler in New York to consul in Los Angeles, with a salary of $18,000 a year. . . .

Despite the brutality of this murder, the exiles were not fearful and often organized picket lines in Washington and New York during the stay of Trujillo, carrying a symbolic coffin and signs asking: "Who murdered Requena?" [Fn. 51, Chap. IV.]

[24] At the closing of this study, this crime continues to be unsolved. But, from the very beginning, the Cuban press judged it a possible political murder (see, for instance, *El País,* August 9, 1955). The magazine *Bohemia,* on August 21, 1955, gave extraordinary importance to this murder, with ample information about this case and reference to other Dominicans killed in the past. [Fn. 52, Chap. IV.]

The Submission of a People

The details given up to this point do not reflect the state of mind of the citizens during the Era of Trujillo. The most serious things are not the illegal arrests, or even the murders; more serious is the total destruction of the spirit of a people. That destruction is obvious in all social structures, especially in the university.

The Dominican people of today are sad, even at their parties. They lack spontaneity, and it is so because from childhood they are used to repressing their thoughts and expressions. A man in public position must feign a Trujillist fervor he does not feel, a common man in the streets must suppress his complaint. The most bitter criticisms of the regime are heard from high officials of the government when they are alone.

After ruling for twenty-five years, Trujillo has succeeded in creating this atmosphere of submission. It was achieved in the beginning by a systematic terror which broke all possible resistance. Later, it was the result of indoctrination of the youth by the schools and the university; the Dominican student does not know what is going on in the world. It is the result of a fawning press, of constant espionage, and of the power of the army and the police. It is especially the result of the frequent humiliations imposed upon the most representative figures; it is rare to find an outstanding Dominican who has not collaborated with the regime in one way or another.

[*A few capsule case studies will illustrate the Trujillist pattern.*]

Rafael Estrella Ureña: nominal leader of the 1930 coup; provisional president of the Republic from May to August, 1930; vice-president with Trujillo on August 16, 1930. He left the Dominican Republic on a pretext in August, 1931, and started a campaign of opposition abroad; in December, 1931, he was dismissed as vice-president by the Congress; in October, 1933, a law declared him a traitor to the Fatherland; for several years he was attacked in the Dominican press. At the end of 1939, Estrella Ureña admitted defeat; he returned to the Dominican Republic on December 2, with his brother Gustavo. In November, 1940, Rafael Estrella Ureña was arrested and indicted jointly with General José Estrella, accused of being guilty in the murder of Martínez Reyna in 1930; his arrest lasted until March, 1941, the time at which the statute of limitations was applied and Estrella Ureña was freed; at once he sent a cable of thanks and adherence to Trujillo. In March, 1942, the police officially accused Estrella Ureña of being a former pro-Fascist; on August 16 of the same year, he was elected a justice of the Supreme Court and accepted. On May 31, 1945, he also accepted an invitation from Trujillo to reorganize his old Republican party and resigned as justice; at once, a campaign against the Republican party was launched in the press. Estrella Ureña died within a few days; Trujillo attended the burial service.

General José Estrella and Mario Fermín Cabral: General Estrella was the commander-in-chief of the military column which at the end of February, 1930, advanced from Santiago and occupied the capital; afterward he was the trusted lieutenant of Trujillo in Santiago, and among other known crimes he committed the murder of Virgilio Martínez Reyna; as of 1934, he was officially appointed as special commissioner of the government in the northern provinces. Mario Fermín Cabral was president of the Senate from 1930 to 1938, organizer and first president of the Dominican party from 1931 until October, 1936, and proposer of the law changing the name of the capital to Ciudad Trujillo. During the illness of Trujillo in 1940, the name of Estrella was mentioned as possible successor. On the day before Trujillo's return from the United States, Estrella issued a proclamation in Santiago hailing his return in the most lyrical terms; one week later he was dismissed and arrested. Trujillo suggested to President Troncoso the nomination of Cabral as governor of Santiago in order to carry on the persecution against General Estrella. On December 19 Estrella was sentenced to twenty years in prison for the murder of Roca. In March, 1941, the statute of limitations was applied because of the murder of Martínez Reyna. At the beginning of June, Cabral was dismissed as governor and also arrested. On August 16 Estrella was pardoned. In December, Cabral was elected a member of the constituent assembly; and in April, 1942, he was elected again as senator. On many occasions since 1941, both Cabral and Estrella have reaffirmed their loyalty to Trujillo. On June 1, 1955, Cabral was elected again as president of the Senate, but on August 16 he was demoted.

Dr. Francisco Benzo: personal physician of Trujillo and secretary of health after April, 1938. During the illness of Trujillo in 1940, Benzo was indiscreet in his comments; Trujillo went out for the first time after his illness in the middle of July; five days later an investigation of the Department of Health was announced. By the beginning of August, 1940, Benzo was in jail subject to numerous persecutions. By a twist in Trujillo's political whims, in May, 1948, he was elected a deputy.

Dr. Manuel de Jesús Troncoso de la Concha: jailed prisoner in July, 1930, in the course of the post-electoral persecutions; vice-president of the Republic in 1938; president after the death of Peynado in March, 1940. He resigned in May, 1942, to allow Trujillo to occupy the presidency three months before the official inauguration. He was president of the Senate from 1943 until his death in 1955.

Pericles A. Franco: in disgrace and without a position for a long time; undersecretary of the office of the Generalissimo in November, 1940;

undersecretary of education in August, 1941; undersecretary of the presidency in May, 1943; undersecretary of interior and police in March, 1944; deputy in July, 1944; president of a new court of appeals in December, 1944. In June, 1945, his son, Pericles, Jr., escaped when the police attempted his arrest, and Pericles, Sr. was arrested in his place; he spent a night in a cell with common criminals, and an attempt was made to use him as hostage to force the surrender of his son. When that failed, he was sentenced to three months in prison for a crime alleged to have been committed many years before. Two months later he was released on parole, but there is still pending against him this incomplete sentence for a common crime.

Ricardo Paíno Pichardo: president of the Dominican party from December, 1938, until May, 1942, and secretary of the presidency from the time Trujillo reoccupied the presidency in May, 1942, until he first fell out of favor in January, 1945; during all these six years, Paíno Pichardo was Trujillo's most trusted man. His first disfavor seemed to be complete, although he was not persecuted. In May, 1945, he was appointed president of the administrative council of Ciudad Trujillo, and in July, 1946, he again became secretary of the presidency for one year. Later on, he faded away. But in June, 1955, he was reinstated as president of the Dominican party.

Virgilio Alvarez Pina: president of the Dominican party from May, 1942, to May, 1950; an honorary general in December, 1947; from 1945 until 1950 he was Trujillo's most trusted man. He fell out of favor in 1950 and was accused in public in May, 1952. In March, 1953, Alvarez Pina was appointed governor of the district of Santo Domingo; in May, 1954, he was named chairman of the commission to organize the festivities of the "Year of the Benefactor."

Manuel A. Peña Batlle: an enemy of Trujillo during the first years of the regime, he joined the Dominican party in March, 1935. But in July he made the mistake of praising the first apparent decision of Trujillo against changing the name of the capital. He was in obvious disgrace after that, boasting, in private conversations, of being an opponent of Trujillo. In August, 1941, he became a professor in the university. Ten days after he was named president of the Chamber of Deputies in April of the same year, he requested that Trujillo immediately occupy the presidency of the Republic. In January, 1943, he served as secretary of interior and police, followed by secretary of foreign relations from September, 1943, to January, 1947. In spite of his violent speech against the Haitians in November, 1943, he was appointed ambassador to Haiti in January, 1947. He died in 1954 while serving as ambassador counselor.

These are only the most outstanding cases typical of the Trujillist style. On the one hand, there is the obvious desire to show that in his regime nobody can last forever as favorite and that even the most important personalities may be persecuted, but later on they are forced again to accept prominent positions in the government. On the other hand, the most serious and significant aspect is the fact that all those persons do not hesitate to accept any positions forced upon them after a punishment; there is not one single case of civic courage, not even among those who were especially humiliated, such as General Estrella.

In any serious dictatorship, there have been purges and punishments: Stalin, Hitler, and Mussolini executed some of their closest associates. But in no other dictatorship has there existed this humiliation of a lieutenant who is punished and a short time afterward accepts another high position in the government. The punishment is the least important thing; the thing that impresses one is the submission.

One could mention the case of a secretary of state who at the time of the Cayo Confites invasion in 1947 told one of his assistants that the plot was very apt to succeed because he himself had seen the deposits of arms the revolutionaries had in Santiago; this secretary never revealed the location of the deposits or the names of the plotters, although afterwards he wrote one of the many condemnations of the invasion. At about the same time, another important officer of the Dominican government, temporarily in the United States, telephoned to some friend of the revolutionaries every few days, asking for information about the invasion, and not as a spy, but hoping for the end of the regime he was forced to serve. This same official complained that in some other countries there existed at least a clandestine resistance fighting back at the dictatorship.

The author has known of many other cases similar to these outstanding ones, because occasionally even the most "Trujillist" Dominican in appearance feels the compulsion to talk sincerely with foreigners. But all of them continue to praise Trujillo in public, and they accept anything Trujillo may decide for their good or their ruin.

Chapter 5: Single-Party System and Controlled Labor Unions

In the Dominican constitution, "freedom of association" is consecrated as inherent in human personality. Article 103 states: "The organization of political parties is free, in accordance with the laws, providing their tendencies conform with the principles established in the second article of this Constitution." And Article 2 says: "Its Government [the Dominican Republic's] is essentially civil, republican, democratic, and representative."

There is no law about political parties in the Dominican Republic. The provisions indirectly applicable are those contained in Chapter 15 of the electoral law, which determines the requirements any political party must fulfill in order to be recognized as such by the central electoral board and be able to participate in the elections: ". . . that it has a membership of not less than 6 percent of the total number of voters who took part in the last general election immediately prior to the request for registration, such members being distributed among at least nine of the provinces of the Republic."

The registration must be requested by the directive council of the party, with submission of the statutes, programs, and symbol of the party. "If the program does not contain doctrines against the public order or good customs, if the proof concerning the number of voters is satisfactory, and the symbol cannot be confused with that of any other party already registered," the central electoral board will decide in favor of the request; otherwise the petition will be sent back with suggestions for its correction.

The labor code regulates in detail the requirements that labor unions must fulfill for their organization and registration with the Department of

Labor for all legal purposes. These unions acquire legal personality by the fact of their registration.[1]

We are again in the presence of an apparent freedom of political and labor association. The only legal restrictions refer to the basic constitutional principles concerning public order and good customs, plus a series of formal requirements for the public activities of political parties and labor unions. In theory, the Dominican constitution is one of the most liberal.

Not until June, 1947, was a law enacted prohibiting communist and anarchist groups, as well as others considered to be similar.

The Destruction of Old Parties

One of the alleged defenses of the Trujillo regime is the Chief's putting an end to previous political chaos, at a time when many caudillos and personalist parties disturbed public order with their selfish ambitions, which again and again incited revolts and even civil wars.

This is true, in the sense that the old system of political parties and groups disappeared as a whole. What is debatable is the final evaluation of this fact.

In 1930, when Trujillo rose to power, there were at least seven political parties in the Dominican Republic. Two of them formed the National-Progressive Alliance, backing the candidacy of Federico Velázquez and Angel Morales; the remaining parties united in the Confederation of Parties backing the candidacy of Trujillo and Estrella Ureña. During the pre-electoral months after the coup of February, an eighth party was organized under the name of National Union, formed by members of the ousted Vásquez administration who decided to collaborate with the new regime.

Among those parties, at least two had a tradition of many years. And more than one had had a brilliant past.

The National party had ruled the country after United States forces left the Dominican Republic in 1924 until the military coup of 1930; it was the personal party of General Horacio Vásquez, the "horacistas." The Progressive party was the personal following of Federico Velázquez, separated from the National party previously, its ally in the 1924 elections, its opponent after 1928, and again an ally in 1930. The Liberal party,

---

[1] The author was legal adviser of the Dominican Department of Labor for several months in 1945–46. During that period, he examined the pertinent documents concerning more than a hundred labor unions and federations; in general the examination was a mere formality to verify that all legal requirements had been fulfilled. [Fn. 3, Chap. V.]

headed in 1930 by General Desiderio Arias, was only a remnant of the old great "Jimenista" party.

The Republican party of Rafael Estrella Ureña was recent, and it also was the product of a small schism in the National party. The Nationalist party served its purpose during the United States occupation, and, in 1930, it split into two groups, one collaborating with Trujillo. The Patriotic Coalition of Citizens had a brief period of success in the 1924 elections. The Independent Workers party pretended to have a moderately pro-labor platform. The new party of National Union was headed by an active collaborator of President Vásquez in the days of the coup ousting him.

All these political parties rapidly disappeared as soon as Trujillo came to power. The first victims were the two parties of the opposition, destroyed between May and August, 1930. But immediately afterward, the parties which backed Trujillo in the elections of May 16, 1930, were also eliminated. By 1931, none of those parties existed, and there was left a new party, also of a personal type: the Dominican party of Trujillo.

The National-Progressive Alliance was forced to withdraw from the electoral campaign a week before the elections of 1930. Very soon afterward all its leaders were in exile, after seeking asylum in foreign legations, and in more than one case after being arrested. There remained only the old caudillo, Horacio Vásquez, too sick to be a threat to the new regime. When Trujillo took the oath as president on August 16, 1930, the two majority parties of the previous period had disappeared permanently.

But, step by step, the parties backing Trujillo were also eliminated. The strongest two were the Liberal and the Republican parties, because of the personalities of their leaders, Desiderio Arias and Rafael Estrella Ureña, both outstanding in the 1930 coup. A few months later, Desiderio Arias was defeated in battle and killed; almost immediately thereafter, Estrella Ureña went into exile of his own will, and the Congress dismissed him as vice-president of the Republic. The remaining parties disappeared by themselves.

In August, 1931, the new Dominican party of Trujillo was officially constituted, and the parties of the Confederation merged with it. In 1933, the "conversions" of former horacistas began.

Since then, there has been only a single party although from time to time a pretense of the existence of opposition parties has been made.

The Simulated Parties of "Opposition"

On more than one occasion Trujillo has issued messages inviting the leaders of the old parties to reorganize them. The best proof that nobody believed in the sincerity of such an invitation was the subsequent silence in response to the first calls.

During World War II, however, and especially at the end of it, the democratic trend was so strong in the Americas that even Trujillo realized the undesirability of the existence of one single party, which suggested a Fascist totalitarian regime. It was necessary to present before the world the existence of opposition parties and even an electoral campaign with the victors and the defeated.

Hence, the observer notes subsequent farces of 1940–41 with the Trujillista party, of 1945 with the reorganization of old parties, especially the Republican, and, more so, of 1946–47 with the brief but energetic campaign of the Popular Socialist party and the Democratic Youth and the simulation of the National Democratic and National Labor parties until the elections of 1947. Let us examine some of the details.

Trujillista party: the name in itself indicates that it was never an opposition party but a replication of identical parties. The idea was launched on October 14, 1940, in a public meeting held in Ciudad Trujillo by the "Guardia Universitaria Presidente Trujillo"; the announced purpose was "to collaborate in the purifying task and in the political re-education of the Dominican people," but it was added that the new party would act within the Dominican party and follow its structure and discipline. The first person applying for membership in the new party was the president of the superior directive council of the Dominican party, Ricardo Paíno Pichardo; three weeks later, Trujillo himself requested admission. He was named the next day as "Supreme Chief of the Trujillista Party."

From the very beginning, there existed a complete identity between the Dominican party and the Trujillista party; identity in program and discipline and in the person of their chief. The purpose of its constitution was twofold: on the one hand, it permitted a symbolic purge of employees, . . . and on the other, it allowed the organization of the women, until then not taken into account, in public life and in the ranks of the Dominican party.

For some time, it was believed that this duality of parties could foreshadow a simulated electoral fight in 1942. From November, 1940, to August, 1941, there were printed, from time to time and with different intensity, news stories about the increasing membership in the ranks of the Trujillista party. In January, 1942, it was said that the party had 153,000 members. In February of the same year, the central electoral board accepted its official registration.

But when the right time came, the Trujillista party confined itself to backing the candidacy of Trujillo for the presidency. On March 12, 1942, the party presented a list of candidates identical to that submitted ten days before by the Dominican party. The certificate of the electoral board after the 1942 elections announced that the total number of ballots was that "received by every candidate on the lists presented by the Dominican and Trujillista Parties."

The Trujillista party faded away after that. For a time, its feminine branch remained, but it was attached to the Dominican party in June, 1942. In March, 1944, this last pretense disappeared, and the branch was integrated as a regular section of the Dominican party.

Reorganization of parties in 1945: on May 28, 1945, Trujillo addressed a letter to Rafael Estrella Ureña (at that time a justice of the Supreme Court, as a member of the Dominican party), inviting him to reorganize his Republican party. A similar invitation was addressed to the old leaders of other historical parties. Those were the days of the victory of the United Nations over fascism.

Estrella Ureña accepted the invitation; he resigned as justice, and in the following days the constitution of several local branches of the Republican party was announced. At once, a strong campaign was launched against Estrella Ureña and his Republican party in the pages of La Nación; the method was subtle, neither the party nor its leader was directly attacked, but one after another the old leaders of the Dominican politics denied having been members of the Republican party or broke away from Estrella Ureña, reaffirming their loyalty to Trujillo. This was the case even with General José Estrella, punished and jailed a few years before, and even with Gustavo Estrella Ureña, brother of the leader of the Republican party and exiled for years with him. The maneuver ended three and a half months later, when Rafael Estrella Ureña died on September 16. From then on, nobody spoke further about the Republican party.

The leaders of the other old parties were more cautious or remained in the shadows after a verbal acceptance that nobody believed. A year and a half later, the National Democratic party, whose organization was announced in June, 1945, by Rafael A. Espaillat, was revived; however, nobody mentioned this party again until the beginning of 1947.

Popular Socialist party: activities to force the public organization of communism in the Dominican Republic started in secret about the end of 1945. They culminated about the middle of 1946 when several exiles of this ideology came back from Cuba.

Democratic Youth: this group, formed almost exclusively by university students, was spontaneously born by taking advantage of the apparent guarantees offered by Trujillo during his play with the Communists. It never deserved official recognition, but it suffered the consequences of the subsequent repression.

National Labor party and National Democratic party: the idea of organizing both parties was launched in 1945, more or less at the same time that Trujillo addressed his invitation to Estrella Ureña; there is documentary evidence concerning the National Democratic party and its titular leader, Rafael A. Espaillat. But the idea was set aside for the time being, and it was not put in practice until it seemed necessary as a counterbalance to the activities of the Popular Socialist party.

The first time that the National Labor party was mentioned in public was in June, 1946; its leader was Francisco Prats Ramírez, until then president in name of the Dominican Confederation of Labor. On August 31 a message of the party explaining its program, which was obviously an answer to the recent message issued by the Popular Socialist party, was printed. There is no more mention of the Labor party until the elections in December for the constituent assembly, in which the party received two seats. On March 31, 1947, there was announced the list of candidates for the next general elections in May, a list headed by Prats Ramírez as presidential candidate. What was never made clear was the political program of the party and of its candidates, nor the minor difference with the Dominican party. Even more remarkable, on October 24, 1946, Prats Ramírez published a lyrical piece dedicated to Trujillo on his birthday.

On the other hand, the National Democratic party was revived at the last moment to take part in the 1947 elections. On January 31 Rafael A. Espaillat issued a manifesto to the country announcing his "return," although he did not say that he had been until then a minister counselor at the embassy in Washington. The central electoral board admitted the registration of the new party in March, and in the same month the list of candidates, headed by Espaillat for the presidency, was announced.

The nominal existence of those two "opposition" parties allowed the pretense of a tripartite electoral battle in the elections of May, 1947. That did not mean that they were interested in giving the appearance of an electoral campaign; on the contrary, a few days before the elections, the press printed the adherence of all deputies to Trujillo's candidacy and among those adherents was the opposing candidate Prats Ramírez.

Trujillo, of course, won the elections. But a seat as minority deputy from Santiago was given to Francisco Pereyra of the National Democratic party, and another minority seat . . . was given to Sra. Consuelo de Prats Ramírez of the National Labor party. The active role of both parties ended with these elections, although the pretense was maintained in the Chamber until 1952. . . .

Both defeated presidential candidates were "elected" deputies some time later, when the two elected deputies for those parties "resigned." Francisco Prats Ramírez replaced his wife three weeks after the new congress was constituted, on September 9, 1947; Rafael A. Espaillat did not replace Pereyra until much later, on August 14, 1951. Both were reelected deputies in the 1952 balloting as candidates of the Dominican party, although Espaillat, who died in June, could not occupy his seat; it should be added that his vacancy was filled, not by any member of the National party, but by Vicente Tolentino who had been until a short time before the president of the Dominican party.

These data are enough to establish the artificial character of the attempts at "opposition" during the period of the victory of the United Nations over fascism, when the existence of one single party was in bad taste. But in the Era of Trujillo there has been one single political party since 1931, the date on which the remaining parties of the past disappeared. This is the Dominican party.

Structure and Ideology of the Dominican Party

The first news about this party appeared in *Listín Diario* on November 20, 1930, three months after the inauguration of Trujillo as president. It was a "Proclamation of the Provisional Superior Directive Council for the Organization of the Party of General Trujillo"; as can be seen, the party started as a personal one.

Its official organization took place on August 16, 1931, one year after the inauguration of Trujillo. He sent a message to the delegates of its first convention, in which he said: "As long as I occupy the first position of the State, I will govern with the men of the Party."[2]

On March 11, 1932, the new party was officially registered with the central electoral board. Its name was now the Dominican party; its director was Trujillo, and Mario Fermín Cabral was the president of its superior directive council. Since this moment, the Dominican party has been the only one in existence, and the old parties have been forced to merge with it.[3] And since the 1934 elections,[4] it has won all contests, usually without any pretended opposition.

---

[2] Trujillo, *Pensamiento,* 1: 122. [Fn. 17, Chap. V.]

[3] Nobody better recognized this merger of all the old parties in the new and unique party than Dr. José E. Aybar, that formerly vociferous opponent of 1930, when he went fully to Trujillo's side in 1933. One of the reasons on which he based his public poll in the pages of *Listín Diario,* proposing the reelection of Trujillo in 1934 without previous elections, was: there is only one party, the Dominican, in which all former parties have merged. *Listín Diario,* March 23, 1933. [Fn. 19, Chap. V.]

[4] In that year the Congress issued a vote of confidence in the Dominican party in February for having named Trujillo as candidate for reelection. *G.O.* 4654; *Bol. Sen.* and *Bol. Cam.,* Feb. 1934. [Fn. 20, Chap. V.]

The date on which the first statutes of the party were approved has not been available for this study; but probably it was in 1931. Later on, several amendments were introduced. The oldest edition of the statutes available in libraries in the United States is that of 1938.

This pamphlet has on its front cover a palm tree, the symbol of the party; a portrait of Trujillo, in his uniform of Generalissimo, with this annotation: "Generalissimo Rafael L. Trujillo Molina, Chief and Director of the Party"; and in the upper corner the motto: *Rectitud, Libertad, Trabajo* (Righteousness, Freedom, Work). It is obvious that this motto was chosen in order that the initials would be those of Rafael Leonidas Trujillo; later on *Moralidad* (Morality), for Molina, was added.

The principles of the party cannot be more vague: ". . . the Dominican Party has been constituted to fulfill a patriotic aspiration of civic conquest of the Dominican people and as a political force to support and accomplish the reform credo of Generalissimo Dr. Rafael L. Trujillo Molina. . . . It declares and recognizes as its only Supreme Chief the Generalissimo and Doctor Rafael L. Trujillo, because he embodies the ideals of all Dominicans with noble thoughts and because his actions have such a Dominican reach and such a projection in history that his life is merged with the existence of our nationality." It means that this is a typically personal party to back Trujillo, without program or doctrine.

This same initial declaration of principles indicates the merging of former parties into one single party, by saying: "When the parties active in the country merged into one single entity to form the powerful political nucleus of the Dominican Party, they accomplished it. . . ."

Let us summarize the most important provisions of these statutes.

Article 5 of Chapter 1 says: "The Dominican Party requires from its members loyalty, enthusiasm, and discipline, and it consecrates and proclaims the principle of presidential reelection." . . . [*Chapters 2 through 4 deal with details of party organization at the lower levels.*]

Chapter 5 regulates the superior directive council of the party. According to Article 21 of the statutes, this council was composed of a delegate from every provincial council, plus a president, all appointed by the chief of the party, who might increase the number of delegates. Deputies and senators may participate with voice and vote in the discussions, but their number does not contribute to making the required quorum. The council elected its superior executive committee, but the president, secretary, and treasurer were directly appointed by the chief of the party.

As can be seen, all presidents of district, county, provincial, and national councils were appointed directly by Trujillo, who at the same time could freely appoint many other members of local councils and all delegates to the superior directive council. This provision was modified in 1945; since then, the superior directive council elects the whole executive committee including the president, but nobody doubts that Trujillo continues to suggest the names of the persons to be elected.

In order that there may be no doubt at all concerning the complete submission of the party and its leaders to Trujillo, Article 27 says: "The Executive Committee shall not decide anything contrary to what is provided in these Statutes, or to the decision of the Chief of the Party. . . . The decisions of the Superior Directive Council or of the Executive Committee may be vetoed by the Chief of the Party."

Chapter 6 regulates the national conventions of the party. The convention shall nominate candidates for all positions to be filled by popular vote; but again it is added: ". . . the Chief of the Party may object to any candidate chosen by a Convention and it shall be the duty of the latter to accept that objection."

The whole of Chapter 7 is devoted to the chief of the party. There is not the slightest doubt about its personal character: "Article 42. The Dominican Party acclaims and recognizes as Chief and Director, the Generalissimo Dr. Rafael L. Trujillo Molina, whose program and political creed of national reform and of aggrandizement of the Fatherland it [the party] makes its own for its accomplishment and fulfillment."

Article 43 enumerates his powers. The most important are "(a) To appoint the President of the Party and all paid employees [this provision was modified in 1945 in reference to the president]. (c) To authorize all expenses of the Party. (e) To indicate orally or in writing . . . the measures he thinks appropriate for the proper functioning of the Party. . . . (f) To exercise the right of veto. . . . (g) To object to candidates. . . . (k) To remove by decree the members of the Party convicted of treason by a Court of Honor.[5] (l) To punish disloyalty with appropriate penalties. . . . (m) To resolve, with absolute authority, any matter not foreseen in these Statutes. (n) To enact rules of procedure or to interpret these Statutes if necessary. (o) The authority of the Chief of the Party cannot be limited or transferred . . . (but he may grant an express mandate, in certain circumstances, to the organs or members of the Party)."

Article 52 later reaffirms these absolute powers of the chief of the party by saying: "The decisions of the County or Provincial Councils and of the Superior Directive Council, in order to be effective, must be approved by the Chief of the Party."

---

[5] For instance, in May, 1935, twenty persons were expelled from the party, for being implicated in the plot against Trujillo in the capital; and in November, 1940, General José Estrella, Rafael Estrella Ureña, and other persons arrested in Santiago were also expelled from the party. [Fn. 24, Chap. V.]

Other provisions of a general character deserve to be emphasized. Article 39, so many times referred to, provides that all elected employees "must submit, in writing, their respective resignations, without date, to the Chief of the Party." Article 56 specifies that, "for the financing of the Party, its members must contribute in the form that the Superior Directive Council decides with the approval of the Chief of the Party"; this provision justifies the official deduction of 10 percent of the salaries of all public employees. Article 65 states that "the Party adopts as a rule that only its members may enjoy the advantages that it [the party] is in a position to offer"; this means that all public employees must be members of the party, and on many occasions such membership shall be required in practice to obtain permits and favorable decisions from the administration.

The president of the superior directive council has the rank of a secretary of state, and the secretary general and the vice-president of the party have the rank of undersecretary. In the second place, the secretaryship of the treasury deducts 10 percent from the monthly checks of all public employees, payable directly to the treasurer of the party, even if an employee, because of extraordinary reasons (foreigners almost always),[6] is not a member of the party. In the third place, to obtain a position as a public employee, one must be a member of the party.

Not only is the Dominican party the only one in the Dominican Republic, but at the same time it is fully integrated in the structure and functioning of the government, in a way typical to totalitarian regimes. It is a rule which is official not only in the party but also occasionally in the government itself.

This totalitarian taste appears also in the order given on September 23, 1937, by the president of the party that members must salute Trujillo by stopping "in front of the Supreme Chief, chest out and the right hand placed over the heart."

The Dominican party, however, is not a minority elite, disciplined and with faith in a credo such as the Communist and some Fascist parties have. In fact, it is rare not to find a Dominican active in public or professional life who is not a member of the Dominican party; it is a mere formality.[7] According to statistics printed by Nanita in the latest edition of his biography of Trujillo, from the establishment of the party in 1931 until the end of 1950, 1,025,883 persons were registered in it. Keeping in mind that the Dominican population, according to the census of 1950, was 2,121,000

---

[6] The author himself can confirm this fact. During the years he lived in the Dominican Republic, where he was a professor at the diplomatic school and legal adviser to the Labor Department, 10 percent was always deducted from his monthly checks, although as a foreigner, he was never affiliated with the Dominican party. This deduction is made independently of income taxes. [Fn. 27, Chap. V.]

[7] It is significant that persons plotting against Trujillo have repeatedly been members of the Dominican party. [Fn. 30, Chap. V.]

inhabitants, and that the ballots cast in the 1952 elections were 1,038,816, it is easy to see that a membership so large decreases its ideological strength. In that total, 659,748 were men, and 336,135 were women; women who, in the beginning, could not be members, but who in 1940 formed the feminine branch of the Trujillista party, attached in December, 1942, to the Dominican party.

A final word may be added about the subsequent presidents of the party. Its first president was its founder, Mario Fermín Cabral, from August 16, 1931 until October 15, 1936; he was at the same time president of the Senate. The second president was Emilio A. Morel, from this last date until the following summer; he had been previously a senator and he resigned that office when he was appointed president of the party, establishing a precedent of separation of functions that would continue in the future. The third president was Daniel Henríquez Velázquez, officially recognized on September 16, 1937, although he had been acting as such a few weeks before; he had been president of the Chamber for a few months. The fourth president was Ricardo Paíno Pichardo, from December 28, 1938, until May 16, 1942, the date on which he was appointed secretary of the presidency when Trujillo initiated his third administration; as president of the party he was, in fact, the strong man of the regime and first lieutenant of Trujillo, even stronger than the president of the Republic, Troncoso de la Concha. The fifth president was Virgilio Alvarez Pina, from May 16, 1942, until the beginning of 1950; he was also the best lieutenant of Trujillo during the last years, but his dismissal as president of the party marked his rapid downfall. The sixth president was Vicente Tolentino, recognized as such on May 12, 1950, and acting until August 18, 1951. The seventh president, who was in power for a very brief period, was José Angel Saviñón, from August 18 to September 4 of the same year. The eighth president was Modesto E. Díaz, from this last date until the middle of 1955. The ninth and present president is again Paíno Pichardo, named on June 10, 1955.

Among all those presidents, three stand out: Cabral, Paíno Pichardo, and Alvarez Pina. The three of them played a very important role in Dominican political life as long as they were presidents of the party. The remaining presidents only fulfilled a routine job.

In summary, the Dominican party has no doctrine, life of its own, or spontaneity, but it is a fundamental part of Dominican political life and Trujillo's best instrument.

The Labor Movement in the Dominican Republic

The labor movement began during the first years of the twentieth century, taking advantage of the freedom which followed the murder of dictator "Lilís"; but the first labor unions were not organized until the United States occupation, with the double purpose of defense of the workers' interests and as an expression of nationalist policies.

A few months after the country was liberated and the new constitutional government of Horacio Vásquez was elected in 1924, the first Dominican law on labor was enacted. This attempt had little success and was declared unconstitutional. This failure, based upon a restricted interpretation of the Constitution and the conviction that any similar legislation would be held unconstitutional, delayed labor legislation for many years.

Nevertheless, the workers' movement went on. New unions were organized, particularly the Dominican Confederation of Labor, constituted on November 17, 1929. Even an Independent Workers' party arose. The provisional government of Estrella Ureña incorporated the confederation on April 10, 1930.

The opening of the Era of Trujillo completely paralyzed the labor development, which was not begun again until fourteen years later and on a different basis. The Independent Workers' party disappeared together with the others, and the confederation stopped its labors.

The labor policy changed. Instead of being a spontaneous movement from below, from the unions up to the government, it was now transformed into a governmental paternalism which came from above; there were concessions by the government in favor of the working class. It meant that the labor movement lost in freedom, but the conditions of the workers were bettered.

The first step was the approval in 1932 of four international conventions prepared by the International Labor Organization.[8] Simultaneously, the first Dominican labor laws that were enforced were enacted in 1932. In 1934 two laws on payment of agricultural wages were enacted; this was the first step toward abolishing a series of abuses in the sugar factories and other enterprises through the use of *vales* (credit slips) as a form of payment.[9]

The year 1940 was important because the first law on minimum wages was enacted; as a consequence, a decree on May 20 established the first national committee on wages, and several later decrees fixed some wage scales; similar decrees were enacted in the following years. As a con-

---

[8] The Dominican Republic had adhered in 1926 to this organization, but it never ratified any of its conventions. The ratification of these four conventions was deposited on Feb. 4, 1933. [Fn. 47, Chap. V.]

[9] This method of payment through *vales* (credit slips), which in fact served partially to cancel debts in the stores of the same sugar factory, has been generally used in many Latin American countries. . . . [Fn. 56, Chap. V.]

trary trend, Law No. 267 of May 10, 1940, must be noticed because, in regulating the organization and functioning of non-profit associations, it restricted the establishment of labor unions.

The year 1942 deserves special mention because in January the Constitution was amended, expressly allowing labor legislation, particularly on matters referring to "maximum work hours, days of rest and vacations, minimum salaries and wages and their form of payment, social insurance, preponderant employment of nationals in any work, and in general, all the measures of protection and assistance by the State that are considered necessary in support of the workers."

Finally, we arrive at the year 1944, which was crucial. It was the final period of World War II, and the high tide of the democratic movement advanced through all Latin America a strong labor movement, infiltrated by Communists, and promoted labor legislation even in countries under political dictatorship. In the Dominican Republic, this trend was reflected in two ways: in the legislative field, an important law on labor contracts was enacted; in the unions, the Dominican Confederation of Labor was reorganized by official encouragement and sent delegates to the congress of the CTAL (Confederation of Workers of Latin America) in Cali, Colombia.

The movement increased in 1945. A law on May 4 created the Secretaryship of Labor and National Economy, in which a department of labor functioned. This department began its work at once and drafted a series of new laws which encouraged the revival of the labor movement. Simultaneously, the law on labor contracts was put into practice, through informal agencies, and also a simple procedure for conciliation and a reinforced corps of inspectors of labor which supervised the fulfillment of the labor legislation.[10]

The development of this trend was revealed not only by the laws, but also in the labor unions. The unions multiplied; at the beginning of 1946, more than 150 were registered with the Department of Labor, plus several provincial federations, and a national federation of sugar workers was

---

[10] The only difficulties arose when the economic interests of Trujillo were involved. The most serious case was the application of the law on annual vacations to the employees of the shoe factory FADOC and to the Dominican Tobacco Company; the problem came from the text of that law, one of the oldest, drafted in such a way that it benefited only "the employees ... receiving fixed wages paid on a weekly, bimonthly, monthly, or any other fixed period basis"; the Department of Labor maintained that this law ought to be interpreted as applying as much to office employees as to laborers, and also that it covered those who, though permanent workers of a factory, were paid on a piecework basis (as was the case of the shoemakers and the cigarmakers). [Fn. 76, Chap. V.]

about to be recognized. Some of these unions and federations, and, of course, the Dominican Confederation of Labor, lacked a life of their own; as mere fronts of the government they lacked initiative. But the old unions, and a few of the new ones, still showed evidence of initiative and strength.

This strength manifested itself in the strike in the sugar fields in January, 1946. A previous attempt to strike, in 1942, had been crushed by the army. The strike of January, 1946, lasted more than a week and ended only after the hurried approval of new scales of minimum wages, which in many cases meant an increase of 100 percent or more over the previous ones. The Dominican government did not dare to face directly such a widespread and militant strike, and settled it at the cost of the sugar industry, although some individual measures of repression were taken simultaneously. But the strike seriously alarmed the government, and after January, 1946, several legislative measures were adopted restricting the activities of the labor unions, especially in the event of strikes. These controls, however, were designed not to impede the game played with the Communist organizations, developed in 1946.

After that it was obvious that the Dominican government followed a clear and strong line. Most of the legislative advantages granted to the workers from above were respected and reaffirmed, until they culminated in the promulgation of the "Trujillo Code of Labor" in 1951. At the same time, the labor unions were controlled, and the Dominican Confederation of Labor was converted into a mere tool in the service of the government.

Today the Trujillo Code of Labor is in force in the Dominican Republic; it contains and summarizes all previous legislation. The simulated Labor party has disappeared. The Popular Socialist party (Communist), as well as other organizations "of similar political trend," have been prohibited. The Dominican Confederation of Labor lacks a life of its own, but it is exhibited in public instead of being banned as it was during the first years of the regime.

The Dominican Confederation of Labor

Dominican labor unions were originally regulated by a United States executive order in 1920, dealing with incorporation of non-profit associations. According to it, the Dominican Confederation of Labor, constituted in 1929, was incorporated the next year during the provisional government of Estrella Ureña.

During the first ten years of Trujillo, the confederation disappeared in fact, and the individual labor unions were reduced to mere benevolent associations. A law in 1940 gave official status to this muzzling of the labor unions, even to the extent that the governor of the province was the president *ex officio* of all provincial labor federations.

This muzzle was partially broken by a law on July 8, 1943, which allowed the Department of Labor to establish a procedural system for the creation of new labor unions. The new law excluded from the general restrictions imposed by the law of 1940 those labor unions recognized by the Department of Labor or incorporated by decree of the executive branch. On the basis of that "recognition," and simplifying the procedure of incorporation established in 1920, the Department of Labor recognized up to the beginning of 1946 the Dominican Confederation of Labor, several provincial federations, and more than 150 individual labor unions.

The Trujillo Code of Labor, presently in force, devotes its Book V to the regulation of labor unions. It is a detailed regulation of the requirements to be met in their constitutions and functioning, but more or less continues the procedure begun in 1945. There is no special mention of the Dominican Confederation of Labor. This silence suggests that the problem of organizing rival confederations, discussed in 1945, remains unsolved. In fact this question has never arisen because of the monolithic structure of the Trujillo regime. Not only is there a single Dominican Confederation of Labor, but it also acts as a governmental tool to supervise individual labor unions.

Some of the leaders of the confederation are veterans of the early labor struggles; today, however, they cooperate with the Trujillo regime. The rebels who insisted on bettering the condition of workers and on maintaining political ideas opposed to or merely divergent from those of the present regime were eliminated.

In general, it is possible to see a two-fold development of activities by the Confederation. In the socio-economic field, it has been a good instrument for progress; more or less intensively, according to periods, it has defended the interests of workers. In the political field, it is again necessary to make a distinction between two types of activities, the national and the international. In the national field, the confederation is a mere tool of Trujillo's government to lead and push the working masses; in the international field, it has had very significant fluctuations which deserve to be briefly mentioned.

In 1944 and in the years immediately following, the Dominican Confederation of Labor collaborated with the CTAL despite the latter's obvious Communist infiltration and control, and Dominican delegates, paid by the government, attended the congress at Cali and subsequent ones. When the American labor unions faced this Communist infiltration and subsequently organized the CIT and the ORIT, the Dominican Confederation of Labor was rejected because of its submission to the Trujillo dictatorship, and it has since remained isolated in the international labor field. The delegates of the Dominican confederation have attended the congresses of the International Labor Organization, where they act merely as obedient servants of the governmental delegates.

For some years now it has been difficult, almost impossible, to follow from outside the life of the Dominican Confederation of Labor; the Dominican press seems not to care about it, except for occasional political activities.[11] At the beginning of 1955, a congress of workers was called on the occasion of the Year of the Benefactor.[12] As expected, this congress, held on May 15 and 16 named Trujillo as the "Protector of the Dominican Working Class" and supported his reelection as president in 1957.

But there is no doubt that the Dominican labor unions and the confederation, at present, are mere political tools of governmental action and control over the labor classes, although, at the same time, they benefit to a large extent the material interests of workers, and one must not ignore the fact that these organizations are a latent force in the future.

Progressive Labor Legislation

Another general characteristic common to most of the Latin American dictatorships today, although there are some exceptions, is the fact that the reverse swing of the political pendulum has not meant a retrogression in recent social advances. Dictators have attempted to compensate for the hate their regimes inspire by concessions granted to the workers. This process is obvious in the Dominican Republic.

The "democratic" maneuvers of 1946 soon evaporated. But the laws in favor of the workers enacted during that period of the continental

---

[11] One of the public activities of the Confederation in recent years was its adherence to the presidential candidacy of Héctor B. Trujillo, in a big meeting held in the palace of the Dominican party, on August 29, 1951. *La Nación,* August 31, 1951.

A few weeks before, the Confederation held another national congress of workers, in which Trujillo was not only praised as usual, but there was sung for the first time the Dominican labor anthem, which goes more or less as follows: "Companions, Trujillo has traced new paths to go by; led by his hand the worker goes, already sure of his great welfare. Let us sing the anthem that the people today listen to with great fervor, because it brings in its vibrant tunes gratitude towards the genial Leader." *La Nación,* May 7, 1951. [Fn. 89, Chap. V.]

[12] The congress was called for May, 1955, with participation by "farmers, businessmen, industrialists, and other representatives of the laboring classes." The topics on the agenda were: "(a) What we, the workers, were before the Era of Trujillo, and what we are now; (b) Benefits received by the Dominican people with the peace in which we live; creations, progress, and heights of national industry, pushed by Trujillo. Also: How the social policy established in the country by the Benefactor of the Fatherland has liberated us from communism; the atmosphere of freedom in which the Dominican people live; benefits of social assistance created by Trujillo; how we are being freed from darkness through the literacy campaign; and, our loyalty to the Benefactor will be without restrictions because of gratitude and because of patriotism." *El Caribe,* Feb. 12, 1955. [Fn. 90, Chap. V.]

democratic tide have been maintained and even improved in some ways. The only drawbacks are certain restrictions in case of strikes and in the composition of the national committee on wages.

Today all those labor laws have been systematized in the Trujillo Code of Labor, enacted in 1951. The official edition of the code lists the different previous laws displaced by it. However, the code maintains in force several other laws. In general it is an act of progressive legislation, more progressive than that of the United States in certain aspects; and its inspiration must be found in Latin American legislation, like that in force in Venezuela and Cuba in about the last fifteen years.

The code regulates also the different organs of the Labor Department, with its inspectors and other employees; the national committee on wages; and the labor courts. In relation to strikes, the code permits them in certain restricted cases, if all procedures of conciliation have previously been attempted and after a notice of fifteen days to the secretary of labor; political strikes, those of solidarity, and those affecting certain services of permanent concern are expressly prohibited.

The Sugar Strike of 1946

It is advisable to close this chapter with a brief case study of the only important strike which took place during the Era of Trujillo. It was a strike in the sugar fields in January, 1946. It happened at the time of the highest democratic tide, and the government did not dare to crush it by force. It was the only time that the labor forces acted with spontaneity.

It was not the only attempt. In 1942 a strike had been attempted in the sugar factory of La Romana but it was crushed by the army. At the end of 1945, the sugar workers began a second strike before the opening of the *zafra* (sugar cane harvesting and milling season); it was stopped through mediation by government officials.

The January strike started early in the morning one Monday. Although it is possible that it received some encouragement from exiles abroad, it was obvious that it was essentially a spontaneous movement by the recently organized labor unions in the *central* [sugar mill] of La Romana. The strike was general in the *central,* and its outward cause was connected with a pending petition for better wages. The government reaction was two-fold; on the one hand, the secretary of labor, the secretary of the presidency, and other high authorities (including the chief of staff, General Fiallo) went to La Romana; on the other hand, the national committee on wages was instructed to consider and approve at once the petitions demanded by the labor unions.

The committee always decided in favor of the labor unions, sometimes with increases of 100 percent over the previous wages. On one occasion, the committee was meeting when General Fiallo appeared to suggest that a new scale of wages approved the day before be increased somewhat.[13] It was agreed to at once. The general impression obtained from the hearings was that the specialized workers of the *central* received wages slightly above the average income of the Dominican workers — as much as five dollars a day in some individual cases. But a very serious problem was offered by the cane cutters because of their great number and because of the fact that they work only a few weeks during the whole year. Before the strike, according to the evidence presented to the committee, they received about fifty cents a day, working from dawn to dusk, and only during the harvest period; their increase came to about one dollar a day.

The fast approval of these new scales placated the temper of the workers, who returned to their jobs. The strike lasted more than a week. No violence occurred, and the labor leaders collaborated in good faith in the work of the national committee on wages.

The government did not undertake any serious reprisal while the strike was going on. But some individual reprisals started afterwards: one leader was indicted for incitement to rebellion and another was forced to seek asylum in the Mexican embassy and later went into exile. The Congress also passed a law restricting strikes and another controlling the membership of labor unions; almost immediately thereafter, the national committee on wages was modified in its membership.

---

[13] The first feeling of the committee when he appeared was one of fear because so many concessions had been made to the workers; but, on the contrary, Fiallo requested an even greater increase in order to pacify the still very disturbed workers in La Romana. The author was a witness of all these hearings, being at that time the secretary of the committee. [Fn. 99, Chap. V.]

Chapter 6: Social Institutions

No political study would be complete if it were limited to an analysis of the functioning of the organs of the state or the political parties. In every nation there are certain social institutions and forces, which press upon and even condition governmental affairs. Business organizations, the press, the church, the army, and other such groups play this role in varying degrees in all countries. In Latin America, three of these forces traditionally have had an outstanding role: the landholders, the church, and the army, without forgetting the customary nursery of liberal ideas and revolutions — the university.

In Trujillo's Dominican Republic none of these social forces has any initiative or even a life of its own. All of them, and some others as well, are absolutely subject to the will of the Benefactor, and at least one of them, the army, is his best tool. In some respects, the Trujillo dictatorship acts like other Latin American dictatorships, especially in its use of the army as the main force of support, but it would be difficult to find such absolute submission of intellectual forces in any other country.

Let us analyze briefly the position of these social forces in the present-day Dominican Republic.

The Army and the Police

In the Dominican budget for 1952 (the latest one for which final figures have been made public),[1] out of a total of $94,576,094.58 expended, $59,193,921.74 was assigned to the central administration. Of this amount, $23,025,497.46 was spent in the Secretaryship of War,

---

[1] *Anuario Estadístico de la República Dominicana, 1952* (Ciudad Trujillo, 1954). [Fn. 1, Chap. VI.]

Navy, and Aviation; this means 38.8 percent of the general expenditures of the nation. At the same time $3,376,454.93 was spent in the Secretaryship of Interior and Police; this means 7.5 percent of the general expenditures.[2] Thus, almost half of the Dominican budget is applied to the maintenance of the army and the police. Especially remarkable is that such an amount is spent on an army that has not fought in an international war since the last Haitian invasions almost a century ago, and that has fought not even a civil war for the last forty years.

The Dominican Republic maintains a powerful army, however, which was supplemented several years ago by navy units and planes.[3] The figures do not appear in the official statistics but it is possible to estimate them roughly by the great number of generals and commanders in service today.[4] The army is not meant to prevent external invasions (although the unsuccessful invasions of Cayo Confites and Luperón could be used as pretexts for its reinforcement); it is an army of internal occupation, a mere apparatus of political domination. In order to be safe, Trujillo established a modern arms factory in San Cristóbal[5] seven years ago.

The army has always been the surest tool used by Trujillo. The 1930 coup was possible because Trujillo was the commander of the army; he forced his election in May through the terror spread by military agents disguised as civilians, and at all times the army has been an instrument of action, flattered and supervised at the same time with special care. The only serious conspiracy in its ranks was that led by Colonel Leoncio Blanco in 1934. In order to maintain the loyalty of his army, Trujillo has

---

[2] For comparative purposes, it is convenient to recall that the budget for the Secretaryship of Defense in 1930 was $1,056,837.86 (*G.O.* 4158). [Fn. 2, Chap. VI.]

[3] *Time,* in its issue of March 14, 1955, stated that the Dominican Republic had just bought twenty-five American jet planes of the recent F-86F Sabre type, at a price of $9,000,000. This purchase means that Trujillo has an air superiority over the entire Caribbean area.
As a symptom of the present Dominican armed forces, it can be pointed out that in the military parade held on May 16, 1955, in Ciudad Trujillo, one batallion of the president's guard, one mixed division of infantry with four regiments and motorized units, one brigade of marines, one group of artillery, and sixteen groups of fighter planes participated. *El Caribe,* May 17, 1955. [Fn. 3, Chap. VI.]

[4] In the same military parade, May 16, 1955, at least one lieutenant general, three major generals, five brigadier generals, and several colonels and captains of the navy were mentioned as participants or attending, besides Generalissimo Rafael L. Trujillo and full General Héctor B. Trujillo. *El Caribe,* May 17, 1955. Several top ranking chiefs of the armed forces were absent, among them Major General Rafael L. Trujillo, Jr. [Fn. 4, Chap. VI.]

[5] This big arms factory has received special attention in the United States press recently. Cf. an article by Robert M. Halle in the *Christian Science Monitor,* reproduced in *El Imparcial* in Puerto Rico, May 26, 1955. Its director is Brigadier General Alexander Kovacs, of Hungarian origin; Halle reported that between 750 and 1,100 men were working under his orders. [Fn. 6, Chap. VI.]

combined the general privileges granted to all its members with the strictest distrust, as revealed in the rotation of its commanders, as well at the top as in local posts.

Let us recall briefly the history of the highest commanders. It has never been possible to say that there has been a single chief of the army; Trujillo has always chosen to maintain a duality, or multiplicity, in which the mechanics are put in the hands of one or more trusted generals, while Trujillo in person has kept in one way or another the final control. If he is president, one of his constitutional powers is to be supreme commander; if he is not president, the special position is created for him.

We should note the rotation of the commanders in the field. When Trujillo became president of the Republic in August, 1930, General Simón Díaz was appointed chief of the army. He had been the colonel who, on the occasion of the February coup, simulated an attempt to stop the revolutionist forces coming from Santiago. Simultaneously, General Antonio Jorge was appointed secretary of war and navy. It is worth noting that none of the generals active in the February coup received military commands; General Desiderio Arias was elected a senator and General José Estrella was elected governor of Santiago. The army remained in the hands of Trujillo through colorless subordinates in his utmost confidence.

But neither of the two remained for long at the head of the army. In January, 1931, the Secretaryship of War and Navy disappeared and was merged in the new Secretaryship of Interior, Police, War, and Navy, entrusted to Lic. Jacinto B. Peynado (General Jorge became a deputy in May and a senator in June, 1931). On April 21, 1932, the secretaryship was entrusted to Virgilio Trujillo, when Peynado became secretary of the presidency.

During the next few years the holders of both positions were replaced. On May 8, 1933, the uncle of Trujillo, Teódulo Pina Chevalier, became head of the joint secretaryship; and his brother-in-law, Colonel José García, was promoted to the rank of brigadier general and appointed chief of the army, with Colonel Federico Fiallo as second chief (General Ramón Vásquez was arrested and sentenced a short time later, and, after many vicissitudes, died about 1940 under suspicious circumstances). Again new changes occurred in October, 1935; first, on the fifteenth, Trujillo in person assumed field command of the army, the navy, and the air force; two weeks later, on the twenty-ninth, his brother, Colonel Aníbal J. Trujillo, was appointed chief of staff and promoted to the rank of brigadier general. Several months later, in August, 1936, the youngest brother of Trujillo, Colonel Héctor B. Trujillo, was named auxiliary chief of staff; and in November he was simultaneously promoted to the rank of brigadier general and the position of chief of staff.

From then on, Héctor B. Trujillo became the trusted instrument of Trujillo in command of the army with one or another title. The Benefactor has shown a trust in this youngest brother which he never showed towards the older brothers. One after the other, Virgilio and Aníbal Julio were removed from the more or less important positions they occupied. Héctor B. Trujillo remained as chief of staff from September 29, 1936, until January 2, 1942, when he was appointed secretary of war and navy upon the restoration of that office. In the meantime he was promoted to the rank of major general, a rank which was new in Dominican history.

The new position of Héctor Bienvenido provoked another subdivision of commands in the army that has lasted until today. The first measure was the simultaneous nomination of the new brigadier general, Fernando A. Sánchez, as auxiliary chief of the army, under the authority of Major General Héctor B. Trujillo, although he was in fact the technical commander of the armed forces. But, in order that nobody should question the real situation, on January 21, 1942, Trujillo himself was proclaimed supreme chief of the army and the navy by President Troncoso. In May, 1942, Trujillo reoccupied the presidency, which meant that he again became supreme chief of the armed forces according to the Constitution; but both Héctor B. Trujillo and General Sánchez kept their positions.

On March 17, 1943, Federico Fiallo was readmitted to the army as general supervisor of the police (at the same time he was named head of many of the special controls created because of the state of war). On December 23, 1943, the title of General Sánchez was modified and he was made chief of staff, but on July 12, 1944, General Fiallo replaced him as such. In November, 1944, Héctor B. Trujillo was promoted to the new rank of general of the army, and Federico Fiallo to major general.

During these years the Dominican armed forces were expanded. In February, 1947, the navy was reorganized, and several ships of considerable strength were purchased.[6] In February, 1948, the air force was also reorganized, and many planes were added. Up to now, the navy has not displayed any special political significance, but from the very beginning Trujillo has been very careful about the commanders of the air force. Its first chief of staff was the youngest brother-in-law of Trujillo, Lieutenant Colonel Fernando Castillo, appointed as such on February 13, 1948; . . . later on, since June 5, 1952, the position was to be occupied by Trujillo's

---

[6] On the occasion of the military parade, May 16, 1955, referred to above, twenty units of the Dominican navy were displayed, including two destroyers (*Trujillo* and *Generalissimo*), two frigates, and five corvettes. *El Caribe*, May 17, 1955. [Fn. 10, Chap. VI.]

son "Ramfis," when he was promoted to the rank of brigadier general (the same day he became twenty-three years old).

In the meantime, compulsory military training was established in September, 1947, which offered a pretext for the creation of "honorary generals" among the top political figures of the regime.

In May, 1952, Brigadier General José García Trujillo, a nephew of Trujillo, was appointed undersecretary of navy and aviation. A year later, July 30, 1953, he was appointed chief of staff of the navy. In September of the same year, the undersecretaryships of war and of navy and aviation were merged under his command. On November 15, 1953, another nephew of Trujillo, Virgilio García Trujillo, was promoted to brigadier general and named chief of staff of the army. And on December 30 the undersecretaryship was again divided, José García Trujillo being named for the army and Antonio Leyba Pou for the navy and aviation. "Ramfis" Trujillo continued to be chief of staff of aviation, and in September, 1953, was promoted to the rank of major general (he was twenty-four years old); a sub-chief of staff was named to help him. The last important changes occured at the end of 1954 and in the first half of 1955. . . .

However, and again in order that no one might doubt who was the true boss when Héctor B. Trujillo became president of the Republic, the Dominican Congress passed a law creating a new position of commander-in-chief of the armed forces of the Republic, a position which since then, by a decree on August 16, 1952, has been held by Benefactor Rafael L. Trujillo Molina. At the same time, and since 1933, he continues to be the highest in the military ranks, with the special title of Generalissimo,[7] a rank which never is equalled by any of the ranks newly created for Héctor Bienvenido and several chiefs subsequently honored.

In consequence, the hierarchy of the Dominican armed forces, at the middle of 1955, is headed by the Benefactor, as much with the rank of Generalissimo as with the position of commander-in-chief of the armed forces. Next to him comes his brother Héctor B. Trujillo, with the rank of general of the army and commander in name of the armed forces as president of the Republic. The third in the hierarchy and, in fact, the active commander of the armed forces is his nephew, Major General José García Trujillo, as secretary of war, navy, and aviation.

These are the most important concrete facts about the commands of the Dominican armed forces. It is obvious that the tactics of Trujillo in

---

[7] *G.O.* 4578. Until the death of Stalin, four "Generalissimos" remained in office: Stalin, Franco, Chiang Kai-shek, and Trujillo; the other three at least fought long years of civil wars. When the Great Cross of Courage was granted to Trujillo in 1937, the only campaign mentioned during his entire military life was the persecution of General Arias in 1931. [Fn. 15, Chap. VI.]

the army have been the same as those used in the civil administration. They show the deliberate purpose of not allowing any general, even the most trusted ones, to be perpetuated in any command which may permit him to organize a personal group of lower chiefs who at any time may become a threat to Trujillo. Since the changes mentioned in the highest commands have been repeated all down the hierarchy, there is no single chief or officer who for long commands a regiment, a battalion, a specialized service, or least of all, a garrison or military base. The army as a whole is the institution upon which the regime is based,[8] but there is not one single chief who may dream of being its commander at any time.

Although the army, as was said before, has never fought any war, its chiefs, and even its officers and soldiers, have received many decorations, some of them of recent creation.[9] They are decorations granted for political loyalty and for daily routine in a task which is not military. The destiny of that army fulfills other purposes. In every important city, of course, and at some other strategic points, there are strong garrisons which at any moment could repel any rebellion or invasion. But their usual job is that of police.

Manning surveillance posts at strategic points at the exits of cities as well as on the roads, the army with great regularity and frequency stops cars and trucks to request the identity cards of travelers and to note vehicle registration numbers.[10] The mounted police who supervise the roads also belong to the army and with their mounted patrols go by night through the populous neighborhoods, occasionally entering public places to request identity cards. The military intelligence, a most efficient espionage agency as much inside the country as abroad, is known to carry on or direct the most notorious acts of violence.

That the Dominican army is strong and has modern weapons is demonstrated by attendance at any military parade. During recent years, its professional character has been emphasized, especially among the young officers. The army not only protects the regime in general, but it

---

[8] An interesting indication of this is the fact that in the list of interviews granted by Trujillo, which *El Caribe* has been publishing almost daily during recent times, there are always mentioned several chiefs of the armed forces, usually headed by the secretary of war, navy, and aviation. [Fn. 16, Chap. VI.]

[9] A law of Nov. 4, 1930, created the "Order of Military Merit." In the last years the new orders of "Navy Merit," "Air Merit," "Police Merit," and "Military Heroism, Captain General Santana" have been created. There is also a "Great Cordon President Trujillo" for officers of the army. [Fn. 17, Chap. VI.]

[10] See *Time*, August 29, 1955. In this article, published on the occasion of the twenty-fifth anniversary of the Era, reference was made to a recent police regulation, also published in the Dominican press, according to which it is prohibited to walk in the streets without a jacket or to enter into Ciudad Trujillo without shoes. [Fn. 18, Chap. VI.]

protects Trujillo personally. The few times he appears in public, officers of his aide corps go before and behind him, ordering the people to stand because "the Chief is coming."[11] A general commands the aide corps, and there is no public ceremony without numerous generals and colonels around him. Even in his trips abroad he is accompanied by them, often dressed as civilians and without apparent publicity; it must be noted that most of these trips occurred when he was not the president of the Republic.

The national police, reorganized in 1936, has less importance than the army, and in some degree it acts with independence. But its command has always been entrusted to a chief of the army, usually a lieutenant colonel with the temporary rank of colonel chief of the police. Almost all the highest chiefs of the army have been at one time chief of the police. Their rotation is even more frequent than among the chiefs of the army. Very few commanders of the police have lasted more than one year in office. Some among them have an unsavory reputation.

The job of the police is more restricted. It supervises and exercises internal political espionage in cities and villages, at the same time prosecuting common criminals and quietly policing traffic in the streets. One of its more efficient sections is that of investigation, which keeps the political files and analyzes the constant receipt of reports about all classes of Dominicans or foreigners, including comments of a secretary of state overheard by his driver or anonymous denunciations motivated by vengeance.

As is easy to see, not even espionage is unified in the Dominican Republic. It is not known which office supervises the whole job; there is the office of the police, that of the army already mentioned, and another in the presidency of the Republic. Often the investigators are watching each other, and more than once one of their leaders has fallen into disgrace suddenly because of denunciation by another service. Neither is it known who is the officer directing this service abroad; sometimes it is an officer of the army, sometimes a civilian, and usually none of them is a professional in the intelligence service. In fact, even Dominicans not belonging to the service hasten to report remarks of a friend, for fear that the friend may be a spy who made the remark to watch his reaction. There have been cases of high officers of the government who were dismissed because they did not report the remark made by another high officer who reported it at once. The Dominican intelligence, including that of the military attachés,

---

[11] When Trujillo decides to take a walk at night with his favorites, the police begin carefully watching Washington Avenue by the sea from the middle of the afternoon, and no one is allowed to remain there for any length of time. The author himself has many times been a witness to this fact. [Fn. 21, Chap. VI.]

does not aim to discover secrets of foreign nations or to profit by their technical progress, but merely to watch the activities of the Dominican exiles and the loyalty of tourists. For this reason, Dominicans in transit through foreign countries show the same cautiousness as those living in Ciudad Trujillo.

Press, Radio, and Television

When Trujillo rose to power in 1930, there were three important newspapers in the Dominican Republic, all of them belonging to private owners and more or less following different political trends. In the capital city, there was the morning paper, *Listín Diario,* owned by Arturo Pellerano and supporting the government of General Horacio Vásquez; and an evening paper, *La Opinión,* owned by Sr. Lepervanche, which backed Trujillo in the 1930 campaign. In the city of Santiago there was another paper *La Información,* owned by Luis A. Franco, of an independent trend and regional orientation.

The two newspapers in the capital have now disappeared. In their place there are two other morning papers, both of them established with Trujillo's money and mouthpieces for his government and policies. *La Información* has survived, but it also supports the official policies.

Listín Diario was a good newspaper of long tradition in the country. From February, 1930, until the May elections it did not hesitate to defend the cause of the National-Progressive Alliance and to denounce the subsequent abuses committed by Trujillo's agents. On May 30 its building was stormed by "a group of civilians in favor of the Coalition." A short time later, its pages became mute to national political news, using a contemptuous silence as the only form of opposition to the new regime. Two and a half years later, in January, 1933, *Listín Diario* began to publish information about Trujillist activities under big headlines; and in March its pages were open to the poll conducted by Dr. Aybar concerning the reelection of Trujillo without previous balloting. Its collaboration was not as yet submissive, and on April 1 its editor was arrested. Eleven days later the unconditional surrender of the newspaper was completed when the assistant editor and son of the owner asked admission into the Dominican party. On April 25 Arturo Pellerano, Jr. was elected a deputy.

From this moment on, *Listín Diario* was the spokesman for the Trujillo regime, and its pages overflowed in a literature of praise. Later on, Arturo Pellerano became president of the Chamber and a senator; he died while a deputy.

La Opinión did not need to change, but nevertheless it was more cautious in its praises. It had been founded in 1922 as a literary magazine and in 1927 was transformed into a daily paper. Both newspapers had good writers on their staffs and received excellent national literary contributions, plus the news transmitted by the best world press agencies.

At the end of 1939, preparations were begun to launch a new newspaper called *La Nación,* with capital put up by Trujillo. It pretended to be an up-to-date paper, which would modernize the style used in the country until then. For this purpose, the services of several exiled Spanish newspapermen were retained, although a Dominican was named its editor. *La Nación* appeared for the first time on February 19, 1940.

Its appearance was better than that of the Dominican papers then in existence. But from the very beginning it was obvious that it would be nothing more than the official mouthpiece of the government. Its circulation was increased by forcing public employees to become subscribers. In consequence, advertising was transferred from *Listín Diario* to *La Nación.* Very soon afterward, it was an open secret that *Listín Diario* could not remain alive without subventions received at the time from the German [12] and Spanish legations. The fact was that *Listín Diario* could not provide competition for long and on January 15, 1942, it was closed; the date confirms the general belief as to German subsidies, because, a month before, the Dominican Republic had declared war on Germany and in consequence the German legation had been closed. *La Opinión* remained as an evening paper, although always carrying on a precarious existence; it was always favorable to the Allies.

The situation remained thus until the beginning of 1946. In January of that year, Trujillo used *La Opinión* for his temporary project of democratization. We already know of the campaign of moderate opposition carried on by this newspaper. But the consequences of this opposition sealed the fate of *La Opinión;* at the middle of 1946, Trujillo bought the paper, and the previous owners left for New York. The paper disappeared permanently at the beginning of 1947.

For one year more, *La Nación* was the only newspaper in the capital and the only good one in the Republic. In April, 1947, another newspaper, *El Caribe,* appeared for the first time. It was no secret that it also belonged to Trujillo, although in the beginning a United States journalist, Stanley Ross, collaborated in the enterprise. Soon afterward, Ross disappeared from the scene, and Germán Ornes Coiscou became editor of *El Caribe.* During the last years, it is obvious that *El Caribe* is better than *La Nación*

---

[12] Its pro-German campaign excelled on the occasion of the victorious battles of 1940. In the days preceding the conquest of Paris, a loudspeaker of *Listín Diario,* installed in the Colón Square, reported the latest news to the public. One of the journalists in charge of this task later became an alternate delegate of the Dominican Republic in the United Nations and finally secretary of foreign relations. [Fn. 26, Chap. VI.]

in content and importance, although both of them coincide in being spokesmen for the regime. The most scrutinized section of *El Caribe* is the so-called Foro Público, made up of pretended letters to the editor that in fact are unofficial warnings from the presidency to those who are suspect, or vituperation against those who have fallen into disgrace. In the rest of the country there are no newspapers deserving the name, and, in fact, no good periodicals at all.

What is the uniform characteristic of the Dominican press? Only one: its fawning over Trujillo. There is no censorship of the press, because it is not required. The facts are so obvious, by just looking at the newspapers and other publications, that they do not need to be proved. But it is advisable for anyone who would like to prepare an anthology of press sycophancy to look through the headlines, reports, and articles of the press. The only difficulty facing Dominican journalists is to find new adjectives for their use: if anyone finds a new idea he is a genius. Occasionally, it is hard for the social writer to be *au courant* with the temporary priorities or disgraces in the family of the Benefactor, so as to use the most glowing adjectives for one, or silence for another who may be in disgrace. It is, of course, impossible to find in the Dominican press the slightest criticism of the regime itself.

With reference to other media of publicity, until a few years ago the radio broadcasting stations were submissive to the regime but they were independent. Today, one of them, La Voz Dominicana, owned by J. Arismendi ("Petán") Trujillo has preeminence. The same person is also the owner of the only television station, which went on the air about ten years ago in the inland town of Bonao, seat of this peculiar brother of Trujillo who in the first years of the regime showed sparks of rebellion. When he founded the station he was a major in the army without assignment; later on he was promoted to honorary colonel, brigadier general, and lieutenant general. The station is today installed in a magnificent building in Ciudad Trujillo, also used as a luxurious night club.

"Petán" deserves to be recognized as the man who contributed to the material advance of the Dominican Republic with a good radio station and the only television station. But the news and propaganda transmitted through them is the same read in the Dominican press.

It must be added that the direction of communications has also the duty to monitor, as much as possible, foreign radio stations, in order to silence with noise those broadcasts that may attack the Trujillo regime. This service was especially active during the years in which this kind of radio offensive was in motion from Cuba and Venezuela.

In summary, there exists no free press or radio in the Dominican Republic. But the problem is not of censorship or gag. It is a problem of asphyxia because it is an almost absolute monopoly in the hands of Trujillo himself or his brother "Petán." [13]

The University and the Students

The Dominicans pride themselves on having the oldest university in the New World, the Pontifical University of St. Thomas Aquinas, created in 1539. Mexicans and Peruvians claim the same honor, affirming that their own universities, organized twelve years later, deserve greater rank. In any case, the Dominican university tradition comes from early colonial days, when the island of Santo Domingo was still the center from which all expeditions for the mainland departed.

That university has suffered many vicissitudes during the agitated political life of the Dominicans. Its president, Núñez de Cáceres, proclaimed the independence of 1821, and the Haitians closed it; some of its presidents have been presidents of the Republic, and in its classrooms were born rebellions against foreign occupations and native dictatorships.

In 1930, a well known physician, Dr. Ramón de Lara, was appointed president of the university, and the National Association of University Students (ANEU) became active there. At the end of 1930, Dr. Lara was expelled from the country. He was later allowed to return, but in 1935 he was jailed as the alleged leader of the plot in the capital against Trujillo. For about twenty years he has lived as an exile in Venezuela. The ANEU was replaced by a militarized organization, the Guardia Universitaria Presidente Trujillo, which was alive only on the occasion of official parades.

What impresses any traveler staying for some time in the Dominican Republic is the silence of the university campus. The Latin American student is noisy, rebellious, and unpredictable in his reactions. All political ideologies flourish in the university and often explode in riots. In countries subject to dictatorship, revolution hatches there in an alliance of professors and students. In the Dominican Republic, the university has the rhythm of a monastic seminary.

During most of the Era, the university was still lodged at the old building near Fortress Ozama; in recent years it has been moved to the

---

[13] The nonexistence of a free press has been confirmed by the Inter-American Press Association in its periodical reports, the latest one made public on March 25, 1955. See *La Prensa*, March 26, 1955. The most interesting report, in reference to the Dominican Republic was the one presented by the board of directors of the IAPA to the congress held in Quito, in July, 1949. It began as follows: "As a consequence of the situation existing since years ago in the Dominican Republic under its present regime of government, there is not a propitious media for the unrestricted exercise of the freedom of the press...." The report included many concrete data, coincident with those exposed in this study. [Fn. 30, Chap. VI.]

new campus of the Ciudad Universitaria on the outskirts of the capital. It shows undeniably the material progress of the recent period, as much in its buildings as in means of teaching. But the education itself is handicapped by the political gag that impedes all discussion of topics which could inspire restlessness; the university is merely a machine to deliver professional degrees.

Its organization is classic: the five traditional faculties of law, medicine, sciences, philosophy, and pharmacy, plus a new one of dental surgery, and the faculty of philosophy, which was organized in 1940. In the past, the degree granted was that of *licenciado* (more or less like the master's degree); today this intermediate degree has disappeared in most of the faculties and the students are graduated as doctors, a routine doctorate in which the thesis lacks any value.

The professors are appointed by decree of the executive. Sometimes the president of the university or the dean of the pertinent faculty suggests a candidate, but often the appointment means only a political reward. All professors must, of course, have evidenced an active adherence to the regime, and more than one has been dismissed because of suspected coolness. The same happens with the positions of the president and the dean. The presidents are always political figures and have frequently been members of Trujillo's cabinet. When Dr. Lara was dismissed in the fall of 1930, he was replaced for four years by another great intellectual personality, Dr. Federico Henríquez i Carvajal. At the beginning of 1935, the latter was replaced by Dr. Manuel de Jesús Troncoso de la Concha (later on, president of the Republic). In June, 1938, the latter was replaced by Lic. Julio Ortega Frier, who had been minister of foreign relations during the settlement of the Haitian massacre. Ortega Frier carried on a notable reorganization, at the same time displaying absolute loyalty to the regime. Two years later, he was replaced by Lic. Virgilio Díaz Ordóñez, former secretary of education and later secretary of foreign relations. In 1943, Lic. Ortega Frier was again appointed as president, with Lic. José A. Bonilla Atiles as vice-president, but the latter had no outstanding Trujillist record and very soon afterward was dismissed before going into exile. Political personalities have also been among the most recent presidents.

These presidents and deans have taken good care of political safety in the university. All Dominican professors must, of course, be members of the Dominican party. They have been forced to answer questionnaires of political investigation, must attend official Te Deums and the principal meetings of the party. In every public demonstration, the university faculty parades as a whole with the president and deans at the head. But much more important than those external demonstrations are the lectures in classrooms. The professors teaching history or mathematics have no difficulties; those teaching current or human problems are in trouble; they must mix their praise of the regime, as required, with silence about events going on abroad. This, among other reasons, is because every professor is fearful that one of his students may be a spy, and more than once that suspicion has been confirmed.

The only period in which there was any agitation within the university was the year 1945. The roots of this movement are to be found in the centennial of 1944, on which occasion the vice-president, Lic. Bonilla Atiles, gathered several students to enact the dramatic piece "La Viuda de Padilla" as the university contribution to the festivities. It is a Spanish drama exalting the rebellion of the Castillian *comuneros* against the new absolutist regime in sixteenth century Spain under Emperor Charles V. Despite its literary weakness, it has many sentences in praise of freedom. The members of the secret society "La Trinitaria" founded by Duarte used it in 1844 as a symbol of their clandestine fight against the Haitian occupation, and Bonilla thought it wise to use the pretext of this historical episode to repeat the symbolic protest against the present regime. The authorities did not suspect the hidden meaning, or, if anyone suspected it, he kept it to himself. The group of students thus selected flourished later in a series of spontaneous centers of study and discussion, which step by step were transformed into cells of a clandestine organization in part discovered by the police in the summer of 1945. Later, these evolved into the political organization "Democratic Youth." At the same time, the incipient Communist movement led by Pericles Franco, Jr., became active.

This movement exploded at the beginning of 1946, when several university students supported the letter of former Vice-President Bonilla Atiles in the pages of *La Opinión,* as already mentioned. The official answer was the mobilization of 2,000 students in March, to pay homage to Trujillo, under the leadership of the Guardia Universitaria.[14]

The first commander of the Guardia was the dean of the faculty of dental surgery, Dr. José E. Aybar. Its lower officers were students active in the Dominican party. This uniformed Guardia organized the Trujillista party at the end of 1940.

Two outstanding facts illustrating the submission of the university to Trujillo involve him personally. Trujillo does not have a university education and there is no evidence that he went further than elementary school; later in life, he did not pursue any intellectual studies or researches.

---

[14] Five years later, in July, 1951, another group of students bestowed upon Trujillo the "Great Collar of Democracy." *El Caribe,* July 10, 1951. It would be endless to mention other gestures of homage and similar demonstrations. [Fn. 32, Chap. VI.]

Nevertheless, in 1934 a law of October 3 authorized the university to grant honorary degrees, and six days later it was made public that the whole faculty had decided to grant the first honorary doctorate to the Generalissimo. Six years later, in December, 1940, he was appointed professor of economy, although of course he never delivered a lecture.

The Secretaryship of Public Education repeats this same political supervision in all levels of instruction, including the few private colleges which exist in the Dominican Republic. While all professors are appointed by the executive, the secretaryship determines the educational standards to be met and the programs to be offered in secondary education in the *escuelas normales* (high schools) and in primary education in other schools.[15] As an example of this close supervision and standard indoctrination, one notes that secondary students must take part in the Trujillist parades, in which the primary students also frequently appear.

In the 1952 budget, $4,230,857.56 was allotted to all the departments under the Secretaryship of Education, from the primary schools to the university; this meant 7 percent of the general expenditures and was less than a quarter of the amount given to the Secretaryship of War, Navy, and Aviation. In order better to evaluate this disproportion, it must be remembered that in the Dominican Republic almost all educational centers are supported by the government; very few are private.

The *Statistical Yearbook* does not give figures for illiteracy. Unofficially, it is said that it is not over 35 percent, a percentage which would be very low for Latin America and seems to be too optimistic. The United Nations, in its preliminary report about the social situation in the world,[16] has not hesitated to report 74 percent illiteracy in the Dominican Republic, basing it on the year 1935, but that is incorrect today. The Pan American Union, in another report printed in 1951,[17] preferred not to mention any figures on illiteracy in the Dominican Republic. In any event, it would be fair to recognize the great advance in the Dominican Republic during the last fifteen years toward decreasing the index of illiteracy, especially through the so-called schools of emergency, even without access to the exact results obtained to date.

There are also some special schools, such as the musical lyceum and the school of fine arts, equally dependent on the Secretaryship of Educa-

---

[15] Since 1940 there is a "Ramfis Prize for Students," awarded every year in the primary schools. *G.O.* 5465. [Fn. 38, Chap. VI.]

[16] *Naciones Unidas, Informe Preliminar Sobre la Situación Social en el Mundo* (E/CN.5/267/Rev.1), (New York, 1952), p. 103. [Fn. 41, Chap. VI.]

[17] Unión Panamericana, *América Frente al Analfabetismo,* Washington, 1951. [Fn. 42, Chap. VI.]

tion. It would seem that pure art is more difficult to control politically, but the decisive influence of that control is noticeable. It is sufficient, for instance, to see the innumerable pictures and statues of Trujillo ordered by secretaryships and other official departments from national or foreign artists;[18] it is even noticeable in the murals by the Spanish painter Vela Zanetti in many official buildings, in which subjects referring to Trujillo are repeated, although they are not the only ones. The same flattery is obvious in the usual dedications of poems or concerts to the Benefactor.

No author could publish a book if he could not be certain that the Dominican party or the Department of Education would buy at least a hundred copies; but in order to assure this sale, the book must be orthodox in appearance, and it is much better if it mentions the name of Trujillo in its pages. Perhaps the outstanding case happened in the literary contest organized by the Department of Education on the occasion of the centennial in 1944. It was an open secret that a great poem written by Lic. Armando Oscar Pacheco about the discovery of the Americas deserved the Golden Flower, but this first prize was declared vacant because neither the jury nor the Department dared to deny a prize to another poem written by Abelardo R. Nanita about Trujillo and his deeds. The solution in the style of Solomon was to declare vacant the Golden Flower and award two citations, one to each poem.

The author of this study was a professor of comparative law during five years of his stay in the Dominican Republic and knows very well the spirit of the students. His students at the diplomatic school (at that time operating in the Department of Foreign Relations) could not hide their reaction every time a reference was made to institutions existing in free countries or when any criticism was made about the totalitarian regimes of the right or of the left. However, the mind and the will of Dominican students in general today are atrophied after twenty-five years of teaching oriented, from the primary schools up, to fawning upon a dictatorial regime.

The Dominican University is completely submissive to Trujillo, and its professors as well as its graduates do not dare give public evidence of any judgment of their own.

The Catholic Church

As in other Latin American countries, Dominicans in general are baptized in the Catholic church at birth. Only a very small minority is

---

[18] Outstanding among the monuments is the "Monument to the Peace of Trujillo" in the city of Santiago, to be dedicated at the end of 1955 on the occasion of the Year of the Benefactor. This equestrian statue was contracted for from the Spanish sculptor, Juan Cristóbal. [Fn. 43, Chap. VI.]

openly Protestant. That does not mean that all Dominicans uniformly practice the Catholic religion or even that they are orthodox in their beliefs. It is normal among middle and upper classes to belong at the same time to Masonic lodges; and among the lower classes to practice a series of superstitions stemming from rites of African origin.

In some Latin American countries, the Catholic church continues to be a socio-political force of great influence, almost always following a conservative trend. In the Dominican Republic, the active participation of the church as such has never been felt in political conflicts, despite the fact that two archbishops have been presidents of the Republic.

When Trujillo became president,* the old Monsignor Nouel was still the archbishop of Santo Domingo.[19] But at the end of 1935, a monk of Italian origin, Ricardo Pittini, was appointed archbishop.[20] His public conduct has been one of total submission to the dictatorship, and, on more than one occasion, he has personally praised Trujillo. The clergy in general have been more discreet in their conduct; they have attempted to keep good, but not too close, relations with the government.

A fruit of government policy was the signature of the concordat with the Holy See on June 16, 1954. It was a project discussed years before, without any result. Trujillo's private life has always shown a complete indifference towards Catholic discipline, despite the fact that he belongs to this faith. He also joined Free Masonry, where it is said that he reached the second degree as brother. One of the conditions the church insisted upon for the agreement on a concordat was a legal procedure of marriage for Catholics on the basis of a religious ceremony and the indissolubility of the conjugal bond. Trujillo has not only been divorced twice,[21] but he forced the approval of a special law on divorce to meet his personal needs. During recent years, however, his wife has exhibited much religious fervor. On January 31, 1947, she issued an appeal to Dominican Catholics in pious terms. Trujillo himself has reached a mature age. All these personal circumstances may have contributed, as much to obstruct the concordat in the past, as to ease its approval in 1954.

---

*He had been president of the Republic for a little more than a year in 1932.

[19] In March, 1933, he was granted a retirement for life paid by the State. *G.O.* 4556. [Fn. 44, Chap. VI.]

[20] *Listín Diario,* Oct. 26, 1935. One of his first public acts was to baptize "Ramfis" (at that time six years old) on Jan. 22, 1936. The previous marriage of his parents at the end of September was a civil one, a ceremony forced by the dual circumstance of both contracting parties being divorced. [Fn. 45, Chap. VI.]

[21] His daughter, Flor de Oro, was divorced five times and married seven. [Fn. 48, Chap. VI.]

Officially, according to the Constitution, there exists complete freedom of conscience and worship, and at the same time there is an unofficial
relationship between the state and the Catholic church. These relations had
been restricted until now to the Te Deums and high masses that are celebrated on the occasion of national holidays or Trujillist festivities. This
situation is not substantially changed by the new concordat. But an important modification has been introduced by giving equal legality to Catholic
and civil marriages, with the important proviso of making divorce impossible for those couples married under church law. The concordat also
grants legal privileges to the Catholic church "according to the Divine Law
and the Canon Law." In reference to the appointment of archbishops and
bishops, the Holy See "will make known to the Dominican Government
the name of the person chosen, in order to learn if there is any objection
of a general political kind against him"; as far as possible, Dominicans will
be selected.

It is too soon to foresee the repercussions that this concordat, with
its partial suppression of divorce, may have in the public and private life
of the Dominicans. It is possible that the number of Catholic marriages
may decrease slightly, in order to keep an open door for divorces which
many years ago became a normal occurrence in the country. But probably
that will not mean any substantial change, because among the lower
classes there have been frequent common-law marriages without any legal
bond.[22] Much more important may be the consequences in public life,
following the unknown negotiations prior to the signature of the concordat.

Until now, the influence of the church in the public life of the Dominican Republic has been small. There is the Catholic Action, but it has no
strength at all. Neither in the Dominican party nor in any of the other
organizations has any ecclesiastical participation or doctrine of Christian
inspiration been observed; neither has there been any antagonism. It would
seem that the Catholic church has not been a factor in the Trujillo regime,
either for good or for bad.

Feminism

It does not seem, either, that the feminist movement, encouraged by
Trujillo in 1940 and 1941, has been an important influence. There was no
spontaneous movement, and least of all a widespread one, of feminine
protest against the traditional legal and political inequality between the

---

[22] According to the *Anuario Estadístico de la República Dominicana, 1952,*
(Ciudad Trujillo, 1954), p. 55, during 1952, 46,451 children were born in the
Dominican Republic; among them 18,605 were legitimate (40 percent) and 27,846
were illegitimate (60 percent). In the same year, 9,163 marriages were performed
and 841 divorces were granted (*ibid.,* pp. 43–55). [Fn. 51, Chap. VI.]

sexes. A few intellectual figures and the wives of political personalities from time to time expressed their opinion in such a respect, but at no time was their desire transformed into a campaign.

When it was obvious that Trujillo thought of flattering the Dominican women by granting them equal rights, at once a rivalry was precipitated among those women with aspirations to the leadership of the movement and the enjoyment of its benefits. Trujillo did not allow those rivalries to cause problems, but from above decided to handle the movement through other persons having his confidence.

The feminist movement was organized as a branch of the Trujillist party at the end of 1940; Isabel Mayer was its most notorious figure during the first political meetings. In 1940, equality of civil rights was granted to women, and in the constitution of January, 1942, equality of political rights was given them. In the elections of May, 1942, women voted for the first time; at the same time three congresswomen were elected. The feminist movement, however, was no more than a summer storm. In practice, the activities of the feminine branch of the Dominican party died through inaction. Until now, no woman has been a secretary of state or has occupied any other of the higher positions.

It is probable that Trujillo began this movement primarily to appear up to date with modern currents of equality between the sexes. But actually these innovations would appear to have no real importance in the political Trujillist field, nor in the general civic one.

Attitude of the Businessmen

It is not easy to evaluate the precise attitude of men of business toward Trujillo's regime. Outwardly, of course, they back it, and it is even possible that, in their conflicting feelings, the security offered by any dictatorship in maintaining order lends predominant weight; but at the same time the individual peculiarities of this dictatorship keep alive suspicion and occasionally provoke antagonism.

In the first place, let us examine the apparent adherence to the regime. One need only see a special issue of *El Caribe* or *La Nación* on the occasion of a national holiday or Trujillist festivity. The full-page advertisements do not offer goods for sale by any store or services to the public by an enterprise; the one message they offer is to praise Trujillo's work.[23]

---

[23] In the latest special issue of *El Caribe,* August 16, 1955, the number of political advertisements increased to seventeen full pages, twenty-two half pages, twenty-six quarter pages, and many small ones. Many of them included pictures of the Benefactor and brother president; some of them were paid for by individuals. [Fn. 58, Chap. VI.]

This kind of advertising has even appeared in the New York press.[24] In the same way, the local chambers of commerce have their special place in Trujillist parades.

But, is there evident any active adherence of these wealthy groups to the regime? It is not evident. There are various reasons for this inertia.

Perhaps the most important one is suspicion. Every one in the Dominican Republic knows that the top businessman in the country is Trujillo, closely followed by his relatives and favorites. There are lines of business in which Trujillo has practically established his monopoly, and it is not even possible to dream of competing with him. In other cases, prosperous businesses of the past have been forced to give him shares,[25] even a majority of the shares. There are known concrete cases of modest businessmen who prefer to simulate the appearance of ruin in their buildings and offices in order not to awake curiosity or cupidity. In other cases, an unofficial agent may visit the owner of a business to offer him "protection" in exchange for participation in his profits.[26]

This suspicion does not reach open antagonism. On one hand, the businessman has the same fear as other citizens, perhaps greater because he has more to lose. A student goes to jail or suffers beatings; a businessman may remain free and yet be ruined by not receiving the necessary and numerous permits required to operate in the Dominican Republic. This control of business is more acute in countries like the Dominican Republic — and in most Latin American countries, which exist upon an economy depending on the export of raw materials and the import of manufactured goods. Most of the big businessmen active in the Dominican Republic are exporters of sugar, cacao, and other tropical products, or they are importers of machinery, textiles, and other manufactures, mostly from the United States; in this game of foreign commerce the government

---

[24] See, for instance, p. 77 of the *New York Times,* Jan. 5, 1955, in which there is a full-page advertisement with the portrait of Trujillo and warm praise signed by the Ozama Sugar Company, Limited, South Puerto Rico Sugar Company and West Indies Sugar Corporation (the two latter had been attacked by Trujillo in January, 1954). An identical advertisement printed in the *New York Herald Tribune,* Jan. 3, 1955, was reproduced in photostat by *El Caribe,* Jan. 5, 1955. [Fn. 59, Chap. VI.]

[25] One of the outstanding cases, widely known in the Dominican Republic, was that of the Compañía Tabacalera Dominicana. After the forced transaction, Anselmo Copello, who previously controlled this company, was appointed ambassador in Washington at the end of 1944 (he died in office a short time later). [Fn. 61, Chap. VI.]

[26] Some of these visits do not come from the boss but from others. For a long time, the agents of one of Trujillo's brothers have been widely known in this respect; it is said that he has more or less controlled truck transportation (there is only a very short railroad in the north of the country), and the marketing of fruits and poultry. Cf. Bustamante, *Satrapía,* p. 14. [Fn. 63, Chap. VI.]

does not need to adopt drastic methods for its pressures, it need only apply in one or another way the laws in force.

The Dominican businessman must be a member of the Dominican party, because in the forms for export or import, there is also a line to be filled in concerning political membership. In addition, many of these businessmen must travel abroad, which requires a passport and an exit permit which depends upon the same official approval. There is no need to decree punishment, or even to deny permits; it is enough to delay the matter forever by red tape in the government offices.

Another reason for uneasiness is the complicated taxes imposed on foreign commerce. Businessmen seek, of course, to transfer those taxes to the consumers and suffer no loss. But often they feel the brunt of new taxes, and they even whisper that the amounts collected may not always find their way to the national treasury, since there are no receipts.[27] This game was especially practiced during World War II, when the scarcity of many imported products allowed the government to establish quotas which benefited the businesses controlled by Trujillo, his relatives, or his favorites, in detriment to those businessmen who were more independent politically.

Another reason for antagonism may be mentioned, based upon personal feelings of the families of "aristocratic" tradition. Trujillo has not forgotten the scorn they showed towards him in the period before he was president; especially the fact that he was rejected as a member of the exclusive Club Unión. After becoming president, Trujillo exacted his social reprisals by forcing his election and reelection as president of the Club Unión before closing it by an apparent decision of the membership. There still remain memories of past brilliance among the oligarchic class, which was formerly prominent in official receptions; the oligarchy today is submissive and apparently collaborates with the regime, but they do not forget and in their private conversations like to recall the humble origin of the Benefactor and his favorites.

During recent years, another reason for a certain uneasiness has been obvious, although it has never assumed the importance reached in Perón's Argentina. This is a consequence of the steps taken by Trujillo in favor of the workers in order to attract them.

Taking into consideration this complex picture, it is easier to understand the diffidence of the wealthy classes towards Trujillo's regime. Deep

---

[27] Importers of textiles, for instance, have been forced for several years to pay in cash and without receipt to a special "Control," 10 percent of the value of rayon and cotton goods and 15 percent of the value of woolen goods. A similar system has existed for other lines of imports and exports. [Fn. 65, Chap. VI.]

in their thoughts, it is possible that they prefer him to the insecurity of a revolutionary change; weighing advantages and inconveniences, it may be that, after all, the stronger argument is the conviction that they are making money even though this negative acceptance is not transformed into active collaboration. The big businessmen do not interfere in public administration, and most of them are very careful not to accept the highest positions or place themselves in the foreground.

This cautious attitude is noticeable not only among businessmen, but also among professionals. There are eminent lawyers who finally decided to join the active Trujillist ranks (like Troncoso de la Concha, Ortega Frier, and Peña Batlle),[28] but most of the outstanding lawyers limit themselves to membership in the Dominican party and at most, accept secondary positions in the regime in order to be on the safe side, lest they be accused of being enemies of Trujillo. Because of the very nature of their profession, physicians have been more protected; their collaboration usually is limited to their being professors in the university, and by rotation, secretaries of health. Engineers and architects are more involved in the activities of the regime, because its program of public works and construction has offered them sources of income; but they also prefer to refrain from occupying public positions. It is significant to check the names of legislators, secretaries of state, and governors in the Dominican Republic. In the list it will be difficult to find big businessmen and prestigious professionals.

This situation is repeated in the foreign companies, which used to be the most powerful in the Dominican economic field before the beginning of the present regime.[29]

---

[28] In the collaboration of these three lawyers with the regime, one must obviously understand the need of protecting in this way the economic interests of the powerful companies they had as clients. Especially outstanding was the case of Peña Batlle, lawyer of the Vicini family (of Italian origin), which was included originally in the "Black List" issued by the Allies at the beginning of the war and later on removed from it at the request of Trujillo. Then its lawyer became active in the regime and subsequently occupied the presidency of the Chamber, the Secretaryship of the Interior and that of Foreign Relations, after having prided himself on being an "opponent" of the regime for several years. [Fn. 69, Chap. VI.]

[29] Until very recently, Trujillo appeared to respect these foreign companies more than native businessmen. But in 1954, obvious signs were noted that he had decided to force them to submit also, and even to displace them. At the beginning of that year, Trujillo personally attacked openly certain United States-owned sugar *centrales*. The reason for this attack must be found in the new sugar *centrales* owned privately by Trujillo which were opened during recent years.

Later on came the culmination of previous attacks upon the Electric Company (*Bol. Cam.*, April, 1946), in the form of its purchase at the beginning of 1955 by the Dominican government for $13,200,000. *El Caribe*, Jan. 17, 1955. At the end of 1954, it was also announced that the government would buy the telephone company. *El Caribe*, Dec. 26, 1954. [Fn. 71, Chap. VI.]

Chapter 7: Personal Style of the Benefactor

Any study of Trujillo's political regime would be incomplete without the human touch. Because it is such a personal dictatorship, a brief analysis of the man himself is required.

None of the features reported in this chapter are exclusive to Trujillo alone. Since history began, the vices of megalomania, nepotism, and graft have been common in the tyrannical courts of the world. But it is somewhat surprising that in the middle of the twentieth century, all these aberrations reappear in a small island of the Caribbean.

In order to summarize this chapter, it would be enough to transcribe any of the footnotes printed in the Dominican Republic every time that Trujillo's picture is reproduced. In the United States, President Roosevelt was referred to as F.D.R. and President Eisenhower is simply "Ike." In the Dominican Republic Trujillo is: His Excellency Generalissimo Doctor Rafael Leonidas Trujillo Molina, Honorable President of the Republic (when he is such), Father of the New Fatherland, Benefactor of the Fatherland, Restorer of the Financial Independence of the Republic. Now that he is not the president, mention of his name is longer because it calls for an "ex" and there must be added commander-in-chief of the armed forces. Occasionally mention must also be made of him as First Worker of the Republic, or First Teacher, or First Journalist.

If we turn from his person to the country itself, any of the smaller maps will show that the capital is Ciudad Trujillo, that there is a Trujillo Province, another Trujillo Valdez Province, and that the highest mountain is called Trujillo Peak. On more detailed maps we can find even small villages with names taken from the royal family, and in the plans of the cities are multiplied similar names of streets, squares, and buildings. The same happens on postage stamps, in the lyrics of the *merengues* (national dances), and in the advertising of the national lottery.

This personal megalomania is duplicated in business. There are few businesses of great importance in which Trujillo or members of his family do not appear in one way or another.

It would be possible to simplify the many titles of Trujillo into a single one: he is the First Landholder of the Republic; the whole country is his estate. Instead of governing, he manages the country as a private estate; today he may appoint someone as his trusted foreman, and tomorrow send him to the "doghouses."

Megalomania

The material on this subject is so copious that the difficulty is to summarize it in a few paragraphs. One can begin with the official and permanent titles of Trujillo, required to be repeated by protocol in the same order they are mentioned here.

The rank of Generalissimo was granted to him by a law of May 26, 1933.* The degree of Doctor (honoris causa) was granted by the university faculty on October 8, 1934. The title of Father of the New Fatherland was conferred by a law of May 5, 1955. The title of Benefactor of the Fatherland was conferred by a resolution of Congress on November 8, 1932. And the title of Restorer of the Financial Independence was granted by law on November 2, 1940.

It may be added that a law of October 11, 1935, created and described with full detail the insignia of the rank of Generalissimo, and another on September 2, 1950, modified slightly the insignia of Benefactor. In the same official category may be included the law of April 16, 1940, which ordered that mention be made in any public document or letter of the date of the "Era of Trujillo" in which it is written.

In a lower level, but also official, belong many other titles and ranks periodically bestowed upon Trujillo when he is not president. Among these may be cited supreme chief of the army and navy and commander-in-chief of the armed forces of the Republic. In the same vein have been his repeated appointments as ambassador extraordinary every time he goes abroad on a pleasure trip, and even his brief nomination as Dominican delegate to the United Nations at the end of 1952, and as secretary of foreign relations at the beginning of 1953, for the sole purpose of giving him the required official prestige during his stay in the United States.

One may also add his nomination as professor of political economy at the University of Santo Domingo in December, 1940, and all the honorary

---

*The meticulous documentation provided by the author for all details in the following pages has been omitted.

titles casually mentioned in the press without exact indications of their source, such as "First Teacher" and "First Journalist."

The list would be endless if one cared to enter into lesser details. In October, 1931, he was proclaimed "Meritorious Son" of the city of San Cristóbal, and in April, 1939, San Cristóbal itself received the official title of "Meritorious City" because Trujillo was born there. In December, 1936, it was decided to celebrate each January 11 as the "Day of the Benefactor." In October, 1938, Congress voted to commemorate each October 24, the day of his birthday, and in March, 1941, decided to celebrate every August 16 as the anniversary of the beginning of his Era. Let us add the many days of national holiday each time Trujillo comes back from a trip abroad. Special mention must be made of this present year of 1955, declared to be the "Year of the Benefactor" to commemorate the twenty-five years of his Era; on this occasion, on August 16, still another decoration has been bestowed upon him, the "Great Collar of the Fatherland" adorned with twenty-five jeweled pieces, one for each year.

There is another kind of Dominican honor. In the first place there are the Orders of Merit created in his own name, titles, or deeds: such as the Order of Trujillo, created on June 13, 1938, whose Great Collar was reserved exclusively for him; the Order of the Generalissimo created the same month for members of the army; the Great Cordon of President Trujillo created in February, 1953, for the same purpose; the Medal of February 23 (date of the 1930 coup) created in June, 1937, whose first presentation was to Trujillo; and the Trujillo Prize of Peace, created in October, 1938, although it was never awarded. In the second place, some Dominican decorations have been exclusively created for Trujillo, besides his insignia of Benefactor and Generalissimo, such as the Great Cross of Courage, bestowed upon him in February, 1937 and other non-official decorations offered to him by professional groups from time to time, including the Great Collar of Democracy given to him by students in 1951, and a symbolic lyre presented by the musicians. The highest decorations of all Dominican honorary Orders, such as those of Juan Pablo Duarte, Cristóbal Colón, Military Merit, Navy Merit, Air Merit, Police Merit, and the very recent Order of Heroism, Captain General Santana, have all been awarded Trujillo.

Prominent among these Dominican honors are the naming of geographical places after Trujillo. Especially remarkable was the rebaptism of the capital (called Santo Domingo de Guzmán since it was founded by Columbus in 1496) to Ciudad Trujillo by a law of January 11, 1936. Next, one may recall the creation of the Trujillo Province by a law of October, 1932, although it did not come into force until it was approved by the constitutional reform of 1934; the creation of the provinces Benefactor and Libertador in 1938; the creation of the province San Rafael in 1942; and the attempt to name another province, created in 1949, "The New Era." The Trujillo Valdez Province is not mentioned here, because it refers to Trujillo's father.

One should be reminded of the contradiction presented by all these new names to one of the oldest laws of the regime, the one promulgated on December 10, 1930, according to which it is prohibited to give names of persons to streets, villages, and towns, unless those persons have been dead for at least ten years; all these nominations for Trujillo (or his relatives) require, in each case, a special law abrogating in part the one of 1940. In 1944, this law was supplemented with another, promulgated on June 28, according to which no statues or monuments may be erected honoring national or foreign personalities without previous authorization by Congress; the latter approvals, since then, have often been multiplied in favor of Trujillo and his relatives. Let us only recall the great Monument to the Peace of Trujillo, scheduled to be inaugurated at the end of 1955.[1] Similar authorization has been granted to print postage stamps bearing the image of the Benefactor.

One may mention other different types of honors of various kinds such as: setting a plaque with his name in every building constructed during his administration (September, 1933); placing his bust in both chambers (December, 1936); a plaque in the Baluarte del Conde (Monument to Independence) honoring him (September, 1940); engraving his name, together with those of the Fathers of the country, in the same Baluarte (November, 1940); proclaiming him "the first and greatest of the Heads of State" (June, 1938); according him a vote of gratitude on the occasion of the centennial of the Republic (February, 1944), just to name a few. There existed already a "Trujillo Museum" with his personal souvenirs (for the time being located in a special room of the national museum).

Trujillo has also earned literary awards: in July, 1938, the "Annual Prize for the best book" was presented to him; and in June, 1955, he was named active member of the Dominican Academy of Language (being in consequence a correspondent member of the Spanish Royal Academy).

Finally, some words about his foreign decorations. The first he received as president was the Great Collar of the Order of the Liberator, sent to him by the Venezuelan dictator, Juan Vicente Gómez, in 1931. Since then, these decorations have multiplied, some of them from peculiar sources and with peculiar titles. We have an official list of those received

---

[1] The idea was launched twelve years ago. *La Nación,* Sept. 27, 1943. [Fn. 38, Chap. VII.]

until 1947, because during that year Trujillo decided that Congress should pass a general authorization to wear them, despite the fact that until then he had dispensed with this constitutional requirement for all Dominicans heretofore accepting foreign decorations. Here is the list of the decorations mentioned in that resolution of Congress, dated January 26, 1947:

Great Cross of the Order of Elizabeth the Catholic (Spain); Great Cross of the Order of the Holy Sepulchre; Golden Medal of the Pan American Society (New York); Great Cross of the Order of Carlos Manuel de Céspedes (Cuba); Great Cross of the Order of Honor and Merit (Haiti); Great Cross, with diamonds, of the Order of the Sun (Peru); Band of the Order of the Republic (Spain); Great Cross of the Order of St. Gregorius Magnus (Holy See); Collar of the Order of Merit (Chile); Collar of the Order of the Aztec Eagle (Mexico); Great Extraordinary Cross of the Order of Boyacá (Colombia); Great Collar of the Order of the Liberator (Venezuela); Great Cross of the National Order of the Condor of the Andes (Bolivia); Great Medal of Extraordinary Merit (Lebanon); Great Cross of the Order of Merit with Band of three tassels (Ecuador); Great Cross of the Order of Vasco Núñez de Balboa (Panama); Great Cordon of the National Order of the Legion of Honor (France); Great Cordon of Merit of Charity of the French Order of the Cross of Blood; Great Cross of the Order of Honor and Merit of the Cuban Red Cross; Great Red Cordon with White Edges of the Order of the Diamond Jade (China); Great Cross of Honor and Devotion, Knight Commander, of the Sovereign Order of Malta; Order of Navy Merit, first class (Cuba); Great Cross of Medhuia (Morocco); Great Cross of Academic Honor of the Inter-American Academy of Washington; Abdón Calderón Star (Ecuador); Great Cross of the Ecuadorian National Order of Merit; Great Cross of the National Order of the Southern Cross (Brazil); Great Cross of Paraguayan Merit; Great Cross of the Netherlands Lion; Medal in Commemoration of the Pan American Flight for the Lighthouse to Columbus (Cuba); Medal in Commemoration of the First Centennial of the Death of the Colombian Father of the Fatherland, Fco. de Paula de Santander; Collar of the Order of San Martín.[2]

One may assume that the list is complete until the beginning of 1947, although in several publications and biographies of Trujillo other lists have appeared.[3] One may also imagine that from 1947 to date the collec-

---

[2] Trujillo uses his Order of Trujillo to reciprocate these decorations. [Fn. 51, Chap. VII.]

[3] Gilberto Sánchez Lustrino, *Trujillo: El Constructor de una Nacionalidad* (Havana, 1938), p. 282, adds his appointment as Comendador of the Order of the Italian Crown, which was conferred on him in 1928 before becoming president. [Fn. 52, Chap. VII.]

tion has increased considerably. Among the latest decorations announced
are those accorded to Trujillo during his most recent trip to Europe in the
summer of 1954: the Spanish dictator bestowed upon him the Collar of the
Order of Elizabeth the Catholic and the Pope granted him the Great Cross
of the Pian Order. In order not to omit anything, let us add that in 1952
the Peruvian writer, Sayán de Vidaurre, offered Trujillo the Great Collar
of his Order of Democracy.

It is doubtful that any dictator has ever collected such a picturesque
series of titles, decorations, and honors. Trujillo appears especially happy
whenever somebody exercises his imagination to extend this marathon.[4]

Graft

Each of the books written against Trujillo[5] devotes several pages to
the details of his businesses, as do the reports of impartial newspapermen.
This aspect of his fabulous activity is an open secret in the Dominican
Republic, but as is usual in all such known secrets, the difficulty lies in
proving it with sources and figures. It will be impossible to make a complete estimate until the day his regime disappears and the files are open for
inspection.* In the meantime, on occasion, partners whose interests have
been harmed speak out, and occasionally even former favorites do the
same after they have fallen into disgrace, although in most instances they
are still fearful or hopeful of returning to favor and business.

Among the books against Trujillo, the one offering the most concrete
data is *Una Satrapía en el Caribe,* signed under the pseudonym of Gregorio
R. Bustamante. The author of this study has read two letters written from
Mexico to New York, requesting an English translation of the book, in
which the true author was identified by name as a former private aide of
Trujillo. Therefore, his facts should deserve greater credence than the
vague or incomplete data mentioned in other books, although "Busta-

---

[4] The uniforms used by Trujillo are beyond description and must be seen to
be appreciated. It is illuminating, for instance, to see the picture printed in the
Spanish newspaper *ABC* of Madrid, on June 10, 1954, reproducing the occasion
in which Franco, dressed in a sober Spanish uniform, is embracing Trujillo, wearing
a two-pointed hat with white feathers. The most interesting feature of this picture
is the restrained smiles of some of the high Spanish officers who watch the scene.
[Fn. 56, Chap. VII.]

[5] On the other hand, the authors favoring Trujillo are carefully silent of this
aspect of his personality and activities. [Fn. 57, Chap. VII.]

* Although the author did not live until that time, the inspection he anticipated
did not prove possible in the Dominican Republic even after the assassination of
Trujillo. The situation differed significantly in post-Perón Argentina because of the
comprehensive "audit" made of that dictator's peculations by the distinguished
Argentine economist, Raúl Prebisch.

mante" may not be entirely trusted due to personal circumstances,[6] and to the fact that he fails to mention some businesses of Trujillo which are generally known in the Dominican Republic today. A concise and factual list of these present businesses was made public in 1953 by a writer in the *New York Times*, Herbert L. Matthews, after a trip to the Dominican Republic and other Latin American countries.[7]

Today, the simplest proof that can be offered as to Trujillo's acquisitions is the plain arithmetical estimate: multiply the years he has spent in several public offices by his official salary in each;[8] if one takes the results, adding all probable interests and returns of normal investments, and compares these with the ostentatious luxury exhibited by him, and his known expenditures, it is obvious that the latter cannot be explained except by a miracle or Aladdin's lamp.

As stated, Trujillo is the first businessman of the Dominican Republic. It is also fair to recognize that some of his businesses have benefited the general economy by establishing factories or enterprises in the Dominican Republic that represent an improvement over earlier foreign monopolies. But each and every one of these businesses has brought personal profits to Trujillo, and their success has often been obtained through monopolies imposed from above, thanks to his hold on power. On occasion, his partners are his relatives or favorites.

Let us consider some of these businesses. In every case, at least a reference can be made to authors who have already mentioned them without being sued for libel.

Salt Production. All authors, especially those Dominicans who were contemporary to the rise of Trujillo to power in 1930, mention as his first business the monopoly over salt, imposed by a law in 1932. Before 1930, the salt deposits in the south of the island were exploited by a company controlled by the Michelena family. The law of 1932, on the allegation

---

[6] As mentioned, this book seems to have been printed in 1949 by the Guatemalan government, which tried as much to conceal this fact as it did the identity of the author. Later on, the person mentioned as the true author wrote another book, favoring the Benefactor, which he signed with his own name. [Fn. 58, Chap. VII.]

[7] Herbert L. Matthews, "Dominicans thrive at cost of liberty," *New York Times,* March 28, 1953, p. 7. [Fn. 59, Chap. VII.]

[8] His annual salary as chief of the army was $4,560 in the 1930 budget (*G.O.* 4158), and his annual salary as president was $8,400 in the 1931 budget (*G.O.* 4316). There is no individual mention of personal salaries in recent budgets, but general assignments for salaries in each department. Bustamante estimates the capital of Trujillo in 1949 at 250 million dollars (p. 137) and his minimum annual income since 1938 at 30 million (p. 152). Matthews says: "It is a parlor pastime in Ciudad Trujillo to guess how much the Generalissimo has secreted abroad; everyone agrees the total must be fabulous." [Fn. 60, Chap. VII.]

that the salt deposits "are threatened with being exhausted," prohibited the taking of more salt from them even by concessions previously granted to private citizens and city councils; it established a tax additional to those already in existence amounting to fifteen cents for every bag of fifty kilograms of salt. Immediately afterward, a Compañía Salinera C. por A. [equals: Inc.] (Salt Company) of a private character but under official protection, was organized. All authors agree, as do the Dominicans in general, that this company was mainly a private business of Trujillo and the initial base for his fortune.[9]

The Insurance Business. Another of the oldest businesses of Trujillo mentioned in many books is the Compañía de Seguros San Rafael (Insurance Company), organized at the end of 1932 after the law on work accidents was passed. In this case, the name of the company indicates that Trujillo is the owner, as does the fact that its first president was Teódulo Pina Chevalier, an uncle of Trujillo and a member of his cabinet at that time. This company at once became a monopoly in fact, almost absolute, and there was no hesitation in putting out of business a United States company previously organized with similar objectives. The Compañía San Rafael does not have today a complete monopoly over all insurance in the Dominican Republic, but it is sufficient for its success to have the copious benefits obtained from insurance against work accidents;[10] we must add that for many years this law on accidents was the only one existing in the Dominican Republic favoring the workers.

The Milk Business. The first large, viable business enterprise of Trujillo was one that had been traditional in the island from colonial times on — the raising of cattle and the sale of their products. Anyone who goes to the Dominican Republic may see in the city of San Cristóbal the very large estate, Hacienda Fundación, where the dictator likes to spend many of his days and often takes his guests of honor to see his cattle and horses. Trujillo is without any doubt the biggest farmer in the Dominican Republic, and for many years he was able to obtain substantial returns from the sale of milk and other cattle products in normal competition. But about twelve years ago the Dominican government imposed an official control on milk sales that in fact gave Trujillo at least a priority to the extent of his production in the Hacienda Fundación and other farms under his private ownership. It is the so-called Milk Central, legally estab-

---

[9] Jimenes-Grullón, *Una Gestapo en América* (Havana, 1946), p. 204, estimated in 1940 that Trujillo was making $400,000 a year from this salt income. [Fn. 64, Chap. VII.]

[10] Jimenes-Grullón, *ibid.,* p. 210, in 1940 estimated the total annual income of this company at $150,000, with a minimum of expenses. [Fn. 68, Chap. VII.]

lished on the grounds of guaranteeing the purity of the milk and the health of the consumers; in consequence, in the Dominican Republic there is no free and direct sale of milk, but the farmers must sell their milk to the government institution that resells it to the public.[11]

Meat Industry. Directly related to this actual monopoly over the milk sales, is another business based upon cattle raising, the sale of meat. In the beginning, it too provided a legitimate income to farmer Trujillo, more or less in competition with other cattle raisers in the country; at that time, the cattle were freely slaughtered in municipal abattoirs. But again, about twelve years ago, an official step was taken which gave priority to Trujillo's cattle through the so-called "Industrial Slaughterhouse" and a stock company for the sale of its model meat; this time the stand-in man used in this business was a brother-in-law of Trujillo. The meat business has another side, that is, the sale of live cattle to the slaughterhouses of the Dutch Antilles and other islands in the Caribbean, in which the ships of the Compañía Naviera Dominicana were used for transport.[12]

Tobacco. When Trujillo became president, there were in the Dominican Republic two competitive companies producing cigarettes, the Tabacalera Dominicana, whose main stockholder was Anselmo Copello, and El Faro a Colón, chiefly owned by the honorary consul of Italy, Amadeo Barletta. The second company was practically eliminated after the 1935 plot, when it was alleged that Barletta was a co-plotter. He was sentenced to prison and later pardoned because of pressure by the Italian government. Copello was more submissive and agreed to transfer to Trujillo a great number of shares in his company; he was named Dominican ambassador in Washington at the end of 1943. The Compañía Anónima Tabacalera, as it is now called, has today a monopoly over national production and is protected against foreign competition by severe import duties.

The Lottery. This is a normal source of public income in Latin American countries and many times an obvious source of graft. In the Dominican Republic, it existed before the rise to power of Trujillo, but he reorganized it by law and put at its head his brother-in-law, Ramón Saviñón Lluberes, who retained its administration until 1953. The statistics of his administration were not made public in detail.

New Industries. It is not necessary to give much space to this topic, because the founding of these businesses would be considered legitimate,

---

[11] Bustamante, *Satrapía*, p. 138, states that in 1949 the producer sold the milk at three cents a liter, and the *central* doubled its price to the consumers. [Fn. 70, Chap. VII.]

[12] Bustamante, *ibid.*, p. 150, estimates at $800,000 a year Trujillo's income from this industry. [Fn. 73, Chap. VII.]

even though they have always profited from the fact that Trujillo is at the same time the ruler of the country. There are many cases of new industries established in the Dominican Republic with Trujillo's private capital, which appear as *Compañías anónimas* (stock corporations) managed by some of his favorites. For instance, the Aceitera Dominicana (Dominican Oil Factory); the Cervecería Nacional (National Brewery), having as front man Trujillo's brother-in-law, Francisco Martínez Alba, and Paíno Pichardo, at the time he was the favorite; the cement factory, organized about 1947, in which the front man was another favorite, Manuel de Moya; and other small factories like those of fruit juices, sacks and cordage, chocolate, and other such commodities. In more than one instance, in the organization of these factories, technicians have participated who contributed their industrial patents in exchange for a share in the profits and who sooner or later have been forced to leave. Often these factories have partly aided the general economy of the country because their products seem to be cheaper than those imported, but in this price differential it must always be taken into account that they enjoy official protection through high import duties and also that the main beneficiary is always the country's greatest capitalist, investor Rafael L. Trujillo Molina. . . .

Natural Products and Exports. Similar tactics have been used by Trujillo in the harvest and export of certain Dominican natural products. Usually mentioned is the production of rice which has increased during the Trujillo Era in such a way that the Dominican Republic, which used to be an importer of rice, now exports it, a change which benefits the national economy, but is said also to benefit the private pocket of Trujillo, this time as a partner of the Syrian-Lebanese firm of Badouit and Dumit. Another instance is found in wood products, in a family enterprise shared with the Robious brothers (one of them a brother-in-law of Trujillo and for a long time the chief of the military medical corps), which started in an apparently legitimate acquisition of very large forested areas in the Central Range through schemes admissible according to the land law.

Dominican Navy Company. In order to handle all this great export business, Trujillo organized his navy company under the management of Colonel McLaughlin, who remained in the country after the United States marines left and is the father of Héctor B. Trujillo's fiancee. Before World War II this company owned the only two Dominican ships, *Presidente Trujillo* and *San Rafael,* which traded in the Caribbean mostly in cattle and other cargo for the Dutch islands of Curaçao and Aruba in a profitable joint venture.

Official supplies and similar business. It is said that Trujillo, through different persons, has profited from providing official supplies for the army, and other services required by its members, such as shoes, medicines, and laundry. It is also said that he had infiltrated and profited from utilities of general and necessary consumption, such as the water aqueducts and the sale of charcoal.

Newspapers. *La Nación* and *El Caribe* were established with Trujillo's capital, although he may have offered some shares to certain friends in order to simulate the convenient stock corporation.

Banking Business. It is not possible to give exact details of the personal participation of Trujillo in the new Dominican banking system. The fact that the Central Bank and the Agriculture and Mortgage Bank are of recent creation and complicated functioning does not permit a sure conclusion. It is said that one of their activities proceeds as follows: Trujillo lends money to these banks in order that they lend money to private borrowers, and Trujillo receives a substantial part of the interest paid by these borrowers to the banks;[13] this means that it would be an apparently legitimate business were it not for the origin of the whole system and the combination of ruler-money lender. It is also said that, on a petty scale, money of the Trujillo family has oiled the mechanics of the so-called *banquito* (small bank), in facilitating the sale, at the beginning of every month, of the future salary of public employees minus a discount.[14]

Sugar. Until about seven years ago, Trujillo had not been able to tap this main source of wealth in the Dominican Republic. The sugar business was entirely in the hands of United States companies, except for a few *centrales* owned by the Vicini family of Italian origin. At the end of World War II, Trujillo decided to enter this business, establishing new *centrales* of his own or acquiring others of previously small importance. The sugar factory that received most attention in the press was the Central Río Jaina,

---

[13] This fact has been reported in reference to the distribution of lands among the *colonos* (peasants) of the five sugar factories belonging to Trujillo and was proclaimed with applause in the Dominican press at the end of 1953. *La Nación,* Nov. 10, 1953. This offered a pretext for the immediate attack launched against the United States-owned *centrales* of La Romana. According to this report, Trujillo sold the lands to the *colonos,* who received for this purpose money lent by the Agriculture and Mortgage Bank. Trujillo made the necessary deposits in the bank to facilitate the loans, receiving the legal interest. In this way, the whole operation benefited Trujillo at both ends, and he also reaped the praises. [Fn. 101, Chap. VII.]

[14] None among the public employees is sure of his post and each knows that he may be dismissed at any moment; in order to cover this risk, there has developed the custom of selling the official salary at the beginning of the month to lenders who advance the salary and take the risk of not recovering the full amount if the employee is dismissed, in exchange for a percentage discount. The result is a vicious circle, because almost all employees have sold their salaries, and on the twenty-fifth of every month they get it diminished by the discount. In the Secretaryship of Foreign Relations at the time of Lic. Despradel, only one of the undersecretaries and two or three technical employees did not sell their salaries. The sale and discount is handled officially by the accounts department of every Secretaryship. [Fn. 102, Chap. VII.]

proclaimed as "the biggest in the world," that made necessary the construction of a new port at the mouth of this river.

An obvious sign of the importance that this new aspect of Trujillo's private activities may have in the future is the great publicity given in the press to the opening of this *central* and port, the promulgation of the law to support sugar, the campaign launched against the protection benefits given to Cuban sugar production by the system of quotas in the United States market (this campaign has included personal negotiations by Trujillo himself during his latest trips to the United States),[15] and the attacks launched at the beginning of 1954 against the United States-owned *centrales* of La Romana.

The enterprise of Río Jaina has recently been increased into a shipyard center with $50,000,000 capital, of which 55 percent belongs to Trujillo and his partners and 45 percent to the American businessman, George W. Gibbs.

This gives a brief list of Trujillo's businesses most commonly mentioned, both in published books or in private conversations, as being totally or partially his property. To this can be added the numberless estates and houses. It would be an endless task to mention other enterprises benefiting his relatives and occasionally, by rotation, his favorites.[16] Some day it will be possible to know the statistics of his capital and annual income; rumors give fabulous estimates and also state that a great part of these profits are not deposited or invested in the Dominican Republic but in the United States and other foreign countries. The only thing which is possible to verify is the extravagance of Trujillo's daily life, which would be absolutely impossible within his official salary and normal activity as a private investor.

Bustamante, in his books, gives more concrete details (with individual references to the pertinent *Official Gazettes*) of some of the official measures which facilitated these fabulous enterprises.[17] The main one was the control of imports and exports established during World War II, using

---

15 Rubber stamps have been used by the post offices in canceling envelopes. Paid advertisements have been published in the United States press; cf. p. 65 of the annual issue of the *New York Times* about Latin American economy, Jan. 6, 1954, where it was stated in definite terms: "Although Dominicans buy 75 percent of their imports from the United States, they can sell the U. S. only 4.7 percent of their sugar." This inequality comes from the law on quotas for sugar imported into the United States, which favors Cuba (plus Puerto Rico as United States territory); almost all the Dominican sugar is exported to England. [Fn. 107, Chap. VII.]

16 In some cases, it is possible to evaluate the degree of disgrace incurred by these favorites by determining whether, at the time they are dismissed from their political posts or immediately afterward, they keep or lose their positions as paid stand-ins for Trujillo in his private business. [Fn. 111, Chap. VII.]

17 Bustamante, *Satrapía*, pp. 153–55. [Fn. 113, Chap. VII.]

as a pretext the abnormal state of the continental economy; this general control was directed by Frank Parra, a relative of the Martínez Alba family whose most prominent member is Trujillo's wife. Besides the general control, many other individual controls were established in different branches, especially of imports, most of them under General Federico Fiallo; a consequence of this system was the concession of monopolistic quotas or priorities to those firms backed by Trujillo's capital, or those benefiting his relatives and favorites. Some of these controls are still in force at the time of closing this study, ten years after the end of the war.

It need scarcely be added that Trujillo is free of taxes.[18]

Only in this way is it possible to explain the private residences Trujillo has around the entire country, his trips to foreign lands, his parties on a multimillionaire's scale, his capricious purchases (like the flying "yacht" and the Pegaso car), his gifts, and his propaganda abroad. This is in sharp contrast with President Troncoso de la Concha who never allowed himself the smallest extra expenditure, despite the fact that he was one of the best lawyers of the country, long before Trujillo could dream of being the owner of the Hacienda Fundación.

Nepotism

At the time of finishing this study, August, 1955, the President of the Dominican Republic is a brother of Trujillo, Héctor Bienvenido; the secretary of war, navy, and aviation (and as such possible successor to the presidency) is a nephew of Trujillo, Major General José García Trujillo; his oldest son, Rafael L. ("Ramfis") Trujillo, Jr., is chief of staff of the air force (at age twenty-six, and since he was twenty-three); his other son, Rhadamés (twelve years old), has the rank of honorary major; his oldest brother, Virgilio, is ambassador inspector of embassies, legations, and consulates; his brother J. Arismendi ("Petán") has the rank of honorary lieutenant general; his brother Pedro is an effective brigadier general; his illegitimate brother, Luis Rafael, is a major; his nephew, Brigadier General Virgilio García Trujillo, is general inspector of the navy; another nephew, Dr. Luis Ovidio Ruiz Trujillo, is undersecretary of public education and fine arts; a brother-in-law, José García, is a senator; another brother-in-law, Luis E. Ruiz Monteagudo, is a deputy; and other members of the family hold high positions, either in the government or in business.

---

[18] Herbert L. Matthews states: "There are other important sources of revenues that could be mentioned. The *Jefe* and his immediate family are exempt from the tax laws. The Generalissimo's vast sugar holdings do not pay taxes, while the United States concerns recently had a new and heavy tax placed on them." [Fn. 114, Chap. VII.]

This nepotism of Trujillo was obvious very early. In his first administration, beginning in 1930, several relatives already had prominent positions: his uncle, Teódulo Pina Chevalier, was a secretary in the cabinet, his brother Virgilio was a deputy, and another uncle, Plinio Pina Chevalier, was also a deputy. In the following years, the careers of his brother Virgilio, his other brother Aníbal Julio, his uncle Teódulo Pina Chevalier, and the promotion to deputy of his father, José Trujillo Valdez (until his death in 1935), were remarkable. But two of the younger members of the family were the ones destined for brighter and more permanent careers: the youngest Trujillo brother, Héctor Bienvenido (twenty-two years old in 1930), and Trujillo's son, "Ramfis" (born at about that time); and we must not forget the picturesque career of his oldest daughter, Flor de Oro, and her first husband, Porfirio Rubirosa. In recent years, the military career of his nephew, José García Trujillo, is outstanding, plus the beginning of his children Angelita and Rhadamés as new stars.

"Ramfis," Rafael L. Trujillo Martínez, Jr., the oldest son of Trujillo, was born in 1929, when his mother was married to a Cuban who rejected him as his son. Subsequently, Trujillo recognized him as his own. While still an illegitimate child by an adulterous union and with his father still married to his second wife, "Ramfis" was appointed a colonel of the army in 1933, when he was four years old. In 1935 Trujillo married the mother of "Ramfis," María Martínez Alba, and "Ramfis" became legitimate. In 1938, he was promoted to brigadier general. In 1943 (being fourteen years old), he resigned this rank, and entered as a cadet in the army. In 1949 he appeared officially as a captain in the aide corps of his father; at the same time he was a student in the school of law. At the end of the year he was named inspector of embassies and legations with the rank of ambassador (he was twenty years old). At the end of 1951, he was promoted to honorary lieutenant colonel. In January, 1952, he was promoted to colonel. On June 4, 1952, the day he reached twenty-three years of age, he became brigadier general and chief of staff of the air force. One year later, he was promoted to major general. Simultaneously he graduated as doctor in law and received the highest decorations of the Orders of Trujillo, Duarte, Colón, Military Merit, Navy Merit, Air Merit, and Police Merit. His name was given to a park in the capital city and to many other places in the whole Republic, while his picture was printed on a postage stamp when he was a toy general.* '

---

* On December 17, 1969, a car driven by Ramfis in Madrid, Spain, struck one driven by the Duchess of Albuquerque, member of a family of ancient Spanish lineage. The Duchess was killed instantly and Trujillo was seriously injured. He died of complications, resulting from the accident, on December 27, 1969. In 1965 Ramfis had been sentenced in absentia by a Dominican court to thirty years' imprisonment at hard labor for involvement in the earlier alleged murder of political prisoners in the Dominican Republic.

Héctor Bienvenido Trujillo, the youngest brother of Trujillo, was born in 1908. When the 1930 coup occurred, he was twenty-two years old and completely unknown. A few months later, in March, 1931, he was a captain and named military attache to several European countries. In July, 1935, he became a major and received the Order of Military Merit. In October of the same year he was promoted to lieutenant colonel. In August, 1936, he was advanced to colonel and named auxiliary chief of staff (his brother Aníbal Julio was the chief). In November, 1936, he became a brigadier general and chief of staff. In September, 1941, he was promoted to major general. In January, 1942, he was named secretary of war and navy, when this secretaryship was reestablished. From October to December, 1942, he suffered a brief punishment (apparent leave of absence), but in November, 1944, he was promoted to general of the army (a newly created rank). From March to October, 1951, he was provisionally trusted with the executive power (during a leave of absence taken by his brother, the president). He was inaugurated president of the Republic on August 16, 1952. He is the only adult member of the family who has not fallen into disgrace (save for the brief reproof in 1942), and during the last twenty years he has always occupied the highest posts in the army, only exceeded in command by his brother, the Benefactor.

Flor de Oro Trujillo and Porfirio Rubirosa have often been in the limelight. It is necessary to link the histories of both, because the bright and peculiar career of Porfirio started with his marriage to the oldest daughter of Trujillo. Flor de Oro (Spanish translation of the name Anacaona, the famous Queen of Jaragua at the time of the conquest) was born of the first marriage of Trujillo, before he became an officer of the army. Porfirio Rubirosa was an officer in the aide corps of President Trujillo, when they married in December, 1932. Rubirosa was appointed undersecretary of the presidency in April, 1933, and undersecretary of foreign relations in July of the same year. In May, 1934, he was elected a deputy in the new congress. The next year he made a brief trip to New York, just days before the murder of Sergio Bencosme. Appointed secretary of the Dominican legation in Germany in June, 1936, he was sent with Paíno Pichardo on a special mission to the coronation of King George VI of England the following March. A short time after his appointment as secretary of the Dominican legation in Paris in May, 1937, he was divorced by Flor de Oro. Their lives separated, but the political star of Porfirio did not fade.

Flor de Oro married for the second time a Dominican, Dr. Ramón Brea, who in October, 1940, was appointed minister in Mexico; they were divorced a short time after. Flor de Oro was appointed secretary of the Dominican legation in Washington, and was married, for the third time, to an American captain in the medical corps of the United States, who died a short time later. In January, 1944, Flor de Oro was promoted to minister counselor in the new Dominican embassy in Washington, followed in May by her marriage, for the fourth time, to a wealthy Brazilian, Antenor Mayrink Veiga. About two years later, they were divorced, and Flor de Oro subsequently married twice again, both times to Frenchmen. After the fifth divorce, Flor de Oro returned to the Dominican Republic where she lived in retirement for several years, apparently in disgrace with her father. In 1954, she was married for the seventh time to a Dominican singer, López Balaguer.*

In the meantime, Rubirosa remained in the Dominican legation in Paris for several years; he was active during the Spanish civil war, together with Minister Virgilio Trujillo, and at this time began to acquire his great fortune. He endured German occupation in France and married the French actress, Danielle Darrieux. In September, 1947, he was married to the American millionairess, Doris Duke, his third marriage. In November of the same year he was named Dominican ambassador in Buenos Aires, and in December, 1948, was transferred as minister to Italy. He divorced Doris Duke later. In February, 1953, he was appointed minister counselor in Paris, and then returned to the Dominican Republic, where he introduced the game of polo and became a close friend of "Ramfis." At the end of 1953, he was dismissed as a diplomat, apparently because of his latest scandals and their repercussions in the world press. But a few weeks later he was reappointed as minister counselor in Paris at the time of his marriage to the American millionairess, Barbara Hutton, in the Dominican consulate general of New York, with "Ramfis" acting as best man. A very short time later the couple became estranged and Porfirio openly began his new romance with actress Zsa Zsa Gabor. At the beginning of 1955, Porfirio requested his divorce in the Domincan Republic, offering as witness a clerk in the New York Dominican consulate. Rubirosa continues to be a minister counselor in Paris.†

---

* The statement above that two of Flor de Oro's husbands were Frenchmen is inaccurate as attested by the following complete listing:
1. Porfirio Rubirosa, Dominican, army officer and diplomat
2. Ramón Brea Messina, Dominican, doctor
3. Maurice Berck, American, doctor and army officer
4. Antenor Mayrink Veiga, Brazilian, businessman
5. Charles Stehlin, American, air force officer
6. Paul Louis Guérin, French, manufacturer
7. José Manuel López Balaguer (nephew of President Joaquín Balaguer), Dominican, radio singer
8. Miguel Ferreras, Cuban (U.S. citizen), fashion designer

† Rubirosa was killed in an automobile accident in Paris on July 5, 1965, at age 56. As mentioned in the text, his five wives had included Flor de Oro Trujillo, Doris Duke, and Barbara Hutton. He had held Dominican diplomatic posts in France, Argentina, Italy, Cuba, and Belgium.

Rhadamés and Angelita Trujillo are the youngest children of Trujillo and María Martínez. María de los Angeles del Corazón de Jesús was born in Paris in 1939. On May 13, 1953, when she was almost fourteen years old, she was appointed ambassadress extraordinary as a member of the special mission to the coronation of Queen Elizabeth II of England, together with a cousin of hers of the same age and honorary "general" Manuel de Moya; on her way back she received the homage of the Spanish dictator Francisco Franco. Since then she has become a star in Dominican social life. At the closing of this study, she has just been named "Queen of the Fair of Peace and Confraternity of the Free World" which will close the festivities of the Year of the Benefactor. Leonidas Rhadamés was born in December, 1942; ten years later, in June, 1952, he was appointed an honorary major of the army. He accompanied his father during his latest trips, in 1953 and 1954, to the United States and Europe, dressed in military uniform. At the closing of this study, the suspension bridge under construction near the capital has been named for him.*

Trujillo's oldest brother, Virgilio, was elected a deputy in 1930, followed in May, 1932, by his appointment as secretary of interior, police, war, and navy, a position he occupied until January, 1933. In June, 1935, he was named Dominican minister in Paris, where he remained until the beginning of World War II and participated actively in the sending of European refugees to the Dominican Republic. Afterward he fell into disgrace with his brother for many years, although he was never openly persecuted. In the 1952 elections they appeared in public together again, and Virgilio was mentioned as "ambassador." At the closing of this study, he has just been named inspector of embassies, legations, and consulates.†

Aníbal Julio Trujillo in May, 1932, appeared as a major of the army, at the time he replaced his brother Héctor B. as military attache in several European countries. In October, 1935, with the rank of colonel, he was named chief of staff; two months later, he was promoted to brigadier general. In October, 1936, he became a deputy for one month and in November he returned to the army as "honorary general" and personal aide to his brother, the president. He was elected a deputy again in May, 1938, but resigned in June, 1939. He was reelected in August, 1940, resigning again in October, 1941. In January, 1945, he was elected a senator, a position he resigned in October. After that he disappeared from public life, until in December, 1938, his death "in an accident" was announced.

---

*Rhadamés was arrested at Touillet, France, on July 28, 1964, charged by six other children of Trujillo with having removed almost all of an estimated $150 million deposited in family funds in Swiss banks. He was extradited to Switzerland but a Swiss court dismissed the charges against him on November 27, 1964.

† Virgilio died in Madrid, Spain, in July, 1967.

José Arismendi ("Petán") Trujillo for many years was mentioned as a "major" although he had no command of troops. In February, 1934, he replaced his brother, Aníbal, as military attache in Europe, apparently after having had a quarrel which came close to rebellion with his brother the president. "Petán" has never been prominent in official life, but he has been very active in business life. He is at present the owner of the best radio station and the only television station in the country. About 1946, he was promoted to colonel; in November, 1951, to brigadier general; and on January 1, 1955, to lieutenant general, always without any command of troops.*

Another Trujillo brother, Romeo, better known as "Pipí," never has had an official life, but he has special businesses. Pedro, almost as young as Héctor, has followed a military career less bright than those of other brothers, but in September, 1953, he also was promoted to brigadier general. Luis Rafael, an illegitimate child born of the last years of Trujillo Valdez, has appeared since 1954 in pictures together with the Benefactor, each time designated with the rank of a major.

Trujillo's father, José Trujillo Valdez, was elected a deputy in February, 1932, and regularly reelected in 1934. When he died occupying this position in June, 1935, three days of national mourning were ordered, followed by his burial in the Chapel of the Immortals in the cathedral. His name was given to a new province created in January, 1945, and postage stamps were printed with his picture (under a *lipijapa* [panama] hat). He was called "Dallocito" because of his frequent pressures on judges, thus referring to the "Dalloz" series of French sentences commonly used in the Dominican courts to interpret the law in force.

Sra. Julia Molina de Trujillo, the President's mother, is a very discreet woman and without vanity despite the many honors bestowed upon her by her son; she ranks as First Lady of the country even when her son is not the president; her picture has also appeared on postage stamps.

María Martínez Alba, the third and present wife, married Trujillo in September, 1935, but she had become the mother of "Ramfis" in 1929. In 1945, she began a series of articles called "Moral Thoughts" in *La Nación,* which, in 1948, were edited as a book in Mexico, and in 1954 translated into English. In 1947 she opened a play of her own, "Falsa Amistad." In 1951, it was suggested that she be granted the degree of honorary doctor but the idea was not carried out. In 1955, she was named "First Woman of the Americas in the Dominican Republic." She has been the First Lady of the Republic since 1935, even when her husband is not

---

* José Arismendi died on May 6, 1969.

the president; in 1954, she was officially received by the Spanish dictator Franco.

Bienvenida Ricardo [Ricart] was the second wife of Trujillo, from 1927 to 1935; they had no children during those years, and this was the pretext used for the divorce. She remained in obscurity after 1935. Aminta Ledesma was the first wife, married when Trujillo was very young; it is impossible to find data about her.*

The brothers-in-law have likewise come into prominence. Trujillo has four sisters, Marina, Julieta, Nieves Luisa, and Japonesa. Marina is married to José García, who, at the beginning of the Era, was a colonel and in May, 1933, was appointed chief of staff with the rank of brigadier general. In December, 1934, he was named secretary of interior, police, war, and navy and promoted to major general. In the 1942 elections, he was elected a senator, a position he keeps to date; he has been secretary of the Senate from 1952 to 1955.

Julieta is married to Ramón Saviñón Lluberes, director of the national lottery until August, 1953, and "honorary colonel" since December, 1949. Nieves Luisa is married to Fernando M. Castillo, one of the oldest air pilots in the Dominican Republic, who in February, 1948, was appointed chief of staff of the air force for a year, at the time being a lieutenant colonel. He is at present a colonel and military attache in Washington. Japonesa is married to Luis R. Ruiz Monteagudo who has almost always been a deputy.

The two uncles, Teódulo Pina Chevalier and Plinio Pina Chevalier, both were prominent in 1930, Teódulo as secretary of labor and communications, and Plinio as vice-president of the Chamber. The career of Plinio has been colorless, mostly as a high official of the Dominican consulate general in New York or as commercial attache in the embassy at Washington. The career of Teódulo until his death was more brilliant; he was several times a member of the cabinet, even secretary of state of the Office of the Generalissimo in 1940, a senator, and a diplomat, and had the rank of "colonel."

The two sons of Major General García are the outstanding nephews, José and Virgilio García Trujillo. They are officers of the army, promoted to the rank of brigadier generals in 1948 and 1952 respectively, and later on to major generals. José during recent years has been chief of staff, undersecretary of navy and aviation, chief of staff of the army, undersecretary of war, navy, and aviation, again undersecretary of navy and aviation, again undersecretary of war, navy and aviation, and the secretary

---

* Some information is to be found in Crassweller, *Trujillo*.

at the time of closing this study. Virgilio has been colonel chief of police before becoming brigadier general, and, since 1952, the chief of staff of the army. At the end of 1954, he was dismissed as such and demoted a rank in consequence of the killing of ten robbers of the Royal Bank of Canada in Santiago, but he was appointed inspector general of the navy. Another young nephew, Dr. Luis O. Ruiz Trujillo, was appointed under-secretary of education in December, 1953.

These data are sufficient to prove the special care displayed by Trujillo towards members of his family. This general nepotism does not mean, however, that his relatives do not also feel the lash of personal authority so characteristic of the regime. His son "Ramfis" seems to be the only weakness in the dictator's iron armor. Even Héctor B. Trujillo, who, since 1936 has been his main lieutenant in the army, since 1942 his main lieutenant in the government, and since 1952 president (in name) of the Republic, was warned at the end of 1942. The remaining brothers, especially "Petán," Virgilio, and Aníbal Julio, suffered periods of disgrace, disgrace which has also been obvious towards Flor de Oro during recent years. Another peculiar exception is Porfirio Rubirosa, despite his divorce from Flor de Oro; but this exception must have exceptional justifications.

Sycophancy and Servility

At the beginning of the new academic year at the diplomatic school of the Dominican Republic, an admission test was given to evaluate candidates. One year, the most difficult question referred to the "Pre-Columbian cultures in the Americas"; one candidate did not hestitate to answer that "the most important pre-Columbian culture in the Americas is the Dominican Republic during the glorious Era of Trujillo." The episode does not end here; later, in the meeting of professors to qualify the candidates, several among the Dominicans refused to reject this candidate because "he had mentioned the Chief."[19]

This anecdote reveals perfectly the general atmosphere of sycophancy and servility existing in the Dominican Republic under Trujillo. That this student had learned nothing in the primary and secondary schools about the aboriginal cultures in the New World meant only a void in his education; but, more significant, he had been trained at the same time in the official worship of Trujillo.

One cannot say that this technique of propaganda follows totalitarian aims, because it is not directed towards any state ideology but simply towards personal sycophancy. But its methods repeat what was usual

---

[19] The author was a witness of this episode, as professor at the diplomatic school. Other witnesses now live outside the Dominican Republic. [Fn. 118, Chap. VII.]

practice in Stalinist Russia or Hitlerite Germany. All the apparatus of propaganda and education is oriented to indoctrinate the mind with the idea that Trujillo is a genius to whom everything is due.

For examples of such sycophancy, it is sufficient to walk through the streets of Ciudad Trujillo or of the smallest village, to look through the pages of the newspapers and books, or to listen to the lyrics of many songs. Trujillo — Trujillo — Trujillo!

His picture appears everywhere and nothing besides his picture. The sign "God and Trujillo" continues to mark the house of the late President Peynado; "Trujillo Forever" repeat the advertisements of the national lottery. Nothing is carried on in the Dominican Republic which is not "by the initiative of the Generalissimo."

Mejía, in his *Vía Crucis de un Pueblo,* pp. 289–90, transcribes an unbelievable anthology of thoughts dedicated to Trujillo, which were printed in *Listín Diario* of January 17, 1938; and on pp. 312–14 others which appeared at different dates.[20]

Servility shines especially in the "royal court"; among the rotating favorites, always with a buffoon; among the members of his family; among his harem. The case is known of a prominent secretary of state who was humiliated at a meeting of the cabinet, but reacted by saying "The Chief is fair even when he punishes." On the occasion of the centennial in 1944, the secretary of education himself was seen checking the seats one by one in the presidential loge before the arrival of Trujillo and looking in the corners to be sure that there were no hidden bombs. United States newspapers in 1952 printed a picture of Ambassador Thomen fixing the cuff buttons in Trujillo's shirt before he entered the office of Secretary Acheson. The nature of this study prevents us from entering into other peculiar details, too well known in the inner circle of favorites, but which sometimes spread widely to other groups. Only one sentence of his official biographer, Nanita, needs special quotation: "He enjoys women. He treats them with softness, delicacy, and gallantry. Their conversation seduces him, their company pleases him. The pretty face of a woman is for him the best card of introduction."[21]

This servility is more evident than ever now that he is not officially the president. A decree on August 24, 1952, after the inauguration of his brother Héctor, provided that in the future the general rules of protocol

---

[20] Two volumes, totaling 955 pages, were printed in 1938, containing individual praises to Trujillo, *Pensamientos a Trujillo* (Santiago, n.d. [1938.]).

[21] Abelardo R. Nanita, *Trujillo,* 5th ed. (Ciudad Trujillo, 1951), pp. 88–89. [The English-language version of Nanita's biography offers this passage in slightly different but similarly adulatory language. Cf. Nanita, *Trujillo* ("New English Version"), (Ciudad Trujillo, 1954), p. 92.] [Fn. 120, Chap. VII.]

would not be in force in reference to the Benefactor and that every time he attends a ceremony special rules would be ordered to meet the case. In this way it is possible to understand once and again that the Benefactor has official preeminence over the president and his picture is the biggest in the press.[22] The press reports the interviews granted almost daily by the Benefactor to the highest officers of the government, but is silent as to the visits received by the president. Even the Bible has been reworded in his praise.[23]

Sometimes this sycophancy becomes accidentally bitter irony as, for example, in the sign at the entrance of the insane asylum at Nigua: *"Todo se lo debemos a Trujillo"* (We owe everything to Trujillo).[24]

---

[22] In several issues of *El Caribe* (see Dec. 17, 1954, Jan. 1, Feb. 1, May 14, and June 22, 1955) pictures of the two brothers were printed on the front page, a big one of the Benefactor and a small one of the president; in other issues and more frequently, the press does not publish the picture of the president, it is enough to print that of the Chief (this happens almost daily). A peculiar case was the double reproduction in *El Caribe,* May 17, 1955, of the same picture taken during the military parade commemorating the twenty-fifth anniversary of the first election of Trujillo; in one print of the whole picture both the Benefactor and the president appeared, and another, but identical print, only the Benefactor appeared; both prints were on the front page. The same happens in official publications; for instance, in the *Anuario Estadístico de la República Dominicana, 1952* (Ciudad Trujillo, 1954), so many times referred to this study, a picture of Benefactor Trujillo appears first of all and another picture of President Trujillo comes next. [Fn. 122, Chap. VII.]

[23] A pamphlet printed by the Dominican Department of Social Insurance [Caja Dominicana de Seguros Sociales, *Seguridad Social* (Ciudad Trujillo, 1953), p. 40] reworded Psalm 23 of the Bible in this way: "Trujillo is my shepherd; I will lack nothing. . . . I will have no fear; because Trujillo will be with me." In a lecture delivered in 1945 at the Dominican Party Palace, a praising comparison was developed between San Cristóbal, birthplace of Trujillo, and Bethlehem, birthplace of Jesus. [Fn. 123, Chap. VII.]

[24] The author himself saw this sign. [Fn. 125, Chap. VII.]

Chapter 8: Repercussion of International Politics

[*In their 1955 setting, Galindez's observations of Trujillo's conduct of international relations are set forth.*]

In this study of Trujillo's political regime it is not possible to enter into a detailed analysis of his international policy. But it would be difficult to have a complete picture of the historical evolution of his Era during these twenty-five years, and a deep understanding of certain internal events, if one did not have always in mind the development of world affairs.

One of the characteristics of Trujillo's regime — as with other Latin American dictatorships, though not all of them — is that it lacks a standard of its own in world politics and tries to follow closely the line marked by the United States. That does not prevent the Dominican Republic from being forced on occasion to face special problems in the convulsive area of the Caribbean and also to face the actuality of sharing an island with Haiti.

A brief analysis of this mimetism of being a political chameleon following great international currents, and of the pressure exercised by political events in neighboring countries, will help to a better understanding of some paradoxical aspects of Trujillo's regime.

The Convulsive Relations with Haiti

In the Secretaryship of Foreign Relations of the Dominican Republic there is a very secret room in which are kept the special files of documents referring to Haiti. The key is in the hands of the chief clerk himself. This secrecy in the archives is proof of the very delicate state of relations between the Dominican Republic and Haiti at all times.

During the nineteenth century, those relations were often bellicose, with the Haitians demonstrating the greater aggressiveness and power. The

Dominicans displayed heroism in facing this during several invasions from the west. In the twentieth century, the Dominicans are undoubtedly stronger both in numbers and military power, and the problem has been transformed into a human conflict that will become more and more insoluble every day. The two nations share a small island, which is not wealthy; the Dominican Republic occupies two-thirds (19,000 square miles) and Haiti one-third (10,500 square miles); the Dominicans number more than two million inhabitants and the Haitians more than three million, which means a proportion of two to three;* besides that, the western part occupied by Haiti is poorer than the eastern part held by the Dominican Republic. The illegal influx of Haitians crossing the border to escape starvation is the natural consequence of this situation.[1]

The border is artificial, and on more than one occasion attempts were made to fix it by international treaties. In January, 1929, Dominican President Horacio Vásquez signed a treaty with Haitian President Borno. But very soon after Trujillo became president, there was obviously a desire to modify the terms of this treaty by another one, perhaps definitively. Remarkable events of those negotiations were the two meetings between the Dominican president and the new president of Haiti, Stenio Vincent, in October, 1933; the immediate consequences were the formation of a mixed commission entrusted with a study of the reform of the 1929 treaty, the trip of Trujillo to Port-au-Prince in November, 1934, and the visit of Vincent to Santo Domingo in February, 1935, and finally the signature of a new treaty in March, 1936, the exchange of ratifications taking place on April 14 of the same year.

It seemed then in 1936 that the cause of misunderstandings between the Dominican Republic and Haiti had disappeared permanently and that friendship mutually bound both presidents, at least officially. This situation lasted a long year;[2] but at the end of 1937 there exploded the most serious incident between the two countries in almost a century.

---

* UN estimates of population in 1968 were: Dominican Republic, 4,029,000; Haiti, 4,674,000.

[1] One of the "solutions" offered to this problem was made public in the book *Curso de Derecho Internacional Público Americano* (Ciudad Trujillo, 1943), p. 113, by its author Carlos Sánchez i Sánchez, a professor of international law at the University of Santo Domingo. He proposed to transfer the excess of Haitian population to another place in the world under an international trusteeship. [Fn. 2, Chap. VIII.]

[2] One of the alleged reasons for the worsening of relations was the fact that the Haitian government refused to deliver to Trujillo's government the Dominican exiles living in Haiti. They were forced to stop their political activities and leave the country after the signature of the 1936 treaty, but that allowed them to continue their campaign in Cuba and other countries. Cf. Hicks, *Blood in the Streets,* pp. 100–101. [Fn. 5, Chap. VIII.]

The massacre of Haitians by Dominican soldiers in October, 1937, has not yet been given serious study. There are vague and scandalous references,[3] a few official documents which attempt to ignore the facts themselves,[4] and some isolated reports in the press of those days.[5] The greatest secret continues to be the reason for the massacre. Let us summarize the known facts, according to the sources available today.

It seems that the massacre took place on October 2–4, 1937. But the first reports did not circulate through the world until almost three weeks later. In the Dominican Republic they were silenced for more than a month. It is said that the first report was issued from Puerto Rico, according to news brought by travelers just arrived from Haiti. The *New York Times* published its first report on October 21 without mention as yet of figures of fatalities.

These first reports, appearing in the American press with interviews with newly exiled Dominicans, alarmed Trujillo's government which was already confident of having solved the "incident" through the agreement of October 15,[6] according to which the Dominicans promised to investigate the events and to punish the guilty parties. Its first notice was an official release from the Dominican legation in Washington, reproduced by the *New York Times* on October 23 in which was made public a joint declaration by the Dominican acting secretary of foreign relations, Joaquín Balaguer, Jr., and the Haitian minister in Ciudad Trujillo, stating that relations between Haiti and the Dominican Republic "have not been impaired."

---

[3] Cf. chapters 11–14 of Hicks, *Blood in the Streets*. Prominent among the personal witnesses of the facts was the bishop of Cap-Haitian, Monsignor Jan, who took care of many dying and mutilated victims who were able to cross the border. [Fn. 6, Chap. VIII.]

[4] The official United States documents, impartial because of their source, have been recently made public by the Department of State in *Foreign Relations of the United States, 1937* (Washington, 1954), 5:133–41. The official Dominican and Haitian documents are easy to consult in many governmental publications, as well as partial references in studies published by both sides in the incident. Among the Dominican studies, two are remarkable: *La Frontera de la República Dominicana con Haití* (Ciudad Trujillo, 1946), which is an official publication, and Virgilio Hopelmán, *Nuestra Vida Exterior* (Ciudad Trujillo, 1951), pp. 281–98 (concerning the 1937 incident), and other pages. Remarkable among the Haitian studies is that of the historian Jean Price-Mars, *La Republique d'Haiti et la Republique Dominicaine* (Port-au-Prince, 1953), 2:310–16. Also interesting is the report made by Trujillo himself in his annual message to Congress, Feb. 27, 1938. Trujillo, *El Pensamiento*, 2: 240–44. [Fn. 7, Chap. VIII.]

[5] In this study, the source of information will be limited to the *New York Times,* as impartial, and to *Listín Diario,* as Dominican. A good journalistic report of those days was written by Quentin Reynolds, "Murder in the Tropics," *Collier's,* Jan. 22, 1938, p. 14. [Fn. 8, Chap. VIII.]

[6] This agreement was not made public on this date. Only later would the Dominican government insist on its existence and force. [Fn. 11, Chap. VIII.]

The scandal had, however, already achieved international publicity, and the great news agencies had sent correspondents to investigate what had happened. The *New York Times* on the twenty-fifth printed on its front page a cable stating that at least 300 people had been killed and about the same number wounded during the events, but it was feared that the total of victims could reach 1,700. At the same time great excitement of tempers was reported among Haitians, so much that the secretary of interior had been forced to make public a strong warning threatening to punish any vengeance taken against Dominicans living in Haiti. This report also earned an official denial made public in a joint statement by the Dominican and Haitian ministers in Washington.[7]

Ten days later the United States Department of State showed its concern over the situation. Haitian Minister Lescot had had an interview with Sumner Welles, but he refused to comment on its terms and limited himself to saying that he had no more data about the killings than those printed in the United States press. In this report, coming obviously from an official source, mention was made for the first time of the inter-American procedure of conciliation that the United States government would be ready to back, but it was also said that the latter would not take the initiative. A further simultaneous release from the Dominican minister insisted that the "incident" was closed, and denied any movement of Dominican troops towards the border.

A careful analysis of all news made public at that time, plus later comments, seems to indicate that in the Haitian government two trends existed. President Vincent not wanting to antagonize Trujillo had attempted to reach a compromise on the terms suggested by the Dominican government, namely an investigation of the events by Dominican authorities. On the other hand, Secretary of Foreign Relations Léger wanted to announce the facts in public and invoke the inter-American procedures in force. Finally, the growing scandal strengthened the attitude of Léger.

By November 9 it was claimed unofficially that the number of people killed was 2,700 and that 3,000 had been forced to flee from the Dominican Republic. That same day, for the first time, and a month after the events, the Dominican press published the first reference to the incident, in terms of a denial: ". . . the incidents of the northern border have not at all the character of an international disagreement, neither do they take on an importance and gravity susceptible of hurting the good relations created between the two neighbor Republics."[8]

---

[7] Since then, the Haitian minister, Elie Lescot, has been accused of being in connivance with Trujillo; he had been Haitian minister in the Dominican Republic before being appointed as such in Washington. [Fn. 12, Chap. VIII.]

[8] *Listín Diario,* Nov. 9, 1937. [Fn. 14, Chap. VIII.]

The *New York Times* reported on November 10 that Secretary Léger had denounced to United States Undersecretary Sumner Welles the confirmed killing of 1,000 Haitians and possibly up to 5,000; at the same time the Haitian legation confirmed the gravity of the events, reversing its previous attitude, and the Dominican legation attempted again to lessen that gravity. News brought to Havana by travelers coming from Haiti or Santo Domingo was also published.

On November 12 the Haitian government officially requested the good offices or mediation of the governments of the United States, Mexico, and Cuba. President Roosevelt on November 14 addressed himself directly to Presidents Vincent and Trujillo, expressing his regret for "the controversy which has unfortunately arisen between our sister Republics" and offering the good offices of the government of the United States together with those of Cuba and Mexico.

Trujillo did not yet admit defeat. His answer to Roosevelt by cable on the fifteenth stated that "up to this time the Haitian government has not given the Dominican government any notification or indication enabling it to know with what the controversy deals," and for this reason he could not yet refer to the inter-American procedure of conciliation. Simultaneously the Dominican congress approved two laws declaring as "traitors to the Fatherland" several Dominican exiles who were active in the United States in trying to use the massacre of Haitians to attack Trujillo.

A circular cable by Cordell Hull on December 14 summarized the events of the preceding weeks. In this document it was said that, (a) the ministers of the United States and Cuba in the Dominican Republic had had an interview on November 22 with President Trujillo to notify him of the Haitian request for mediation; (b) simultaneously, the Dominican government had appointed special envoys to the three governments in charge of the mediation; (c) on December 2–3 high officials of the two disputing states and the three mediating powers had met in the Mexican embassy in Washington in order to have an informal exchange of opinions about the controversy, and in this meeting four conclusions had been reached: (1) the loss of life of an undetermined number of Haitian citizens had occurred in the Dominican Republic, (2) the direct negotiations between the two governments concerned had thus far been unproductive, (3) negotiations by informal conversations by the three invited powers had likewise been unproductive, and (4) the incidents had assumed an international aspect; (d) in consequence, it was proposed that a commission composed of representatives of the United States, Mexico, and Cuba would go to Port-au-Prince and Ciudad Trujillo to investigate the events; (e) and (f) the Haitian government had accepted this proposal but the Dominican government had temporized; (g) the Dominican memorandum had been referred to the Haitian government; (h) the

Haitian government had answered on December 14 officially requesting that the Gondra Treaty of 1923 and the Inter-American Convention for Conciliation of 1928 be put in operation.

The American press in those days confirmed the increasing gravity of the situation. The *New York Times* printed statements by President Vincent fixing the number of persons killed at 8,000. Trujillo attempted his usual tactics of paid propaganda by means of a full-page advertisement in the *New York Times* on December 17 with reproduction of all documents adduced by the Dominican government in its favor. But on the next day the newspaper itself commented editorially with a sober summary of all the facts, ending in a comment backing the new Haitian petition based upon the inter-American treaties of 1923 and 1928.

Trujillo admitted defeat at last on December 18 in a cable addressed to President Roosevelt. The Dominican government accepted the procedure of conciliation and thanked the United States government for its efforts. The *New York Times* on the twenty-first gave a figure of 12,000 Haitians killed, and mentioned details of the massacre in sixty-five Dominican towns. The *Times* on the twenty-second reported the petition made in the House of Representatives of the United States by Congressman Hamilton Fish, ranking Republican member of the committee of foreign affairs, requesting that the United States government withdraw its recognition of the Dominican government if the latter would not yield in its intransigent attitude.[9]

The end of the story is generally known. The sessions of the commission of conciliation took place in January, 1938; the Dominican Republic agreed to pay a general indemnification of $750,000 to the Haitian government; it was stated on March 1 that the Dominican government had already paid a first installment of $250,000. The Dominican press announced at the middle of March that 16 persons had been sentenced to thirty years in prison for the murder of 134 Haitians and 12 Dominicans.

Someday it will be possible to know the inside details of the discussions, first in the informal commission to mediate at the beginning of December, 1937, and later in the commission of conciliation at the middle of February, 1938. For the time being, it is only possible to affirm that there was a massacre of Haitians and that the Dominican government paid

---

[9] Hicks, *Blood in the Streets,* pp. 125–31, reproduced quite concrete data about this congressman, who later appeared as a registered agent of Trujillo, handling bank deposits whose source was proved to be the account of the Benefactor in the National City Bank of New York. See also Carmita Landestoy, *¡Yo También Acuso!* (New York, 1946), p. 145. [Fn. 30, Chap. VIII.]

an indemnification of $750,000 for it. The number of victims is not certain; the latest figures officially announced reported 12,000 people killed as a minimum; other private sources mention 20,000 and even 25,000. The mystery about the direct cause for the massacre is still greater.[10]

The massacre had obvious repercussions in the internal politics of the Dominican Republic. By the middle of 1937 the political campaign to reelect Trujillo as president in May, 1938, was in full steam. During the Haitian-Dominican controversy nothing was said about it. Suddenly, *Listín Diario* on January 10, 1938, made public a statement by Trujillo announcing that he would retire to private life. On May 16 Lic. Peynado and Troncoso de la Concha were elected president and vice-president of the Republic. There is no doubt at all that the massacre of Haitians stopped the second reelection of Trujillo and seriously endangered his continuity as the boss.

For the first time in the Era of Trujillo, an event of international importance had repercussions in the domestic politics of the Dominican Republic.

Other international complications of wider reach and seriousness, however, allowed Trujillo to reaffirm himself and come back to the presidency. During this second period of his administration, his relations with Haiti had never been so strained as in 1937, but more than once they had again caused uneasiness and even inter-American conflicts, alternating with periods of better relations and at times political flirtation with the new rulers.

The election of Elie Lescot as president of Haiti in 1941 was received with joy by Trujillo and the Dominican government;[11] the subsequent brief bettering of relations between the two countries was revealed in the appointment of André Chevalier as minister in Ciudad Trujillo (he was proud of being a relative of Trujillo through his grandmother Ercina Chevalier) and in some visits of protocol. But in the following years relations worsened again, although the reasons were never made public.

---

[10]*Ibid.,* pp. 105–6, mentions as the immediate cause of the 1937 massacre a speech by Trujillo in person, on the evening of Oct. 2 in Dajabón. [A graphic account of the massacre and additional information about it is given in Crassweller, *Trujillo,* pp. 154–60 and *passim*]. [Fn. 35, Chap. VIII.]

[11] Trujillo met Lescot on the border on September 4, 1941. *La Información,* Sept. 5, 1941. The meeting was a personal one, and President Troncoso did not attend. On the occasion of the election of Lescot, it was said that Trujillo had helped him with funds. More details about the relations between Trujillo and Lescot can be found in Bustamante, *Satrapía,* pp. 194–99; see also Price-Mars, *La Republique d'Haiti,* p. 317. [Fn. 37, Chap. VIII.]

They did not become better when Lescot was ousted in January, 1946, and President Dumarsais Estimé was elected a few months later; on the contrary, a new period of increasing strain between the two governments began one year later.

This second crisis between Trujillo and another Haitian government is less known because it did not end in blood, but it also required the intervention of inter-American agencies.[12] According to later accusations by the Haitian government, the story started in the fall of 1947 when Haitian Colonel Astral Roland allegedly conspired with Trujillo and his secretary of interior, Anselmo A. Paulino,[13] in order to prepare a coup against President Estimé. After several incidents, Roland was indicted as a traitor in January, 1949, while he was being given asylum in the Dominican Republic. One month later Roland began a campaign against the Haitian government using the radio broadcasting station "La Voz Dominicana," owned by J. Arismendi "Petán" Trujillo. The subsequent investigation proved that during all this period of plotting by Roland, the latter was in close touch with Secretary Paulino.

On February 23, 1949, the Haitian ambassador to the Organization of American States introduced a memorandum denouncing all these activities. The Council of the OAS expressed its hope that good relations between the two republics would be reestablished. In consequence, both governments signed a joint statement on June 9. However, Roland and a companion repeated from La Voz Dominicana their incitements to rebellion against the Estimé administration; this campaign culminated in the death on December 19, 1949, of one Haitian plotter and the arrest of others. In face of such a situation, the Council of the OAS was forced to order an investigation in the field at the beginning of 1950 (related to another and wider investigation of the Caribbean situation as a whole).

This investigation took place on the petition of the Haitian government on January 3, 1950, invoking the inter-American treaty of Rio de Janeiro. In this denunciation, the secretary of the Dominican legation in Port-au-Prince and the Dominican charge d'affaires were mentioned by

---

[12] Again it is convenient to use the official reports, this time of the Organization of American States (OAS), *Anales de la Organización de los Estados Americanos* (referred to as *Anales de la OEA*), II–2, 1950, pp. 133–51, and the complete Report of the commission of investigation of the Organ of Consultation, submitted to the Council of the OAS in the session of March 13, 1950. See also Price-Mars, *Republique d'Haiti,* pp. 332–34. [Fn. 42, Chap. VIII.]

[13] Paulino was a specialist in Haitian affairs after the incident of 1937; and in this new period the favorite of Trujillo. [Fn. 44, Chap. VIII.]

name as agents of the Trujillo administration in the plot. It was affirmed that part of the plot was to set fire to the building of the legation and to beat some of its employees in order to offer a pretext for Trujillo's intervention in Haiti. It was thought that the Dominican president had plans for the unification of the whole island under his command.

The culmination of these events is coincident with the general run of plots in the Caribbean and the granting of special powers by the Dominican congress to Trujillo in order to declare war against countries not named. All this complicated situation was the subject of investigation by a commission, appointed by the Council of the OAS under the chairmanship of Uruguayan Ambassador José A. Mora, which sat in Port-au-Prince and Ciudad Trujillo at the end of January. Its report on March 13 more or less confirms the facts which were used as grounds for the several contradictory accusations issued by the governments involved in the controversies. In reference to Haiti, the report stated that Roland and Alfred Viaud had conspired against the Haitian government with the help of certain Dominican authorities, among whom Secretary Paulino was mentioned by name.

As a result of this investigation and report, the tension decreased, not only between Haiti and the Dominican Republic but in general in the whole Caribbean area. However, the Haitian government of Estimé did not benefit by it since it was ousted on May 10. Five days later the Dominican government recognized the new military council that provisionally assumed the Haitian administration.

Later, the relations between Haiti and the Dominican Republic seemed to improve again. On February 19, 1951, President Trujillo met the new Haitian president, Colonel Paul Magloire. In the middle of April, 1952, the future Dominican president, Héctor B. Trujillo, visited Haiti officially.

Any official bettering of relations between the two governments, however, cannot, of itself, make the serious problem between them disappear, because its nature is not so much political as demographic. It is a question of two republics that are quite distinct and with a history of hatred, sharing a small island. There are racial factors that may not be ignored, but especially there are more pressing reasons of human life that every day will become more and more acute. The Dominican government has attempted to stop the peaceful invasion of Haitians by reinforcing an artificial border by means of new cities, agricultural colonies, and penitentiaries, by organizing smaller administrative units which may allow better control, and by erecting a series of military fortresses. But the pressure persists and will increase in the future, because the increase of the Haitian population moves at a faster pace than the improvement of their standard of living.

The panegyrists of Trujillo applaud him for having solved the Haitian problem. Writers who are enemies of Trujillo use the massacre of 1937 to attack him, but they keep a cautious silence in reference to the general problem of relations with Haiti as it means a problem for the future no matter who is the ruler. Trujillo occasionally has tried to face it wisely with a policy of colonization in the border areas. At other times, he could not control himself and faced it with his typical methods of violence.

The European Refugees

Let us go back in time, to follow the international policy of Trujillo since the massacre of Haitians and its consequences. His international "image" was bad. He needed to do something which could win over foreign opinion to his side. He thought he had found the solution in the troubled European situation, which offered him a ripe field to present himself as protector of the persecuted.

Many European countries were full of political refugees in 1938, especially Jews who had escaped from the Nazi dictatorship. To study the problem and possible solutions, an intergovernmental committee met at Evian [France], on July 6, 1938, on the initiative of President F. D. Roosevelt. The Dominican Republic was represented there by its minister in Paris, Virgilio Trujillo and two other diplomats. On behalf of their government, they declared that the Dominican Republic was ready to receive 50,000 to 100,000 refugees "to be established there, either in agricultural work or in commerce or industry, and even in the field of the liberal professions," if the Dominican government did not have to assume any obligation for the financing of this emigration."[14]

This offer began to be put in operation the next year. It did not benefit so much the Jewish refugees for whom it was originally planned, but rather the Spanish refugees spread throughout the world at the end of the civil war on April 1, 1939. Two different groups of refugees thus arrived in the Dominican Republic in 1939 and 1940, plus a few other isolated cases of different origin.

The immigration of Spanish refugees was organized, in general, according to an agreement with the SERE (Service for the Evacuation of Spanish Republicans), an office established in Paris by the government of the Spanish Republic to evacuate its hundreds of thousands of refugees to

---

[14] Hoepelmán, *Nuestra Vida Exterior* (Ciudad Trujillo, 1951), pp. 312–13. [Fn. 58, Chap. VIII.]

countries where they could reconstitute their lives.[15] It is estimated that between 4,000 and 5,000 Spanish refugees arrived in the Dominican Republic in about half a year (from November, 1939, to May, 1940),[16] plus a few more who arrived individually before and after that period.[17] In the case of the Jews, the immigration was financed by powerful United States organizations. On January 30, 1940, a contract was signed between the Dominican government and the Dominican Republic Settlement Association (DORSA), dealing with establishment of an agricultural colony in Sosúa, for which land was provided by the Dominican government and financial assistance in general by United States Jews.

Both immigrations were a failure, even worse among the Spaniards.[18] In the case of the Jews, it may be said that the Dominican Republic was only a waiting place for them, where they could stay until United States visas as immigrants came through. In the meantime, the Sosúa colony functioned quietly and some individual professionals made their living in several towns of the Republic. Even worse was the case of the Spaniards, because of lack of organization. It is necessary to make a distinction

---

[15] The number of Spaniards who crossed the French border at the end of the civil war is estimated at 500,000. Many returned, little by little, to Spain, but more than half were forced to remake their lives abroad. The SERE was organized in Paris for such a purpose by the government of the Spanish Republic; at the beginning this evacuation went principally to Mexico, but that country temporarily closed admissions when World War II started; in this critical situation, the SERE entered into negotiations with the Dominican legation in Paris. For this reason, most of the Spanish refugees arriving in the Dominican Republic could not adapt themselves to the country; they did not go there on purpose, they were forced to go because of the circumstances of the moment. [Fn. 59, Chap. VIII.]

[16] Probably there is no complete enumeration of all the refugees who arrived in the Dominican Republic. The first ship with Spaniards, the *De la Salle,* arrived in the middle of November, 1939, with about 500 persons; in December, January, February, and March, four more ships arrived with an average of over 700 persons each. About a hundred more arrived individually (among them the author of this study). Later, about 200 more came from Martinique. The same lack of statistics exists about the Jewish refugees, but they were much fewer in number. [Fn. 60, Chap. VIII.]

[17] These individual refugees were those who went to the Dominican Republic of their own will. Most of them were professionals who could have adapted themselves easily to the new land had it not been for the subsequent mass immigration. Those who first arrived were obtaining technical positions or positions in the educational field. At the same time, the deposit of fifty dollars belonged to them so they could survive during the first weeks. [Fn. 61, Chap. VIII.]

[18] The Brookings Institution in the United States conducted a study about the Jewish immigration in 1942 that was unfavorable. The Dominican Government answered officially in a pamphlet printed in English under the title *Capacity of the Dominican Republic to Absorb Refugees* (Ciudad Trujillo, 1945).
In general, see Bustamante, *Satrapía,* pp. 204–9 for criticism of the results; and any of the recent books praising Trujillo (such as those by Fernández Mato and Almoina) for favorable comment. [Fn. 64, Chap. VIII.]

between some individuals who received technical positions in the University and other departments of the administration, and the collective groups who were taken to the agricultural colonies. None of those colonies was able to survive, to a large extent because their members were not farmers and even less adaptable to the tropical climate.

Within a few months after their arrival, the refugees faced a mass problem of acute privation, in some cases of starvation, and at the end of 1940, help was requested from a new unofficial organization of relief for Spanish refugees established in Paris and Mexico, JARE [Junta de Auxilio a los Republicanos Españoles]. Dominicans wanted the Spanish authorities in exile to invest capital in the Dominican Republic by means of small industries that could offer work for the refugees, but the decision was to evacuate gradually most of the refugees from the Dominican Republic.

On the other hand, the Dominican government realized very soon that it had committed a serious political error in receiving those who went into exile for having fought Franco and his dictatorial regime. The last French ship able to escape from Bordeaux just before the German occupation spent several days facing the port of Ciudad Trujillo but its hundreds of passengers were not allowed to land. Meanwhile, the Dominican press launched the first attack against the Spanish immigration. Later, immigration was permitted for a few more individual refugees who had come in the meantime to the French colonies of the Antilles, but it can be said that by about the middle of 1940 the doors of the Dominican Republic were closed to European political immigration. The offer made in Evian was reduced to one percent; very soon after, an unfortunate minority.

The refugees who were able to remain in the Dominican Republic took pleasure in proclaiming their gratitude and fondness towards the Dominicans, who accepted them from the very beginning as brothers. They have not faltered in proclaiming the same appreciation towards the Dominican authorities who in 1939 and 1940 granted the necessary visas to enter in the country.[19] Perhaps Trujillo, not realizing the political nature of such an immigration, made a mistake when he suggested it. But his greater mistake came later when he destroyed the beneficial effect of this measure through individual attacks and persecutions.

There was a small Communist minority which intervened cautiously in internal politics in the Dominican Republic, but the great majority abstained from such activity, although at the same time they refrained

---

[19] See a letter by the author printed in the *New York Times,* Feb. 11, 1953, in answer to accusations made by Trujillo in a press conference held in New York, stating that most of the Spanish refugees who arrived in the Dominican Republic were Communists; the U.P. distributed a summary of this letter throughout Latin America. [Fn. 67, Chap. VIII.]

also with rare exceptions, from praising the dictator.[20] A chosen minority collaborated loyally in the technical work carried on by the Dominican administration; a greater number tried to adapt themselves to the life of the country, working in all kinds of professional activities even if they were not their own original ones, and more than one married a Dominican and established a home there. In general, the Spanish refugees integrated themselves easily with the Dominicans because they had a common language and origin, which was not the case with the Jews. However, by the end of 1945, most of the Spanish refugees had already departed from the Dominican Republic (the last ones for Venezuela during that same year, approximately 1,000 in number). There are many individual cases of refugees who could have remained in the country but were forced to leave by political reprisals.

At the end of World War II, Trujillo attempted to encourage immigration of Italians, and at present additional Spaniards are coming. . . . The wish to exploit international propaganda continues to confuse this policy because of the simultaneous and pressing demographic necessity of stopping the human flood from Haiti.[21]

World War II

Trujillo has been accused several times of having felt sympathy towards the Fascist regime before World War II, but there is no evidence of this. However, it was obvious before 1939 that German agents had complete freedom of action in the Dominican Republic. Their chief was Karl Hertel, covered under the guise of sales representative for several German imported products. There had also existed a suspicious Dominican-German cultural institute (apparently interested in the "flora" of the Samaná Bay).[22]

When World War II broke out, the feelings of the Dominicans split openly. Some applauded in the Colón Square the news broadcast by a loudspeaker of *Listín Diario* (subsidized by funds from the German

---

[20] The main exception was José Almoina, who accepted the position of private secretary to Trujillo and later wrote a book praising him, *Yo Fuí Secretario de Trujillo* (Buenos Aires, 1950). That was no obstacle to his having previously written another one against Trujillo, *Una Satrapía en el Caribe,* under the pen name of G. R. Bustamante. Two other "Republican" Spaniards who wrote books in favor of Trujillo, R. Fernández Mato and P. González Blanco, were not refugees of 1939. [Fn. 68, Chap. VIII.]

[21] Since 1939, there has been an evident desire to increase the white population, and if possible to establish agricultural colonies in the border area. The great difficulty is that, because of climatological reasons, this region is one of the less suitable for settlement by European farmers. [Fn. 71, Chap. VIII.]

[22] The Samaná Bay is in the northeastern end of the island, and it was discussed as a possible refuge for submarines; this was later proved to be incorrect. [The United States in the 1870's had tried unsuccessfully by treaty to gain a naval base site in Samaná Bay.] [Fn. 72, Chap. VIII.]

legation) about the German advance in 1940; on the other hand, *La Opinión* was alway pro-Ally. The government proclaimed an official neutrality.

The atmosphere began to change in the second half of 1940 and in 1941, when the United States took an attitude clearly anti-German. In December, 1941, Trujillo was not the president and was in New York. It has already been noted how the Dominican congress waited several hours in recess, ready to approve the petition by President Troncoso to declare war on Japan on the eighth and on Germany and Italy on the twelfth, as soon as a cable from Trujillo should arrive with the expected instructions.

In September, 1939, the Dominican Republic had declared its neutrality in the European war "but stated that it will follow the policy of the United States in any way they may go." This has always been the obvious line of Trujillo's international policy, complete mimetism of the United States, although this is reflected more in words than in actions. It is reasonable to assume that this criterion was much influenced by the obvious displeasure of the Department of State after the massacre of Haitians in 1937.

When war was declared in December, 1941, several German and non-German agents in the service of the legation were arrested at once; but Karl Hertel was respected as "attaché" in name.[23] The war offered a reason for establishing general and special controls on exports and imports. During the first months of 1942, the Dominican Republic lost its only two cargo ships, the *San Rafael* and the *Presidente Trujillo,* torpedoed respectively in the Caribbean Sea and near Martinique. Such was the repercussion of World War II in the Dominican Republic;[24] at no moment was there a question of sending troops to the fronts.

---

[23] These German agents were transferred to the United States. No Italian is known to have been arrested. A Dominican businessman, Esteban Prieto, was arrested because he was a representative of Japanese imported goods. *La Nación,* Dec. 13, 1941. The rumor spread through the capital that when war was declared on Japan, the secretary of foreign relations faced the problem that he had no available Japanese diplomat to whom he might communicate the declaration of war, but somebody remembered that Prieto was acting as honorary consul; that same rumor affirmed that such an honorary position was also the reason for his subsequent arrest, although the United States legation intervened immediately afterward to put an end to such a senseless situation. [Fn. 75, Chap. VIII.]

[24] A comical incident was the assault by the Dominican army on a neutral Swedish ship, which was in the port of Ciudad Trujillo when the war was declared, remaining there for a few days waiting for sailing instructions. It seems that the Dominican government misunderstood a decision taken in Washington by the Inter-American Defense Council in the sense of confiscating the ships that had taken asylum in the ports of the Americas since 1939; the decision referred to German ships (or any other enemy vessels), but the cable did not enter into details. The Dominican government held the Swedish ship for a few hours but was forced to return it immediately. [Fn. 78, Chap. VIII.]

But the fact of being at war allowed Trujillo to intervene in all of the organizations of the United Nations, as much during the war period as when they were transformed into permanent entities in peace time. This policy continued to be one of complete imitation of that of the United States, so much so that in 1944 the Dominican government invited Soviet Russia to attend the festivities of the Dominican centennial, and in August, 1945, a Dominican minister was sent to Moscow at the same time that Trujillo gave unconditional praise to the Russian government. In the same way, he launched an offensive against communism as soon as the United States entered that phase of the "cold war" after 1947.

The Dominican Republic declared war in 1941 because Trujillo wanted to be on good terms with the United States government. The island was one link more in the chain tying the United States with Brazil and Africa. But the Dominican government did not collaborate in any active way in the Allies' effort. European exiles were not even permitted to celebrate the victory in 1945.

The Political Situation in the Caribbean

Too many pages would be required to make a complete study of the political crosscurrents agitating the area of the Caribbean during the twenty-five years of the Trujillo Era. Nine small republics in Central America and the Antilles, plus the island of Puerto Rico, comprised the area, with two large republics, Venezuela and Mexico, nearby. It would be an exceptional country indeed that did not suffer during that period from agitated political fluctuation, and many went from dictatorship to democracy to dictatorship. Their tiny size and closeness have provoked a crisscrossing of interest and forces, in which the exiles attempt to attack the dictatorships of their own countries and often dictatorships and democracies help each other against the others.

The Dominican Republic is located in the heart of that volcano, and its exiles have jumped from country to country according to the course of events in all of them. Let us attempt to summarize the period and its most outstanding events.

At the beginning of the Era, the first Dominican exiles took refuge in Haiti and Puerto Rico; they were not only the closest countries but neither the dictatorship of Juan Vicente Gómez in Venezuela nor that of Gerardo Machado in Cuba allowed them to take refuge in those countries at that time. When the treaty between Haitian President Vincent and Trujillo was signed in 1936, the Dominican exiles were forced to abandon Haiti, but at that time the doors of Cuba and Venezuela were already opened after the disappearance of both their dictators.

The fact that Puerto Rico was a United States territory precluded the Dominican exiles from reflecting a belligerent attitude there, although they were not limited in their individual freedom. In the case of Cuba and Venezuela, their activities increased or were limited according to the relations between Trujillo and the subsequent governments of those countries. In 1943, a general meeting of exiles took place in Havana;[25] Trujillo knew of it beforehand but nothing important happened at the time.

When Cuban President Ramón Grau San Martín was inaugurated in 1944, Trujillo sent a very important special mission, perhaps attempting to be on good terms with the new ruler because his last relations with Batista had not been friendly.[26] But it was soon obvious that the exiles had greater freedom of action under the new Cuban Auténtico government; and the Dominican press began to attack Grau San Martín.[27] At the same time, the relations between Trujillo and Venezuelan President Isaías Medina Angarita had not been very friendly, and the first news about the revolution of October, 1945, in Caracas was received with joy in Ciudad Trujillo. But the subsequent surprise at finding Rómulo Betancourt in power, the assault on the Dominican legation in Caracas, the breaking of diplomatic relations by the new Venezuelan government, and the immediate campaign by radio on the part of Dominican exiles launched a hostility between Dominican Republic and Venezuela that lasted three years.

In the period after the end of World War II, the democratic tide reached a climax. The Dominican press and radio attacked Grau San Martín and Betancourt but the Dominican exiles received unofficial protection from the Cuban government. Even the threats of Trujillo were powerless to prevent it. Hence, the Cayo Confites invasion was prepared in Cuba with the indubitable complicity of its authorities.

By that time, another government had joined the anti-Trujillo alliance, that of Guatemala, and after 1948, that of José Figueres in Costa Rica. In this latter case, the fact that several Dominican members of the Cayo Confites group had intervened in the Costa Rican civil war was a decisive factor.[28] When the Acción Democrática government was ousted

---

[25] See *Quisqueya Libre,* July, 1952. [Fn. 81, Chap. VIII.]

[26] *Patria,* the publication of Dominican exiles in New York, reproduced in January, 1954, a photostat of a circular addressed by the Dominican Office of Foreign Relations to officers of the foreign service on August 6, 1944, ordering them not to attend any party given for former President Batista because he had "always acted as an enemy of the Republic and its illustrious Head of State." [Fn. 82, Chap. VIII.]

[27] Bustamante, *Satrapía,* pp. 164–77, gives many details of the machinations of Trujillo in Cuba against the Grau San Martín administration. [Fn. 83, Chap. VIII.]

[28] One of them was Horacio J. Ornes, later on commander of the revolutionary plane landing at Luperón; Ornes had been Dominican chargé d'affaires in Costa Rica. Some of the arms readied for the Cayo Confites invasion were used by the Figueres forces in the civil war. One of the first measures taken by the provisional government of Figueres was to break relations with the Dominican Republic. [Fn. 87, Chap. VIII.]

in Venezuela in November, 1948, this alliance was reduced to Cuba, Guatemala, and Costa Rica. In the meanwhile, Trujillo had joined forces with the Nicaraguan dictator Anastasio Somoza.[29]

The climax of this intrigue occurred in 1949, at the time of the unsuccessful Luperón invasion. This time, the invaders departed from Guatemala. It was not possible to prove complicity on the part of the Cuban government, and it seems certain that the Costa Rican government did not intervene. But by 1949, the political tide in the world had changed, and Trujillo himself felt strong enough to accuse the governments of Guatemala, Cuba, and Costa Rica in the Council of the Organization of American States; at the same time, the Haitian government was accusing Trujillo in the same Council. The commission of investigation visited the five countries, and its report confirmed the facts denounced by all the parties involved.

Since 1950, there has been no evidence of any overt aggression like that of Cayo Confites and Luperón, but the state of political tension in the Caribbean has not decreased, although the balance of power has been substantially altered. Venezuela is now a country friendly towards the Dominican Republic. Since 1952, Cuba has also been friendly and has forced some Dominican exiles to leave that country;[30] Trujillo now praises Batista, forgetting past attacks. Until the summer of 1954, Guatemala was a stronghold of Dominican exiles, especially the Communist ones. Today the attacks of Trujillo are mostly turned against President Figueres of Costa Rica and Governor Luis Muñoz Marín of Puerto Rico.[31] On the other hand, it has been said, without proof until now, that Trujillo inter-

---

[29] When the puppet president installed by Somoza in Nicaragua in May, 1947, was not recognized by the governments of the Americas, the Dominican ambassador was the only one who dared to defend the Nicaraguan government in the governing board of the Pan American Union. The friendship between Trujillo and Somoza would culminate later in the latter's attendance at the inauguration of Héctor B. Trujillo as president in August, 1952. [Fn. 88, Chap. VIII.]

[30] The leader of the Dominican Revolutionary party, Juan Bosch, went to Costa Rica, a fact that increased the animosity of Trujillo toward Figueres. [Fn. 93, Chap. VIII.]

[31] At the end of 1954, there was distributed (even in the United States) a pamphlet printed in the Dominican Republic attacking Muñoz Marín and other democratic leaders of both Americas. It was a reproduction of a series of articles published in the Dominican press when the Inter-American Association for Democracy and Freedom granted its annual citation to Muñoz Marín; this citation was delivered to him on July 25, 1954, by a committee headed by Miss Frances R. Grant, secretary general of the association, and having among its members the Costa Rican delegate to the United Nations, Rev. Benjamín Núñez; most of them were accused of being pro-Communist.

In reference to the attacks against President Figueres, perhaps the most violent one appeared in *El Caribe,* Jan. 27, 1955 (on the occasion· of the invasion of Costa Rica from Nicaragua); it was an editorial on the front page and an alleged letter of Figueres to a Nicaraguan in 1950. [Fn. 95, Chap. VIII.]

vened in some way in the invasions of Guatemala in 1954 and Costa Rica in 1955.

It is not possible to undertake a deeper analysis of this changing situation in the Caribbean. But the mere existence of a prolonged dictatorship in the Dominican Republic, without any possibility of internal reaction, is forcing the activity of the exiles from neighboring countries into a complicated game of alliances that change according to the political events of the whole area. It is not possible to study the Dominican dictatorship without having in mind these complications of an international character, a fact that demonstrates at the same time the potential danger it carries for other countries. One of the aspects of this reality is the numberless paid agents of the Dominican government in foreign countries, usually there to spy on the activities of the exiles, and one cannot forget the three, possibly four, Dominican exiles who have been liquidated in New York and Havana.

The Dominican Republic in the International Community

The most recent list of inter-American treaties signed and ratified to date, published by the Pan American Union on September 1, 1954, indicates that the Dominican Republic has deposited more ratifications than any other country — sixty-three out of a possible ninety-one. Panama was the second with fifty-six, the United States had ratified forty-nine, and Argentina was last with only eleven. This detail is a good symptom of another of Trujillo's preoccupations, that of displaying a good role in international life. But at the same time it confirms something else that has been obvious in different places in this study, that is, that international treaties are ratified without attention to their content.

Of course, the Dominican Republic approved without hesitation the Universal Declaration of Human Rights (Paris, 1948) and the similar Inter-American Declaration (Bogotá, 1948). And yet many of their main principles are ignored in the daily political life of the country.

This internationalist preoccupation of Trujillo became manifest from the time of his first administration, despite the scarcity of his financial resources. In the annual message presented to Congress on February 27, 1931, the establishment of a new legation to the Holy See was announced, as well as three more consulates in Europe; the annual message of 1932 announced the accrediting of ten new heads of missions, a permanent delegate to the League of Nations, and several consuls. Today the Dominican Republic maintains embassies and legations in almost all western countries. It has a permanent delegation to the United Nations and a permanent ambassador in the Organization of American States, and regularly attends international conferences.

In general, the international policy of the Dominican Republic tries to follow step by step the currents coming from Washington. At very few times does it show a policy of its own, unless it involves a question of problems closely related to internal politics; the usual exceptions refer to that convulsive situation in the Caribbean and especially its relations with Haiti. Another case in some ways exceptional, often for reasons of national politics, has been its defense of Franco's Spain in the United Nations.

This case of Franco Spain presents a fresh aspect of the dissimulation typical of the Trujillo regime. In the First General Assembly of the United Nations, the Dominican delegation voted against the resolution adopted in December, 1946, recommending the withdrawal of heads of missions from Madrid. At that time, the Dominican Republic was represented in Spain by a minister, and during 1947 he was kept as such in Madrid. But just on the opening day of the Second General Assembly of the United Nations, the Dominican government announced that it had withdrawn its head of mission to the Spanish government in fulfillment of that resolution. A few days after the end of this Second General Assembly, the Dominican government reappointed the same diplomat as head of mission in Madrid, but promoted him to the rank of ambassador. In the Fifth General Assembly, in 1950, the Dominican delegation took the initiative in favor of the Franco regime, together with other delegations, most of which represented Latin American dictatorships.[32] Since Trujillo's trip to Spain in the summer of 1954, he has sponsored the admission of Franco Spain to the United Nations (despite the constitutional resolution adopted in San Francisco and reiterated during the first part of the First General Assembly held in London).

Another significant case was the attitude towards the Korean War. As soon as President Truman decided to fight against the Communist aggression, the Dominican government made public its unconditional backing; the backing was repeated when the United Nations adopted its first collective measures. The Dominican Republic never went further, however, than those oral statements and never sent troops to Korea. Only at the end of the conflict, when the negotiations for a truce were almost completed, did Trujillo state to the United States press that he was ready to send Dominican troops against Communists in Korea.

---

[32] The first Dominican petition was introduced by a letter dated August 10, 1950, addressed to the secretary general of the United Nations (A/1314). Its first project of resolution was officially deposited on Sept. 16 (A/1363). The joint project, together with the delegations of Bolivia, Costa Rica, El Salvador, Honduras, Nicaragua, and Peru, was deposited on Oct. 3 (A/Ac.38/L.4). [Fn. 103, Chap. VIII.]

In the opposite direction, another interesting initiative on the part of the Dominican Republic appeared in 1954 in the international field. It deserves emphasis because it shows again the priority of internal political interests over the appearances of internationalism. On September 25, 1954, the Dominican congress authorized the executive to denounce two inter-American treaties, those of 1928 and 1933 on diplomatic asylum. Such asylum is an institution so traditional and strong in Latin America that even the Peruvian dictatorship of General Manuel Odría was forced to respect it in the years-long case of Haya de la Torre;* and Trujillo himself was also forced to respect it in several cases that have developed since 1945, although in more than one occasion that asylum provoked diplomatic uneasiness.[33] Today the Dominican Republic is the only Latin American country which does not recognize the right of political asylum, although fifteen years ago the official propaganda attempted to credit to Trujillo the doctrine of political asylum as something of his own.[34]

All such international policy is decided by Trujillo without any control from Congress as the Constitution provides.

Both the embassies and the consulates usually have the primary purpose of praising the person of the Benefactor with the same zeal exhibited in the Dominican Republic by the legislators or the press.

In the inter-American regional area, one must add as final data the "Trujillo Project for a League of American Nations," introduced in December, 1936, by the Dominican delegation to the special Conference for the Maintenance of Peace, held in Buenos Aires. This project had

---

* Víctor Raúl Haya de la Torre was the leader of the Peruvian national revolutionary party APRA, an organization which had long been at serious odds with the Peruvian army. Haya, who between 1945 and 1948 enjoyed an unwonted degree of political freedom and even activity, found the situation suddenly reversed as the result of an army coup in October, 1948, which instituted a military *junta* led by General Odría as a replacement for the Peruvian civilian regime. Haya immediately had to go into hiding and early in 1949 took political asylum in the Colombian embassy in Lima. Because the Odría regime refused for years to grant him a safe-conduct to leave the country, he was forced to remain in the embassy for more than five years, until the early months of 1954, when the Peruvian government permitted him to depart.

[33] When the case of "Chito" Henríquez and his father occurred in 1945, *La Nación* on June 22 printed an official note on the matter attacking the Venezuelan government of Medina Angarita; some weeks later, the three chargés d'affaires of Venezuela, Colombia, and Mexico, who had granted asylum to several boys, were forced to leave the Dominican Republic as *personae non gratae*. [Fn. 110, Chap. VIII.]

[34] On the occasion of the Spanish civil war, the Dominican legation at Madrid granted asylum to a few persons, as almost all embassies and legations did. For many years, the official Dominican propaganda proclaimed this gesture, calling it "the Trujillo Doctrine of Humanitarian Diplomatic Asylum." See Hoepelmán, *Nuestra Vida*, pp. 298–302; Henry Helfant, *La Doctrina Trujillo del Asilo Diplomático Humanitario* (México; 1947). [Fn. 111, Chap. VIII.]

great success in the Dominican Republic, where doctoral dissertations were written on it, but it went from conference to conference and no government paid it any attention until it had to be withdrawn in 1945 at the Chapultepec Conference, when plans for the present Organization of American States were seriously approached.

Relations with the United States

A main guiding principle in the international policy of the Dominican Republic is to follow the currents coming from Washington, occasionally with more enthusiasm and extremism than is shown by the generators themselves.[35] But this imitation of the United States administration, whether Democratic or Republican, does not mean that Dominican speakers hesitate to attack high officials of the United States State Department if they have shown any dislike towards Trujillo's dictatorship.

Two cases may be mentioned. On June 3, 1944, a career diplomat, Ellis O. Briggs, presented his credentials as the new United States ambassador in Ciudad Trujillo. Because Briggs had been associated with Ambassador Spruille Braden in Cuba and his deep democratic feelings were well known, he lasted only a few months in the Dominican Republic. Two years later, Ambassador Braden became assistant secretary of state for inter-American affairs, during the precise period in which external pressure against Trujillo was increased and the Cayo Confites invasion was prepared. Even today the Dominican press attacks jointly Braden, Briggs, and other United States officials calling them "pro-Communists."[36] The successors of Braden as assistant secretary for inter-American affairs were Edward Miller and John Moors Cabot, the first a Democrat and the

---

[35] In the Third Meeting of Consultation among American Foreign Ministers held at Rio de Janeiro in January, 1942, when the problem was to defeat the resistance of Argentina and Chile in order to obtain a joint breaking of diplomatic relations with the Axis powers, the Dominican delegation went to the extreme of requesting a joint declaration of war; of course, this proposal was withdrawn.

Also, in the same sense, it is fitting to call to mind that in November, 1945, the Dominican congress passed a resolution to change the name of Dajabón (the border town soaked with the blood of Haitians in 1937) into Ciudad Roosevelt. It seems that the United States embassy did not like such an honor; the change of name was not carried out. [Fn. 115, Chap. VIII.]

[36] The most serious attack, because it was an official one, was the speech made by the secretary of foreign relations of the Dominican Republic, Joaquín Balaguer [a later president], in a joint meeting of both legislative chambers on Sept. 17, 1953. El Caribe, Sept. 18, 1953. One of the latest press attacks was an editorial in El Caribe, July 28, 1955, on the occasion of some strong anti-Communist statements made by Braden in the United States. It was also reported to the author that the Dominican government had intended to put a plaque on the Monument to the Peace of Trujillo, to be inaugurated at the end of 1955, in which the names of Braden and Briggs would appear together with those of other "Communist" enemies of Trujillo; the idea was discarded because of the reaction provoked in diplomatic circles. See also, El Caribe, May 1, 1955. [Fn. 117, Chap. VIII.]

second, a Republican. Neither of them had any obvious attitude against the Dominican regime although it is possible that they had ideas of their own on the matter. Nevertheless both were equally attacked by Dominican speakers, always insinuating "pro-Communist" sympathies.[37]

Similar attacks have recently been made against United States publications as important as the *New York Times* and the weekly *Time*, as a consequence of news and comments adverse to Trujillo appearing in their pages.

What is curious is the fact that one of the prominent Americans acting obviously in the service of Trujillo as a lawyer, is Joseph E. Davies, a former United States ambassador in Moscow who was convinced about the fairness of the Stalin purges. Davies has never been called a "pro-Communist"; on the contrary, Trujillo takes pleasure in receiving his hospitality and returning it when he is in Washington.[38]

Among former officers of the Department of State, there is one whom Trujillo has never forgiven, although he — former Undersecretary Sumner Welles — is no longer attacked openly, undoubtedly because of his attitude at the time of the Haitian massacre. In contrast, the attempt was made years ago to glorify Secretary of State Cordell Hull, putting him on the same level with Trujillo because both of them were signers of the 1940 treaty which freed Dominican customs from United States control. It is one of the positive deeds to be noted on the credit side of the Trujillo administration. The attempt was repeated at the death of Hull in July, 1955.

Another cause for uneasiness between the Dominican government and that of the United States is not political but economic. It is the quota system for the import of sugar into the States, which hurts the interests of Dominican exporters.

---

[37] One of the accusations against Miller was issued by Ramón Marrero Aristy, as a member of the commission to support sugar, in a statement to *El Diario de Nueva York,* Sept. 2, 1951, reproduced by *El Caribe,* Sept. 5, 1951. The accusations against John Moors Cabot were officially issued by the Dominican government on May 19, 1953 (cable by U.P. from Ciudad Trujillo on the twentieth); this accusation was denied at once by the United States Department of State but the Dominican Foreign Office on the twenty-second repeated it. See also *Time,* June 1, 1953. [Fn. 118, Chap. VIII.]

[38] On the occasion of the latest trip of Trujillo to Washington, in October, 1954, he offered a reception to the press on his private yacht in order to express his ideas about "communism" and to repeat the usual accusations against former officers of the United States Department of State. His guest of honor on this occasion was former Ambassador Joseph E. Davies. *Hispanic American Report,* October, 1954. Davies appeared also next to Trujillo in a picture taken on the occasion of a party given in the Dominican embassy in Washington, during his long stay in the United States two years before. *La Prensa,* Dec. 24, 1952. [Fn. 120, Chap. VIII.]

To sum up, in general the Trujillo regime takes pride in presenting itself as the best ally of the United States, even by paid advertising, as, for instance, that which appeared on page 61 of the special issue of the *New York Times,* January 6, 1954,[39] about the Latin American economy. In fact, the Dominican Republic is a formal ally of the United States. On April 17, 1953, the Dominican congress approved, without discussion, a military agreement between the two countries.

The serious question is this: does the alliance between the people leading the fight of the free world and one of the most absolute tyrannies of the present time mean an increase of strategic safety for the United States or does it mean a liability that the other enemies of freedom can take advantage of?

Relations with Other Countries

In the inter-American field, the Dominican Republic maintained in 1955 diplomatic relations with all countries except Costa Rica. That does not mean that all those relations are cordial, and it is always necessary to make fine distinctions between friendly dictators and democracies that reduce relations to the minimum required by protocol, and those that are indifferent. At times, a close Dominican approach to Perón was intimated, but it did not materialize because of the subordination to the United States, which has been pointed out.

In the European field, Spain and England are predominant for different reasons. England continues to be the main purchaser of Dominican sugar;[40] it is a strictly commercial interest, which never had political repercussions. In the case of Spain with that generally affective tie that binds the Latin American countries to the "Motherland," there have been added during recent years special political reasons of friendship between Trujillo and Franco that do not need to be explained; this friendship was reinforced by Trujillo's trip to Madrid.[41] There is also in the Dominican

---

[39] The page had a picture of Trujillo completely filling it, and as a footnote a brief message of his saying: ". . . The people of the United States have, and always had, in the Dominican Republic a true friend with a clear conception of the solidarity that ought to prevail between neighbors. Our country identifies itself with the United States and other free nations completely in the worldwide fight against communism. This union, inspired by the same ideals of liberty and democracy. . . ." [Fn. 122, Chap. VIII.]

[40] In 1951, England bought 458,574,319 kilograms for $57,988,346; and in 1952 it bought 444,226,878 kilograms for $42,553,890. *Anuario Estadístico de la República Dominicana, 1952* (Ciudad Trujillo, 1954), p. 435. [Fn. 125, Chap. VIII.]

[41] A special issue of the unofficial Spanish magazine *Mundo Hispánico* (Supplement to No. 81 of 1954) was devoted to commemorate this trip, with many pictures. [Fn. 126, Chap. VIII.]

Republic a strong Spanish colony of businessmen, who, almost as a whole, adhered to the Franco side during the Spanish civil war and even had a uniformed branch of the Falange Exterior.[42] This colony survived the immigration of Republican refugees during World War II, a period in which Trujillo was careful not to show special friendship towards Franco, also for obvious reasons.

Among the remaining European nations, France continues to have a relative cultural influence, especially among lawyers because of the fact that the Dominican codes are a translation of the Code Napoleon, and the decisions of French courts and the doctrine of French authors are used in Dominican courts.[43] Before World War II, Germany began to have some influence, but today it is in abeyance.

---

[42] The secretary general of this Dominican branch of Falange Exterior was named Manuel Resumil Aragunde (married to a sister of R. Comprés, brother-in-law of Trujillo's wife, later on a Dominican citizen, and in 1955 secretary of industry and commerce). In the publication organ of the Casa de España (Spanish House) of Ciudad Trujillo appeared pictures of these Falange groups, in uniform and raising hands in the Fascist salute. . . . [Fn. 127, Chap. VIII.]

[43] The French codes, in force since 1845 (previously the Haitian codes of 1825 were used), were translated into Spanish in 1884. The Dominican courts try to keep up to date with the decisions of the French Supreme Court of Justice; and any lawyer who is worth his fee has in his office the *Repertoire Dalloz*. [Fn. 128, Chap. VIII.]

Chapter 9: The "Anti-Communism" of Trujillo

In October, 1954, Trujillo made a brief trip to the United States, the last one until now. On this trip, he made repeated statements to the press offering the United States his experience and files about Communist infiltration in the Americas. In particular, he offered them to a House subcommittee of investigation, at the time under the chairmanship of the Republican Congressman Patrick J. Hillings.[1]

For some years now, all of Trujillo's propaganda in the United States, including paid advertising in the New York press, has presented him as the first anti-Communist of the Americas.[2]

Trujillo is not the only Latin American dictator who today presumes to use the excuse of anti-communism to justify internal violations of basic freedoms in a political system very similar to the Stalinist one. Nor is the Dominican Republic the only Latin American country where the Communists have not hesitated within recent years to play ball with any kind of government, even a dictatorial one.

However, it would be useful to round out this analysis of the political regime of Trujillo by exploring the position of communism in the Dominican Republic, noting the fluctuating line pursued both by the Communists and Trujillo according to world politics, and also to define what Trujillo — and other Latin American dictators — understand by "communism" and "Communists."

---

[1] Report by Joseph Hirshaw from Washington, distributed by INS, on Oct. 12, 1954. [Fn. 2, Chap. IX.]

[2] When Georgi Malenkov resigned as Prime Minister of the USSR at the beginning of 1955, *El Caribe* printed an editorial saying that Trujillo had already foreseen this one year before, thanks to his profound knowledge of communism. [Fn. 3, Chap. IX.]

In addition to the data already mentioned, almost all of it based upon documentary evidence, there are additional data which cannot be supported by documentation, but about which the author knew or witnessed personally during his stay in the Dominican Republic.[3]

Communism is only an episode, a secondary aspect, in the Era of Trujillo. Nevertheless, the lesson it presents is useful in interpreting his style and in understanding his present attitude. Especially does it aid in evaluating some of his accusations against his Dominican opponents abroad or against disinterested critics.

Background of Communism in the Dominican Republic Until 1945

It is not possible to state precisely when the first Communist ideas arrived in the Dominican Republic. None of the first leaders of the Dominican Confederation of Labor before 1939 appear to have had Communist tendencies or even sympathies. Officially, the first reference to communism in the publications of the Dominican government appeared in a law dated November 4, 1936, repressing communism and other doctrines of the same kind. To interpret what was meant at that time by "communism," no further clue is given than a decree on April 5, 1937, prohibiting the return to the country under penalty of arrest of Dr. Juan I. Jimenes-Grullón, because he was in Cuba "dedicated to ignoble and unjustified Communist activity." Jimenes-Grullón, one of the boys arrested two years earlier in Santiago and sentenced as an alleged participant in the plot against Trujillo, was later pardoned and exiled. He is the author of two books,[4] in which he does not reveal any pro-Communist ideas. This law of 1936 was abrogated on December 22, 1937, by request of Trujillo.

Nevertheless, the first Communist ferment must have arisen in the Dominican Republic about this same time, perhaps as a consequence of the Spanish civil war that divided public opinion into two groups and many shades. At the end of 1939, there already existed some Communists and pro-Communists, and there were even indications of an incipient organization. One person who in those days openly defended the Spanish Communists, even attacking the non-Communist anti-Franco groups, was José Angel Saviñón, last editor of the publication *República* which appeared during the Spanish civil war as an anti-Franco paper in a general sense but obviously of pro-Communist trend in its later issues. Also

---

[3] Especially in the second half of 1945 and the beginning of 1946, when the author was legal adviser to the Department of Labor. [Fn. 5, Chap. IX.]

[4] *La República Dominicana* (Havana, 1940), and *Una Gestapo en América* (Havana, 1946). [Fn. 8, Chap. IX.]

obvious was the simmering of advanced ideas among a group of Dominican intellectuals who later became adherents of Trujillo.

At the end of 1939 and the beginning of 1940, several Spanish
Communists arrived in the ships bringing the mass immigration of refugees. Their proportion in relation to the whole number of exiles was small,
but they soon began acting with their usual techniques. The members of the
party retained their organization, most of the time clandestine, although
about 1944 they published a summary of the topics discussed in a local
congress of the party and for a considerable time a refugee named Cepeda
acted as open leader of the Spanish Communists in the Republic.

More apparent and dynamic were the activities of several Communist
fronts housed in the building officially used by the so-called Centro
Democrático Español (Spanish Democratic Center) in the capital and
also operating branches in several other towns. They issued two publications and held public meetings which some Dominicans attended. When
the sugar strike was attempted in 1942, the Dominican police ordered the
general arrest of the Spanish Communists, but they were later released.[5]
Their activities were not curtailed until 1945.

Among future Dominican Communists who seem to have been initiated through contact with Spanish Communists may be mentioned "Chito"
Henríquez, although he later completed his indoctrination in Cuba. But
the chief Dominican Communist leader, Pericles Franco, Jr. ("Periclito"),
was indoctrinated in Chile, where he was a scholarship student until the
beginning of 1942. As the war spread to the Americas, Periclito returned
to the Dominican Republic, where he acted with extreme cautiousness for
some time thereafter. He began to be more active only in 1944, when the
first groups of students were organized, groups that, step by step, began
their clandestine activities in 1945. During this period, it is possible that
the first communist cells were already organized, but within the university
the future Communists mingled with the future members of Democratic
Youth, who did not evolve towards communism.

"Periclito" began openly to act as a Communist in exile, traveling
first to Colombia. Later he traveled through different countries, and in
Chile he printed a pamphlet, *La Tragedia Dominicana,* with an introduction by the Communist poet Pablo Neruda. In this pamphlet he spoke of
groups in clandestine opposition to Trujillo, using names typical for Communist fronts, such as Frente Democrático de Liberación Nacional
(Democratic Front for National Liberation).

---

[5] Instead of the Communists, two Socialist leaders and one Republican leader
were expelled at that time; all of them were heads of local branches of the JARE,
openly anti-Communist and taking care of Spanish refugees. [Fn. 11, Chap. IX.]

José Angel Saviñón in 1945 became an active Trujillist, first as president of the Congress of Youth, and very soon afterward, as civil aid to the president. The restless intellectuals of 1940 were more discreet in their development, but one by one, they also began to take governmental positions.

Outside the actual activities of the Communists, it is worthwhile noting that delegates of the Dominican Confederation of Labor, with expenses paid by the government, attended in 1944 the notorious congress of the CTAL (Latin American Confederation of Labor, under the chairmanship of Vicente Lombardo Toledano) in Cali, Colombia, where the Communists completed their control of this organization.

Trujillo Sends a Minister to Moscow and Praises the USSR

In the meantime, the Dominican Republic, as a member of the United Nations, had become an ally of the USSR. In the beginning this meant nothing in the international policy of the Dominican government, but as the centennial approached in 1944, the government desired that a Soviet diplomat be present. The difficulty was that the Dominican Republic had no diplomatic relations with Moscow, and the Secretaryship of Foreign Relations hence had problems at the beginning. Nevertheless, an official invitation was sent by the Dominican government to that of the Soviet Union.

During the centennial festivities in February, 1944, the USSR was represented by Minister Dimitri Zaikin and Secretary Victor Ibertrebor. In consequence, the red Soviet flag was exhibited in the Jaragua Hotel together with the flags of the other countries represented, and Trujillo at the end of the centennial gave decorations to the two Communist diplomats.

In June, 1945, after the surrender of Germany, Trujillo decided to establish diplomatic relations with the USSR and to appoint a Dominican minister to Moscow. For this purpose, he sent a message to the Senate on June 11 submitting the nomination of Dr. Ricardo Pérez Alfonseca. It was a long message, and today, when Trujillo depicts himself as the champion of anti-communism, it seems especially curious. The second paragraph read:

The appointment of this distinguished diplomat, who passed the entire war period in Europe as head of our mission to the suffering and heroic city of London, to inaugurate the first Dominican Legation with permanent residence in Moscow, constitutes an act signifying the sincere desire of the Dominican Government officially to regularize and to make closer our relations that in fact have always existed between the Russian people and the Dominican people, on the basis of mutual respect and cordiality. Since long before the current war, ships flying the Soviet flag came to our ports on commercial missions, and received a friendly welcome from our authorities and people; Russian artists have been among us as ambassadors of the rich musical talents of this people; books by Russian authors, from the past to the present, from Turgenev to Stalin, occupy important places in our bookstores and public libraries, where they have always been at the free disposal of everybody; rhythms and melodies of the great Russian musicians, from Glinka to Shostakovich, are popular in our artistic circles.

In two additional paragraphs, Trujillo praised the Russian resistance during World War II, and in a third he recalled the attendance of the two Soviet diplomats during the centennial. Then came another paragraph, which today is the most curious one, because of the unlimited praise he gave to the USSR as one of the great forces of the democratic world, no more, no less:

As a result of its noble and powerful contribution to the victory of the United Nations in Europe, and of the imminent constitution, in the historical Conference of San Francisco in California, of the World Organization for the maintenance of peace, security, justice, and cooperation, the *Soviet Union,* whose material force has been extended to the service of a high cause, *will always be recognized as one of the great forces for good and progress that the democratic world may count upon.*[6]

Dr. Pérez Alfonseca spent one year, more or less, in Moscow. The USSR never reciprocated by appointing an envoy to the Dominican Republic. About 1947, Dr. Pérez Alfonseca was recalled from Moscow. A short time afterward, Trujillo became the champion of "anti-communism." In the meantime, his domestic play with Dominican Communists took place.

The Period of the Popular Socialist Party

A Communist organization by the name of the Popular Socialist party made its appearance in 1946 and became active for several months. The first episode was the peculiar activity of Manuel Frías Meyreles at the end of 1945.[7] He appeared for the first time in a demonstration, organized by United States citizens at La Romana on the occasion of the Japanese surrender, which he attended waving the red Soviet flag. In consequence, he was later arrested for a brief period by the police, and still later requested asylum in the Mexican embassy. The Dominican government offered him a position as labor adviser in the Secretaryship of Labor and Economy, which he accepted and held for several weeks.

---

[6] The italics in this and the above quoted paragraph are not in the original. [Fn. 17, Chap. IX.]

[7] The author was a witness of some of the activities of Frías Meyreles, being at the time the legal adviser of the Labor Department. Other activities were directly mentioned to the author by Frías Meyreles himself or by direct witnesses. Only the outstanding events are given here. [Fn. 19, Chap. IX.]

His movements could hardly be more unexpected; very soon afterward, he began to express himself as secretary general of a clandestine Communist party. At the same time, the secretary of the presidency and the president of the Dominican party discussed with him the possible public organization of the Communist party.[8] In consequence of his intervention in two strike attempts he was finally dismissed from his position as adviser. He was invited to take a trip abroad with expenses paid by the government under the pretext of meeting labor leaders of Cuba and Mexico. This game around Frías Meyreles was known only to a narrow circle, but the speech he made in La Romana during the first strike attempt, at the end of 1945, caused an extraordinary repercussion — some people thought he might be an *agent provocateur* of the government. It is possible that the Dominican government, equally with the clandestine Communists, used Frías Meyreles as a guinea pig in order to test the strength and motives of the other side.

Despite these first maneuvers, the Dominican Communist party continued to be a clandestine one up to the beginning of 1946, when the general strike in the sugar provinces was called in January. In consequence of this, Frías Meyreles, who had returned from abroad a few weeks after his departure, was arrested and indicted. At the same time, the president of the federation of labor of San Pedro de Macorís, Mauricio Báez, was also arrested for a few days. Immediately after the strike he received asylum in the Mexican embassy and later went into exile in Cuba.

Of the second episode of this process, there also remains no public documentary evidence, although it is generally known in the Dominican Republic. The government was still interested in forcing the public organization of the Communist party, and during the second half of 1946 an unofficial agent, Ramón Marrero Aristy, was sent to Cuba to discuss with exiled Communists their return to the country and also the public organization of their party. The most significant aspect of these negotiations is that no attempt was made to discover the Communists hidden within the Dominican Republic, but that problems were discussed only with the declared Communists abroad.

The terms of the agreement have not been made public. But the best proof that the agreement itself existed is the fact that the exiled Communists returned, and that their party was immediately organized and became active in the second half of 1946, using the many guarantees offered officially by Trujillo as president. It is interesting to note that the chief leader

---

[8] The author himself heard a telephone conversation between Frías Meyreles and Secretary Vega Batlle to this effect, although he heard only Frías Meyreles' words. These negotiations were confirmed by other high officers who knew of them directly. [Fn. 21, Chap. IX.]

of the Dominican Communists, "Periclito" Franco, did not return until the last moment, and his arrival marked the climax of the game played by both sides.

The first public news in which reference was made to Dominican Communists was a release by the Secretaryship of Interior and Police on March 15, 1946, ordering them to appear within five days to regularize the existence of their party. This attempt failed. Three months of silence followed, during which negotiations must have proceded. The first sign that something was boiling was the letters of President Trujillo on June 15 to the secretary of interior and to the attorney general instructing them to respect all constitutional guarantees of the free expression of opinion and the organization of political parties. Nine days later, Trujillo addressed a message to the Dominican exiles inviting them to return. At the same time *La Nación* printed an editorial saying: "Those people must not return!" From this moment, a double play was in evidence: while Trujillo, as president, offered guarantees, other forces reacted against those who abused the guarantees.

On August 18 *La Nación* made public a presidential pardon affecting, among other prisoners, Communist leader Fredy Valdés. In *La Nación* on the twenty-seventh appeared a manifesto of the newly named Popular Socialist party; among the signers were Mauricio Báez and Ramón Grullón, returned from Cuba, and Fredy Valdés, freed from jail. The same newspaper commented in a frontpage editorial: "What better answer as to the existence of a democratic government, than the fact that their leaders may express themselves in such terms?" This comment reveals one side of the game. But on the next day, the same newspaper printed an attack by six persons (employees of the government) insulting the signers of the manifesto.

At the end of September, a national congress of workers was held. Communists Báez and Grullón participated in it and were elected members of the executive committee. At the beginning of October, the Communists requested the official registration of their party. The secretary of interior sent the petition to the central electoral board; Alvarez Pina, as president of the Dominican party, asked its members to be on the watch "to prevent the dissolving Communist action." The central electoral board refused the registration, and Trujillo intervened, recommending giving facilities to the Communists in order that they might legalize the party.

This letter from Trujillo was highly interesting because of the praise he gave the Soviet Union and even his favorable comment about the Communists themselves. He said in the first paragraph:

Communism, whose existence in the Dominican Republic is already a real factor of positive consequence, has its indubitable origin in the organizations of the Soviet Union, and in order to evaluate it, as a maker of socio-political activities, it would be unfair to forget the sacrificial cooperation that they offered to Democracy during the last World War.[9]

In another paragraph Trujillo repeated one of his reasons for such a game:

> Their existence among us is also a strong and eloquent denial to those slanderers who, without grounds, accuse the Dominican Republic of not being governed by a democratic regime.

The Communists themselves hasten to express appreciation of this letter. But Alvarez Pina strongly opposed their recognition. The fact merits attention that no other groups among the exiles or in the country received similar guarantees for organizing a political party. The obvious purpose was to have on hand a Communist party. Nobody was fooled by the spontaneous appearance of the National Labor party. But at the beginning of October, another group unexpectedly popped up that was not composed either of Communists or of exiles returning from abroad — the university boys and girls of the Democratic Youth, who were bitterly attacked at once.

The subsequent activities of both groups culminated in a meeting held in Ciudad Trujillo on October 26, during which Trujillist *agents provocateurs* attacked the meeting place and incited street riots. This meeting offered a pretext for the first repressive measures by the government.

In summary, these are the outstanding events marking the public process of the organization of a Communist party in the Dominican Republic. Subsequent events may help to explain the ends sought by the Dominican government in this period immediately following the victory of the United Nations in World War II.[10]

---

[9] The italics are not in the original. [Fn. 26, Chap. IX.]

[10] The interpretation of this process remains a matter of conjecture so long as it is not possible to consult documents that remain secret, for the time being, on both sides. Two facts seem obvious: (1) The Dominican government encouraged and negotiated by different means the organization of a Communist party in the Dominican Republic; (2) Communist leaders collaborated willingly in this plan, and during its development they refrained from attacking Trujillo. As a possible explanation of this project, it seems wise to realize that the Dominican government had several ends in mind: (a) to expose a possible clandestine Communist organization in the Republic, suspected since 1945; (b) to give the appearance of liberty even to extreme ideas during the period of a high democratic tide; (c) to present the Dominicans with this simple dilemma: either Trujillo or communism (it may be that this idea did not exist at the beginning). It is more difficult to interpret the ends hoped for by the Communists; it seems that in the beginning they rejected the first overtures, but later on they thought it wiser to plant seeds for the future (the arrival of "Periclito" at the last moment of the game may be the most significant detail as far as their side is concerned). [Fn. 27, Chap. IX.]

Repression of Communism Since 1947

At the beginning of 1947, the first signs of a change in the policy of the government became obvious. Alvarez Pina, in a series of attacks and accusations printed in La Nación,[11] headed a movement of "public opinion" requesting the suppression of the Communists.

In March, the Communist leader "Periclito" Franco returned to the Dominican Republic. His return was typical of the Communist method, because a few days later a purge took place in the ranks of the party and "Chito" Henríquez was expelled.

The accusations against Communists and non-Communists were repeated in April, and there even occurred attacks in the streets against several students of the Democratic Youth. A short time later, those members of the Popular Socialist party and Democratic Youth who were not able to get asylum in time, were arrested.

Law No. 1443 on June 14[12] put an end to the process by prohibiting communist, anarchist, and other groups opposing the civil, republican, democratic, and representative system of the government of the Republic. A previous decree on June 9 had created the "Commission to Investigate Anti-Dominican Acts."

Since June, 1947, communism has been illegal in the Dominican Republic. The term "Communist" has been applied over and over to anyone criticizing Trujillo's regime. It is interesting to finish this analysis by exhibiting some evidence of what is understood officially as "communism" and "Communist."

Among the personalities accused of being Communist or protecting Communists are former assistant secretaries of state for Latin American affairs in the government of the United States (Spruille Braden, Edward Miller, and John Moors Cabot). In 1953, a student from Princeton University interviewed Trujillo in New York[13] and asked if all of Trujillo's

---

[11] La Nación, Jan. 29 and Feb. 18, 1947. It is significant that the Communists attempted until the end to follow this double game. An article by "Periclito" Franco printed in the January, 1947, issue of their mouthpiece in Cuba, Noticias de la República Dominicana, said: "This obvious contradiction between the terrorist offensive which victimizes the people and the democratic statements by Trujillo, provokes this question: Is the Fascist V. Alvarez Pina the one who rules in Santo Domingo, or are Trujillo's words but a smoke screen? . . . The events during the next few days will give us the answer." (Reproduced together with a bitter criticism of this Communist attitude, in Boletín ARDE, No. 19, Jan. 13, 1947.) [Fn. 28, Chap. IX.]

[12] G.O. 6641; Bol. Sen. and Bol. Cam., June 1947. The full text of the law, translated into English, was reprinted in a full-page advertisement in the New York Times, Jan. 6, 1954, p. 63. [Fn. 32, Chap. IX.]

[13] The author has in his files a copy of this interview, which was never printed. [Fn. 35, Chap. IX.]

opponents were Communists. Trujillo's answer, through his interpreter, Manuel de Moya, was direct: "Yes, they are all Communists. . . . No patriotic Dominican who loves his place of birth would try to overthrow its stable, beneficial government except Communists." On January 11, 1954, the newspaper *El Caribe* printed an open letter to the editor under this headline: *"¡Fuera ese rojo!"* ("Out with that red!"). In the letter, Prof. José Ramón Báez of the school of sciences was denounced for having criticized in his lectures a recent law favoring tenants, because he thought that this law hurt his interests as owner of many houses. There are many evidences that in the Dominican Republic today there is an effort to apply the term "communism" to any criticism of the present regime.

In a word, Trujillo played with the Communists for his own purposes at the end of World War II; now, he uses anti-communism as his instrument to persecute or to slander his opponents and critics.

Chapter 10: The Positive Results of Trujillo's Regime

A brief evaluation of both favorable and critical points of view regarding the regime is desirable.

A number of books have been written in Trujillo's praise, and there are many official publications offering considerable statistical data about the positive work of the regime.[1] It is possible to channel all this material into the three fields in which Trujillo's regime has accomplished positive results: maintenance of public order, material progress, and cultural progress, as well as the rationalization of his methods, using Trujillo's own words and those of some of his official spokesmen.

Maintenance of Public Order

Today there is peace in the Dominican Republic. In a country characterized during a century of independence by repeated rebellions and civil wars, there has not been one civil war during the twenty-five years of the Era of Trujillo. The rebellion of General Arias in 1931 and the landing of Luperón in 1949 were easily defeated, and other conspiracies have been discovered in time. The army and the police keep absolute order, and Trujillo has been able to maintain the loyalty of those public forces.

The order in the political scene also exists in private life. Only one important hold-up has occurred in a quarter of a century, that of the branch of the Royal Bank of Canada in Santiago de los Caballeros on November 6, 1954, but the robbers were arrested immediately. There

---

[1] See the several volumes of *Anuario Estadístico de la República Dominicana,* and the annual *Memorias* of each department of the administration. [Fn. 2, Chap. X.]

are common criminals, but they are not dangerous, and usually are discovered and punished by the authorities.

The roads of the country are made safe for travelers by military police and motorized policemen. It is possible to travel into the interior, in the forests and the mountains, without fear of surprises. The streets are not dangerous at night. The only unexplained deaths are those of a political character, and the clues always point to the authorities themselves. The only confiscations that cannot be justified are those benefiting the regime or its leaders.

Material Progress

Considerable material progress, obvious to anyone who knew the Dominican Republic before 1930 and returns today, is reflected both in the extensive building and in the national budget. Perhaps the greatest success of Trujillo has been the balancing and the progressive increase of the budget, the liberation of the customs in 1940, the payment of the external and internal debts, and the maintenance of a new national currency at par value.

The budgets speak for themselves. When Trujillo became president in 1930, the budget for that year was $6,608,555; the budget approved for 1955 was $108,124,235, sixteen times greater. Moreover, the increase has been without deficits. On the contrary, it has occurred with a simultaneous cancellation of previous debts. The increasing curb has been maintained since 1932, was accentuated in 1945, and has jumped since 1947.

That budget naturally corresponds to a general increase of acquisitive power in the Dominican Republic, even though it has been beneficial for businessmen. Goods to an amount of $15,229,219 were imported in 1930, and exports totaled $18,551,841, leaving a favorable balance of $3,322,-622. In 1951, imports amounted to $58,595,441 and exports to $118,-712,052, leaving a balance of $60,116,611. During the following year, however, a serious change occurred, because imports rose to $96,900,591 and exports decreased to $115,366,736, leaving a balance of only $18,-466,145. At the same time, gross national sales in 1936 amounted to $16,279,130 and in 1952 to $161,359,165. Wages, however, did not increase in the same proportion. In 1936 wages paid amounted to $4,561,184 and in 1952 to $28,784,562. In 1952 the highest wages paid in the capital were $3.56 a day (in air transport) and the general average was around $2 a day.

External and internal causes (such as the expansion of foreign trade after World War II, the maintaining of internal order) have been responsible for this improvement in Dominican economy and finances. But it is necessary to analyze briefly the content of the Dominican-United States treaty of 1940, which freed the Dominican customs.[2]

The treaty was signed on September 24, 1940, in Washington; Cordell Hull signed for the United States and Trujillo, as ambassador extraordinary, for the Dominican Republic. The Dominican Congress ratified it in October, and the United States Senate in February, 1941; the exchange of ratifications took place on March 10. This treaty modified and abrogated the convention of 1924, which had been another modification of the previous conventions of 1905 and 1907, which offered a pretext for the United States occupation of 1916–24. In the 1924 convention, the external debt of the Dominican Republic had been consolidated at $25,-000,000, and the United States kept the right to appoint a general collector of customs and all the employees required to collect the custom duties, the total of which was mainly devoted to pay the interest and the annual amortization of the debt.

Government income rose during the Vásquez administration to the amount of $15,385,843 in 1929, but the world crisis of the next years (coincident with the first Trujillo administration) forced a decrease to less than half in 1931. At that time the Dominican external debt was $16,320,500, and the government was forced to pass a law of emergency on October 23, 1931, modifying substantially the terms for the payment of that debt. At the same time, serious restrictions in the payment of salaries to public employees were ordered and other public expenses were curtailed. This abnormal situation led to the readjustment of the external debt in 1934,[3] which facilitated the terms of amortization and gave necessary respite to the Dominican government for the rehabilitation of its finances after the crisis. However, United States control over the Dominican customs continued to weigh heavily.

The suppression of this control was the main purpose of the 1940 treaty. As a result, the general office of the customs collector and all United States employees were eliminated, and the customs returned to Dominican control, with the right to regulate its own administrative-financial life. On their part, the Dominicans agreed to pay monthly the

---

[2] A good but brief study of this treaty and its background is Joaquín Balaguer, *El Tratado Trujillo-Hull y la Liberación Financiera de la República Dominicana* (Bogotá, 1941). [Fn. 6, Chap. X.]

[3] *Ibid.*, pp. 92–97. Trujillo himself signed a long book with the title of *Reajuste de la Deuda Externa* (Santiago, 1937); the authorship of this book and of the plan itself has been attributed to several technicians of both Americas. The official point of view of the United States may be consulted in Dept. of State, *Foreign Relations, 1931,* 2:110–37; *ibid., 1933;* 5:589–671; and *ibid., 1934,* 5:189–211. [Fn. 11, Chap. X.]

interest on the external debt and an annual amortization as a preferred credit, plus an agreement to pay greater amortizations if the annual income of the government were more than $12,500,000.

The transfer of the customs took place on April 1, 1941. Since that time, the annual income of the Dominican government has exceeded the minimum of $12,500,000 and since 1944 has increased considerably. In great part, this increase was due to new custom taxes. In 1950, the Dominican government was able to announce the full payment of its external debt, and in 1953 the cancellation of the internal debt.

That this success can be attributed to the Trujillo administration is undeniable. In the Dominican Republic all the credit has been given to the Benefactor (promoted in 1940 to the Restorer of Financial Independence), while the successful role of President Roosevelt's Good Neighbor policy has been ignored.

Also in the economic-financial field may be noted the organization of the Dominican Bank of Reserves, based on the local branch of the National City Bank of New York, purchased in 1941 by the Dominican government; the organization in 1945 of the Agriculture and Mortgage Bank; the banking reorganization in 1947; and the establishment of a new national currency in 1947, which is still maintained more or less at par with the dollar.

In the field of Dominican material progress may be emphasized the intense program of public works, initiated in 1934 by the Dominican government as soon as funds were available, and increased during the last ten or fifteen years. One of these works was the man-made port of Ciudad Trujillo, completed in 1936. At the same time, one may mention the repair of main roads and construction of secondary roads, several canals, the airfield in the capital and small fields inland, and many public buildings. A detailed list of all this construction may be found in any of the books printed in praise of Trujillo.

One might also add on the positive side the legislation enacted in favor of the workers, the creation of some national industries, and a relative improvement in medical and health services.

The material progress of the Dominican Republic during the Era of Trujillo is very obvious. What is lacking is a comparative study of its distribution, an analysis of its benefits to the masses. One must overlook the luxurious buildings of the capital and delve further into life in the poverty-striken *bohíos* (peasants' houses). This is also a negative criticism and will be considered in the following chapter.

Cultural Progress

Although it has not been very important, a certain cultural if not spiritual progress may be added to the positive balance of Trujillo's regime. That is to say, the increase in the number of educational and cultural institutions, taking into account only their material aspect and excluding the factor of their political control.

The university has received that support. In 1940, the faculty of philosophy was reestablished. Since 1946, new buildings of the University City have been inaugurated. Its library is today the best in the Dominican Republic. Although the increase in the number of its students may be due in part to the general increase of the population, it must be emphasized, nevertheless, that in the academic year 1936–37 the total of enrolled students was 328, in the academic year 1941–42 it increased to 900, in the academic year 1946–47 it grew to 1,558, and in the academic year 1951–52 it rose to 2,449. There is no doubt that this increase in university enrollment is due to the intensification of primary and secondary education.

At those levels, the increase of students has kept a proportion more similar to demographic growth, but it is also satisfactory. In the academic year 1936–37 there were 112,722 students, in the academic year 1941–42 there were 130,032, in the year 1946–47 there were 232,099, and in the year 1951–52 there were 259,664. Simultaneously, the number of schools increased from 898 in 1936–37 to 2,747 in 1951–52. There are no official statistics available about the emergency schools to fight adult illiteracy and it has already been said that the unofficial ones seem too optimistic. But it is also obvious that during recent years considerable progress has been made in reducing the index of illiteracy that in 1935 reached 75 percent of the total population.

In order better to evaluate these statistics, it is necessary to add that the official census of 1950 indicated a total population of 2,121,000.

Together with these regular schools and the university, one must add other special schools created during the Era of Trujillo, such as the music school, the school of fine arts, the diplomatic and consular school, which lasted a few years, and the vocational school.

There must also be mentioned other cultural institutions of several kinds, created or reorganized, such as the national symphonic orchestra, the national archives, the library of the university, the projected gallery of fine arts, the Ateneo Dominicano, and the academies, and the encouragement given to painters, sculptors, and writers. The murals by Vela Zanetti in many public buildings are outstanding. More than one Dominican writer or artist has been appointed to diplomatic positions as a practical way of helping his creative activities.

Even the publication of two good, new newspapers like *El Caribe* and *La Nación* and the establishment of the radio-television station, La Voz Dominicana, means progress, although it is diminished in its results because of the biased propaganda.

Not all the cultural advances of the last years came from governmental initiative. Some private bookstores also deserve praise; some of
them, like the Librería Dominicana, organize cultural lectures. There are
also groups of poets such as "la poesía sorprendida" and individual poets
such as Moreno Jiménez, Incháustegui, Mieses Burgos, Carmen Natalia,
and Oscar Pacheco; novelists such as Marrero Aristy, Damirón, and López
Penha; and short-story writers such as Juan Bosch. Some among them
finally surrendered to the regime, but others were forced into exile. There
are also cultural centers like "Los Amantes de la Luz" in Santiago de los
Caballeros, and private colleges, like the Instituto Escuela and others
belonging to religious orders.

The Doctrinal Defense of the Regime

The Dominican press, legislators, diplomats, and Trujillo's biographers have daily eulogized his work. However, a constructive defense
of the regime answering the criticism of its enemies is very rare. The best
two attempts to defend the regime on doctrinal bases are a speech by
Trujillo himself in 1950 and another by Secretary of Foreign Relations
Balaguer in 1953.

It is, of course, possible to trace the successive purposes of Trujillo
and occasionally the defense of his activities in many other speeches,
messages, and annual reports (most of them already collected in several
volumes).[4] But the speech he made on October 2, 1950, to the delegates to
the Thirteenth Pan-American Health Conference[5] has the advantage of
being an explanation of the Dominican past and a defense of his own work
during twenty years. He also answered some of the criticisms levied
against his regime. With variations, it was the same line followed by
Balaguer three years later.

In that 1950 speech, Trujillo gave a brief summary of Dominican
history, emphasizing the development of the external debt and the subsequent Dominican-United States conventions. It seems that the economic
difficulties of 1930 were for him the best justification of his conduct, even
of the February coup, about which he succeeded in confusing the degree of
his own participation ("Subversive elements were preparing the rebellion
and some of them started civil war"). In face of such an attitude, Trujillo
wanted to maintain peace at any price as "an instrument of the revolution
itself." As an organ for such a policy, the Dominican party arose:

I did not have in mind another political party, but the integration of a
Dominican social sub-structure by itself able to fulfill the vital program of

---

[4]See Rafael L. Trujillo, *El Pensamiento,* 11 volumes. [Fn. 15, Chap. X.]

[5] Rafael L. Trujillo, *The Evolution of Democracy in Santo Domingo* (Ciudad
Trujillo, 1950). Also in Spanish. [Fn. 16, Chap. X.]

general transformation which would decide the life of the country as a national entity.

He referred to the criticisms made against the existence of one single party, which he rejects:

The Dominican Party was originally established by the same members of the old factions, disbanded because of fatigue and lack of faith in their own goals. . . . I have ruled the country with men coming from all political groups existing before 1930 and with others absolutely free from any ties with such groups.

He referred to the necessity of crushing the rebellion of old leaders in 1931.

Trujillo did not explain the program of the Dominican party, but he explained in full the work of his administration and its different aspects. It is a good summary, often with precise figures and data. It dealt with the Dominican-United States treaty of 1940, the settlement of the border problem with Haiti (avoiding the 1937 incident), financial and banking legislation, labor legislation, the agricultural program, public works, education, and finally the army. He referred also to the plots against the Dominican government in 1947 and 1949, which he charged to an alliance inspired by Communists, in conjunction with the United States press. "Communism found us alone, but with plenty of courage to face its purposes and stop its influence in the Caribbean."

It is advisable to read this speech if one wants to have a picture in its entirety of the positive work of Trujillo's regime. Its omissions are remarkable, but it is skillful. The most interesting insinuation is the defense of his disciplined regime because of the need of maintaining peace as a necessary base to solve acute economic problems in a country destroyed by continuous conflicts in the past. The greatest omission is any mention about possible evolution of the regime towards an effective democracy.

More skillful and also bolder was the speech made by the secretary of foreign relations, Dr. Joaquín Balaguer, before the two legislative chambers in a joint meeting on September 17, 1953, on the occasion of the liquidation of the internal debt of the Republic.[6] Balaguer implied that the Cayo Confites and Luperón invasions were the "beginning of a wide conspiracy of Communist infiltration in the Americas that is still going on." He based all his statements on a detailed answer to the aide memoire which the United States assistant secretary of state for inter-American affairs, Spruille Braden, delivered to the Dominican ambassador in Washington on December 28, 1945, in order to justify the denial of the required export permit demanded by the Dominican Republic to purchase 20,000,000 cartridges for its army.

According to Balaguer, Braden's denial was based upon three con-

---

[6] *El Caribe,* Sept. 18, 1953. [Fn. 17, Chap. X.]

siderations: (1) that such ammunition would be used only to attack some neighboring republic or against the Dominican people themselves; (2) that it would not contribute to continental defense; and (3) that it would not serve to encourage democracy in the Dominican Republic. The Dominican answer at that time was delivered in another document, January 8, 1946, which Balaguer commented on almost eight years later.

In this comment are incidental details, such as a denial of the Dominican guilt in the Haitian massacre of 1937. But the main part is the doctrinal defense Balaguer made of Trujillo's system of government. The fundamental argument continued to be that expressed by Trujillo in 1950: "the seditious habits and the subversive spirit of the Dominicans have been eliminated permanently." However, the most interesting and skillful argument was his defense of the Dominican party, claiming it to be an only party. Balaguer said that it is the party "of the majority" and that its organization "is not exclusive of other parties"; he reinforced his thesis by referring to the case of Mexico where the Institutional Revolutionary party has been ruling for thirty years. Later he gave an interpretation of the Dominican party in much more concise terms than Trujillo himself had done.

"The Dominican Party is not dictatorial because it constitutes the first attempt made in the Dominican Republic to achieve a political program with doctrinal projections." It was constituted in 1931 by the merger of all political parties (he mentioned them one by one) which were victors in the 1930 elections as a confederation. It has not obstructed the development of "independent political ideology such as the labor movement and the feminist movement." It is composed of "representative elements of all political tendencies and rather than being a unilateral party it is really the synthesis of the national will polarized around a government program." Balaguer admitted that it is not a political party such as those existing in the United States, Chile, or Colombia, but he insisted that "it represents a great effort of organization against the personalist and subversive regime of groups without a program."

Immediately afterward, and following Trujillo's 1950 pattern, he explained the governmental work during the Era. He even maintained that the Dominican Republic had helped continental defense. He concluded by referring extensively to the "Communist conspiracy" directed against the Dominican Republic since 1945, when the Venezuelan president broke diplomatic relations, until the invasions of Cayo Confites in 1947 and Luperón in 1949. He attributed the conspiracy to the "sinister figures" of Rómulo Betancourt, Juan José Arévalo, Spruille Braden, Ramón Grau San Martín and Carlos Prío Socarrás.

Just as was true of Trujillo's speech in 1950, this speech by Balaguer in 1953 ignored many aspects of the Dominican regime, but it was the most explicit analysis of some of the criticisms formulated against the regime, especially because of his defense of the Dominican party.

Concerning the positive work accomplished by Trujillo's regime, it is also useful to read some of the doctoral dissertations presented in the Dominican school of law, although all have the defect of being conceived simply as eulogies of the regime.

Chapter 11: Criticism of the Regime and Forces of Opposition

In all the books written by opponents of Trujillo, numberless accusations are presented, almost all of which are entirely correct. But these works completely lack any contribution worthy of a leader who presents his own ideas for the future. They also are silent in regard to the positive results of the regime, especially those which Trujillo and his eulogists capitalize on the most, such as the maintenance of public order in place of the past chaos. In reference to communism, the opposition groups are divided, and while one sector does not hesitate to denounce the Communists, both in principle and because of the Dominican experience, another segment still believes in a possible united front.

In the interior of the Dominican Republic it is impossible to express openly any criticism or any plans of opposition; the only criticisms are in whispered confidences, rumors of violence, and ironic jokes. For several years now, there seem to have been no further conspiracies or even organized clandestine groups. The opposition expresses itself openly in exile, in published books, periodicals, and occasional street demonstrations. On only two occasions, has the activity of these groups abroad culminated in organized expeditions, both of which failed, that of Cayo Confites in 1947 and that of Luperón in 1949. In both expeditions, the participants included political personalities known before they went into exile, some organized groups like the Dominican Revolutionary party, and independents acting in good faith; nor were there lacking those opportunists who sooner or later went over to the dictator's side and made a career for themselves. The Communist party did not take part in these two expeditions, but followed its own line.

It would be fitting to close this study by summarizing the fundamental trends expressed in the criticisms of Trujillo's regime and by suggesting the distribution of opposition forces by groups and parties. Also it will be well to give an analysis of the two great conspiracies engineered abroad, and the possibility of evolution or collapse that the regime offers. The sources at times are documentary and public, others are confidential statements made by persons whose names cannot be given.

Criticism of the Regime

In general, the books and publications of the opposition contain only mere statements of accusation, facts of violence, and instances of the corruption of the regime. There are good studies, such as those by Jimenes-Grullón; others are full of data but presented in objectionable language that prejudices the work, such as Bustamante's; some are strong works, but concern themselves mostly with bloody facts, such as the one by Hicks and the Requena novel; some are partially useful, such as Mejía's. Still lacking in all of these is the thorough analysis of the regime as a political system, a dispassionate approach to its negative results, and the proposal of better solutions for the future. It is still possible, however, to extract from written works and especially from numberless oral discussions, a background of constructive criticism.

Let us first analyze the positive results of the regime: in the first place, its maintenance of public order. In appearance, that order seems perfect — but it is actually the order of the cemeteries. Opponents of Trujillo claim that order is not enough, if it is not accompanied by freedom. For those who repudiate the abuses of the regime but yet prefer the present system to the fear of new civil wars, the most reliable opponents of the regime point out that the Dominican Republic maintained order *with* freedom during the last Vásquez administration from 1924 to 1930, and that Trujillo himself was the one who disrupted it by the February, 1930, coup. They point out also the fact that all dictatorships inherently present the danger of greater disruptions of order because, following the death or the ousting of a personal regime that leaves nothing behind, there is no other outlet except a bloody revolution or a chaotic explosion. Perhaps the greatest failure of Trujillo has been in failing to exploit his complete control over the Dominican Republic to permit it slowly to evolve towards democratic procedures which could provide an outlet from the present regime of force, without explosions or violence. But this is the common sin of all personal dictators, who always believe they are indispensable.

In the Dominican Republic there is order but there is no freedom. There may be senseless persons whose only aim is to oust the dictator, but most Dominicans would like to have order with their freedom; and the most valuable leaders, as much among those fighting in exile as among

the few apparently collaborating with the regime, think that it is possible
to realize this in the future.

In this respect, there is another detail, delicate because it affects the
future not only of the Dominican Republic but of all Latin America. During recent years, Trujillo — and many other Latin American dictators —
does his best to present the Dominicans this argument and dilemma: my
only enemies are the Communists; I am saving the country from the Communist danger; it is either my regime or chaos controlled by Moscow. Thus,
involving anti-communism, he reinforces his dictatorship. This dilemma
and its resulting confusion is very serious. In doctrinary terms, it is untrue
and contradictory, because these regimes are at least as dictatorial as
those of Communist control, and they are coincident in many details,
although the purpose and ideological bases may be different. In practice,
it could become the best propaganda for Communists.

Because these Latin American peoples, often subjected to dictatorship, know only the one they suffer, and the distant Communist dictatorship is presented to them from two contradictory directions, if the only
choice offered to them is between a native dictatorship that already crushes
them or a try at Communist control, which is today part of the opposition
and which offers them a solution for all their needs, the temptation may
become too attractive to resist. The only efficient possible solution which
could confront communism is a positive policy which offers a solution of
social problems, with justice and freedom — that freedom missing equally
in Communist regimes and Latin American dictatorships.

In the second place, let us examine the material progress of the Era
of Trujillo. Some of his bitter opponents refuse even to acknowledge that
there has been any, but wise persons admit this progress and, in some
cases, applaud the results gained by Trujillo, as, for instance, in the 1940
treaty or in the financial reconstruction of the country. But they probe
more deeply in their analysis by pointing out the unequal distribution of
the benefits. The most severe criticism is usually aimed at the personal
peculations carried on by Trujillo, his relatives, or favorites. Another more
general criticism is in comparing the external aspect of the great buildings
for use by the government and the Dominican party with the standard
of living among the masses. These critics admit the value of the social legislation enacted during recent years, but they also point out the vast
difference between the present life of the workers and the luxury enjoyed
by the heads of the regime.

One of the most astute criticisms is based upon a comparative study
of the appropriations in the budget. Any one of the annual budgets could
be used for this purpose; let us consider the one for 1952, because it is the
latest one analyzed in official publications. The general expenditures of

the central administration that year reached the sum of $59,193,921.74. Of this total, the largest amount went for the benefit of the Secretaryship of War, Navy and Aviation with 38.5 percent; another 7.5 percent went for the Secretaryship of Interior and Police. This means that almost half of the budget was invested in forces entrusted with the maintenance of public order, or the repression of freedom. Eleven percent was divided among the different branches of the government itself (legislative chambers, courts, Secretaryship of the Presidency, Secretaryship of Foreign Relations); and 13 percent was allocated to the Secretaryship of the Treasury.

On the other hand, the departments designed to benefit the people directly received only the following percentage of allotments: 9 percent to the Secretaryship of Public Works; 7 percent to the Secretaryship of Education; 7 percent to the Secretaryship of Health; 3.5 percent to the Secretaryship of Agriculture; and 3.5 percent together to the Secretaryships of Economy-Commerce and of Labor.[1] These figures speak for themselves and reveal the emphasis placed by the Trujillo administration on the different needs of the nation. They are even more eloquent if one takes into account that there are no separate budgets for the provinces, and that municipal councils do not cover most of the basic services like education and large projects of public works.

Although the *Anuario Estadístico* is not very reliable in reference to wages, because it reports only those in the capital, where they are always highest, it is also possible to make a rough estimate of the general standard of living by carefully analyzing the official figures. According to the 1950 census, the Dominican population was 2,121,000;* that year, the official figure for the total amount of wages paid in the whole Republic was $18,938,028, and the number of employees or workers who received that sum was 48,332. This means that the average annual income for employees and workers did not come to even $400, a little more than one dollar a day.

---

[1] The budget for the current year 1955 (*G.O.* 7787), whose total amount of general expenditures estimated is $15,000,000 higher than in 1952, indicates that the percentage for the Secretaryship of War, Navy, and Aviation has been decreased to about 30 percent and those for the Secretaryships of Education and Public Works have been increased to about 10 percent.

In order to get a better evaluation of the hypertrophy of military expenditures in Trujillo's budgets, it is convenient to keep in mind that the last budget approved during the Vásquez administration, for 1930 (*G.O.* 4158), in a total amount of $6,470,210 for general expenditures, the appropriations for the Secretaryship of War equaled 16.3 percent; those for the Secretaryship of Education, 15.9 percent; and those for the Secretaryship of Public Works, 14.9 percent. [Fn. 1, Chap. XI.]

* The *Anuario Estadístico* may have been in error in this figure; the *Statistical Abstract of Latin America* credits the country with a population of 2,135,782 in 1950. If the larger population figure is accurate, it would still further reduce the statistic of average annual income.

Within this average are also included employees with high salaries, which means an even lower average for ordinary workers.

Since the total number of employed persons mentioned is about 2 percent of the whole population, it follows that the great majority of peasants whose income is very low has not even been taken into consideration, plus the obvious fact that each of those employed maintains a family, most often a large one. In order to evaluate the rise in wages during recent years, one should also bear in mind that, according to official figures, the cost of basic consumption has risen more than 250 percent in the last fifteen years.

Tourists who visit Ciudad Trujillo and live in the Jaragua Hotel do not see the misery in the poor districts or the *bohíos* of the countryside. The economic wealth of the Dominican Republic has increased ten times or more during the Era of Trujillo, but its apparent improvement has benefited only a minority and has not solved the needs of the great masses of population.

In the third place, let us turn to the cultural progress. The preponderant criticisms admit advances in the fields of education, culture, and the communications media. But these point out also, as they do in reference to public order, that those advantages are more than neutralized by the losses in freedom of expression, by the biased propaganda, and by the perversion of minds trained in sycophancy to the dictator. It means little to have more students in the university if the university does not train men as citizens, while the press and the radio can be the worst instruments of deterioration because of their large areas of influence.

It is not possible to give more extensive comments on and criticisms of the regime, because this would only mean entering into needless detail as to its methods: faked elections, forced resignations of legislators and judges, a single party, controlled labor unions, lack of political freedom, violence, domination by the army, graft and nepotism.[2]

The Opposition in the Dominican Republic

It is doubtful that opposition groups exist within the Dominican Republic. Police vigilance is too rigid. But, at the same time, it is obvious that many are waiting only for the right moment.

---

[2] Prof. Russell H. Fitzgibbon of the University of California, in 1945, 1950, and 1955 conducted a poll among several specialists in the United States, on the political and social levels of the different Latin American countries. The results of the first two polls were made public and analyzed in 1951 (R. H. Fitzgibbon, "Measurement of Latin American Political Phenomena: A Statistical Experiment," *American Political Science Review*, XLV–2, June, 1951, pp. 517–23). In the three polls, the Dominican Republic was ranked second from the last, followed only by Paraguay. [Fn. 4, Chap. XI.]

The only period during which this clandestine organization of the opposing forces was felt was in 1945; the events of 1946 confirmed their existence, but also exposed most of the leaders. More than one, however, has remained in hiding.[3]

Conversations with Dominicans of all kinds during the six years in which the author lived there, and during nine subsequent years of frequent relations with exiles and travelers, have convinced the author that most of the opposing forces are not organized under the discipline of any party, neither have they a concrete doctrinal program. Their only goal at present is to put an end to the regime. Only a small, organized Communist minority is in existence, but it does not seem to be dangerous for the time being.

The opposition adopts vague forms of general uneasiness, in addition to more concrete attitudes. This last group merits consideration. Intellectuals predominate in it, occasionally with idealistic preoccupations. Another obvious sector is the workers. A general characteristic of this Dominican opposition is that in most cases it does not hesitate apparently to collaborate with the regime, waiting for a propitious moment to act. Almost all those who gave their confidences to the author in opposition to Trujillo were members of the Dominican party, and quite a good number had high positions in the government, even cabinet-level.

Some of these persons have contacts, more or less periodically, with the exiles. Both the Cayo Confites and the Luperón invasions were backed by armed revolutionary groups within the Republic ready to join the invading forces as they landed.

Although at times the exiles speak bitterly of those in the Dominican Republic who have collaborated with Trujillo,[4] the fact that the regime has lasted twenty-five years will make it necessary that for any future change, whether by evolution or by revolution, use must be made of many of these people who apparently were collaborationists with the regime.

The Opposition in Exile

Some exiles, such as Dr. Angel Morales, have lived abroad for twenty-five years. Each year the number of those who must escape for one reason or another increases. Death is the cause of many losses. However,

---

[3] A few months ago, a Dominican professional called the author by telephone; he had been one of the lieutenants of Bonilla Atiles during the clandestine activities of 1945 and was never discovered. To a discreet question about the situation in the country, he did not hesitate to answer: *"Los que eran, siguen siendo"* (Those who were [active enemies of the regime] continue to be). [Fn. 5, Chap. XI.]

[4] This happened when former vice-president of the university, Lic. Bonilla Atiles, arrived in New York in 1946 as an exile. [Fn. 6, Chap. XI.]

discouragement does force some to return to the Dominican Republic, more or less shamefully. No one knows the exact number of exiles, but it is large. Some have decided to adapt themselves to the countries to which they went. Most of them continue to wait hopefully, while a minority remains actively against Trujillo's regime.

There are quite large groups of active exiles in New York, Cuba, Puerto Rico, Venezuela, Mexico, and some Central American countries. The political fluctuations of these countries force some of the leaders to change residence from time to time.

During the early years of the regime, the leaders who escaped concentrated in Haiti and Puerto Rico. When dictator Gerardo Machado fell in 1933, many of them went to Cuba; later, Venezuela was a center of attraction after the death of dictator Juan Vicente Gómez. In New York, there has always been quite a large number. Since 1940, Cuba has been perhaps the most active center, and in 1943 a general congress of exiles was held, attended by the most prominent leaders living in several countries.

The Cuban Grau San Martín administration from 1944 to 1948 and the Prío Socarrás administration from 1948 to 1952 allowed the exiles more freedom of action, which in 1947 was translated as unofficial complicity in the Cayo Confites invasion. Venezuela also from 1945 to 1948 was a center of attacks by radio stations during the Betancourt and Gallegos administrations. Costa Rica seems to be a propitious place since the victory of Figueres in 1948, but it has never been used for launching any attacks.

On their part, the Dominican Communists concentrated in Guatemala, especially from 1950 until the fall of the Arbenz administration in the summer of 1954. Previously, during the Arévalo administration, Guatemala had been used as the launching place for the non-Communist invasion of Luperón in 1949.

Politically, those exiles are divided into many shades. Perhaps the two groups best organized are the Communist party (Popular Socialist party) and the Dominican Revolutionary party (anti-Communist). Occasionally other groups, without any party discipline, are formed around some leader of prestige, or with unifying aspects that the Communists easily infiltrate.

The official headquarters of the Dominican Revolutionary party is in Cuba, with the publication *Quisqueya Libre* as its organ. Its directive council is formed by several persons who are rotated in periodical elections; its present head is Angel Miolán. One of its better known leaders is the writer Juan Bosch, living at present in Chile (after having been for a long while in Cuba, and then for a shorter time in Costa Rica). This party has an active section in New York, headed by Nicolás Silfa, which prints a periodical bulletin, usually mimeographed, and organizes street pickets. The PRD (Partido Revolucionario Dominicano) has more than once made public its political plans for future action. It also participated actively in the Cayo Confites invasion. It is an openly anti-Communist group, although at the same time socially advanced, and is in close relationship with inter-American democratic organizations such as the ORIT [Organización Regional Interamericana de Trabajadores] and the IADF [Inter-American Association for Democracy and Freedom.]

The Communist party seems to continue under the leadership of "Periclito" Franco, Jr. During the years it was free to act in Guatemala, it printed a monthly publication, *Orientación,* openly Communist and anti-American. Since the summer of 1954, it has not acted publicly, although it apparently is attempting to reorganize in Mexico, where Ramón Grullón has lived for years.

The groups without discipline of party but centered around a leader are several in number. The most interesting seems to be the one following more or less the leadership of Dr. Angel Morales. Morales lives in Puerto Rico, but his influence reaches New York and other places. In New York, this group had as its one visible head, Juan M. Díaz. It has adopted several positions, according to circumstance and time. About 1945 and 1946, it collaborated with the former vice-president of the university, Bonilla Atiles, in the group called ARDE which issued from time to time its own *Bulletin.* Later, some of them issued another publication, *Patria,* coedited by Díaz and Requena (until the murder of the latter in 1952). They have not offered any doctrinal program, although its most representative leaders occasionally write valuable articles. They have no sympathy for the Communists, but they have not broken with them as openly as has the PRD, and some of its individual members do not hesitate to collaborate with Communists in united fronts. Among the personalities who may be mentioned in this amorphous group, besides Angel Morales, are Dr. Leovigildo Cuello, J. I. Jimenes-Grullón, Dr. Ramón de Lara, Ing. J. C. Alfonseca, and others.

Another independent sector includes men of action, who were prominent in the invasions of Cayo Confites and Luperón. Perhaps the most dynamic was Miguel Angel Ramírez, an officer in the Cayo Confites expedition and in Figueres' forces during the Costa Rican civil war in 1948, chief of staff of the Luperón invasion, exiled later in Guatemala although he has never been a pro-Communist, and jailed for several months after the fall of Arbenz. Another is General Juan ("Juancito") Rodríguez, nominal chief of both invasions although it may be that his command was due to the fact that he had put up most of the money expended in buying arms.

Also to be mentioned is Horacio J. Ornes, chief of the plane which landed in Luperón, a prisoner for more than a year, and exiled at present in Mexico.

Finally, there are the united fronts, always using non-Communist personalities, more or less colorless, which makes it hard to determine the exact degree of their infiltration by Communists.

During recent years, this Communist problem has complicated the joint action of exiles, even beyond that of the usual personal quarrels. Some exiles believe that at this time all efforts must be concentrated against Trujillo and that it is not desirable to lose the collaboration of anyone at all. Other exiles keep in mind the actual international situation, well knowing Communist tactics. Thinking of the Dominican future, they reject any relationship with Communists or fellow-travelers.

Activities of these exiles differ according to periods, but their main task is always directed to propaganda, especially in denouncing abuses by Trujillo's regime. Whenever they have occasion, they exploit errors made by Trujillo. This was especially true after the massacre of Haitians in 1937. In the United States, they often use the tactic of street picket lines in protest, either when Trujillo spends days or weeks in New York or Washington, or if the embassy or New York consulate is having some celebration.

The active conspiracy always had its main headquarters in some place outside the United States, although in the last instance the necessary weapons and munitions were clandestinely bought in the States. The organization and failure of the two invasions attempted in 1947 and 1949 deserve a brief report.

The Invasions of Cayo Confites and Luperón

The expedition of Cayo Confites was prepared during the summer of 1947. Several reasons made this possible. On the one hand, it took place in the historic period after the end of World War II, at the height of the democratic tide which had already ousted other dictators in Latin America. On the other hand, were the events then occurring in the Dominican Republic, including the student movement of 1945, the sugar strike of January, 1946, the reaction provoked by the short-lived campaign of *La Opinión,* the later agitation in 1946, and the final conviction that the regime would not evolve into a more democratic order. Also — and this was perhaps the factor that coordinated all elements — the escape of "Juancito" Rodríguez from the Dominican Republic with part of his wealth took place in 1947.

Rodríguez was a landholder in La Vega, a "General" of the old order, and, as a legislator, an accidental collaborator with Trujillo. In

1947, he fell into disgrace and was persecuted; his estates were confiscated, but he was able to escape and take with him a good part of his funds. Thanks to these funds, he could think of organizing an expedition sufficiently strong to land in the Dominican Republic. The date scheduled for the attack was around August sixteenth, that being the day on which Trujillo for the fourth time would take his oath as president. The purpose was to impede this, as a symbol, at any cost.

From the very beginning, the conspiracy had the aid of the Cuban Grau San Martín administration and more or less benefited from a benevolent unconcern on the part of United States authorities. The point of concentration for the invaders was Cuba; Dominican revolutionaries arriving from New York and several Latin American countries gathered there, as well as citizens of other countries, including mercenaries. They were trained first on the estate belonging to the Cuban Minister of Education, José Manuel Alemán. Later they were transferred to a deserted island, Cayo Confites, for which the expedition was named. Politicians of prestige belonging to different trends did not hesitate to take part in the expedition in one way or another. Three ships for the invasion as well as weapons and munitions, and even light bombing planes, were purchased in the United States. Communists did not participate in the expedition as such and later condemned it.

In the beginning, the revolutionaries tried to keep it a strict secret, but this was impossible to maintain for long. The Cayo Confites expedition was an open secret for several weeks, of which the revolutionaries failed to take advantage, for attack. At the end, United States authorities could no longer ignore the smuggling of arms, nor could the Cuban government continue to condone the preparations. Almost at the same time as the purchase of United States weapons was prohibited, the trainees in Cayo Confites were informed that they must disband.

With all their hopes crumbled, the invaders decided to set out at any cost. The three ships sailed. Under these circumstances, the expedition was suicide. It did not even reach its objective; the Cuban fleet seized the small convoy the next day. The invaders were arrested for a few hours and later returned to their normal residence (except those implicated in the smuggling of United States arms). The Dominican courts tried them later in absentia, and sentenced them to prison, using as evidence the reports printed in the Cuban and Puerto Rican press.

There are no printed reports as to the later use of the arms. But there is enough evidence to state that they finally landed in Guatemala, and that the light weapons, at least, were used during the Costa Rican civil war of 1948, in which Ramírez, Ornes, and several other members of the Cayo Confites expedition also participated in favor of Figueres.

Apparently some of the Dominican and Nicaraguan exiles who fought in Costa Rica hoped that the victory of Figueres would be the starting point for the subsequent liberation of their countries. This hope was never realized, and the Dominicans transferred their field of operations to Guatemala, in contact with other agents in Mexico and Cuba. Thus began the preparation for the second expedition, known under the name of Luperón.

This time the secret was kept from the press, although not from Trujillo. Attack was by air, and fewer persons participated in it. Again "Juancito" Rodríguez was the chief of the invaders. The idea was to depart from Guatemala, to land simultaneously in several points in the Dominican Republic, and to join revolutionaries within the country itself. Several planes departed from Lake Izabal in Guatemala on June 19, 1949. The one under the command of Horacio Ornes Coiscou had special instructions to land in the small port of Luperón in the evening. Other planes landed in the Mexican island of Cozumel as instructed, but they failed to follow the orders sent from Mexico City and were interned there by military authorities.[5]

The landing took place without incident, but in the town there was a guard of Trujillo's army (afterwards promoted to lieutenant) who hastened to cut off the electric power. In the darkness, the two groups, into which Ornes deployed his forces, shot at each other. The invaders realized that something had failed in their plans and attempted to fly again, but in the darkness they took the wrong direction and ran aground on the beach. At the same time Trujillo's coastguard appeared and began firing. The seven remaining invaders hid together in the mountains, trying to reach the Haitian border. They were never able to get near it, and at dawn on the twenty-second were surrounded by Trujillo's troops. Ornes and four more had the good luck of being surprised first and were made prisoners, thus being spared from the coastguards' bullets.

Apparently the Dominican government needed several prisoners in order to stage a trial, during which they could accuse of complicity the governments of Guatemala (correct in this case), Cuba, and Costa Rica (this appears to be incorrect). Since 1949, there have been no further expeditions against the Dominican Republic; neither are there reports of any serious conspiracies.

The Cancer of Any Personal Dictatorship

It remains only to speculate on one aspect of the Trujillist forces themselves. All personal dictatorships carry in themselves a cancer which

---

[5] The author has spoken with, among others, Horacio Ornes, commander of the plane which attacked Luperón. [Fn. 14, Chap. XI.]

destroys them as the years go by — the ambitions of possible successors. In a democratic regime, the death of a head of state (even that of Roosevelt in 1945) does not impede the normal transition to a new period. But after a dictator, nothing is left of any organized method of development, because the dictator, during his lifetime, took pains to arrest that development. But all of them are mortal after all.

Until now, Trujillo has been able to exert complete control over his collaborators, who are named or dismissed without any of them daring to rebel. But no matter what the future may hold, Trujillo's Era is inevitably approaching its end. Trujillo is sixty-two years of age, and it is obvious that he is thinking of assuring a dynastic succession through his son "Ramfis";[6] it is a natural dream in any father, and in Latin America there was a precedent in the Paraguayan dictator Carlos A. López* in the nineteenth century. But this is also difficult, even in the Dominican Republic of Trujillo. Moreover, the hypertrophy of the regime itself will make it more difficult, if at a given moment all ambitions break out. There are today too many generals and even more than one rear admiral; it is not impossible to imagine conspiracies to oust Trujillo alive, but it is even more probable that many ambitious individuals are already dreaming of future succession.

We cannot speculate as to the end of Trujillo; that rests only with God. But even at this point, it is possible to estimate the probable consequences of a regime based upon the personal will of one man, in which the powers of the state and the socio-political institutions are mere façades without a life of their own. Normally, the end of the present dictatorship should mean a time of chaos, in which the present apparatus cannot be maintained because it is spurious. It may resolve in a personal fight, in which a strong man will attempt to exploit the system for his own benefit. But sooner or later in the Dominican Republic there will arise the possibility of democratic reorganization.

The greatest danger in the Dominican Republic is that nothing has been left standing. There are no political parties, no leaders with authority, and no doctrines. Everything must begin again from the very beginning, and it is probable that it will be begun by new men without political training. The experience of Guatemala during the last ten years offers a lesson that no Latin American people may ignore. The fall of dictator Ubico left behind a vacuum that men of good will with ideas of democracy and justice attempted to fill. They started from the same void in which the

---

[6] See, for instance, *Time,* Nov. 29, 1954. [Fn. 21, Chap. XI.]
* Who was succeeded by his son, Francisco Solano López.

Communists weave their net; the difference is that the Communists know what they want and they seek it with discipline.

Trujillo still has time to rectify his direction in part by permitting a democratic development in which the political parties and leaders of tomorrow would be trained. However, a knowledge of his character induces one to think that this evolution will never enter into his mind, and he will persist in envisioning a dynasty initiated by himself. This danger is perhaps the gravest charge that history will record in its final judgment about the Benefactor.

Conclusions

The author considers that the data presented and analyzed in this study permit him to state the following general conclusions, which will be subsequently developed:

1. The political regime existing in the Dominican Republic is a dictatorship, or rather tyranny, of a personal order.

2. Its special characteristic — in common with almost all Latin American dictatorial regimes — is the use of apparent constitutional democratic forms that are actually perverted to its ends (elections, Congress, courts, constitutional reforms).

3. In common with other classic dictatorial regimes, it suppresses political freedoms and uses the army as its main support.

4. In some respects, it has adopted the modern methods of totalitarian regimes, such as the single party, controlled labor unions, and the techniques of propaganda. But it lacks an ideological basis and program.

5. It attempts to adapt itself to the international trends of the western world, although it does not feel them. At the same time, it is directly pressed into, and exerts pressure upon, the convulsive politics of the Caribbean.

6. During recent years it uses "anti-communism" as a justification, but it did not hesitate in the past to play with the Communists — just as have other Latin American governments.

7. On the human side, this picture is completed by Trujillo's megalomania, nepotism, and the sycophancy and servility of his rotating favorites.

8. Like any regime of force, it has maintained order and has achieved a certain progress, mostly of a material nature.

9. This progress is offset by civic degradation.

10. The future of the country may well be chaotic, because there are

neither socio-political forces nor democratic instruments to facilitate a normal succession the day the tyrant disappears.

Explanation of These Conclusions:

Some of these conclusions are obvious in themselves once the facts presented in the different chapters of this study are known, but some of them require further explanation in order to make more precise the ideas involved.

1. The Political Regime Existing in the Dominican Republic Is a Dictatorship, or Rather Tyranny, of a Personal Order

The characteristics typical of a regime of force imposed against the will of the citizens have been obvious since the 1930 electoral campaign. During the first months of the Trujillo administration, it was still possible to find him supported by a coalition of old parties and politicians, but by 1931 a new regime was established, founded upon the Dominican party as the tool. By then, the most important leaders of the February coup had been eliminated and the characteristics of a dictatorial regime were clear. Step by step, the peculiar features of this regime were accentuated, as, one by one, the successive collaborators of Trujillo in the government and the party were replaced.

The facts presented in this study demonstrate that since the first Trujillo administration none of the institutions and freedoms which characterize a democratic regime has existed in the Dominican Republic. On the contrary, the will of one single individual, at first as president and later as chief, has been the only decisive voice in national affairs. This de facto situation has been maintained up to the present.

Is this regime a true dictatorship? It depends on the exact meaning given to this word. If by dictatorship we understand a political regime of force, in which the citizens have no power to express their will and the ruler alone makes decisions, then there is a dictatorship in the Dominican Republic. But history has seen several kinds of regimes fulfilling these broad characteristics. Such were the absolute monarchies of the past, such have been the modern totalitarian states, but all these systems of government had a formal structure deliberately organized in order to justify the omnipotent will of the ruler on the basis of a doctrine. What exists in the Dominican Republic — and in many other Latin American countries — is different; the formal structure of the government pretends to have democratic organs. It is not a dictatorship according to its own rule but rather in violation of the apparent law.

A real dictatorship implies a certain legality. Such a type of regime has existed in Latin America; its best example was that of Dr. José Gaspar

Rodríguez de Francia in Paraguay from 1814 to 1840. Francia looked to the ancient period for inspiration. That ancient age had known both the formal regime of dictatorship and the lawless regime of tyranny.

For this reason, it seems proper to define the political regime of the Dominican Republic — and of other Latin American countries — as a tyranny rather than a dictatorship, because the will of the ruler purposely violates the formal structure of the apparent constitution.

Whether we define it by the more appropriate term of tyranny or the broader one of dictatorship,[1] it is a completely personal rule. Hitler and Stalin had a group of trusted collaborators, although occasionally they were purged, and they were supported by a disciplined party faithful to a doctrinaire program. In the Dominican Republic, the collaborators last only for a short time, and very few have failed to end their offices in political disgrace, although they may return to favor later. The Dominican party has no program which could justify the regime, nor does it even reflect the existence of an elite of fanatics. It is merely a tool handled individually by Trujillo. Neither is his political strength based upon the fact that he is head of the state; he continues to be "boss" even when he selects somebody else to fill his position.

The political regime of the Dominican Republic is based upon the will of one single individual, and such is in obvious violation of the formal Constitution of the country.

2. Its Special Characteristic — In Common with Almost All Latin American Dictatorial Regimes — Is the Use of Apparent Constitutional Democratic Forms That Are Actually Perverted to Its Ends (Elections, Congress, Courts, and Constitutional Reforms)

Like any regime of force, it has some characteristics common to other known systems of government of the past and the present, which might provide all of them an apparent similarity. But it has the special characteristic which precisely identifies the type of political regime developed in Latin America, and which justifies the study of Trujillo's Dominican Republic in this study, as the present prototype of Latin American dictatorships.

This special characteristic is that it externally adopts the constitutional democratic guises of the western world, but in its internal functioning proceeds to pervert them all.

There are periodic elections, but the results are fraudulent. A con-

---

[1] The term dictatorship has been advisedly used in this study, because it is the one commonly referred to. Only in the conclusions is a distinction made in order to clarify the ideas expressed. [Fn. 2, Conclusions.]

gress is elected and functions, but congressmen are removed at will and laws are passed without discussion. Judges are appointed, but no one is secure in his position. Even the Constitution itself is changed at convenience, each time that it seems expedient thus to disguise some new institutional whim of the tyrant.

This perversion of the apparent constitutional set-up was developed step by step during the Era of Trujillo. It may be said that during his first administration only the lower chamber was affected, but elections have been fraudulent since 1934. During his second administration, the Senate suffered the same perversion as the Chamber had before; since the Peynado administration, it infected the Supreme Court of Justice; and in 1942, it involved the presidency itself. The Constitution has been changed three times. These distinct milestones suffice to prove this point, because they involve the very expression of the popular will and the chief elected instruments of the nation.

The key to an understanding of the whole regime is in the Constitution itself. Everything is carried on in accordance with its articles, but the Constitution itself is nothing but a curtain. The replacement of congressmen is made according to Article 16 of the Constitution, and, according to other articles, judges and even the president are replaced, if convenient. However, not even the constitutional semblance is stable. The Constitution has been modified three times during the Era, and on the latest occasion it was merely to alter one article which obstructed a new decision by the government.

Everything in the Dominican Republic is carried out according to the Constitution, a constitution of Western democratic structure, which takes its inspiration from the government of the United States. But the Constitution itself contains convenient provisions to facilitate the perversion of all its basic institutions. Neither do the people elect their officers, nor are the elected officers truly holders of their offices; everything is fiction.

Tyranny thus garbs itself with a democratic constitution in order to violate it the more conveniently.

3. In Common with Other Classic Dictatorial Regimes, It Suppresses Political Freedoms and Uses the Army as Its Main Support

This conclusion, obvious in itself, needs no further development. It is a characteristic common to all Latin American dictatorships, regardless of their varying shades.

In the particular case of Trujillo, it can be pointed out that he rose to power in 1930 as the then chief of the army, and since then he has taken special care of this institution. Almost half of the Dominican budget is appropriated to army needs, although the Dominican army has not participated in any international war for a century. Trujillo always retains the supreme command in his person, even if he may temporarily not be the president of the Republic.

As a parallel, the curtailment of political freedoms had already become obvious with the 1930 electoral campaign. One fact merits attention in Trujillo's regime, namely that the suppression of political freedoms, although occasionally manifesting some bloody details, is generally more subtle because it acts through moral humiliation leaving no incriminating traces.

4. In Some Respects, It Has Adopted the Modern Methods of Totalitarian Regimes, Such as the Single Party, Controlled Labor Unions, and the Techniques of Propaganda, But It Lacks an Ideological Basis and Program

It is not possible to state, in any way, that Trujillo's regime is totalitarian. This is also true of other Latin American dictatorial regimes, with the exception of that of Vargas from 1937 to 1945 and, in part, that of Perón. It lacks a doctrinaire basis, either of the various fascist shades, or, even more, of the communist.

Deliberately or by instinct, however, it has adopted certain methods typical of totalitarian regimes. Some of them are evident, such as the existence of one single party, notwithstanding the occasional simulation of "opposition" parties; the labor movement encouraged by the government in appearance but actually controlled by it; and the techniques of propaganda and indoctrination from the primary schools up through the university. Even the title of *Jefe* (Chief) given to Trujillo has the same odor as *Führer, Duce,* or *Caudillo*. The same may be said of the street demonstrations, the omnipresent pictures everywhere, and, on any pretext, the literature used by press and radio.

5. It Attempts to Adapt Itself to the International Trends of the Western World, Although It Does Not Feel Them; At the Same Time It Is Directly Pressed Into, and Exerts Pressure Upon, the Convulsive Politics of the Caribbean

This conclusion is not so much a characteristic of the regime as such, but the circumstantial motions of self-defense. The Dominican Republic is geographically located only a short distance from the United States and in the center of the Caribbean Sea. This situation, in different ways, conditions many of its political events.

It is not possible to say, as some opponents do, especially the Communists, that Trujillo is a political product of the United States and, even less, that he owes the United States his continuance in power. But it is undeniable that the entire Era has been oriented toward Washington. The negotiations to settle the 1930 coup were carried on in the United States legation in Santo Domingo; Roosevelt's pressure forced the settlement of the Dominican-Haitian conflict in 1937 and its repercussions made impossible the reelection of Trujillo the next year; during World War II the Dominican government did its best to guess the wishes of Washington in order to be a step ahead; in 1945 and 1946 the Dominican government played with communism, as a reflection of the occasional United States alliance with the USSR and the victory over fascism; in 1947 it exploited the "cold war" to its benefit at once; the Dominican delegation acts almost as a United States satellite in the United Nations. Occasionally, some of these international attitudes seem to be contradictory, because they do not follow any individual pattern, but they always disclose the desire to appear as the unconditional ally of the United States.

At the same time and with very different consequences, the Dominican Republic cannot avoid the cross currents of political forces that agitate the Caribbean area in a violent fluctuation of dictatorships, revolutions, and conspiracies. Trujillo has proven himself able to dominate the internal political stage, but the very impossiblity of evolution and change within the Dominican Republic prompts the action of exiles living in neighboring countries. The small geographical area of these countries facilitates the weaving of the complicated net involving alike dictators and revolutionaries in the whole area.

6. During Recent Years It Uses "Anti-Communism" as a Justification, But It Did Not Hesitate in the Past to Play With the Communists — Just as Have Other Latin American Governments

There is no need to dwell extensively on this conclusion which is rather a corollary of the previous one. The difference arises from the fact that this attitude is also obvious in other Latin American countries, which may not have even the same geographical location nor yet dictatorial governments during the period in question.

It is a circumstantial effect of the world situation, as, for instance, when Communists took the initiative by their confusing change of tactics. For political reasons, the Communist line, which had already changed more than once, after 1941, and especially in 1945 and 1946, followed the deliberate aim of collaborating with any types of governments in order to infiltrate them, especially if they were weak or decadent regimes. This was obvious everywhere in Latin America and culminated in the labor activities of the CTAL. In analyzing the game of Trujillo with the Communists in 1946, the strategic deviations of both sides must be equally considered.

On the other hand, the increasing hostility between the United States and the USSR since 1947 has facilitated the "anti-Communist" reaction in Latin America, which, while sincere and democratic in some countries, has, in almost all the dictatorships, been useful only as a cover to justify the suppression of freedom through the subterfuge of calling anyone "Communist" who dared to criticize the incumbent regime.

The game between Trujillo and the Communists never reached the point of actual collaboration, but very few have exceeded Trujillo in the use of the club of "anti-communism" for his spurious purposes.

7. On the Human Side, This Picture Is Completed by Trujillo's Megalomania, Nepotism, and the Sycophancy and Servility of His Rotating Favorites

This conclusion, obvious to anyone who is in the Dominican Republic for only a few days, is only an anecdotic aspect without importance for the qualification of the regime. It is sufficient to mention it.

8. Like Any Regime of Force, It Has Maintained Order and Has Achieved Certain Progress, Mostly of a Material Nature

The regime has remained in power now for twenty-five years. At this point in balancing its results, it is possible to cite to its credit, the maintenance of public order, without the rebellions and even civil wars that in the past were so prevalent; a certain cultural progress; and a material progress, reflected in various public works, in the figures of the government budget, in the liberation of the country from external debts which culminated in the Dominican-United States treaty of 1940, and in general in the improvement of the national economy.

These results appear almost invariably in all regimes of force which are able to retain power for long. But Trujillo deserves recognition especially for the economic stability of his regime up to now, and to a certain degree, for the achievement of greater material progress than that reached by any other Latin American dictator of similar type (in Nicaragua, Honduras, and Paraguay, for example).

9. This Progress is Offset by Civic Degradation

The credits of the regime are overbalanced by the debits. The material and economic progress has not benefited alike the whole population, and the tyrant himself has appropriated the lion's share. It must especially be pointed out, in the column of debits, that the ironclad order is reached through a complete subjection of the individual and that the regime as a whole has brought the deterioration of all civic spirit. This final result is not justified even by an ideology which places the state, the society, or the head of the state above the citizens. It is de facto oppression, without any doctrinal justification.

10. The Future of the Country May Well Be Chaotic, Because There Are Neither Socio-Political Forces Nor Democratic Instruments to Facilitate a Normal Succession the Day the Tyrant Disappears

As in any other personal tyranny, the regime bears in itself the tragedy of its ultimate end. There is no normal outlet for future succession. Regardless of how Trujillo's Era may end, it will leave behind neither instruments of government, political parties, nor other socio-political groups, not even men trained to make their own decisions or able to face new problems. The very hypertrophy of the army could be the cancer putrifying the regime and provoking the struggle for succession.

On the other hand, the Communists could exploit this future confusion to their advantage, by starting from a new zero point at the level of democratic groups without a previous organization or administrative training (the case of Guatemala furnishes a good warning). In the meantime, during the present world struggle, through their propaganda they can capitalize on the apparent alliance between Trujillo and the United States and on the confusion of the arbitrary alternative: either Trujillo or communism.

Editor's Epilogue:
Toward Götterdämmerung

I have a rendezvous with Death
At some disputed barricade,
When Spring comes back with rustling shade
And apple-blossoms fill the air —
I have a rendezvous with Death. . . .

I've a rendezvous with Death . . .
When Spring trips north again this year,
And I to my pledged word am true,
I shall not fail that rendezvous.

— Alan Seeger, 1916*

The Year of the Benefactor marked a pinnacle of power such as few
if any rulers in Latin America could at any time have matched. Trujillo
could echo the Sun King in saying, or at least thinking, *l'état, c'est moi.*
Indeed, he could do it with even more justification than the mistakenly
credited author of the phrase. No serious threat faced him, internally or
externally. The quarter century had seen its crises but one by one they
had been surmounted, and the silver anniversary of the regime found
Trujillo the lord of all he surveyed. One cannot know whether Trujillo had
ever read *The Prince* but surely he had learned its lessons even better than
its author. Machiavelli could have wanted no better pupil than Rafael
Trujillo.

---

* Alan Seeger, "I Have a Rendezvous with Death," *Poems* (New York: Charles
Scribner's Sons, 1916), p. 144. Reprinted by permission of the publisher.

No faint cloud of effective opposition marred Trujillo's skies at home. Potential political opponents were all humbled; ebullient and greedy family members were under control. True, his Argus-eyed intelligence informed him that there was a man up at Columbia University in New York who might try to make trouble — some ingrate who had once enjoyed posts in the Dominican government — but he could easily be taken care of when necessary. As the Year of the Benefactor began, his fellows in the confraternity of dictators occupied the seats of power in many Latin American capitals; Perón was in his twelfth year of once glamorous control in Argentina; in nearer Colombia and Venezuela Rojas Pinilla and Pérez Jiménez continued their tyrannies; in his own Caribbean, Cuba's Batista and Haiti's Magloire definitely belonged to the clan; four Central American presidents (three of them of the military) could be called dictators; and there were Odría in Peru and Stroessner in Paraguay. It seemed as if the hemisphere had been made safe for dictatorship.

Or had it? If Trujillo had read political history — and there is no evidence that that was any less a blank in his reading than was political theory — he might have pondered on the situation in Mexico just forty-five years earlier. The year 1910 was to mark the centennial of Mexican independence and the eightieth birthday of the country's ruler, Porfirio Díaz, whose durability as a dictator would be unmatched even by Trujillo. The year 1910 dawned with every indication that the political credit of the porfirista regime was high and solid — but it would end with Mexico in basic and bloody revolution and Díaz on the way out. Transition for Trujillo would be neither so sudden nor so dramatic — at least not immediately — but the twilight of the god was approaching.

Trujillo undoubtedly thought about transmission of his fief. His preference certainly would have been to bequeath it to Ramfis, for at the end of 1955 the Constitution was amended to make the minimum age for the presidency twenty-five years. Ramfis was then twenty-six. But both by temperament and training, as Crassweller well analyzes, Ramfis was poorly fitted for the succession. The sons of Somoza were better prepared to strut on a tawdry, if tiny, imperial stage.

The International Fair held in the Dominican Republic in 1955–56 was superficially glittering and dramatic but financially a fiasco. Its cost was more than $30,000,000 and the return to the country in tourism and investment was only a small fraction of that amount. As with Kubitschek's construction of the new capital, Brasília, in the vast South American hinterland, the action was a propagandistic success but well-nigh a fiscal disaster.

If the unsuccessful fair helped grease economic skids for the Dominican regime, there were other lubricants as well to facilitate a downward path. Moral deterioration became increasingly evident. Enemies of the dictator had been liquidated before, but the kidnapping and murder of Galíndez in 1956 both failed to achieve its immediate end — prevention of the publication of his study — and also opened a Pandora's box of troubles for Trujillo. It was estimated that the direct cost of the Galíndez case to Trujillo, especially after it became linked with and complicated by the presumed murder of Gerald Murphy, was half a million dollars, most of which went for the retention of a top public relations firm and prestigious and expensive legal and investigative talent. Indirect costs, extravagant but largely futile efforts to refurbish the Trujillist "image" abroad, were estimated to have amounted in the late 1950's to as much as six million dollars.

Symbolic of the dictator's descending path was the emergence of "Johnny" Abbes García as Trujillo's principal adviser. Abbes was a sinister and evil figure, the regime's Iago in a sense, whose baleful hold over the dictator was opposed and resented, but to no effect, even by Ramfis. His moral shortcomings, or deformities, might under more normal circumstances have alerted even Trujillo who, after all, was usually nobody's fool, but the dictator was, as time passed, becoming desperate from the impending pressures that seemed to be closing in on him. Abbes, with his dark talents, seemed to fit the needs of the times. In all probability he had a heavy hand in the abortive attempts made against Presidents Figueres and Betancourt, possibly even in the assassination of President Castillo Armas of Guatemala. His genius was for intelligence work, and surveillance and subversion reached farther and with more sophistication than ever before.

The aphorism that politics makes strange bedfellows was never better illustrated than by the relations between the Dominican Republic and Cuba in the late 1950's. Even though Batista and Trujillo were fellow dictators, both of them pragmatic and opportunistic, each felt the pulls of power politics in different directions. Both faced deteriorating internal situations. Logically, they should have made common cause, but Batista's feeling that he must improve his stance vis-à-vis the United States caused him to be chary of approaches from Trujillo, and the antagonized Dominican then resolved his earlier deep differences with the exiled Carlos Prío Socarrás of Cuba and aided him in his pathetic efforts to topple Batista.

But the greater threat to Batista was from the derring-do of an adventurer in the mountains of eastern Cuba, a man who for a few years was to capture the imagination of Latin Americans as no other man in history had done. The rise of Fidel Castro was, by extension, as much of a menace for Trujillo as for Batista. Granted that the overthrow of the "sergeant named Batista" was the first objective for the charismatic *barbudo,* he even then was tuning the tocsin of revolution against Latin American dictatorship. And what could be a better goal, once Cuba were reduced, than the near-by Dominican Republic? Hence, in a typically opportunistic about-face, Trujillo began throwing his support to Batista against the Bearded One. It availed Batista nothing, and at the beginning of 1959 he followed in the footsteps of Perón and Pérez Jiménez by making the Dominican Republic a first port of call for unemployed dictators.

There is evidence that Trujillo was profoundly surprised and disturbed by the sudden collapse of Batista's regime. What was happening to the "strong men" of the hemisphere? — Remón, Somoza, and Castillo Armas assassinated; Perón, Rojas Pinilla, Pérez Jiménez, and now Batista forced out by uprisings. It seemed, as Tad Szulc aptly labeled it, truly the twilight of the tyrants. Was even the monolith the Benefactor had built up in the Dominican Republic not impregnable? It gave one to think.

Castro's action in 1959 was marked by even less caution than later, and the heady euphoria induced by the dramatic conquest of Cuba soon pointed his adventurism toward the Dominican Republic; he would add the political scalp of Trujillo to that of Batista hanging at his belt. What followed would have been a comedy of errors were it not for all of the lives lost in the successive scenes of the farce-drama. Castro mounted an invasion of the Dominican Republic, by air and sea, in June, 1959, which surely was one of the most poorly kept secrets in all the long annals of warfare. The three landings attempted were promptly crushed and all of the several hundred invaders killed. Cayo Confites and Luperón thus had a third failure added to them. Trujillo had hurriedly collected fifty million dollars by forced taxation as an emergency defense fund for arms (the large part of it went into officials' pockets), but it was unnecessary — the expeditions were almost foreordained to failure. Now it was Trujillo's turn to carry on the tragicomedy.

Cuba severed diplomatic relations with Trujillo's government in mid-summer as the Dominican regime readied its own invasion forces. A seamy United States soldier of fortune, one "Major" William Morgan, was in the middle of the intricate dealings, quite willing to double-cross, or even triple-cross, any of the other parties if his own ends (and pockets) would thereby be served. A Dominican plane landed at night in southern Cuba, unloaded its clandestine munitions, and returned safely to the Dominican Republic. The bait was swallowed. Another planeload of munitions was dispatched. It landed and was unloading. Then the denouement. Some thousands of Castro's men, waiting in encirclement around the small airfield, came out of hiding led by none other than Fidel in person, who had been entertaining himself by listening to the radio conversations between the descending plane and the ground decoys. Of course Castro had a field day in parading and humiliating the captured invaders. Morgan was temporarily lionized; in March, 1961, he was executed.

Politico-diplomatic sparring followed within the precincts of the Organization of American States. The feuding was moved to a higher level in August, 1959, when, at the proposal of Venezuela and Cuba and with the support of the United States, a Fifth Foreign Ministers' meeting was held for five days in Santiago, Chile, to consider the entire surcharged Caribbean situation. Verbal vitriol flowed freely during the meeting, which concluded by resolving against intervention, roughly akin to holding that the New World nations were against sin. Most of the nitty-gritty of Caribbean involvement was swept under the rug, which is to say that other agencies were entrusted with investigation of continuing elements of friction. In the hectic midyear confrontations in 1959 between the Dominican Republic on the one hand and Cuba and Venezuela on the other, the former came out very definitely on the losing side. Castro was still highly popular, Betancourt had emerged as a staunch and heroic figure, and Trujillo's Machiavellianism was becoming ever more apparent.

Prompt Trujillist crushing of the 1959 invasions could not hide the fact that they had aroused some sympathy and even support within the Dominican Republic. Again, Trujillo failed to read the lessons of history. In Cuba, just one and two years before, Batista's panicky striking out at urban middle-class elements that he assumed, often without foundation, were giving aid and comfort to Castro, resulted in crystallizing such sentiment and delivering it into the camp of his enemies. So in the Dominican Republic, Trujillo lashed out indiscriminately and insensately, arresting hundreds and evidencing his own brand of panic. The latent national malaise deepened and fed on itself. There was not yet an impending sense of nationwide explosion, simply a growing bewilderment and frustration. The progressive deterioration of Ramfis and the growing obsession of Trujillo with laudatory actions and reactions stage-managed from the public did nothing to help the situation.

Coupled with the disintegrating political situation was a continued economic decline. Trade and tourism were off; expenditures for arms and a vastly expanded intelligence service went up astronomically; even the weather seemed to conspire in part against Dominican agriculture. Much of the year 1960 was marked by hollow attempts to whip up demonstrations of adulation, by artificial gestures seemingly pointed at a more democratic political structure, and by efforts to shore up an increasingly shaky international position. The climax of the campaign to sell the illusion of a democratic trend to the country and the hemisphere was the resignation of Héctor Trujillo on August 4 from the presidency, ostensibly for reasons of health. He was succeeded by Vice-President Joaquín Balaguer, thus unwittingly cast in a most fateful role indeed. Pathetic attempts to establish "opposition" parties, which the vast majority of Dominicans correctly assumed to be façades and mirages, were also undertaken.

Not the least of the omens of 1960 was provided by the degeneration of relations between government and church. In still another way, Trujillo misread, or failed to read, what recent history might have taught him. In Argentina a few years earlier, the decline of the Peronista regime was both cause and effect of the breakdown of the former cordial entente between governmental and ecclesiastical authorities. Somewhat the same abrasive course of church-state relations had been followed in Venezuela and Colombia as a prelude to the collapse of the Pérez Jiménez and Rojas Pinilla regimes, respectively.

In the Dominican Republic, the dramatic unveiling of the difficulties began at the end of January, 1960, with the reading in all of the country's Catholic churches of a pastoral letter expressing the hierarchy's distress at the excesses of oppression the government had used in countering the invasions of 1959. The fat was now in the fire, or in more dignified terms, the issue was joined. The bad situation became worse. A second pastoral letter early in March established an even firmer position for the church. The hierarchy was buttressed in a way by the fact that a number of its members were foreigners, had no family ties in the Dominican Republic, and were not subject to the various pressures, subtle or unsubtle, that Trujillo could bring to bear on domestic clergy.

The government resorted to small and large harassments, but the stick and the carrot were both employed (the Spanish have an equivalent phrase, *pan o palo*) — the Generalissimo at least once tried a crude attempt at bribery. The hierarchy at one stage was pushed reluctantly into a species of compromise of the growing feud but it was a temporary stance and the friction was soon resumed. Trujillo's vanity, pathological by now, was piqued by refusal of the hierarchy to agree to bestow the title, Benefactor of the Church, on the man already loaded down with so much fulsome adulation but ever coveting more. The government began following a peronista path more faithfully: petty badgering of the church in general, individual priests in particular. Further and dramatic showdowns might have crystallized had not the fatal day arrived before they could take shape.

It was most unfortunate for Trujillo that his relations with the church developed so abrasively. The church structure in the Dominican Republic was no great monolith of strength but, as in many parts of Latin America, the humble were devoted to it, and an attack on it implied an assault on a constituency that otherwise might have provided rather reliable support for the regime. It was self-induced undercutting by Trujillo at a point where he could least afford that sort of erosion.

A sharply more dramatic development in 1960 was the culmination of worsening relations wth Venezuela, reaching a nadir in the attempted assassination of President Betancourt in June. Trujillo had never forgiven Rómulo Betancourt for his association with Cuba in pressing diplomatic action against the Dominican Republic in 1959, with a climax in the Santiago foreign ministers' meeting. In February, 1960, Venezuela again hailed the Dominican Republic before the bar of the Organization of American States to answer charges of gross violations of human rights in the island imperium. The resulting OAS resolution was highly critical and the subsequent investigations by its peace committee — which, ironically, had been reactivated some years before on the initiative of the Dominican Republic itself, after a long period of somnolence — added substance to the charges.

Trujillo's repeated frustrations, and the apparent invulnerability of Betancourt to diplomatic or political aggression, led the Generalissimo to undertake one of the most bizarre attacks ever attempted in the tortured politics of the Caribbean. The sinister Abbes masterminded the plot but the stimulus for it came from Trujillo himself. An exiled Venezuelan navy officer and others were enlisted in the venture. After elaborate preparations, a car containing a large explosive charge was parked on a Caracas street along which President Betancourt's automobile would be driven in a parade celebrating Army Day on June 24. The explosive could be detonated by an electronic device operated from a distance of several hundred yards.

Everything went as planned — except that the tremendous blast, exactly at the scheduled second, killed only an accompanying officer in the President's car (and a bystander) and merely wounded Betancourt himself. Trujillo's luck had soured again. And his tracks in Venezuela had been poorly covered. The plot was quickly revealed and in a matter of days Betancourt was charging Trujillist complicity and Venezuela was demanding a top-level OAS investigation. The upshot, after sensational preliminaries, was a new, two-phase, foreign ministers' meeting in Costa Rica to consider the dual problems of the Dominican Republic and Cuba. In the first, or Dominican, phase the Venezuelan position prevailed; even the sop of Brother Héctor's resignation as president two weeks earlier could not soften Venezuelan determination. The result was a unanimous resolution of condemnation and a decision for a collective severance of diplomatic relations with the Dominican Republic. These severances followed in due course and brought about the complete diplomatic isolation of Trujillo's fief; economic quarantine, he feared, would soon follow.

The spiraling descent of Dominican fortunes did not disturb the surface calm. Trujillo had increasingly exhibited erratic reactions under stress but normally he maintained his icy detachment and aplomb. He allegedly had a growing preoccupation with death and on one occasion, in his last month of life, reportedly told two old companions, "I will leave you soon." The downward path of the regime did revive and stimulate plotting — perhaps those possible premonitions of departure could be hastened to fruition. The final plot matured in the late months of 1960 and early 1961. It was involved and in some respects amateurish. Political decline had not been accompanied by any loss of Trujillo's sexual ability or interest; after all, he was a man who had for years been almost the personification of *machismo* in its literal sense. The conspirators took advantage of this appetite.

On the night of May 30, 1961, Trujillo was scheduled for an assignation with his current mistress at an *estancia* some miles outside the city. He drove there, well armed as usual, but accompanied only by his chauffeur. At the planned point, a carload of conspirators passed him, opened up with machine gun fire, circled and came back. Another carload of conspirators closed in. The chauffeur wanted to turn and head back for the city but Trujillo, wounded though he was, insisted that they must stand and fight. And fight they did. But one bullet is as good as another, and too many of them found their mark in the dictator's body.

Trujillo had not failed his rendezvous.

RUSSELL H. FITZGIBBON

Author's Bibliography

[*The Bibliography reproduces, as faithfully as possible, the "Sources Used for this Thesis" (the Table of Contents included in the manuscript substitutes "Study" for "Thesis") presented in the manuscript as Part III of the Introduction (that portion is omitted in the foreign-language editions published in Santiago, Buenos Aires, and Paris). Editorial changes or additions are enclosed in brackets.*]

It is not yet possible to have access to the archives which in the future will document a study of the Era of Trujillo and its internal working. The official Dominican archives, of course, are closed, save when those who praise the regime are permitted a partial glimpse. The official archives of the United States will be opened for researchers only beginning in 1956, since normally a lapse of twenty-five years is required after events, except in cases accorded special permission. Similar restrictions exist in other countries. At the same time, the materials available in private archives are very sparse, especially as censorship on the Dominican border is extremely strict. Nor do there exist any personal memoirs by the protagonists themselves (except for occasional narratives of a few concrete minor episodes).

Some original documents are available for use. The United States Department of State already has printed some of the documents in its archives both those from its own officers and, occasionally, from Trujillo himself. They appear in the annual series *Foreign Relations of the United States,* of which the latest volume published concerning the Americas is that for 1937. The Organization of American States has also printed some important documents, as have the Dominican government and others, when it is to their benefit; also the United Nations. Occasionally the author has also been able to use documents which either he himself saw during his stay in the Dominican Republic, or which were lent to him by others (even officers of Trujillo's own government).

Aside from these exceptional cases, one must utilize other more public sources for the research, documents intended from the very beginning for public knowledge. Most of these are official or unofficial materials of the Trujillo government itself; only when these are lacking, has it been necessary

in this study to use other sources, some unbiased, others partisan. Some of
these must be considered as direct sources since they are authentic contemporary expositions of the facts referred to. Almost all of these are official publications of the Dominican government or its chief departments, speeches and
messages by Trujillo himself or the highest officers of the Republic, or articles
and news from the Dominican press, which usually is an unofficial mouthpiece
for the regime. Some are official documents issued by the United States Department of State, the Organization of American States, or other governmental or
international organizations. In addition, although exceptionally, a few documents used are those made public by exiles, if they serve to express their own
point of view. Other indirect sources, such as books which favor or oppose
Trujillo, impartial or general books, and non-Dominican publications, have
been used to complete details or to fill lacunae in the direct information.

One may add that other information, perhaps less reliable but at the
same time more impressive, was used, obtained in many conversations that the
author had with Dominicans and many foreigners during more than fifteen
years. At times they had the spontaneity of immediate reaction after an event,
given in sincere confidence; at other times, one could not fully trust them,
either because the recollection was dim after many years or because wishful
thinking had lent a bias to facts and motives.

In every chapter, section, page, and paragraph of this study, the source
from which the data were obtained is mentioned, except in cases which are
sufficiently obvious as to require no mention.[1] However, it is best in this bibliography to make a general mention of the various documentary sources used in
this study. It is by no means a complete list of such sources, and even less, a
bibliography of the era and regime of Trujillo. It is rather a list of the sources
used by the author in his study, most of them available for any other student,
chiefly in the public libraries of the United States.

In many well-known bibliographical volumes, may be found complete
lists of books, pamphlets, articles, and other publications dealing with the
Dominican Republic. Among the most important, for instance, may be mentioned the successive volumes of the *Handbook of Latin American Studies*
published annually since 1935, and the General Catalogue and annual Appendices of the Library of Congress in Washington; and, in the national field,
the *Bibliografía de la Bibliografía Dominicana* by Luis Florén (for fourteen
years director of the library of the University of Santo Domingo).

Below is the classified list, with comments, of the documentary sources
referred to above. Occasionally, others are mentioned in the text of the study
itself, in reference to concrete details. Those commented on are the more
important ones:

I. Primary Sources.

    A. Official publications of the Dominican government:
        Anuario Estadístico de la República Dominicana. Annual publication
        of the Dominican General Office of Statistics since 1936; the
        latest volume available is that for 1952. Ciudad Trujillo, 1954.

---

[1] The author could mention many other facts he knows, either because he was
a witness to them, or because somebody who knew them directly told him the story.
However, facts not based upon indubitable evidence have been omitted.

Boletín del Senado and *Boletín de la Cámara.* Stenographic records of the sessions held in both chambers of the legislature. They are printed monthly, but are often delayed for long periods. Usually they are referred to as *Bol. Sen.* and *Bol. Cam.*

Código Trujillo de Trabajo. (Trujillo Labor Code). Officially edited, Ciudad Trujillo, 1951.

Colección de Leyes, Decretos, y Resoluciones. The main documents issued by the legislative and executive branches are reprinted annually. Usually referred to as *Colección de Leyes.* . . .

Constitución de la República Dominicana, 1947. Official text of the present constitution, printed in the *Official Gazette, G.O.* No. 6569, of Jan. 19, 1947. An English translation was printed by Prof. Russell H. Fitzgibbon in *The Constitutions of the Americas,* Chicago, 1948, pp. 299–320.

Constitución Política, Reformas Constitucionales: 1844–1942. Santiago, 1944, two volumes. All constitutions which have been in force in the Dominican Republic from Independence to 1942, plus other constitutional documents and brief comments.

Declaración de Principios y Estatutos del Partido Dominicano. Official pamphlet without date [1938?]. (Program and by-laws of the Dominican party.)

Gaceta Oficial. Official Gazette in which all laws, many decrees, and other official documents are printed. It appears every few days. Usually referred to as *G.O.*

Other sources of the same kind, less frequently utilized in this study, include the annual *Memorias* (Reports) of the various Secretaryships of State, the *Bulletin* of the Department of Foreign Relations, and other periodical publications of various departments; the texts of many important laws, printed individually in pamphlets; the *Bulletin of the Dominican Embassy* in Washington; and the *Boletín Judicial.*

Similarly, many pamphlets printed by the Dominican Government on various special topics should be included here, such as those used in this study: *Capacity of the Dominican Republic to Absorb Refugees,* Ciudad Trujillo, 1945; *La Frontera de la República Dominicana con Haití,* Ciudad Trujillo, 1946; *Un Proyecto de Ley Trascendental y su Mensaje-Exposición de Motivos. El Hon. Presidente Trujillo Propone la Reforma de la Constitución,* Ciudad Trujillo, 1946; and *La Traición de Sebastián Lora y Oscar de Moya Hernández,* Ciudad Trujillo, n.d. [1951?].

B. Dominican press:

El Caribe. Morning daily newspaper of the capital; appeared for the first time in April, 1948, with characteristics similar to those of *Listín Diario.* During the last years it has come to be the best daily source of information.

La Información. Daily newspaper in Santiago de los Caballeros, with a certain regional character for the Cibao provinces. It existed prior to Trujillo's regime; it has backed him, without acting as an unofficial mouthpiece. Occasionally useful for local events.

Listín Diario. Morning daily newspaper of the capital, existing before
Trujillo's regime; proponent of the party and government of
Horacio Vásquez ousted in 1930, it attempted to ignore the new
regime during the first two years after the violence of the electoral campaign, but in 1933 it went over to Trujillo's side and
became his unofficial mouthpiece; it disappeared at the beginning
of 1942. It is the best source of daily information from 1930 to
1940.

La Nación. Morning daily newspaper of the capital; it appeared for
the first time on Feb. 19, 1940, using, as its capital, funds mainly
supplied by Trujillo; unofficial mouthpiece for the regime since
then. It is the best daily source of information from 1940 until
recent years, when *El Caribe* became the major newspaper.

La Opinión. Evening daily newspaper of the capital; it existed prior
to Trujillo's regime; it supported him in the beginning, but never
served as an unofficial mouthpiece; during the first months of
1946, it carried on a certain moderate opposition; it disappeared
at the beginning of 1947.

In general, some periodicals, such as *Cosmopólita*, and one small
newspaper *El Diario de Macorís*, may be also included here.
Other Dominican publications are without value as sources of
information.

C. Speeches, Messages, Reports, and Plans of Trujillo:

Evolución de la Democracia en Santo Domingo, Ciudad Trujillo,
1950. (And an English translation printed simultaneously.) A
pamphlet containing the major speech made by President Trujillo, in which he explains his political work and ideas, on the
occasion of the XIII Panamerican Health Conference, held in
the Dominican Republic.

*El Pensamiento de un Estadista: Discursos, Mensajes, y Proclamas
del Hon. Dr. Rafael L. Trujillo*, 11 vols. Santiago, n.d. [1946–
53]. Official collection of all his speeches, messages, reports, and
plans from 1930 to 1952. Usually cited as Trujillo, *Pensamiento*.

Reajuste de la Deuda Externa. Santiago, 1937. Lengthy book signed
by Trujillo, explaining his conduct and plans in the face of the
external debt of the Dominican Republic during the first period
of economic difficulties.

There are numberless other printed pamphlets containing speeches
by Trujillo; almost all of them are reprinted in the official collection already mentioned; the most recent may be found in the
daily press.

D. Speeches by personalities of the regime, and manifestos of some of
the Dominican political groups. Among them, secretaries of
state, senators and deputies, presidents of the Supreme Court,
and presidents of the Dominican party. (Most of them may be
found in the Dominican press, or in the official bulletins of
their respective departments.)

E. Foreign official documents:

Organization of American States, *Annals of the . . .* , since 1949;
Bulletin of the Pan American Union, for the previous years;

Investigating Committee of the Organ of Consultation. Result of its Work (Document submitted to the Council of . . . in the session of March 13, 1950); several official documents from the governments of the Dominican Republic, Haiti, United States of America, and other countries, addressed to the OAS and its Council; and some other publications of the Pan American Union (occasionally mentioned especially in the footnotes of this study).

United Nations, Stenographic Records and Official Summaries of Subsequent Sessions Held by its General Assembly, Councils, and Committees since 1946; *Informe Preliminar sobre la Situación Social en el Mundo,* 1952; and several publications concerning Latin America.

U. S. Department of State, *Foreign Relations of the United States.* Official publication of the U.S. Department of State, year by year and in several classified volumes, of some diplomatic documents which are chosen as basic; the latest printed volume concerning the Americas refers to 1937 (Vol. V, Washington, 1954). [Volumes covering 1946 were published in 1969.] Vol. II of 1930, referring to the coup of Feb. 1930, and Vol. V of 1937, referring to the Haitian massacre, are of especial interest for the Era of Trujillo.

In this group, official documents printed by different governments of the Caribbean region may also be included.

F.   Publications of Dominican exiles:

Boletín de Partido Revolucionario Dominicano, Sección de Nueva York. It appears from time to time, mostly in mimeographic form; its editor is Nicolás Silfa.

Boletín Organo de la Oposición a la Dictadura de Trujillo. Printed in New York from August 19, 1946 to April 14, 1947 by Lic. José A. Bonilla Atiles as its editor; after Dec. 2 it added the initials ARDE *(Asociacíon Reivindicadora Dominicana del Exilio).* It contained good factual information about events of this period. Usually cited as *Boletín ARDE.*

Orientación. Organ of the Dominican Communists, printed in Guatemala from 1951 to 1954; its editor was Pericles Franco, Jr. ("Periclito").

Patria. Published occasionally in New York, from December, 1951, until the murder of Andrés Requena in October, 1952; Requena was its co-editor with Juan M. Díaz; it reappeared in October, 1953.

Pluma y Espada. Printed occasionally in New York, by José R. López Cestero as its editor.

Quisqueya Libre. Organ of the Dominican Revolutionary Party, printed from time to time in Havana; its volume III began in July, 1951. Its editor is Angel Miolán.

Tribuna Dominicana. Printed in Mexico since 1954 by Ramón Grullón (former Communist leader during the 1946 campaign) as its editor.

In the past, other publications have been printed, but these have been short-lived. In the same groups, many manifestos and leaflets of opposition groups, in New York and several Latin American countries, may be included.
One may also mention especially *Memoria del II Congreso del Partido Revolucionario Dominicano* (Havana, 1950).

II. Secondary Sources.

    A. Non-Dominican press and agencies:
Cables from UP, AP, INS, and other press agencies.
Bohemia. Weekly, Havana, Cuba.
El Diario de Nueva York. Spanish newspaper in New York, since 1949.
Hemispherica. Printed bimonthly by IADF (Inter-American Association for Democracy and Freedom), New York.
Hispanic American Report. Monthly mimeographed publication of Stanford University, Stanford, California.
New York Times.
La Prensa. Spanish newspaper in New York.
Time magazine (especially its Latin American edition).
In this group may also be included, in general, other American newspapers and magazines (especially those of New York and at times those of Miami), plus other Cuban, Puerto Rican, and Latin American publications. Some magazine articles of exceptional importance are mentioned separately as monographs.

    B. Books favoring Trujillo's regime:
Almoina, José. *Yo Fuí Secretario de Trujillo.* Buenos Aires, 1950. A book similar to those by Fernández Mato and Osorio-Lizarazo. Its author is a Spanish refugee who accepted the position of private secretary to Trujillo from 1945 to 1947. This book has useful data, especially because it covers recent years.
Bessault, Lawrence de. *President Trujillo: His Work and the Dominican Republic.* 3rd ed. Santiago, 1941. The most useful biography in English, although entirely biased in its eulogy; it covers the first six years of the regime.
Fernández Mato, Ramón. *Trujillo o la Transfiguración Dominicana.* Mexico, 1946. Its author is a Spaniard who went to the Dominican Republic in 1944, paid by the Dominican government, to write this book; it is useful from the Trujillist point of view; it has been translated into other languages.
Nanita, Abelardo R. *Trujillo.* 5th ed. Ciudad Trujillo, 1951. The first three editions had the title *Trujillo de Cuerpo Entero;* there is an English translation, *Trujillo, a Full-Size Portrait,* printed in the Dominican Republic (Santiago, 1939). It is the biography of Trujillo most often reprinted; it is very weak as to exact data, a model of sycophancy.
Osorio-Lizarazo, José A. *La Isla Iluminada.* Mexico, 1946. Very similar to the book by Fernández Mato.
Sánchez Lustrino, Gilberto. *Trujillo: El Constructor de una Nacionalidad.* Havana, 1938. The most useful of all the biographies of

Trujillo, because of the concrete data it contains; it is written in praise of Trujillo, but with a certain moderation; it covers the background of the regime and its first eight years.

Many other less important books could be mentioned here, e.g., Pedro González Blanco, *Trujillo*, Ciudad Trujillo, 1946; Henry Helfant, *La Doctrina Trujillo del Asilo Diplomático*, Mexico, 1947; Fabio A. Mota, *Un Estadista de América*, Ciudad Trujillo, 1945; Herman Murray-Jacoby, *The Diplomacy of President Trujillo*, N.p., n.d.; and a very recent pamphlet, Stanley Walker, *Generalissimo Rafael L. Trujillo: A Biography*, New York, n.d. [1955].

It is also worth mentioning other books on concrete aspects of the regime, which although written purposely in praise, reflect some serious study: Joaquín Balaguer, *El Tratado Trujillo-Hull y la Liberación de la República Dominicana*, Bogotá, 1941; and Virgilio Hoepelmán, *Nuestra Vida Exterior*, Ciudad Trujillo, 1951.

(Some of these books and pamphlets, and occasionally others, are referred to in the footnotes of this study.)

C. Books opposing Trujillo's regime:

Bustamante, Gregorio R. de. *Una Satrapía en el Caribe*. Guatemala, 1949. "Bustamante" is a pen-name; the author of this study [i.e., Galíndez] has read two letters, sent from Mexico to New York, requesting an English translation, in which it was stated that this pen-name covers a person who had for some time a confidential position next to Trujillo and later wrote another book in his praise. Other reliable sources affirm that the expenses of printing this book were supplied by the Guatemalan government. Later on, the book practically disappeared from circulation. It is the one containing most informative data, which is natural since its author may have been a private aide of Trujillo; its main weakness is its objectionable language, and the personal circumstances surrounding the author himself.

Hicks, Albert C. *Blood in the Streets: The Life and Rule of Trujillo*. New York, 1946. It is the only work in English; it contains many data, although incomplete; its main weakness is its excessive emphasis of bloody details, and its failure to mention its sources of information.

Jimenes-Grullón, Juan L. *La República Dominicana (Análisis de su Pasado y su Presente)*. Havana, 1940. Analytic study of Dominican history before Trujillo, and an impassioned comment on the first years of his regime; although the author is a political exile, this book is perhaps the most balanced and valuable of all of them.

Jimenes-Grullón, Juan L. *Una Gestapo en América*. Havana, 1946. By the same author; he tells his own experiences in Trujillo's jails from 1934 to 1935; it is the only narrative of this kind, and has all the force of direct testimony.

Mejía, Félix A. *Via Crucis de un Pueblo*. Mexico, 1951. The author is another Dominican exile, and the style at times is passionate;

but it contains adequate and useful data for the first period of the regime.

Requena, Andrés. *Cementario sin Cruces.* Mexico, n.d. [1951?]. The author is another Dominican exile, murdered in New York a short time after the publication of this book. It is a novel, but based upon facts occurring in the Dominican Republic from 1945 to 1947; it presents a good picture of real life, although freely written as any work of fiction.

There are other books against Trujillo, of less importance, e.g., Pericles Franco Ornes, *La Tragedia Dominicana,* Santiago de Chile, 1946, useful in part because of the data it contains about clandestine activities in 1945, its author is a Dominican Communist leader; Carmita Landestoy, *¡Yo Tambien Acuso!* New York, 1946; two pamphlets printed in Havana in 1950 and 1951 under the title *Luperón, Símbolo de Libertad y de Heroismo;* and a pamphlet *Trujillo es un Nazi,* printed in Havana during World War II (n.d.) by the Dominican Democratic Anti-Nazi Union.

It is also in order to mention here the pertinent chapters of some general books on Latin American politics, or special books on the Caribbean dictatorships. The outstanding ones are: Germán Arciniegas, *The State of Latin America,* New York, 1952, Spanish text published later in Mexico and Santiago de Chile under the title *Entre la Libertad y el Miedo;* Wenzell Brown, *Angry Men; Laughing Men,* New York, 1947; John Gunther, *Inside Latin America,* New York, 1941; and William Krehm, *Democracia y Tiranías en el Caribe,* Mexico, 1949.

Aside from these books, several articles appearing in magazines or newspapers also deserve to be cited here:

Draper, Theodore, "Trujillo's Dynasty." *The Reporter,* Nov. 27 and Dec. 11, 1951.

Gunther, John. "Hispaniola." *Foreign Affairs,* July 1941.

Kent, George. "God and Trujillo." *Reader's Digest,* April 1946.

Matthews, Herbert L. "Dominicans Thrive at Cost of Liberty." *New York Times,* March 28, 1953, p. 7.

Thomson, Charles C. "Dictatorship in the Dominican Republic." *Foreign Policy Association Reports,* April 15, 1936.

D. Books providing historical background, or impartial books of general character:

(1)   On the general history of the Dominican Republic:

García, José G. *Compendio de la Historia de Santo Domingo.* Santo Domingo, 1867–69; and *Historia Moderna de la República Dominicana.* Santo Domingo, 1906.

Incháustegui Cabral, Joaquín Marino. *Historia Dominicana.* Ciudad Trujillo, 1946 and 1948.

Mejía, Luis F. *De Lilís a Trujillo.* Caracas, 1944.

Mejía Ricart, Gustavo A. *Historia de Santo Domingo,* several volumes, some of them already printed. Ciudad Trujillo, 1948–. . . .

Monte y Tejada, Antonio del. *Historia de Santo Domingo.* Havana, 1853.

Peña Batlle, Manuel A. *Historia de La Cuestión Fronteriza Dominicana-Haitiana.* Ciudad Trujillo, 1946.

Pichardo, Bernardo. *Resumen de Historia Patria.* Barcelona, 1922.

Price-Mars, Jean. *La Republique d'Haiti et la Republique Dominicaine.* 2 vol. Port-au-Prince, 1953.

(2) On the period of the American occupation:

Henríquez Ureña, Max. *Los Yanquis en Santo Domingo.* Madrid, 1929.

Kelsey, Carl. *The American Intervention in Haiti and the Dominican Republic.* Philadelphia, 1921.

Knight, Melvin M. *The Americans in Santo Domingo.* New York, 1928; there is a Spanish translation, Ciudad Trujillo, 1939.

Welles, Sumner. *Naboth's Vineyard: The Dominican Republic, 1844–1924.* 2 vol. New York, 1928.

General books on the relations between the United States and the Caribbean area, e.g., those by Dexter Perkins, Wilfrid H. Callcott, J. Fred Rippy, Dana G. Munro, and Howard C. Hill.

(3) General books on Latin American history and politics:

E.g., that by the author of this study: Galíndez, Jesús de. *Iberoamérica: Su Evolución Política, Socio-económica, Cultural e Internacional.* New York, 1954. In the field of history, those by John F. Bannon and Peter M. Dunne, Harold E. Davis, Hubert Herring, Frederick A. Kirkpatrick, Ricardo Levene, David R. Moore, Dana G. Munro, Carlos Pereyra, J. Fred Rippy, William S. Robertson, Luis A. Sánchez, and A. Curtis Wilgus. In the field of politics, those by Asher N. Christensen, Cecil Jane, Miguel Jorrín, Austin F. Macdonald, and Mary W. Williams. And a few others in different fields, occasionally referred to in the footnotes, e.g., Jesús de Galíndez, "La Inestabilidad Constitucional en Latinoamerica," *Boletín del Instituto de Derecho Comparado de México,* May-August, 1952, pp. 45–65; Wendell C. Gordon, *The Economy of Latin America,* New York, 1950.

(4) General books on the Dominican Republic, e.g., Otto Schoenrich, *Santo Domingo, a Country with a Future,* New York, 1918; Stanley Walker, *Journey toward the Sunlight,* New York, 1947; and John W. White, *The Land Columbus Loved,* Ciudad Trujillo, 1945.

(5) Dominican books of an objective type, e.g., Luis Florén, *Bibliografía de la Bibliografía Dominicana,* Ciudad Trujillo, 1948; Carlos Gatón Richiez, *La Jurisprudencia en la República Dominicana,* Vol. I, Santiago, 1943; Arístides Sanabia, *Recopilación de las Leyes de Trabajo,* Ciudad Trujillo, 1946; Carlos Sánchez y Sánchez, *Curso de Derecho Internacional Público Americano,* Ciudad Trujillo, 1943; and some doctoral dissertations.

III. Private conversations with, or confidences from:
1. Officers of the Dominican government, including members of the cabinet (especially during the six-year stay of the author in the Dominican Republic).
2. Dominicans active in the clandestine opposition.
3. Dominicans of all kinds and social classes, without political bias.
4. Exiled leaders, and their followers (from 1946 on).
5. Foreigners with business in the Dominican Republic or those who have lived there for some time.

IV. Author's personal experience in the country, from November, 1939, to January, 1946.

Editor's Bibliography

The following bibliography is supplementary to the preceding Author's Bibliography. It is narrowly selective and includes no evaluative comments. Included are titles that throw significant additional light on "the Era of Trujillo," i.e., the period from 1930 to 1961, either published between completion of the author's study and the time of Trujillo's assassination (and a few titles of earlier date) or subsequent to the dictator's death but importantly related to the period of question. Excluded are titles relating to the Dominican Republic but not primarily to the period of Trujillo, for example, a spate of books and articles dealing with the dramatic developments of 1965, and many titles that are too short or insubstantial, even though dealing with the Era, to deserve inclusion. The titles listed are from such varied sources that it has seemed impractical to classify them as is done in the Author's Bibliography.

Alba, Víctor. "República Dominicana: La Herencia del 'Benefactor.'" *Cuadernos* (Paris), 63 (August 1962): pp. 67–72.

Alexander, Robert J. *Communism in Latin America.* New Brunswick: Rutgers University Press, 1957.

———. *The Venezuelan Democratic Revolution: A Profile of the Regime of Rómulo Betancourt.* New Brunswick: Rutgers University Press, 1964.

Ariza, Sander. *Trujillo: The Man and His Country.* New York: Orlin Tremaine, 1939.

Atkins, George P. "The United States and the Dominican Republic during the Era of Trujillo." Ph.D. dissertation, American University, 1966.

Balaguer, Joaquín. *La Realidad Dominicana: Semblanza de un País y de un Régimen.* Buenos Aires: Imprenta Ferrai Hermanos, 1947.

Beals, Carleton. "Caesar of the Caribbean." *Current History,* 48 (January 1938): pp. 31–34.

Bosch, Juan. *Trujillo: Causas de una Tiranía sin Ejemplo.* Caracas: Librería Las Novedades, 1959.

————. *The Unfinished Experiment: Democracy in the Dominican Republic.* New York: Praeger, 1965.

Cestero Burgos, Tulio A. *Filosofía de un Régimen.* Ciudad Trujillo: Editora Montalvo, 1951.

Clark, Gerald. *The Coming Explosion in Latin America.* New York: David McKay, 1962.

Cook, Fred J. "Who Killed Jesús de Galíndez?" *Fact* (New York), 3 (March-April 1966): pp. 42–59.

"Costly Whitewash of Black Charges." *Life,* 44 (June 9, 1958): pp. 105–6.

Crassweller, Robert D. *Trujillo: The Life and Times of a Caribbean Dictator.* New York: Macmillan, 1966.

Damirón, Rafael. *Resumen (a los Enemigos de Trujillo).* Ciudad Trujillo: Editora Montalvo, 1947.

Ernst, Morris L. *Report and Opinion in the Matter of Galindez.* New York: Sydney S. Barron, 1958.

Espaillat, Arturo R. *Trujillo: The Last Caesar.* Chicago: Henry Regnery, 1963.

Ferreras, Ramón A. *Preso.* Santo Domingo: Editorial la Nación, 1962.

Franco Pichardo, Franklin J. *República Dominicana: Clases, Crisis, y Comandos.* Havana: Casa de las Américas, 1966.

Galíndez, Jesús de. "Un Reportaje sobre Santo Domingo." *Cuadernos Americanos,* 80 (March-April 1955): pp. 37–56.

Gallegos, Gerardo. *Trujillo: Cara y Cruz de su Dictadura.* Madrid: Ediciones Iberoamericanas, 1968.

González Blanco, Pedro. *La Era de Trujillo.* Ciudad Trujillo: Editora del Caribe, 1955.

————. *Trujillo, o la Restauración de un Pueblo.* Ciudad Trujillo: Luis Sánchez Andujar, 1946.

Grullón, Ramón. "Antecedentes y Perspectivas del Momento Político Dominicano." *Cuadernos Americanos,* 120 (January-February 1962): pp. 221–52.

Henríquez, Noel. *La Verdad sobre Trujillo; Capítulos que se le Olvidaron a Galíndez.* Havana: Imprenta Económica en General, 1959.

Herraiz, Ismael. *Trujillo dentro de la Historia.* Madrid: Ediciones Acies, 1957.

Inter-American Peace Committee. *Report of the . . . to the Fifth Meeting of Consultation of Ministers of Foreign Affairs,* August 6, 1959. Washington: Organization of American States, 1959.

————. *Report of the . . . on the Case Presented by Venezuela,* June 7, 1960 (processed). Washington: Organization of American States, 1960.

————. *Special Report on the Relationship between Violation of Human Rights or the Non-Exercise of Representative Democracy and the Political Tensions that Affect the Peace of the Hemisphere,* April 14, 1960 (processed). Washington: Organization of American States, 1960.

James, Daniel. *Detrás de la Cortina de Azúcar.* Mexico: Serie Justicia, 1956.

La Souchere, Elena de. *Crime à Saint-Domingue: L'Affaire Trujillo-Galíndez.* Paris: Editions Albin Michel, 1972.

Lieuwen, Edwin. *Generals vs. Presidents: Neomilitarism in Latin America.* New York: Praeger, 1964.

Martin, John Bartlow. *Overtaken by Events: The Dominican Crisis from the Fall of Trujillo to the Civil War.* Garden City: Doubleday, 1966.

Morrison, DeLesseps S. *Latin American Mission: An Adventure in Hemisphere Diplomacy.* New York: Simon and Schuster, 1965.

Organization of American States. *Eighth Meeting of Consultation of Ministers of Foreign Affairs,* at Punta del Este, Uruguay, January 1962. Address by José A. Bonilla Atiles, January 26, 1962. Washington: Organization of American States, 1962.

Ornes Coiscu, Germán E. *Trujillo: Little Caesar of the Caribbean.* New York: Thomas Nelson and Sons, 1958.

———— and McCarten, John. "The Little Caesar on Our Own Front Porch." *Harper's,* 213 (December 1956): pp. 67–72.

Ornes Coiscu, Horacio. *Desembarco en Luperón: Espisodio de la Lucha por la Democracia en la República Dominicana.* Mexico: Ediciones Humanismo, 1956.

Osorio Lizarazo, José A. *Así es Trujillo.* Buenos Aires: Artes Gráficas, 1958.

————. *Birth and Growth of Anti-Trujillism in America.* Madrid: Gráficas Rey, 1958.

Pagán Perdomo, Dato. *Porqúe Lucha el Pueblo Dominicano: Análisis del Fenómeno Dictatorial en América Latina.* Caracas: Empresas Caribe, 1959.

Peña Batlle, Manuel A. *Política de Trujillo.* Ciudad Trujillo: Impresora Dominicana, 1954.

Porter, Charles O. (as told to Geoffrey Bocca). "The Butcher of the Caribbean." *Coronet,* 42 (June 1957): pp. 50–66.

———— and Alexander, Robert J. *The Struggle for Democracy in Latin America.* New York: Macmillan, 1961.

Roberts, Thomas D. et al. *Area Handbook for the Dominican Republic.* Washington: American University, 1966.

Rodríguez Demorizi, Emilio, ed. *La Era de Trujillo; 25 Años de Historia Dominicana.* 20 vols. Ciudad Trujillo: Impresora Dominicana, 1955. Vols. 9–10 (by Rodríguez Demorizi) are *Cronología de Trujillo;* vol. 20 (by Rodríguez Demorizi) is *Bibliografía de Trujillo.*

Rys, John F. "Tension and Conflicts in Cuba, Haiti, and the Dominican Republic between 1954 and 1959." Ph.D. dissertation, American University, 1966.

"The Story of a Dark International Conspiracy." *Life,* 52 (February 25, 1957): pp. 24–31.

Szulc, Tad. "Trujillo's Legacy: A Democratic Vacuum." *New York Times Magazine,* September 2, 1962, pp. 9, 40–41.

————. *Twilight of the Tyrants.* New York: Henry Holt, 1959.

Tannenbaum, Frank. *Ten Keys to Latin America.* New York: Alfred A. Knopf, 1962.

Tejeda Díaz, Teodoro. *Yo Investigué la Muerte de Trujillo.* Barcelona: Plaza y Janes Editores, 1963.

Trujillo, Flor de Oro (as told to Laura Bergquist). "My Tortured Life as Trujillo's Daughter." *Look,* 29 (June 15, 1965) : pp. 44–66, and (June 29, 1965): pp. 52–71.

Trujillo, Rafael L. *The Basic Policies of a Regime.* Ciudad Trujillo: Editora del Caribe, 1960.

Vega y Pagán, Ernesto. *Military Biography of Generalissimo Rafael Leonidas Trujillo Molina, Commander-in-Chief of the Armed Forces.* Ciudad Trujillo: Editorial Atenas, 1956.

Vergés Vidal, Pedro L. *Trujillo, Prócer Anticomunista.* Ciudad Trujillo: Editora del Caribe, 1958.

Viau, Alfred. *La Era de Trujillo: Economía y Finanza.* Ciudad Trujillo: n.p., 1950.

Wiarda, Howard J. "The Changing Political Orientation of the Church in the Dominican Republic." *Journal of Church and State,* 7 (Spring 1965): pp. 238–54.

―――. "Constitutions and Constitutionalism in the Dominican Republic: The Basic Law within the Political Process." *Law and Society Review,* 2 (June 1968): pp. 385–405.

―――. "The Development of the Labor Movement in the Dominican Republic." *Inter-American Economic Affairs,* 20 (Summer 1966): pp. 41–63.

―――. *Dictatorship and Development: The Methods of Control in Trujillo's Dominican Republic.* Gainesville: University of Florida Press, 1968.

―――. "Dictatorship and Development: The Trujillo Regime and Its Implications." *Southwest Social Science Quarterly,* 48 (March 1968): pp. 548–57.

―――, ed. *Dominican Republic: Election Factbook.* Washington: Institute for the Comparative Study of Political Systems, 1966.

―――. *The Dominican Republic: Nation in Transition.* New York: Praeger, 1969.

―――, ed. *Materials for the Study of Politics and Government in the Dominican Republic, 1930–1966.* Santiago, D. R.: Universidad Católica, 1968.

―――. "The Politics of Civil-Military Relations in the Dominican Republic." *Journal of Inter-American Studies,* 7 (October 1965) : pp. 465–84.

Wilgus, A Curtis, ed. *The Caribbean: Contemporary International Relations.* Gainesville: University of Florida Press, 1957.

―――, ed. *The Caribbean: Its Political Problems.* Gainesville: University of Florida Press, 1956.

Index